SHAOLIN 鈴 SISTERS

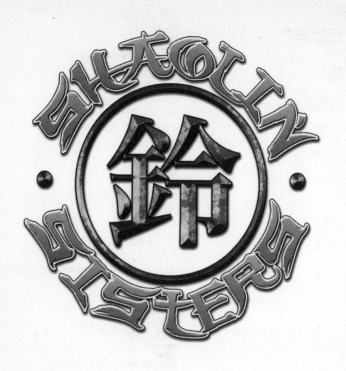

English Adaptation - Alexander O. Smith
Story Editor - Rich Amtower
Retouch and Lettering - Jesse Fernley
Graphic Design - Mark Paniccia
Cover Layout & Logo Design - Patrick Hook

Editor - Rob Tokar
Managing Editor - Jill Freshney
Production Coordinator - Antonio DePietro
Production Manager - Jennifer Miller
Art Director - Matthew Alford
Editorial Director - Jeremy Ross
VP of Production - Ron Klamert
President & C.O.O. - John Parker
Publisher & C.E.O. - Stuart Levy

Email: editor@TOKYOPOP.com
Come visit us online at www.TOKYOPOP.com

A ⭐TOKYOPOP® Manga
TOKYOPOP Inc.
5900 Wilshire Blvd. Suite 2000
Los Angeles, CA 90036

ISBN: 1-59182-233-5

First TOKYOPOP printing: October 2003

10 9 8 7 6 5 4 3 2 1
Printed in the USA

SHAOLIN SISTERS

Volume 5

by
Toshiki Hirano
&
Narumi Kakinouchi

TOKYOPOP®
Los Angeles • Tokyo • London

Cast of Characters

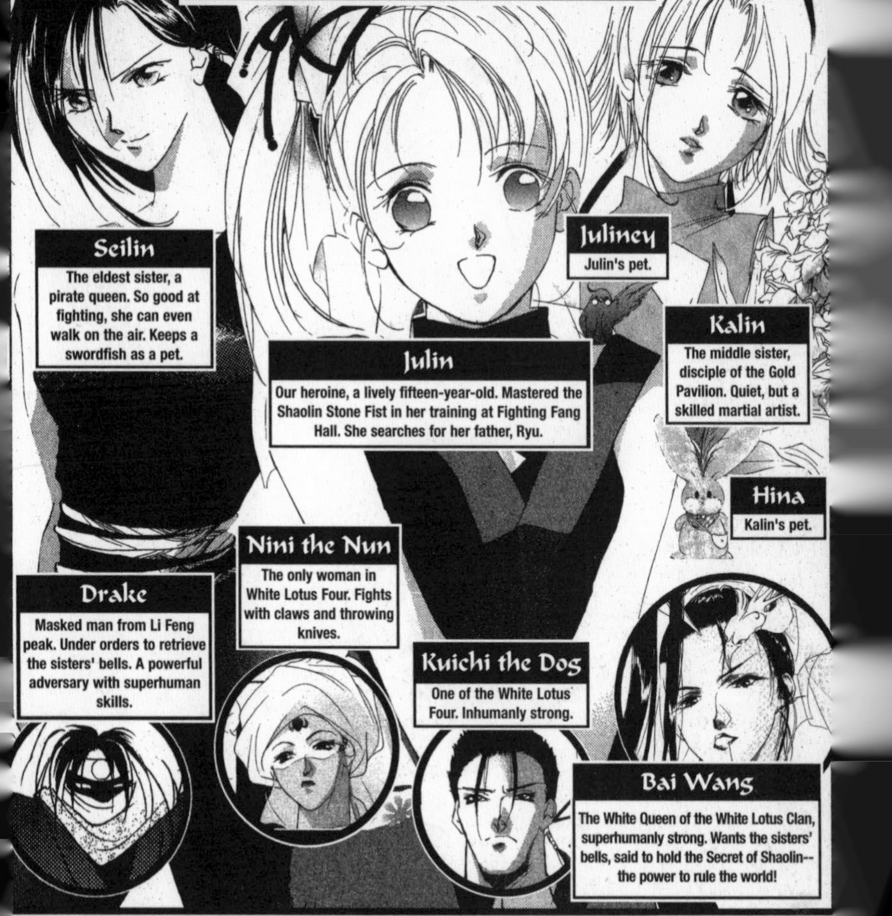
Seilin
The eldest sister, a pirate queen. So good at fighting, she can even walk on the air. Keeps a swordfish as a pet.
Juliney
Julin's pet.
Kalin
The middle sister, disciple of the Gold Pavilion. Quiet, but a skilled martial artist.
Julin
Our heroine, a lively fifteen-year-old. Mastered the Shaolin Stone Fist in her training at Fighting Fang Hall. She searches for her father, Ryu.
Hina
Kalin's pet.
Nini the Nun
The only woman in White Lotus Four. Fights with claws and throwing knives.
Drake
Masked man from Li Feng peak. Under orders to retrieve the sisters' bells. A powerful adversary with superhuman skills.
Kuichi the Dog
One of the White Lotus Four. Inhumanly strong.
Bai Wang
The White Queen of the White Lotus Clan, superhumanly strong. Wants the sisters' bells, said to hold the Secret of Shaolin--the power to rule the world!

STORY SO FAR: It is an age when warriors rule. After an attack by Bai Wang's White Lotus Clan, Julin's master uses his dying breath to inform Julin that she has two long-lost sisters, each of whom possesses a magic bell like her own. Julin embarks on a quest to find them and, after fighting off further attacks from members of the White Lotus Clan, Julin is reunited with her sisters. Bai Wang attacks the sisters on Seilin's pirate vessel, but the battle is interrupted by the mysterious Drake, who also demands the sisters' bells. When the dust settles, Drake is holding Kalin and Julin's bells, and Bai Wang is holding Seilin's bell. After a fierce battle at the White Lotus camp, Julin, Kalin, and the White Lotus Clan chase Drake to Li Feng Peak. Emerging victorious from a hard-fought duel with two of the White Lotus Four--Kuichi and Nini--the two sisters are reunited with Seilin, and the three decide to climb the foreboding peak together. Near the top of the peak, Drake and Bai Wang face off for a third time. Bai Wang is assaulted by a mysterious, sentient force that seems to peer into her very soul, but she manages to steel her formidable will and resist its attack. Farther down on the slopes of the peak, the three sisters face new enemies: Sanji and Shino of the White Lotus Four. The sisters are hard-pressed and near exhaustion when a strange ki power comes welling up from the mountain itself! Will they be able to turn the battle around?!

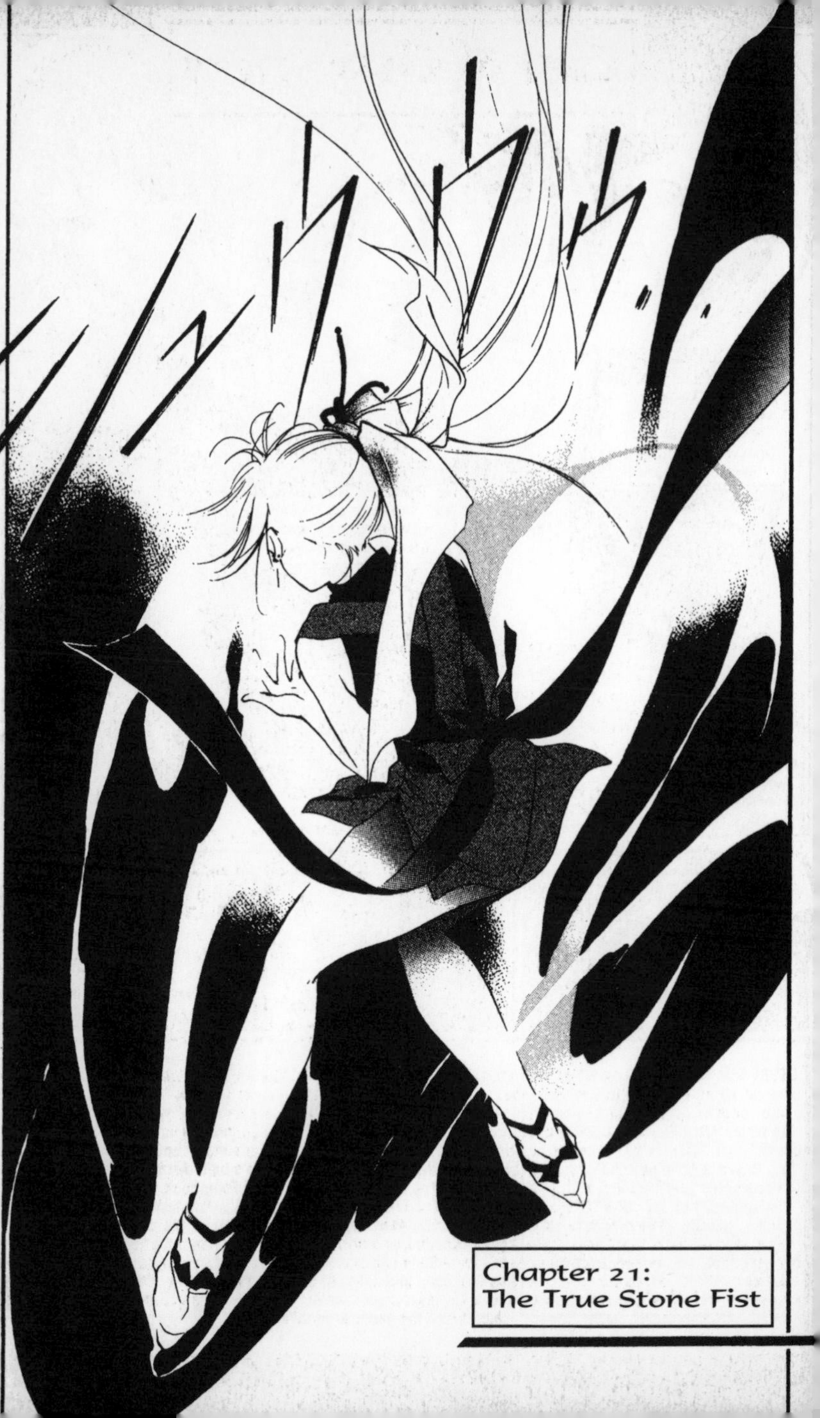
Chapter 21:
The True Stone Fist

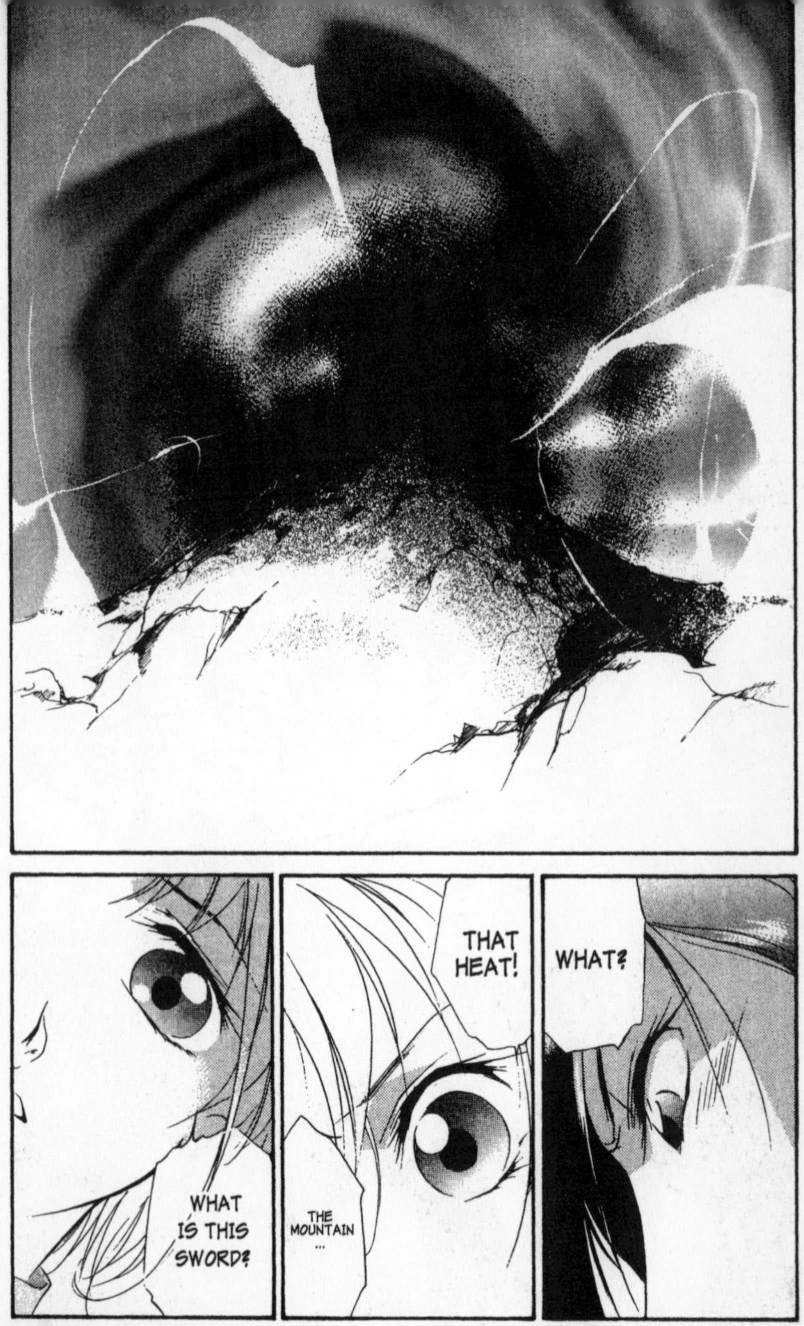
WHAT?
THAT HEAT!
THE MOUNTAIN ...
WHAT IS THIS SWORD?

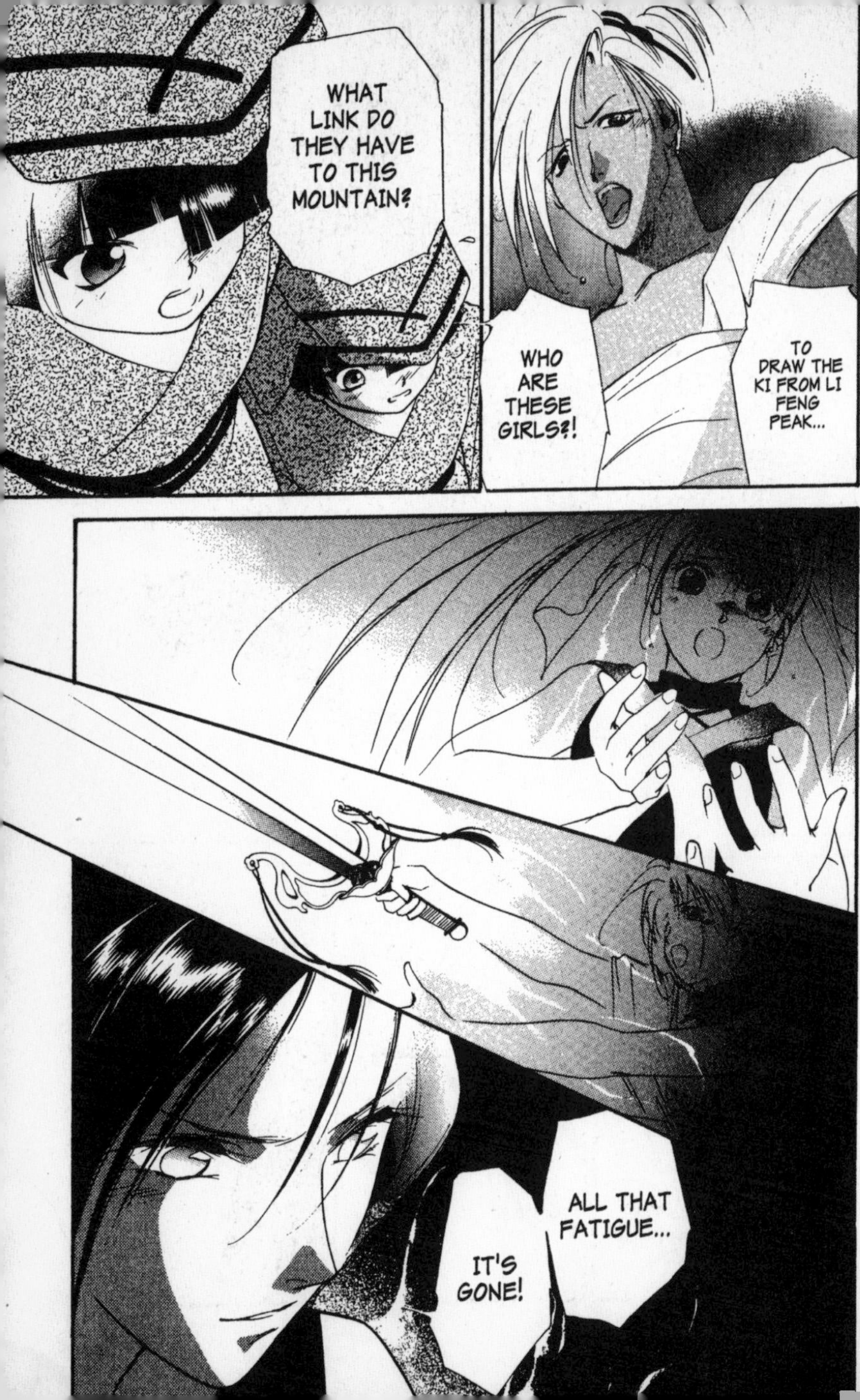
TO DRAW THE KI FROM LI FENG PEAK...
WHO ARE THESE GIRLS?!
WHAT LINK DO THEY HAVE TO THIS MOUNTAIN?
ALL THAT FATIGUE...
IT'S GONE!

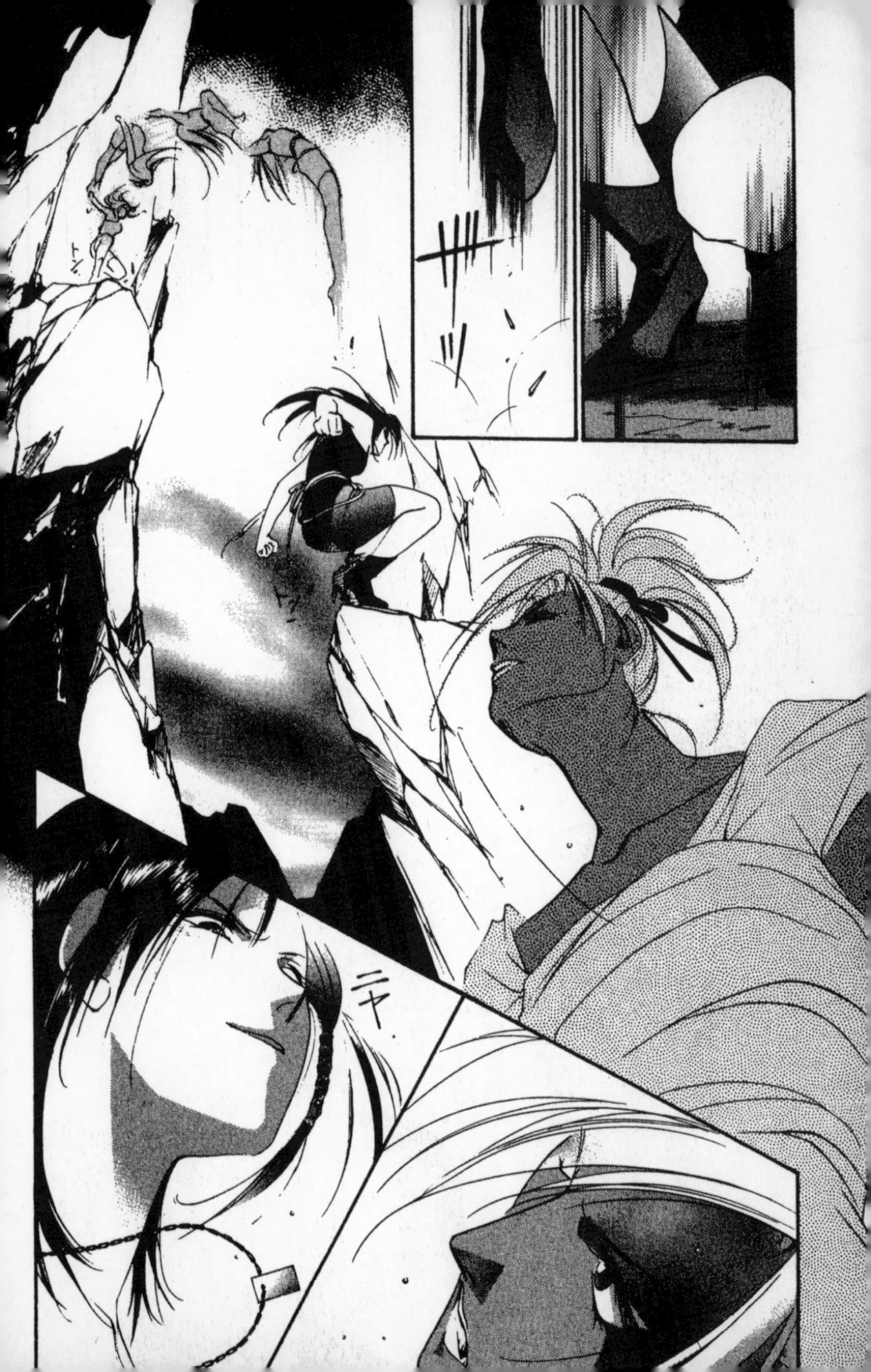
ザッ
トン.
ニヤ

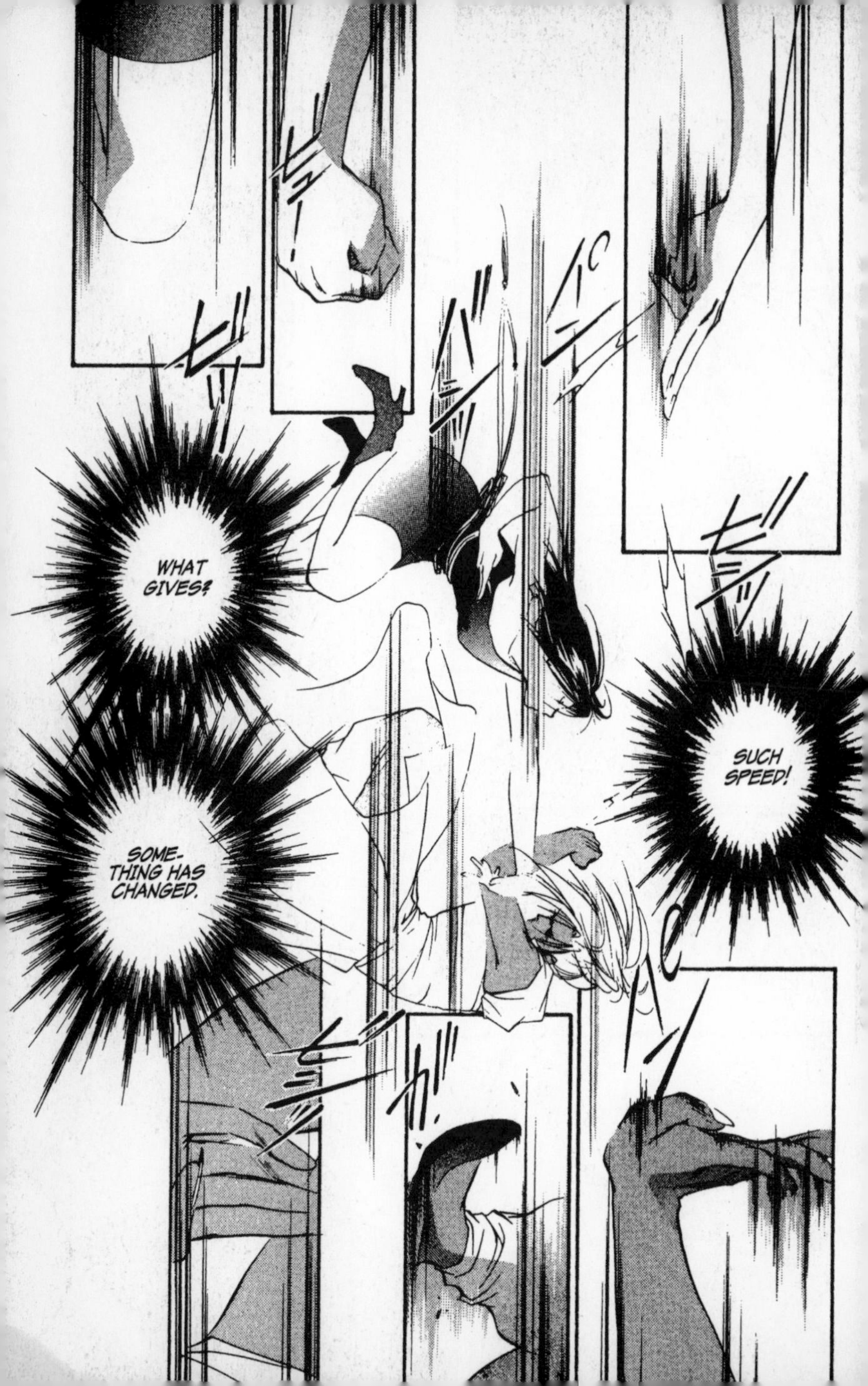
WHAT GIVES?
SUCH SPEED!
SOME-THING HAS CHANGED.

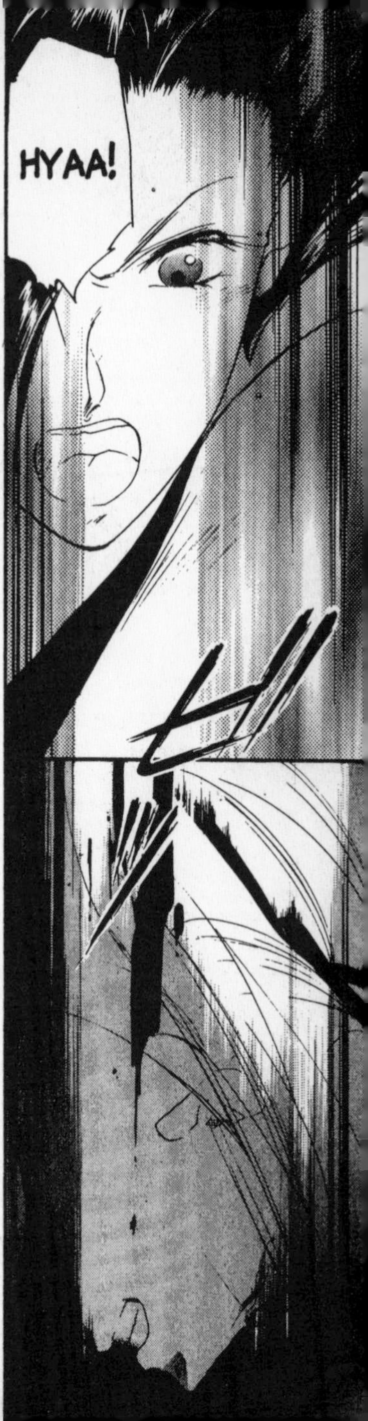
HYAA!
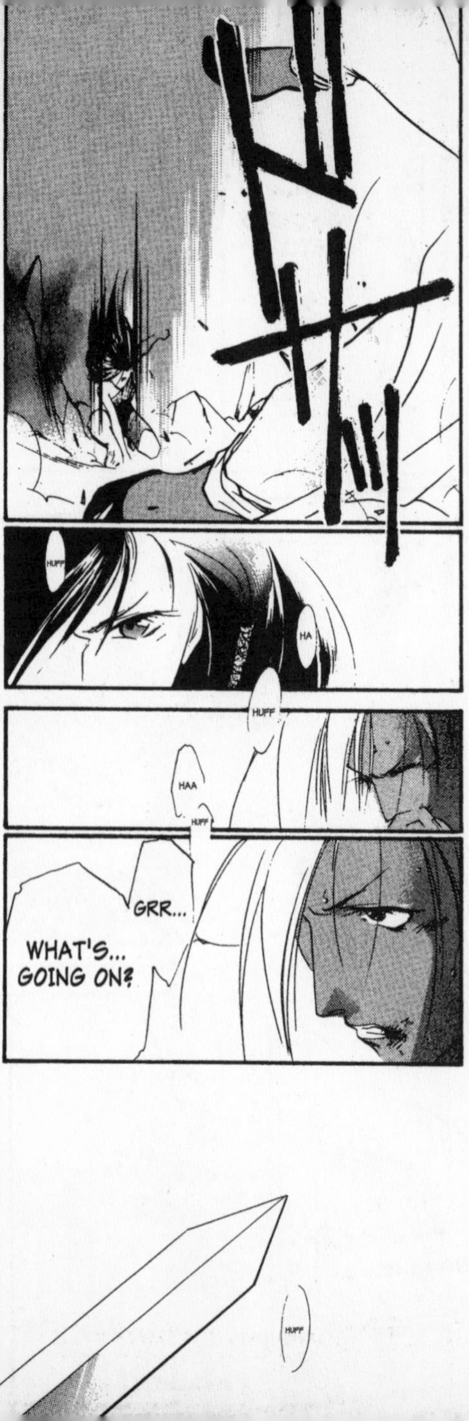
HUFF
HA
HUFF
HAA
HUFF
GRR...
WHAT'S...
GOING ON?
HUFF

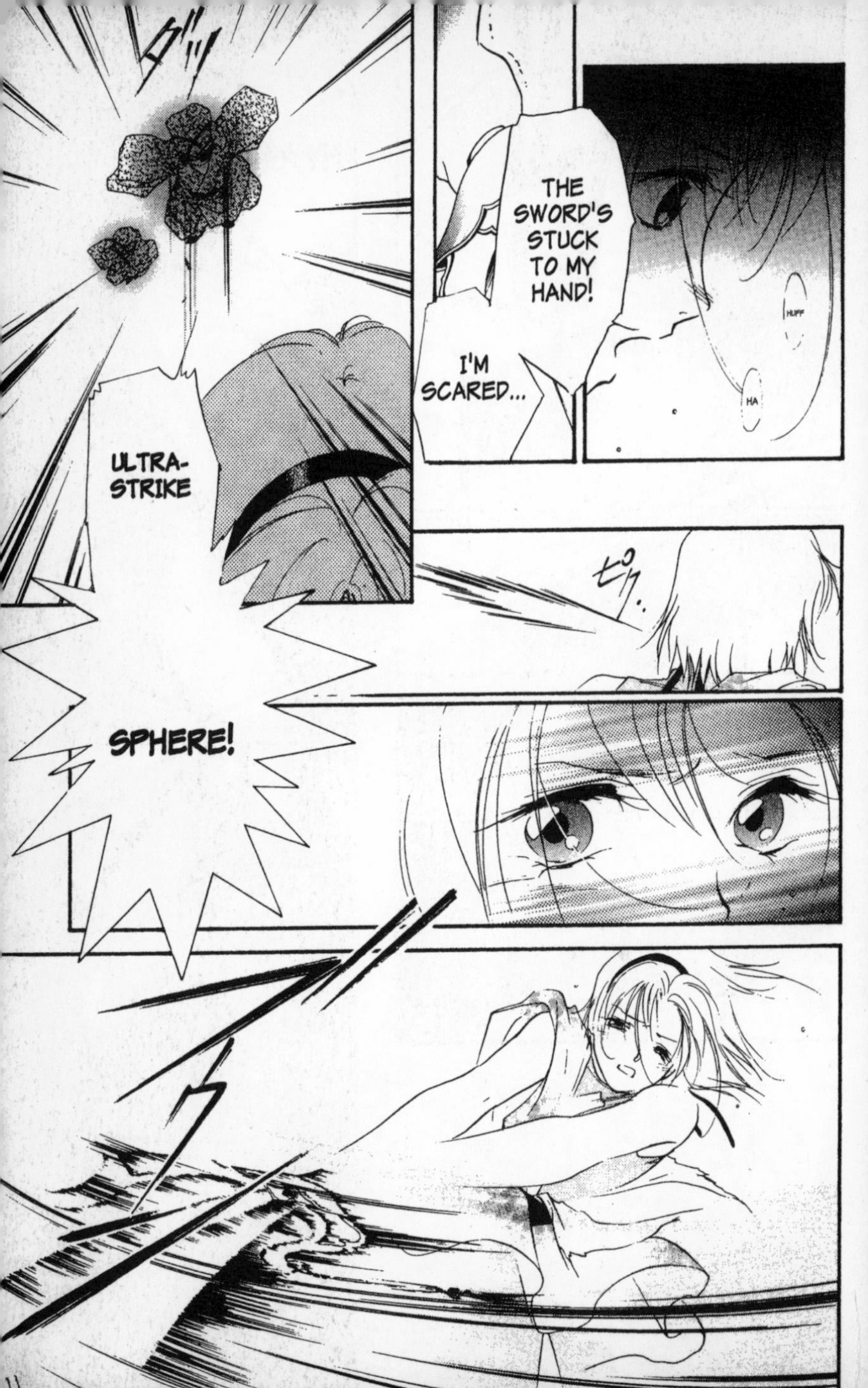
HUFF
HA
THE SWORD'S STUCK TO MY HAND!
I'M SCARED...
ダッ
ULTRA-STRIKE
ピク..
SPHERE!

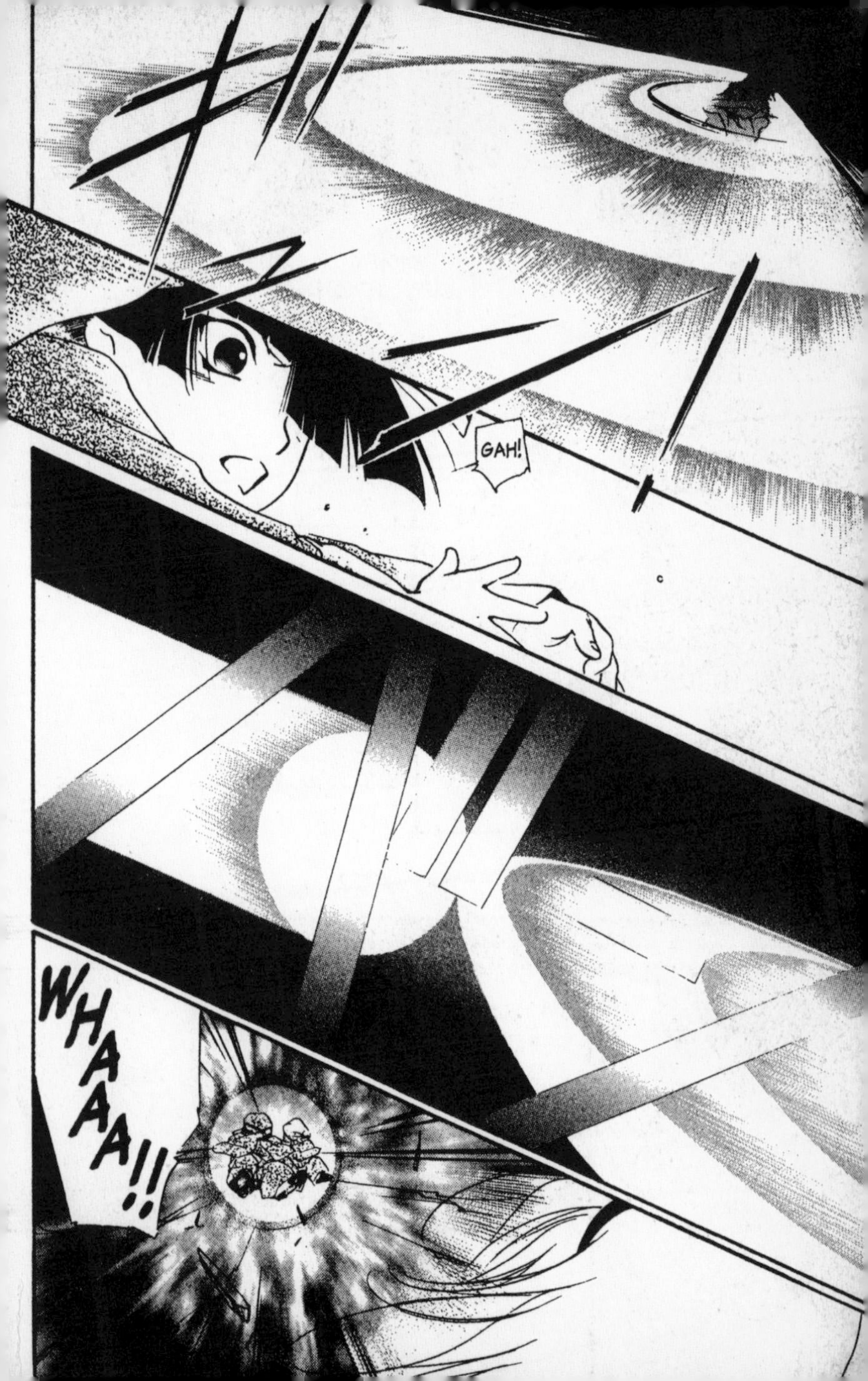
GAH!
WHAAA!!

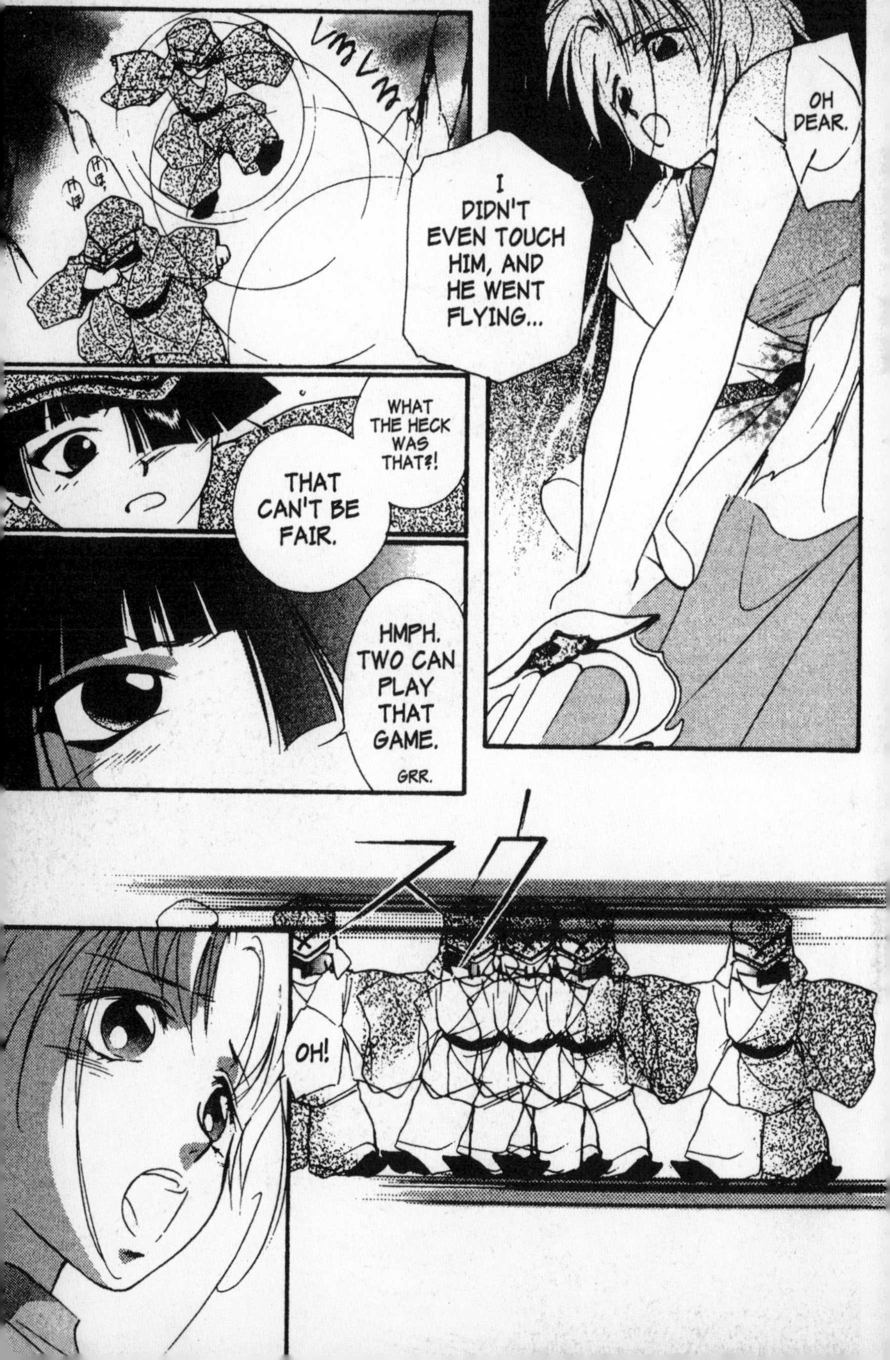
OH DEAR.
I DIDN'T EVEN TOUCH HIM, AND HE WENT FLYING...
WHAT THE HECK WAS THAT?!
THAT CAN'T BE FAIR.
HMPH. TWO CAN PLAY THAT GAME.
GRR.
OH!

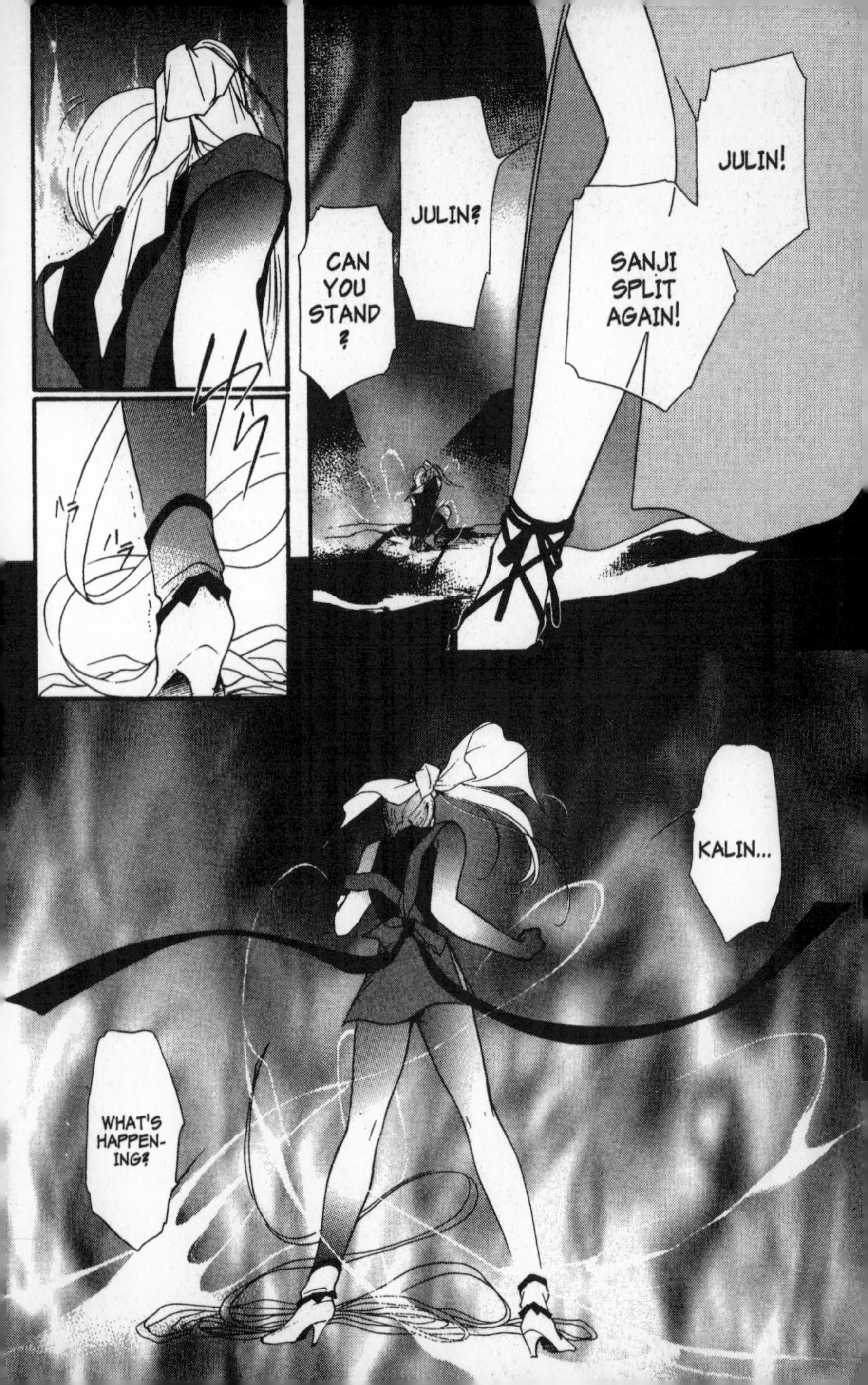
JULIN!
SANJI SPLIT AGAIN!
JULIN?
CAN YOU STAND?
KALIN...
WHAT'S HAPPEN-ING?

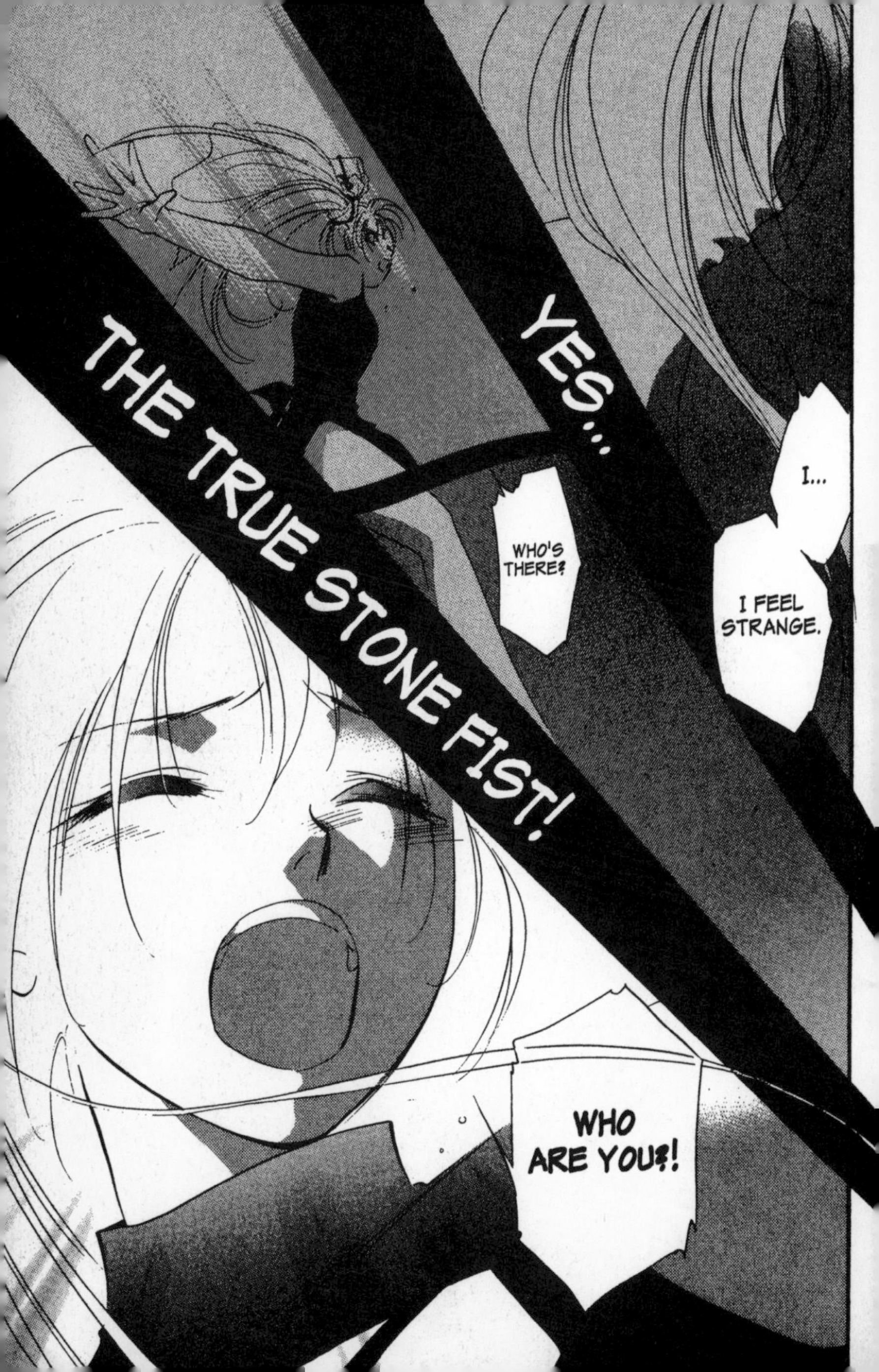
I...
I FEEL STRANGE.
WHO'S THERE?
YES...
THE TRUE STONE FIST!
WHO ARE YOU?!

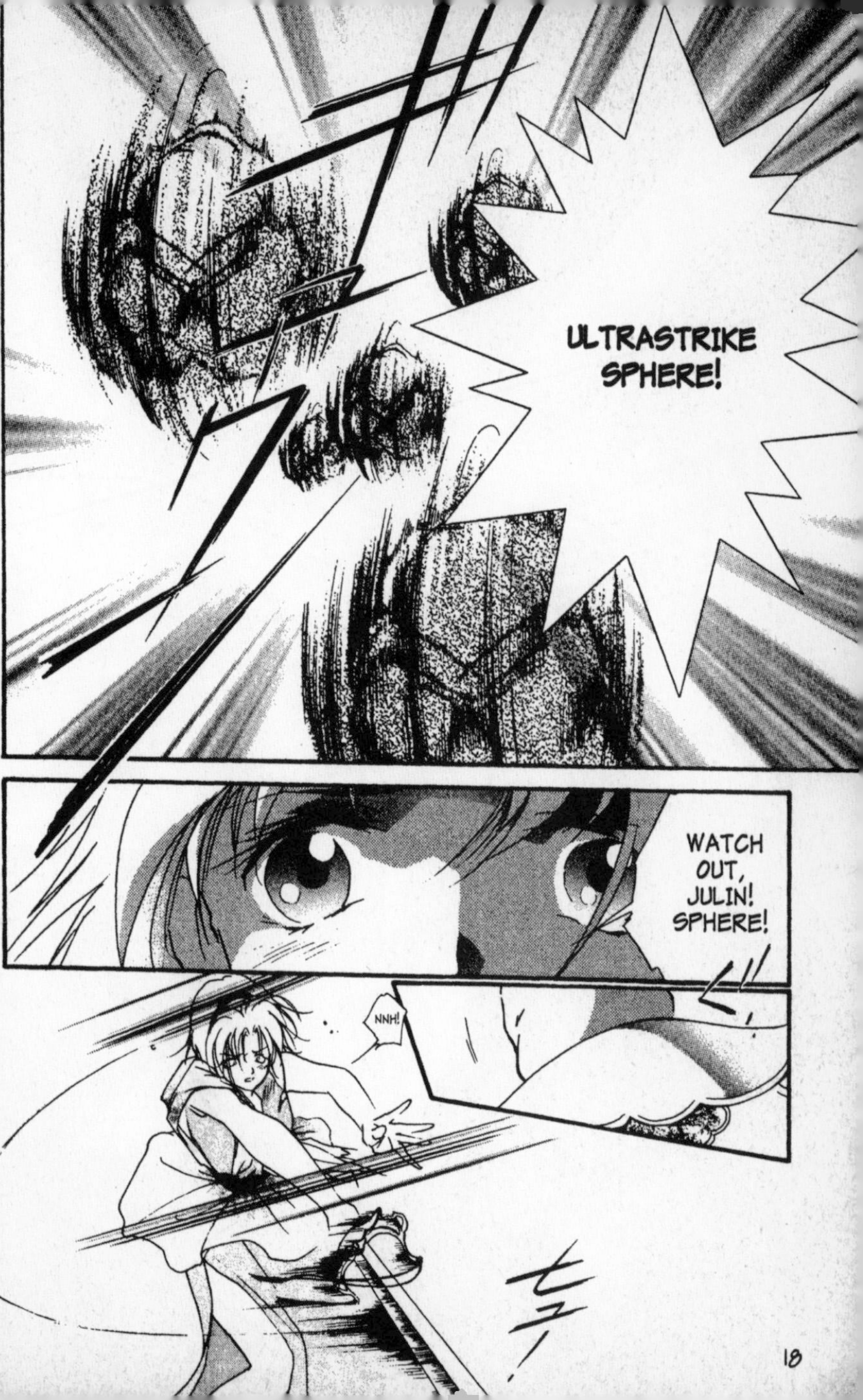
ULTRASTRIKE SPHERE!
WATCH OUT, JULIN! SPHERE!
NNH!

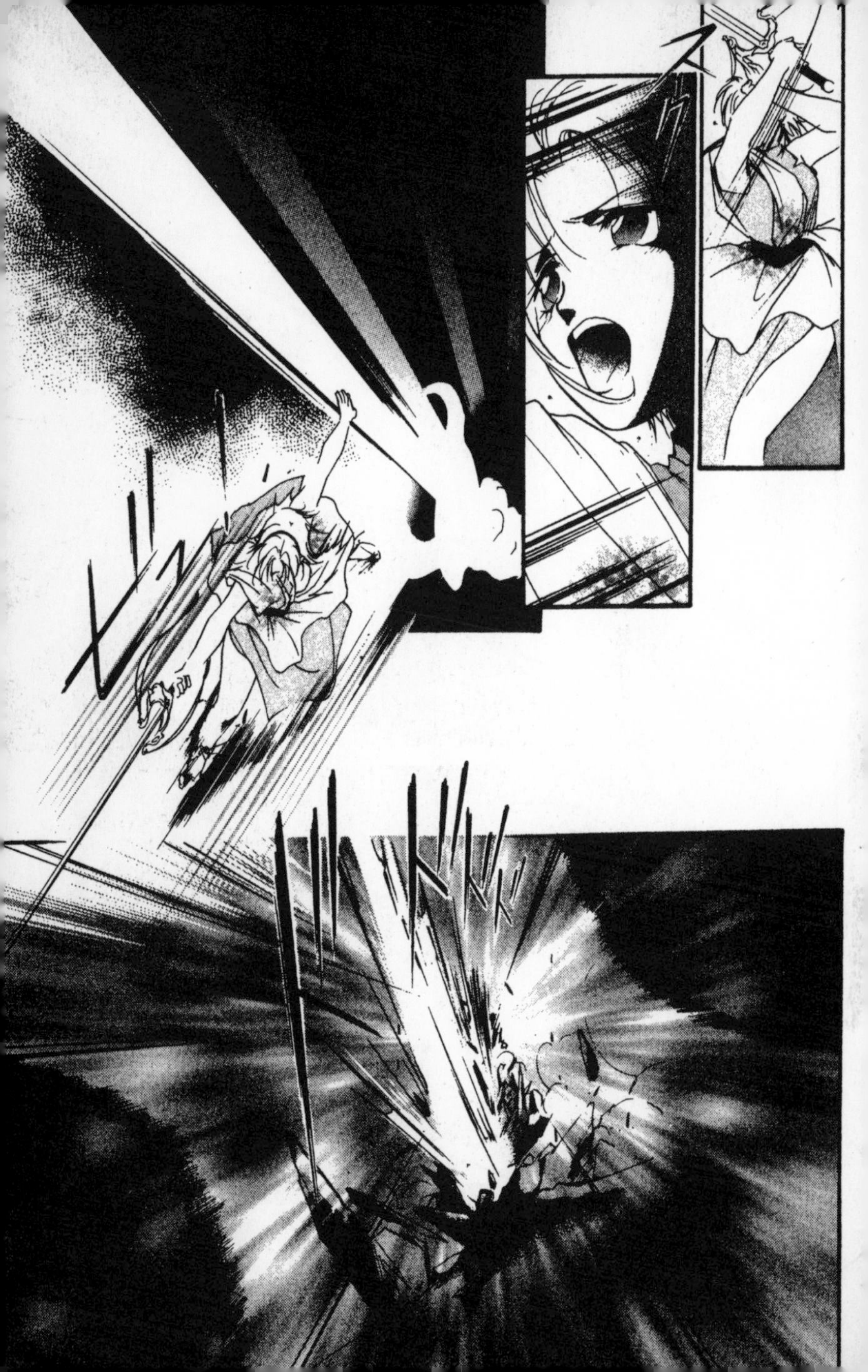

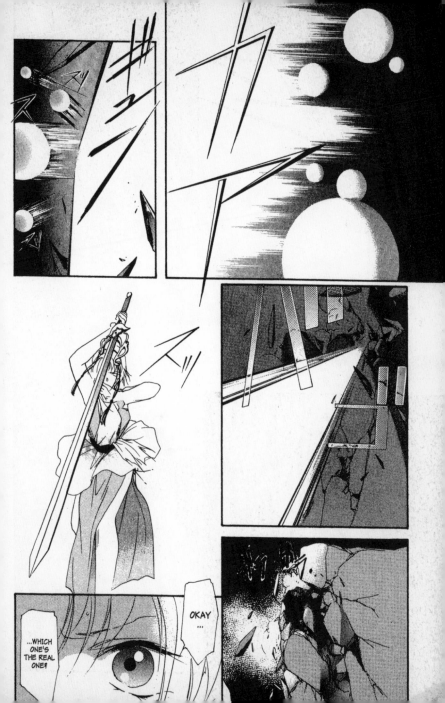

OKAY
...

...WHICH
ONE'S
THE REAL
ONE?

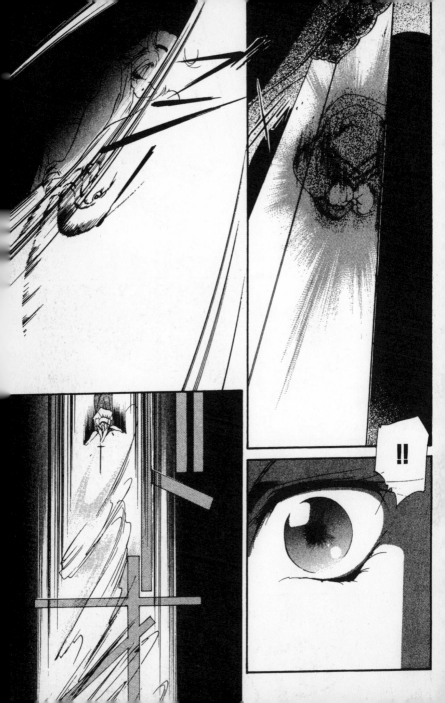

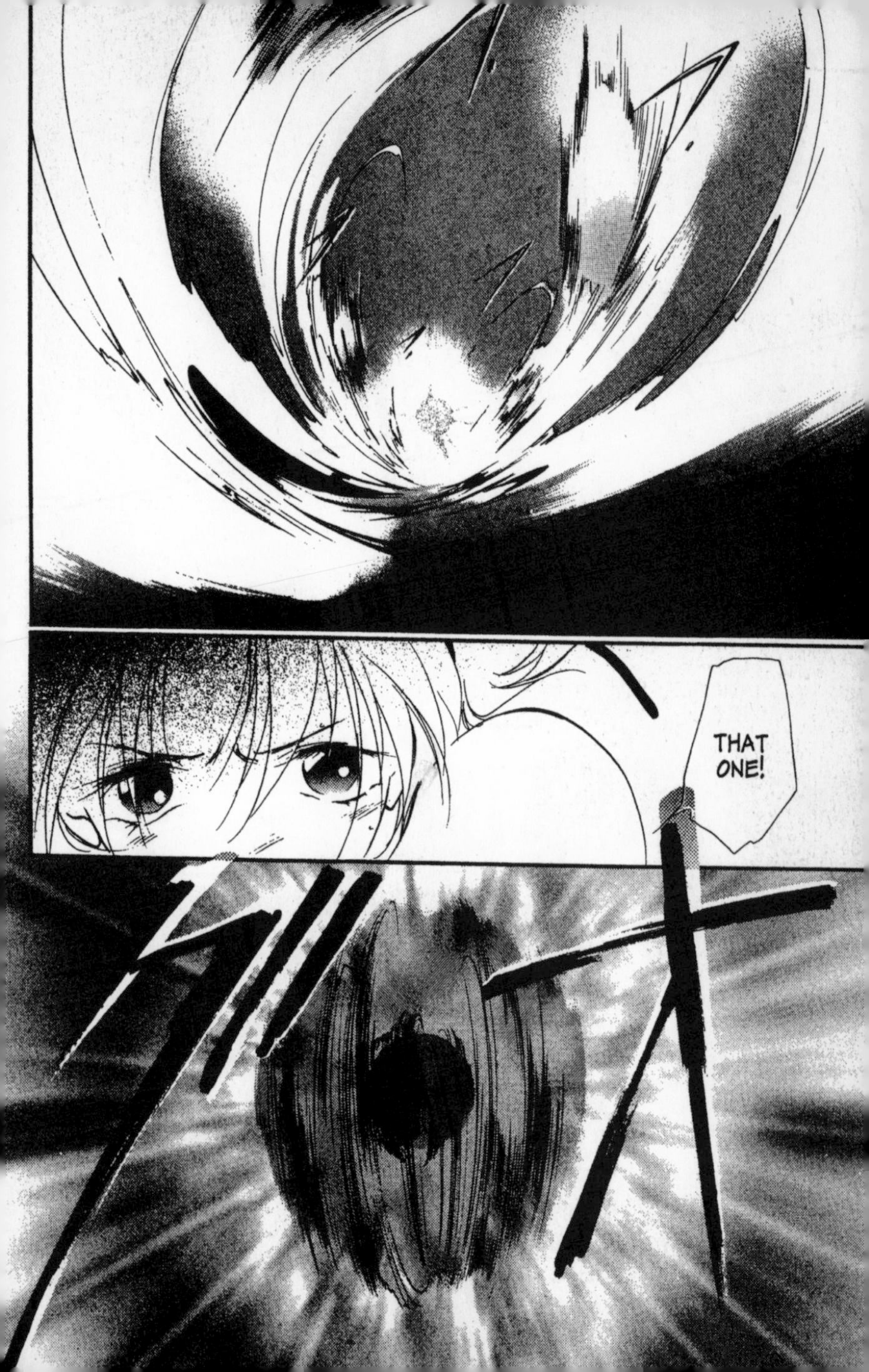
THAT ONE!

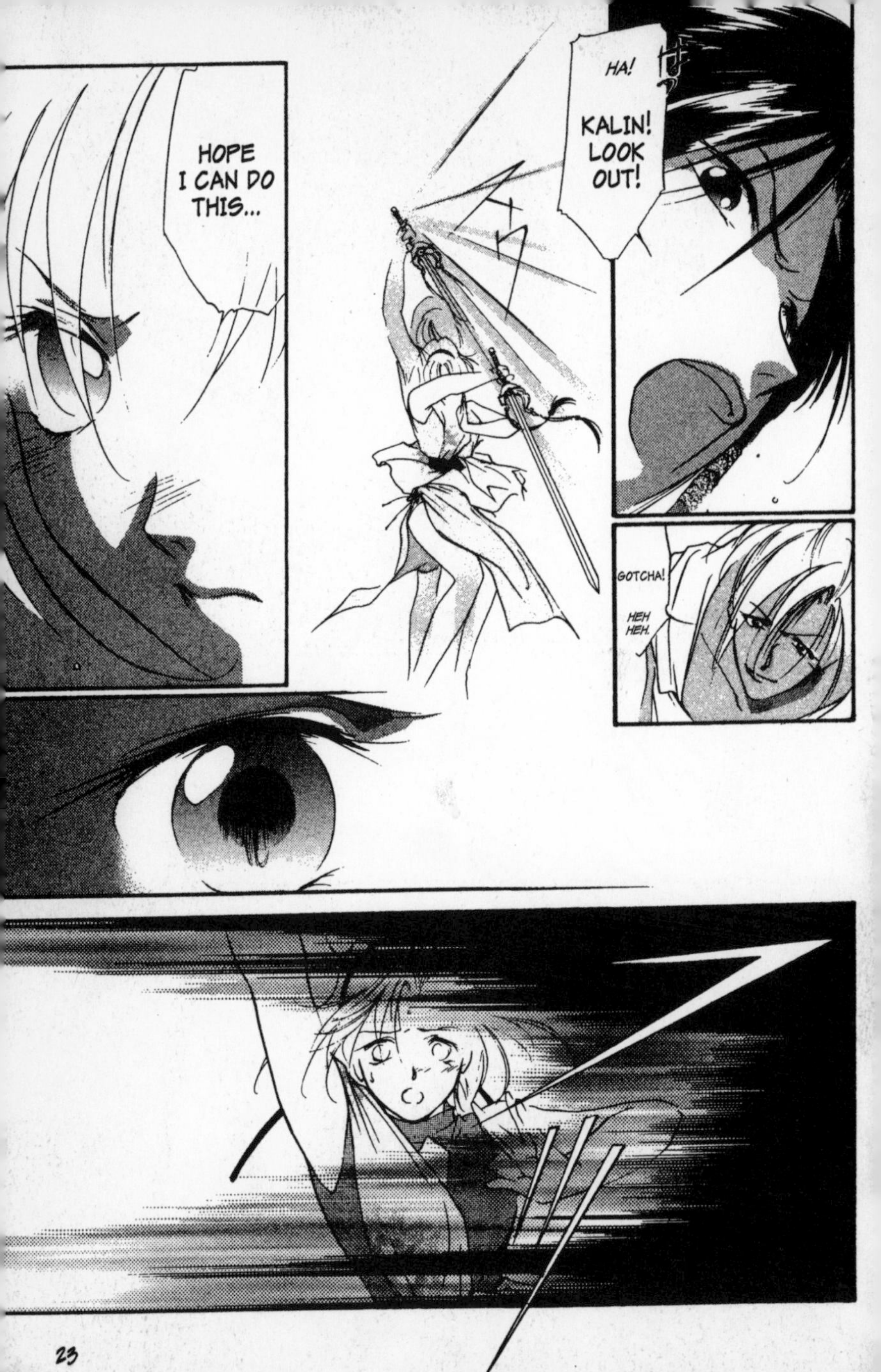
HA!
KALIN! LOOK OUT!
HOPE I CAN DO THIS...
GOTCHA!
HEH HEH.

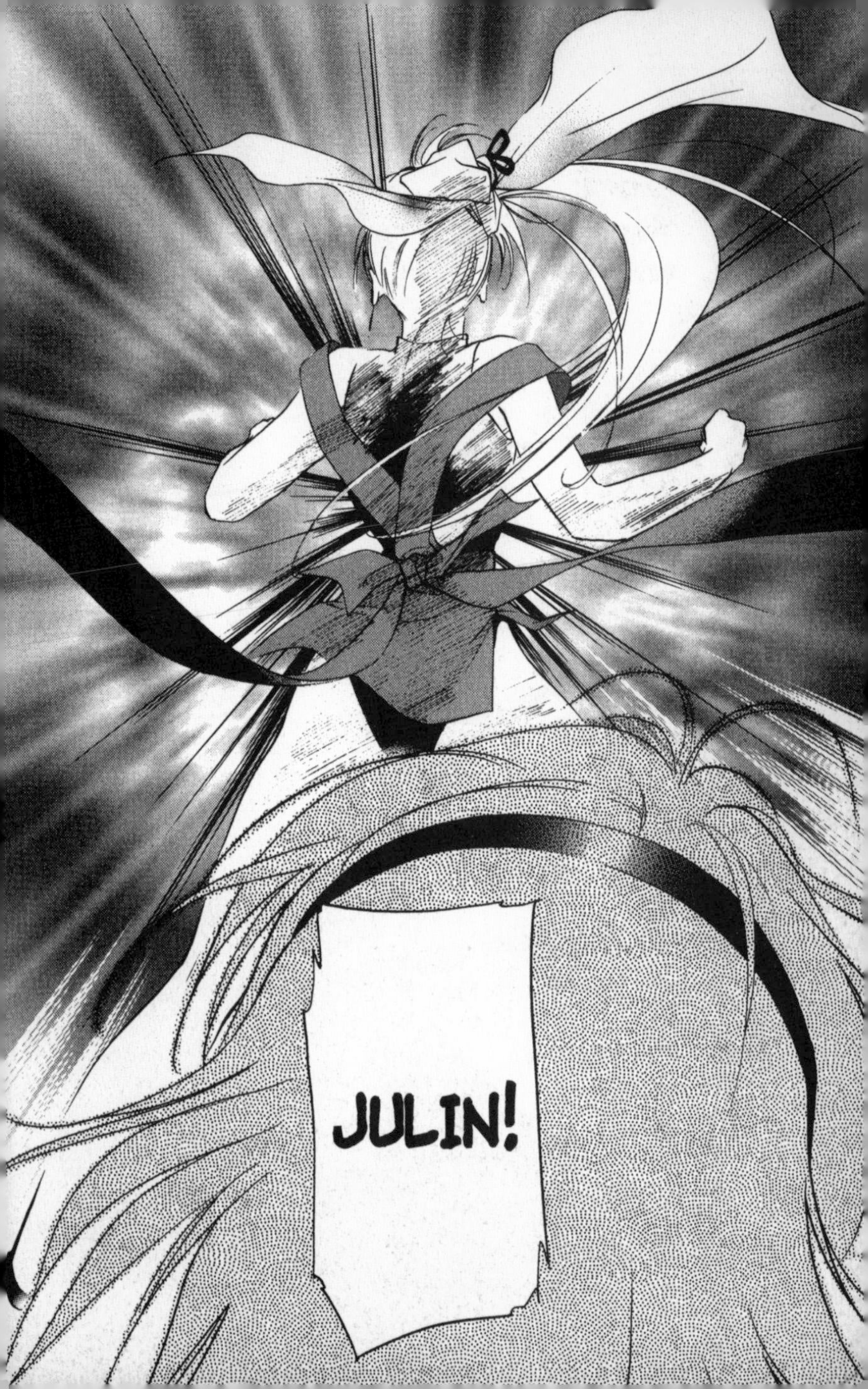
JULIN!

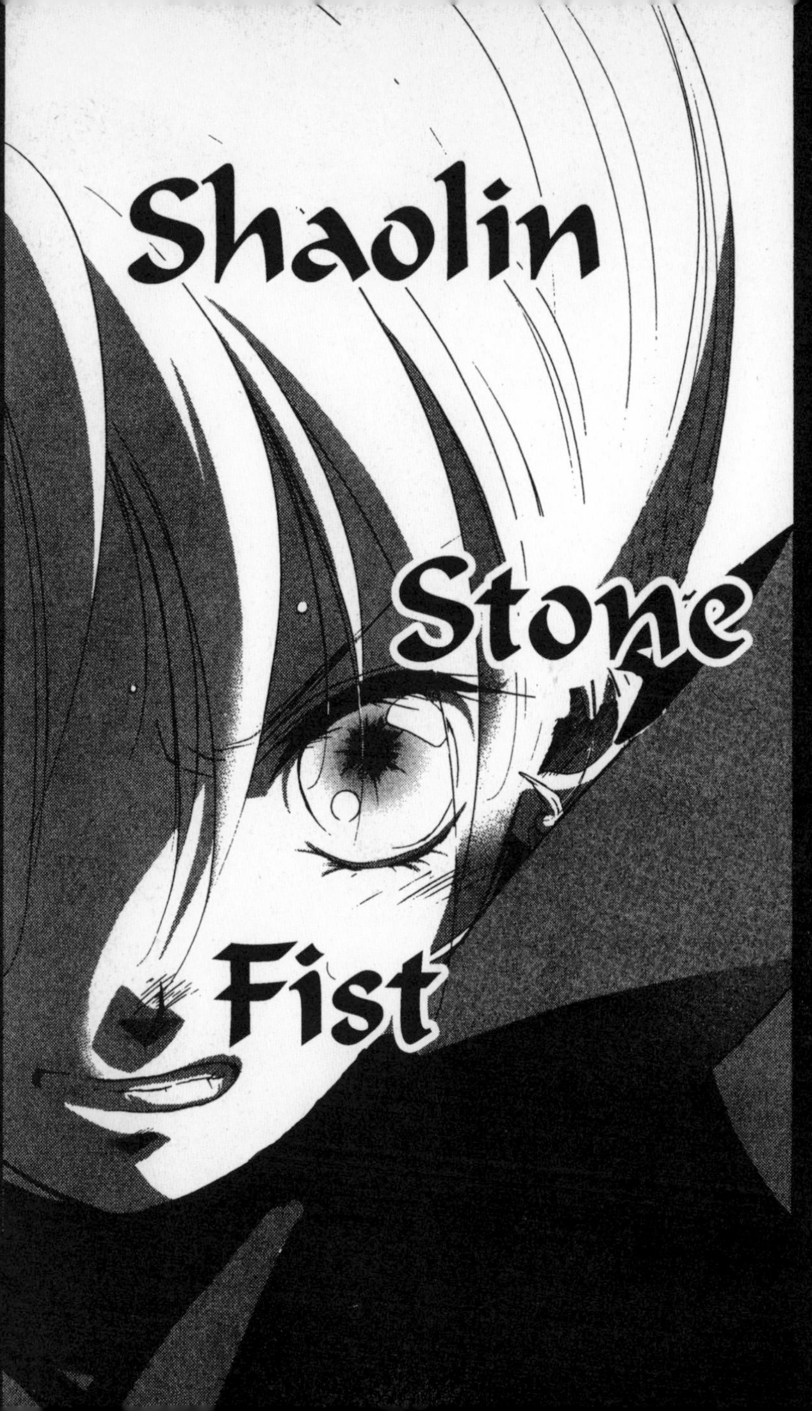
Shaolin
Stone
Fist

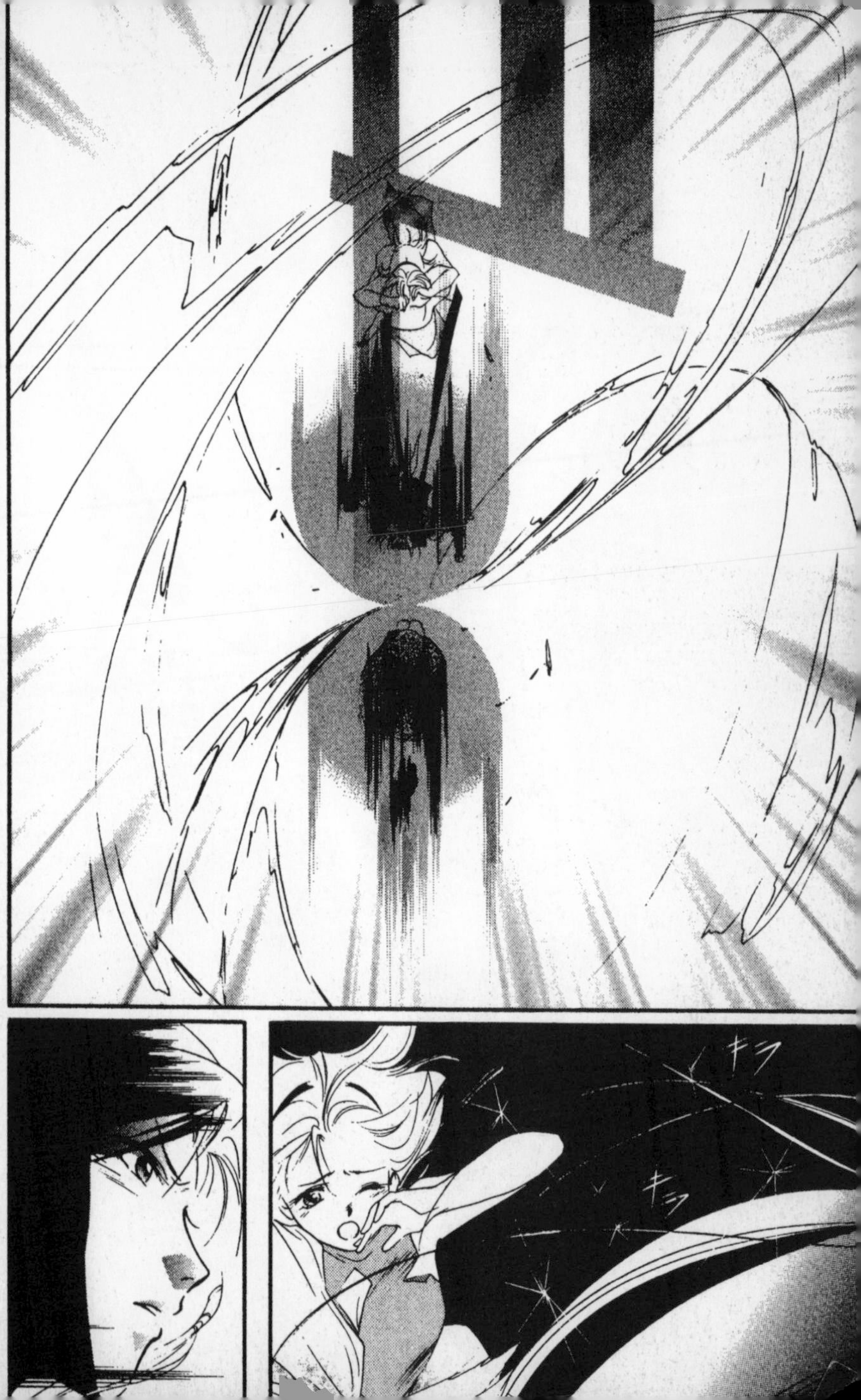
キラ
キラ

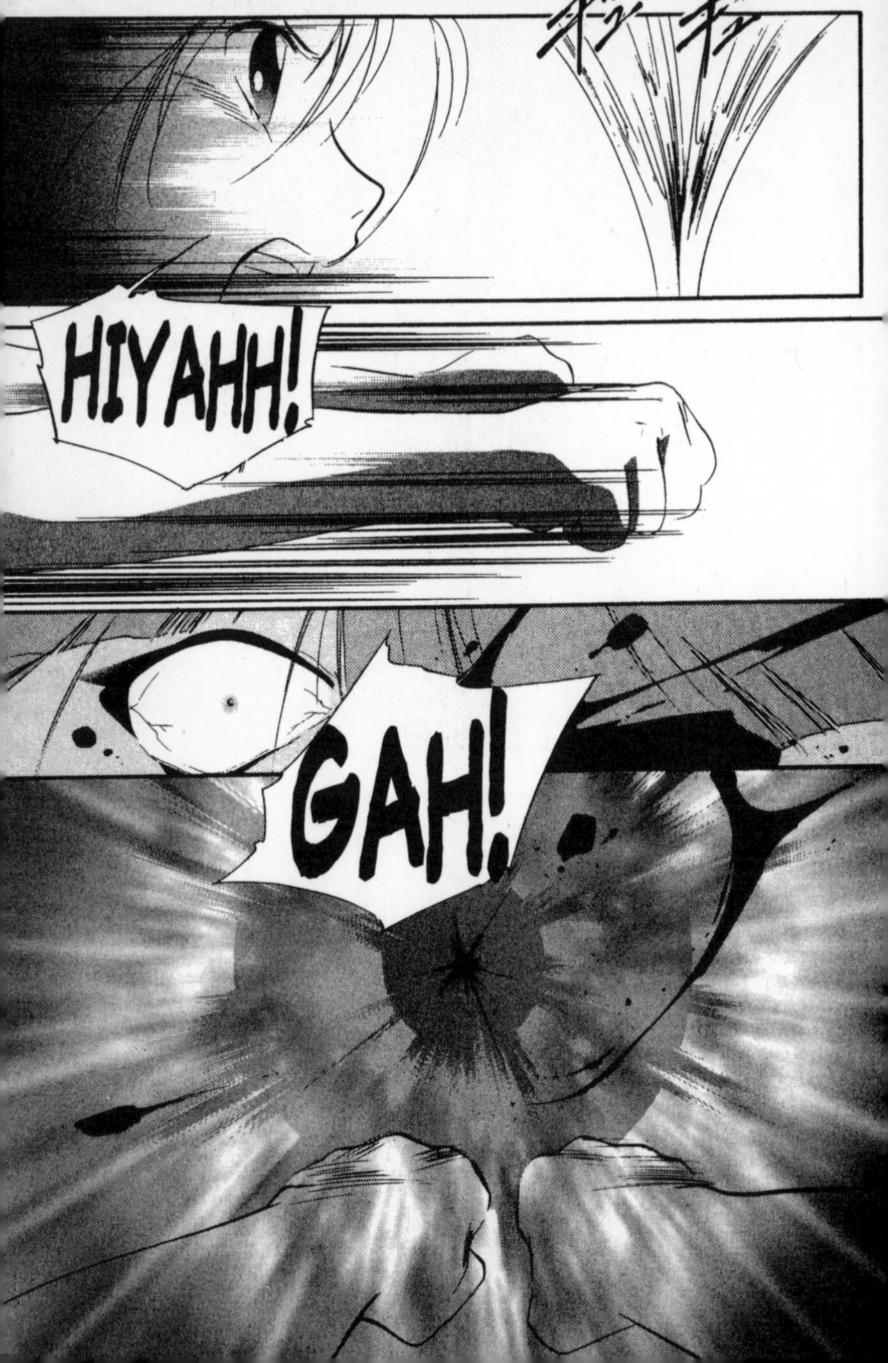
HIYAHH!
GAH!

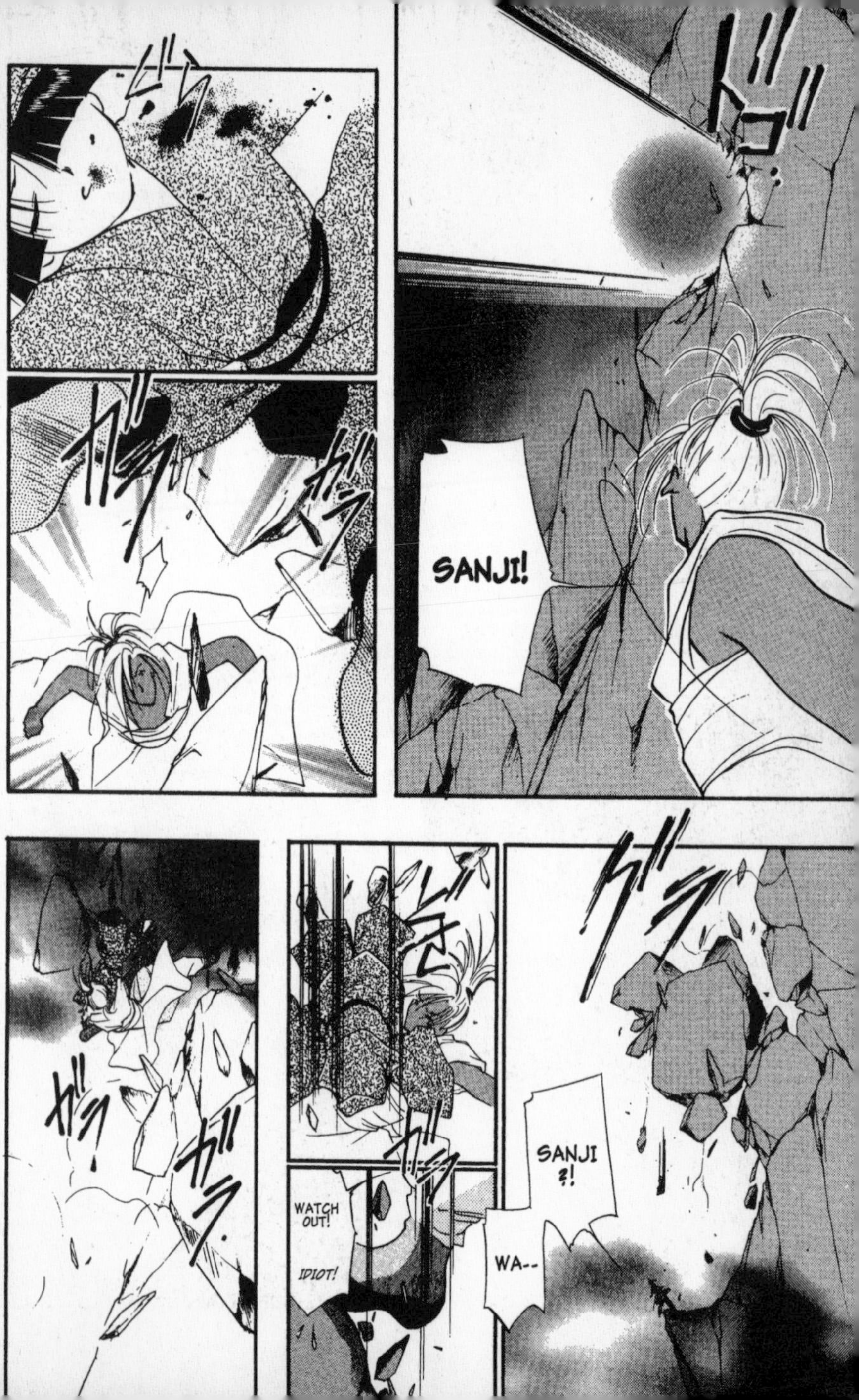
SANJI!
SANJI ?!
WA--
WATCH OUT!
IDIOT!

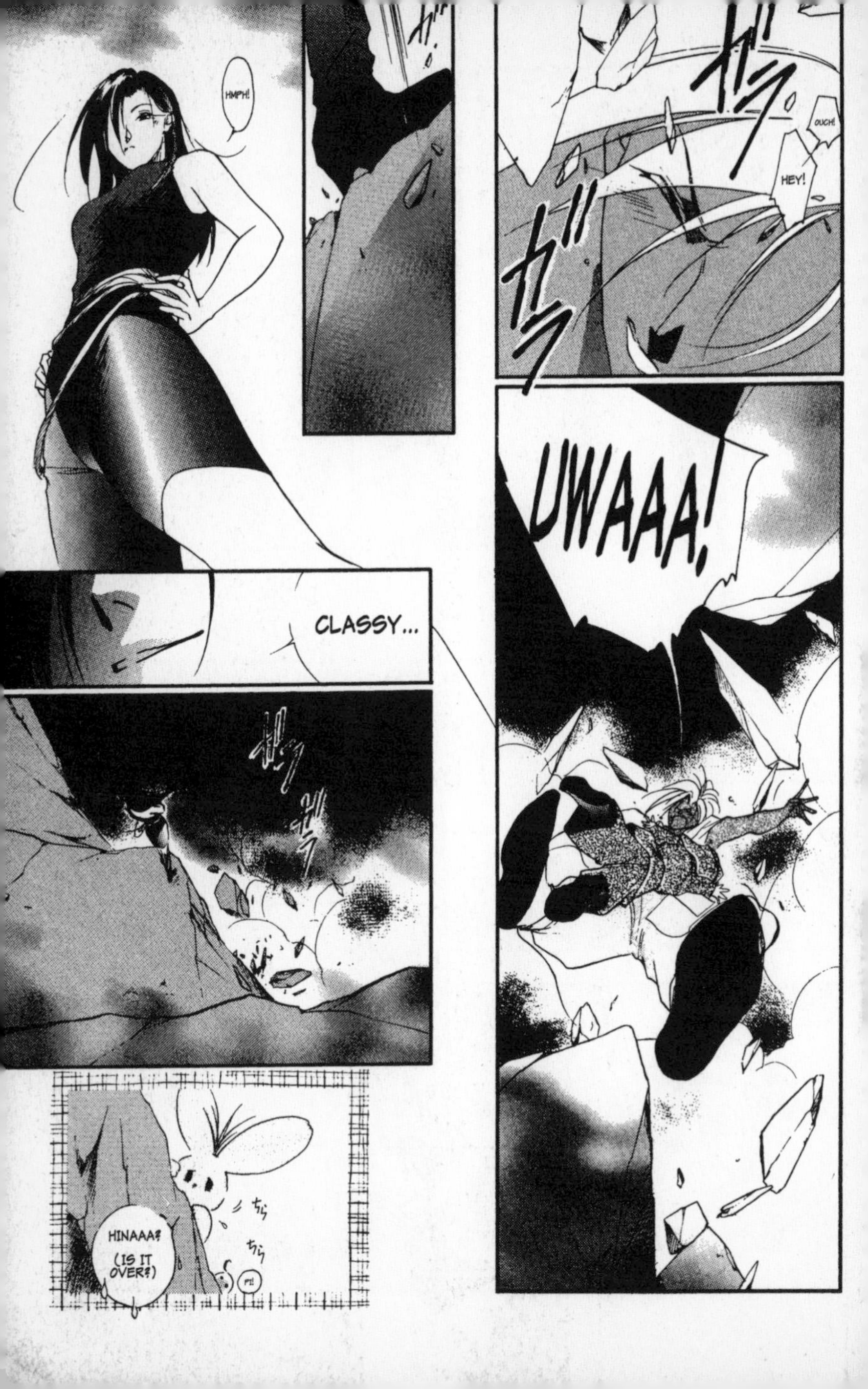
OUCH!
HEY!
HMPH!
UWAAA!
CLASSY...
HINAAA? (IS IT OVER?)
FI!

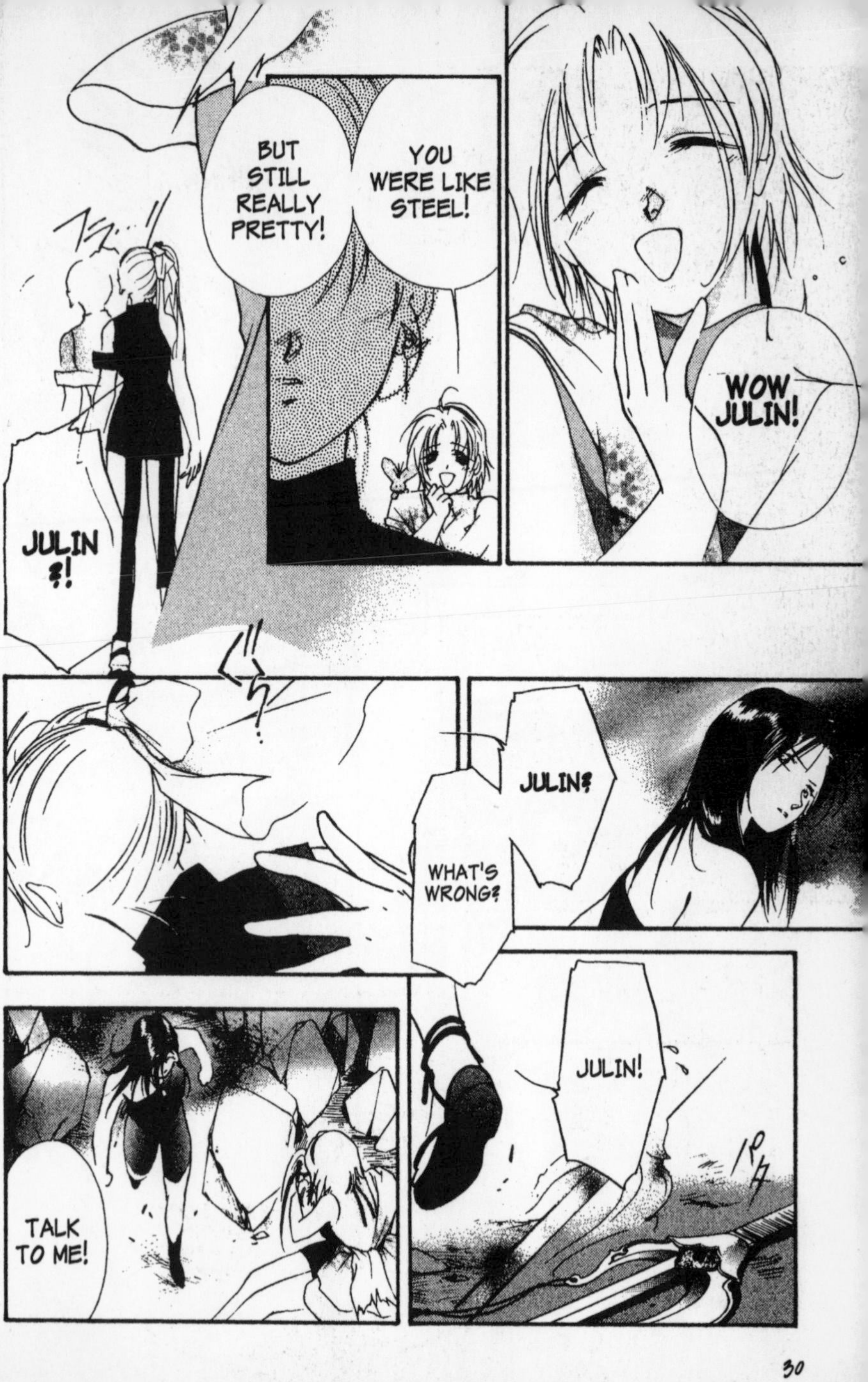
WOW JULIN!
YOU WERE LIKE STEEL!
BUT STILL REALLY PRETTY!
JULIN?!
JULIN?
WHAT'S WRONG?
JULIN!
TALK TO ME!

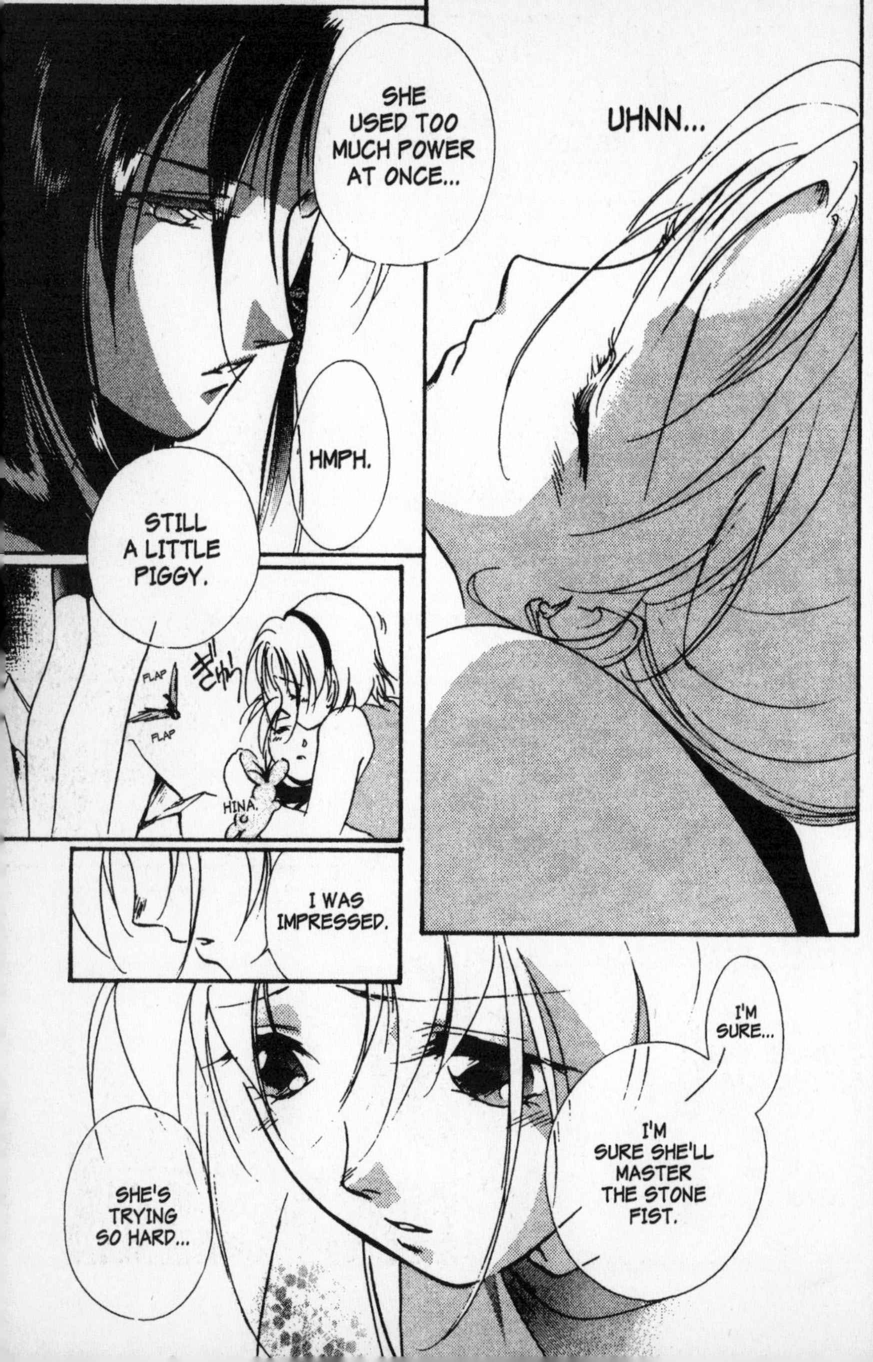
UHNN...
SHE USED TOO MUCH POWER AT ONCE...
HMPH.
STILL A LITTLE PIGGY.
FLAP
FLAP
HINA.
I WAS IMPRESSED.
I'M SURE...
I'M SURE SHE'LL MASTER THE STONE FIST.
SHE'S TRYING SO HARD...

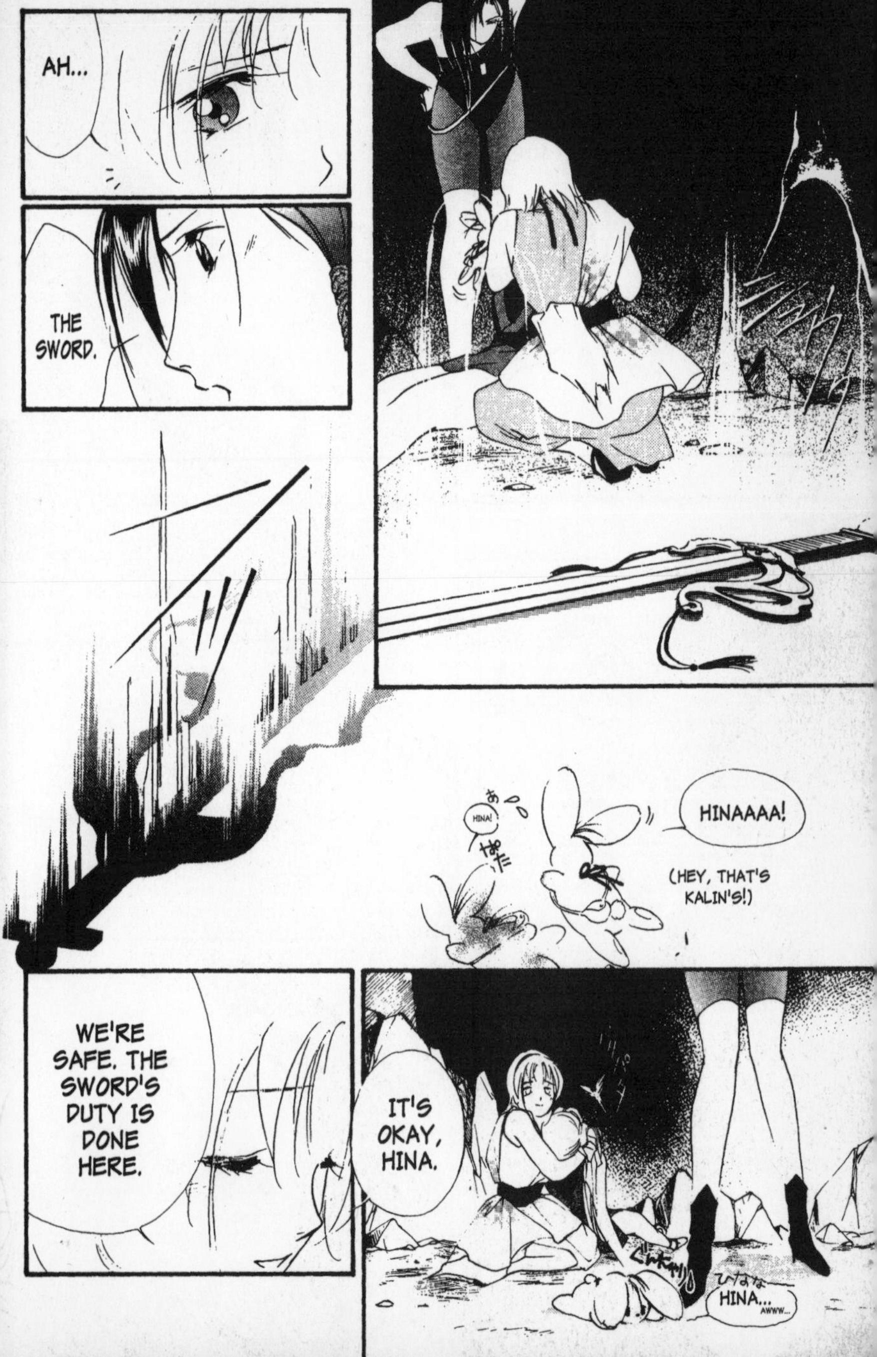
AH...
THE SWORD.
HINAAAA!
(HEY, THAT'S KALIN'S!)
HINA!
IT'S OKAY, HINA.
HINA...
AWWW...
WE'RE SAFE. THE SWORD'S DUTY IS DONE HERE.

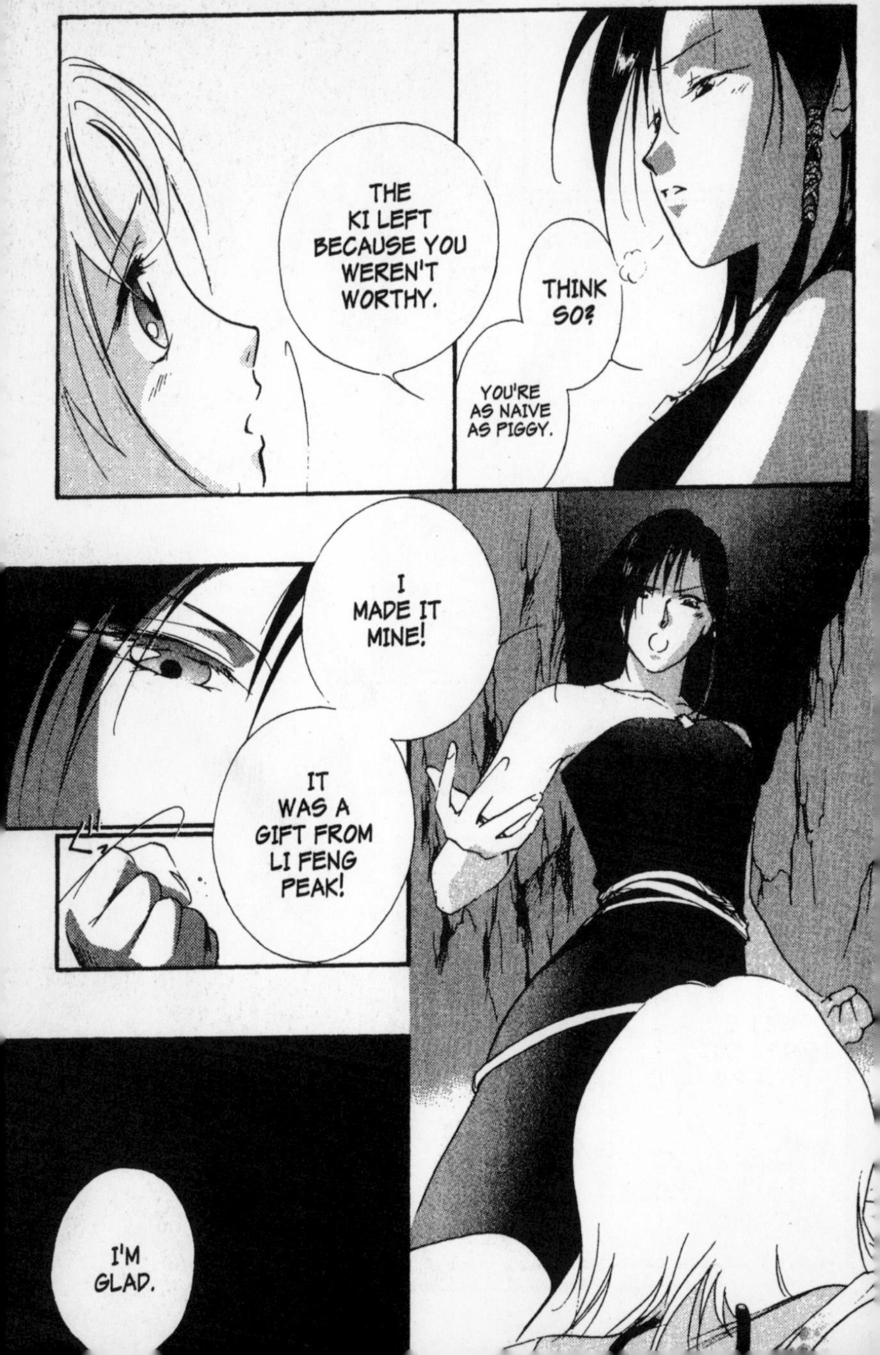
THINK SO?
YOU'RE AS NAIVE AS PIGGY.
THE KI LEFT BECAUSE YOU WEREN'T WORTHY.
I MADE IT MINE!
IT WAS A GIFT FROM LI FENG PEAK!
I'M GLAD.

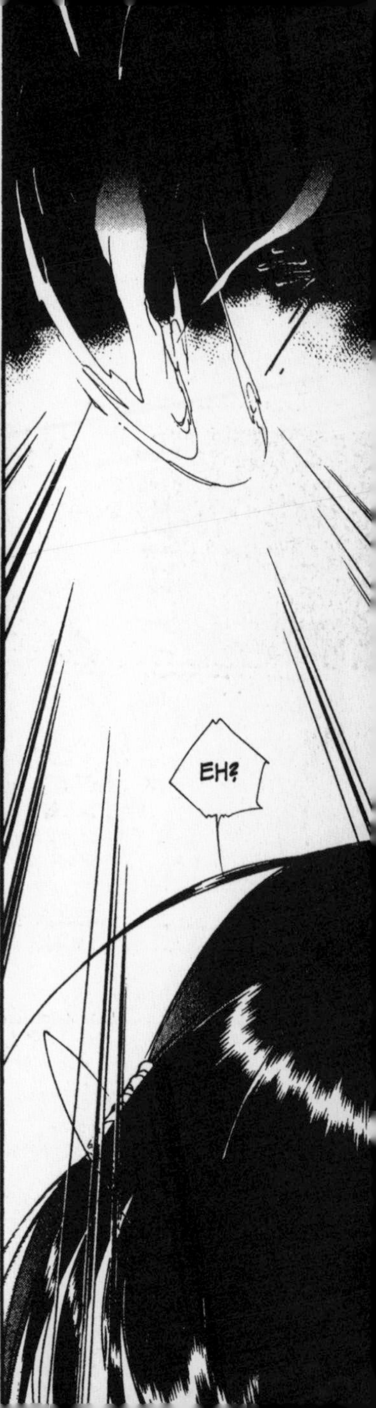
EH?

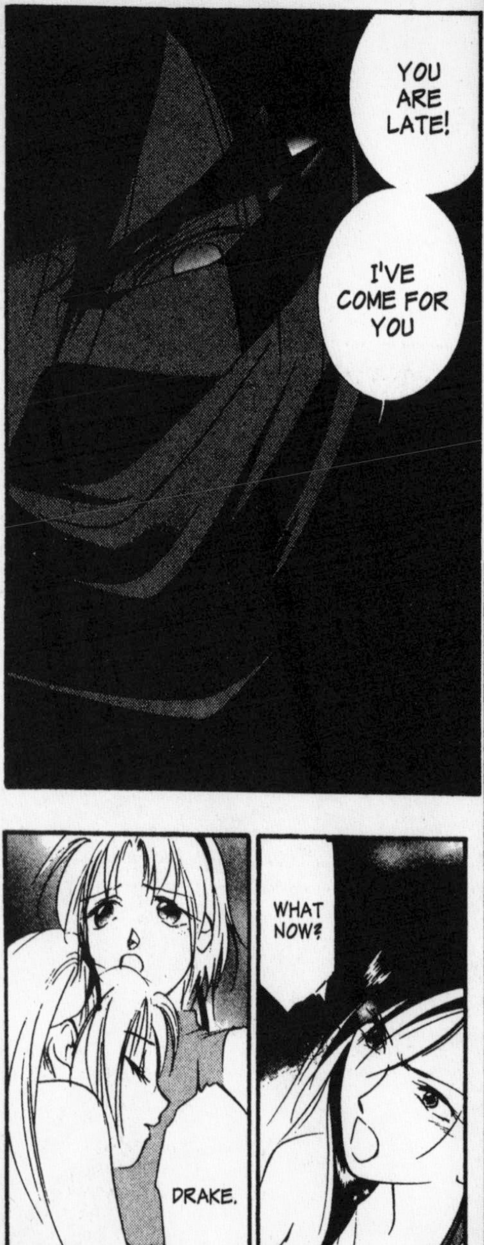
YOU ARE LATE!
I'VE COME FOR YOU
WHAT NOW?
DRAKE.

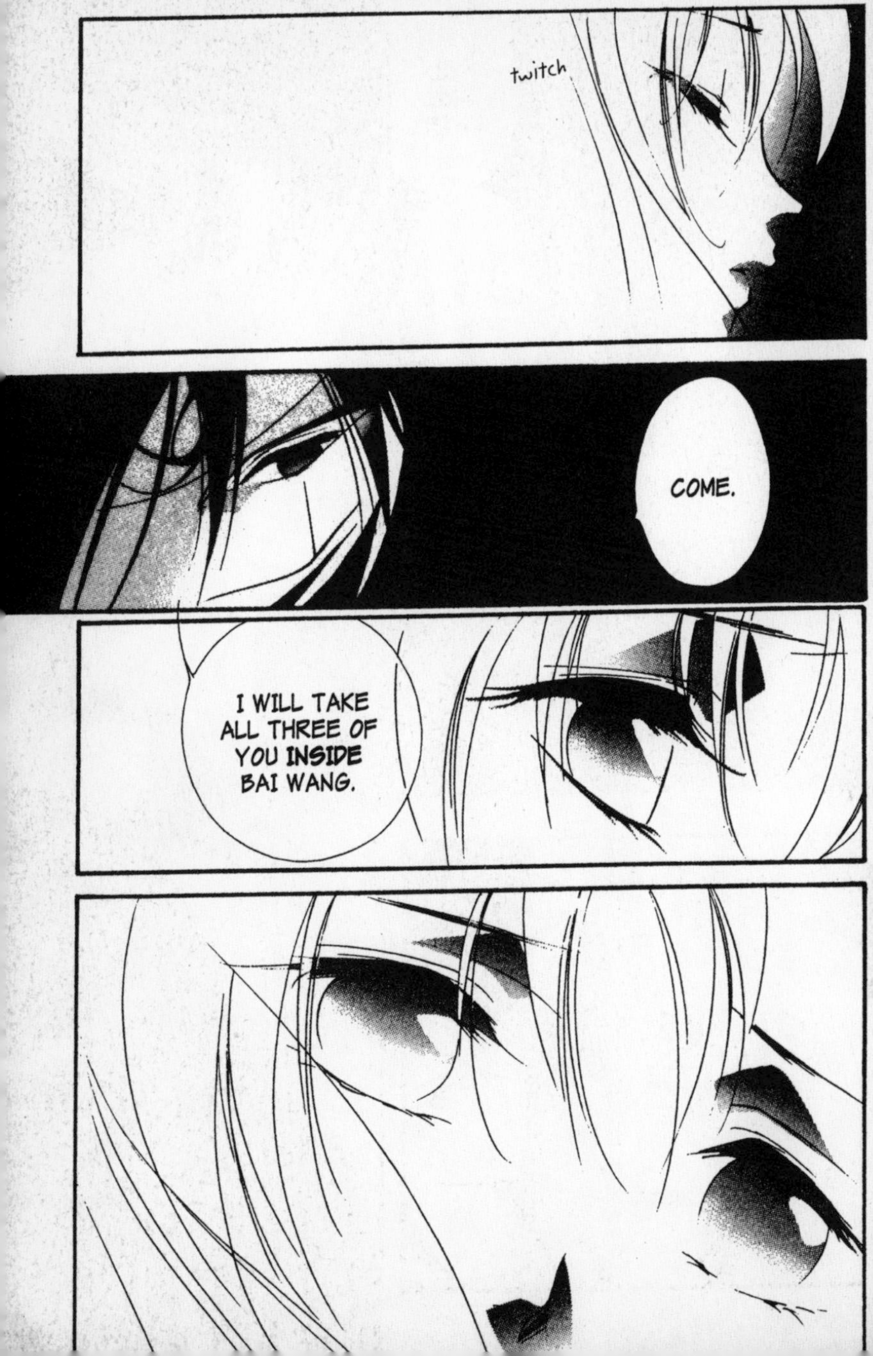
twitch
COME.
I WILL TAKE ALL THREE OF YOU INSIDE BAI WANG.

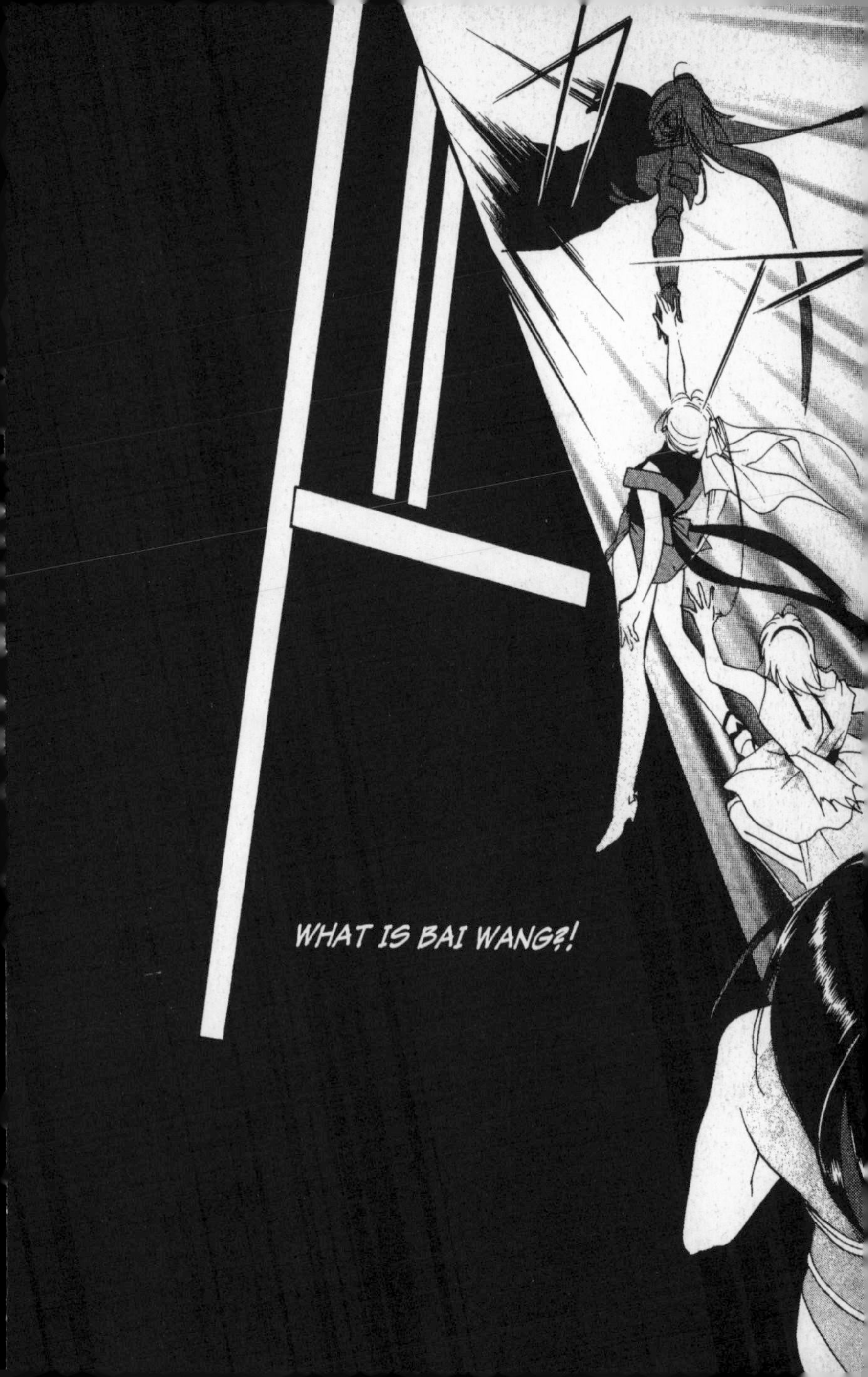
WHAT IS BAI WANG?!

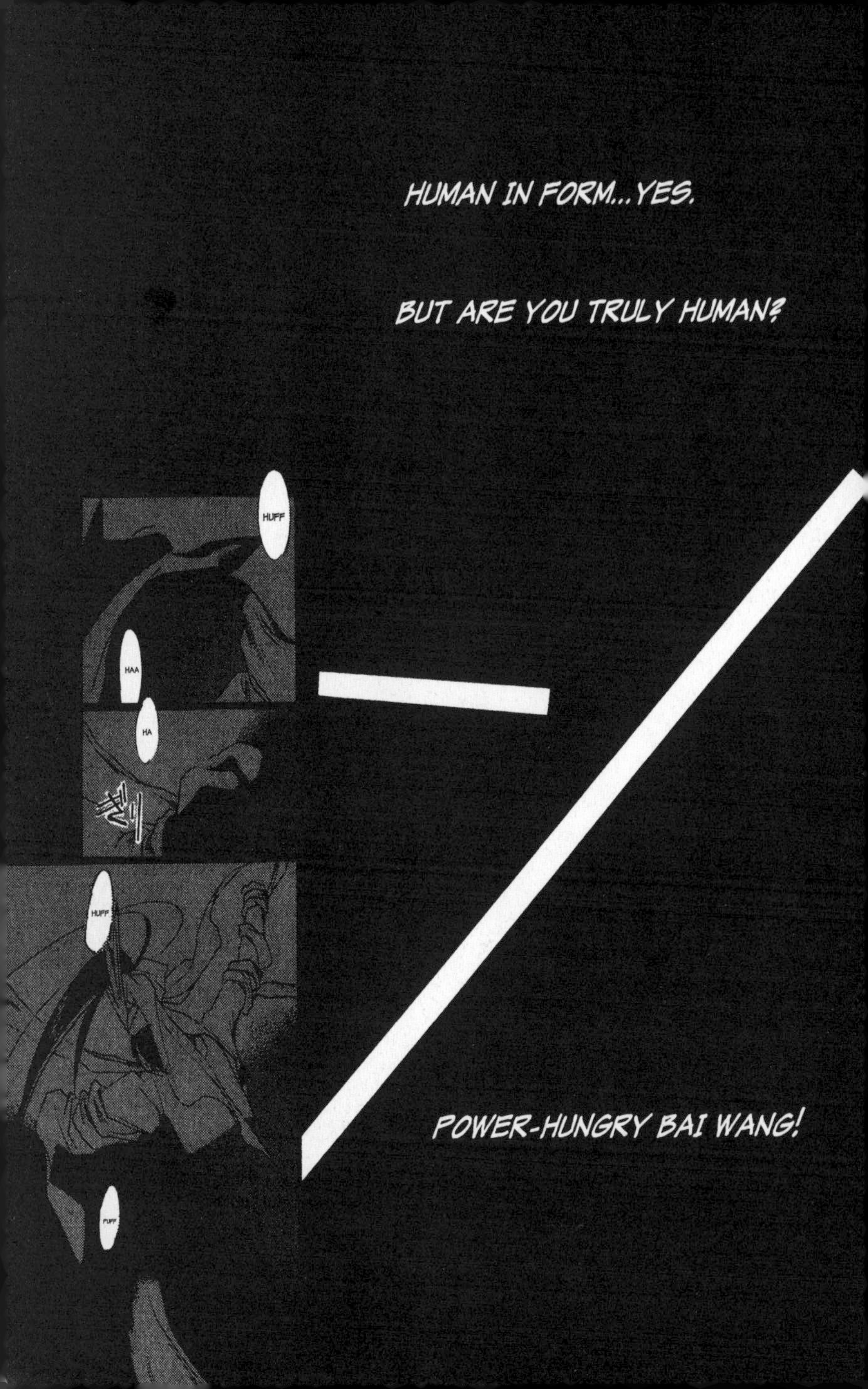
HUMAN IN FORM...YES.
BUT ARE YOU TRULY HUMAN?
POWER-HUNGRY BAI WANG!
HUFF
HAA
HA
HUFF
PUFF

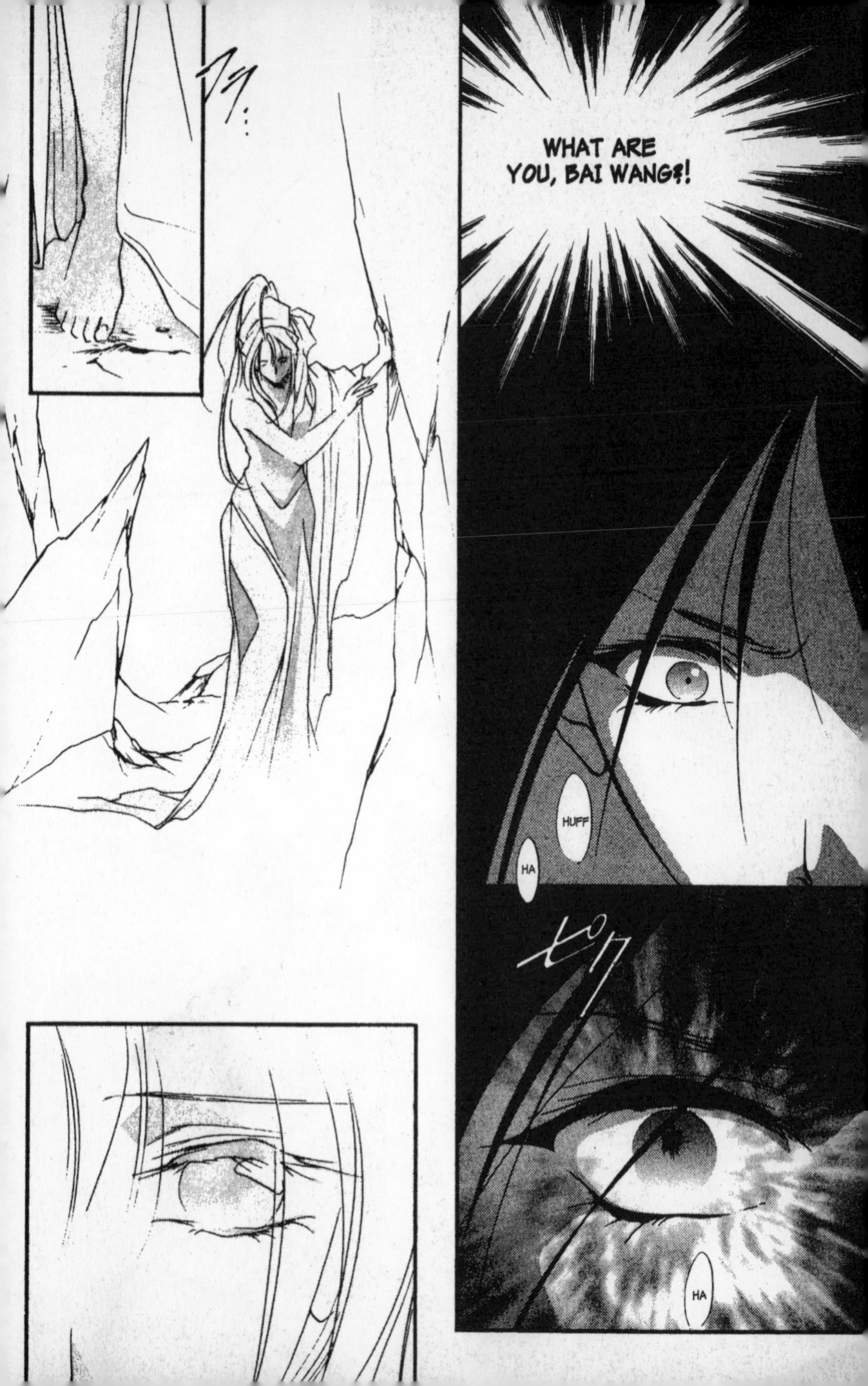
WHAT ARE YOU, BAI WANG?!
HUFF
HA
HA

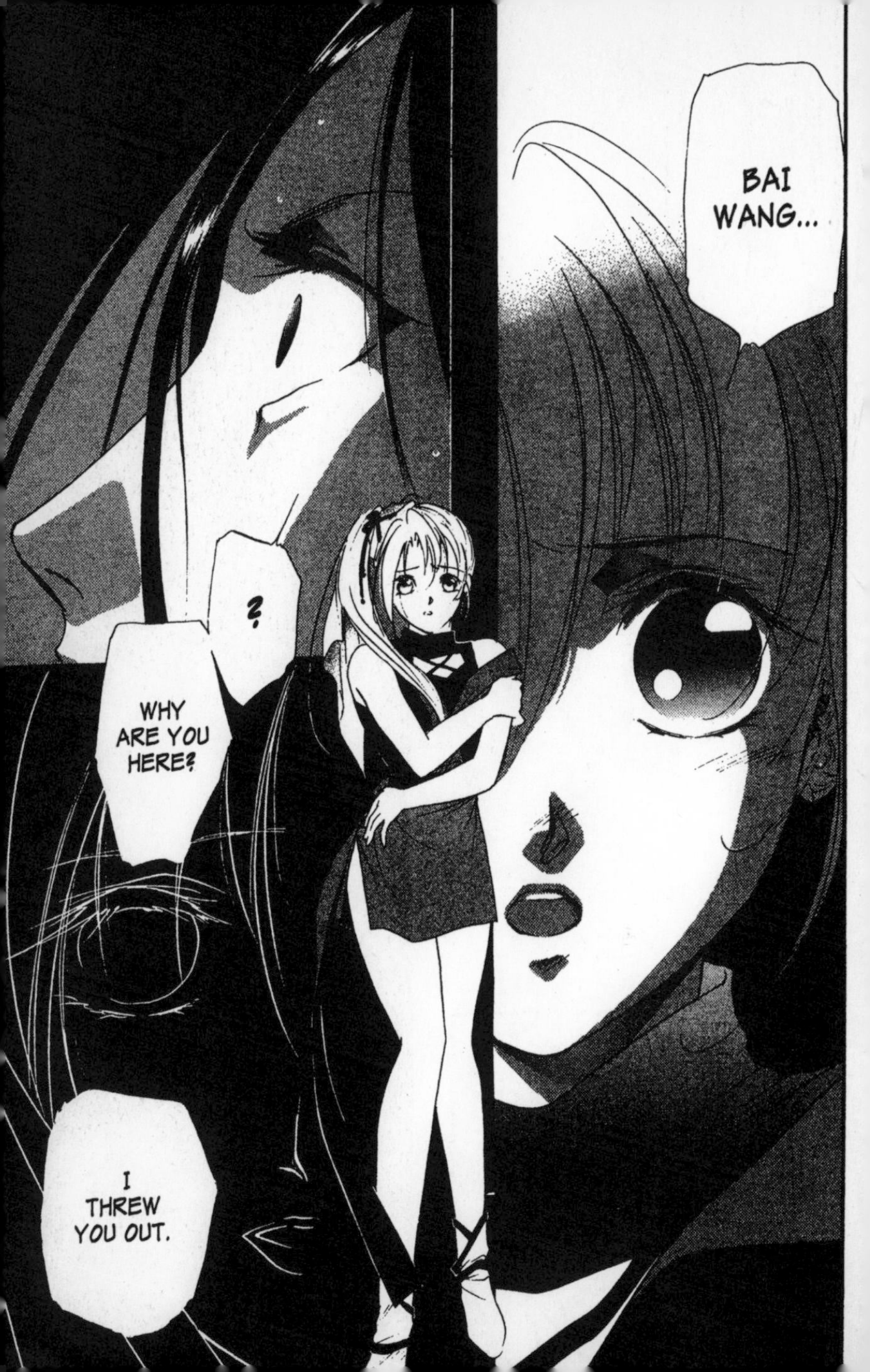
BAI WANG...
?
WHY ARE YOU HERE?
I THREW YOU OUT.

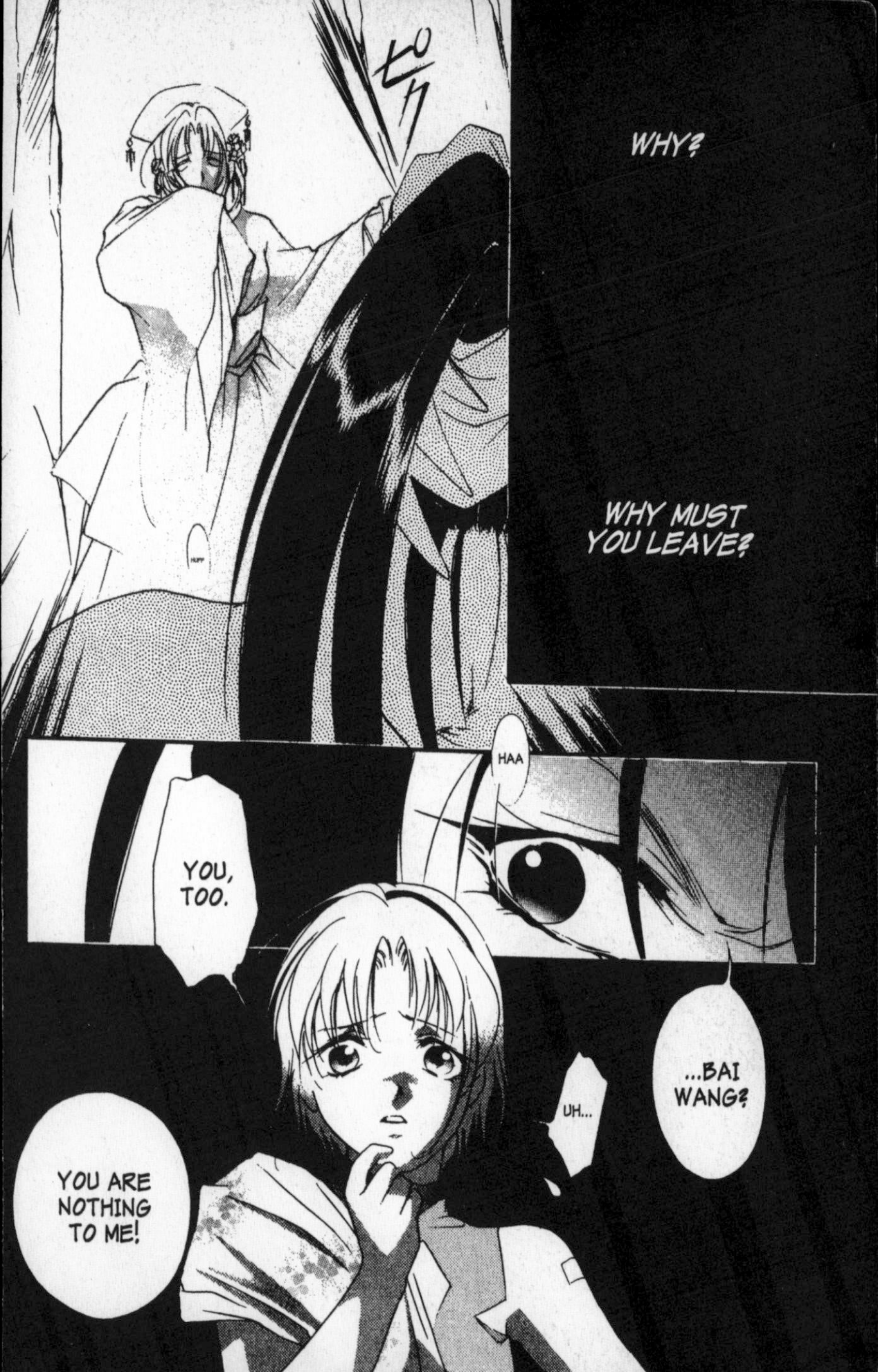
WHY?
WHY MUST YOU LEAVE?
HUFF
HAA
YOU, TOO.
...BAI WANG?
UH...
YOU ARE NOTHING TO ME!

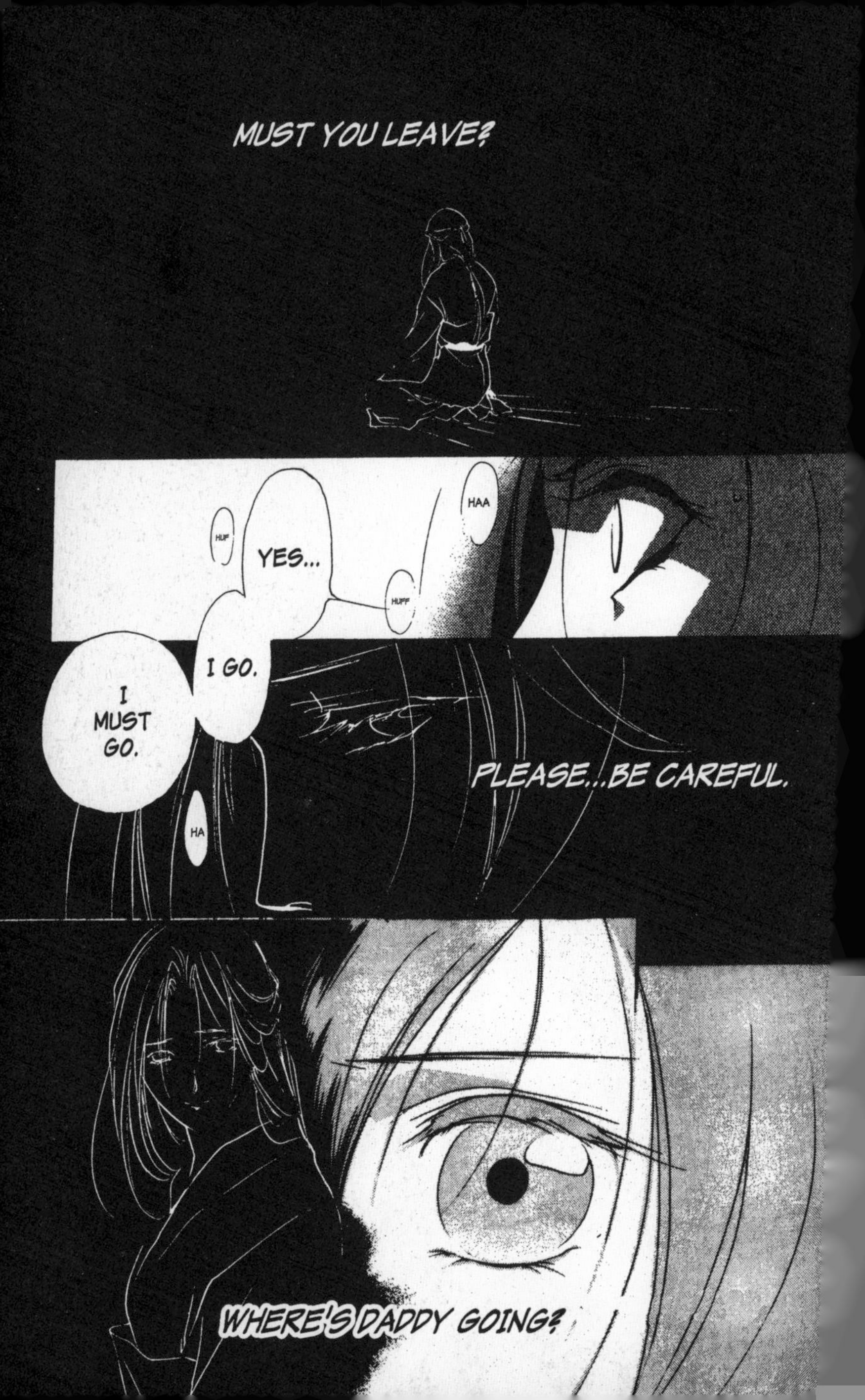
MUST YOU LEAVE?
HAA
YES...
HUFF
HUF
PLEASE...BE CAREFUL.
I GO.
I MUST GO.
HA
WHERE'S DADDY GOING?

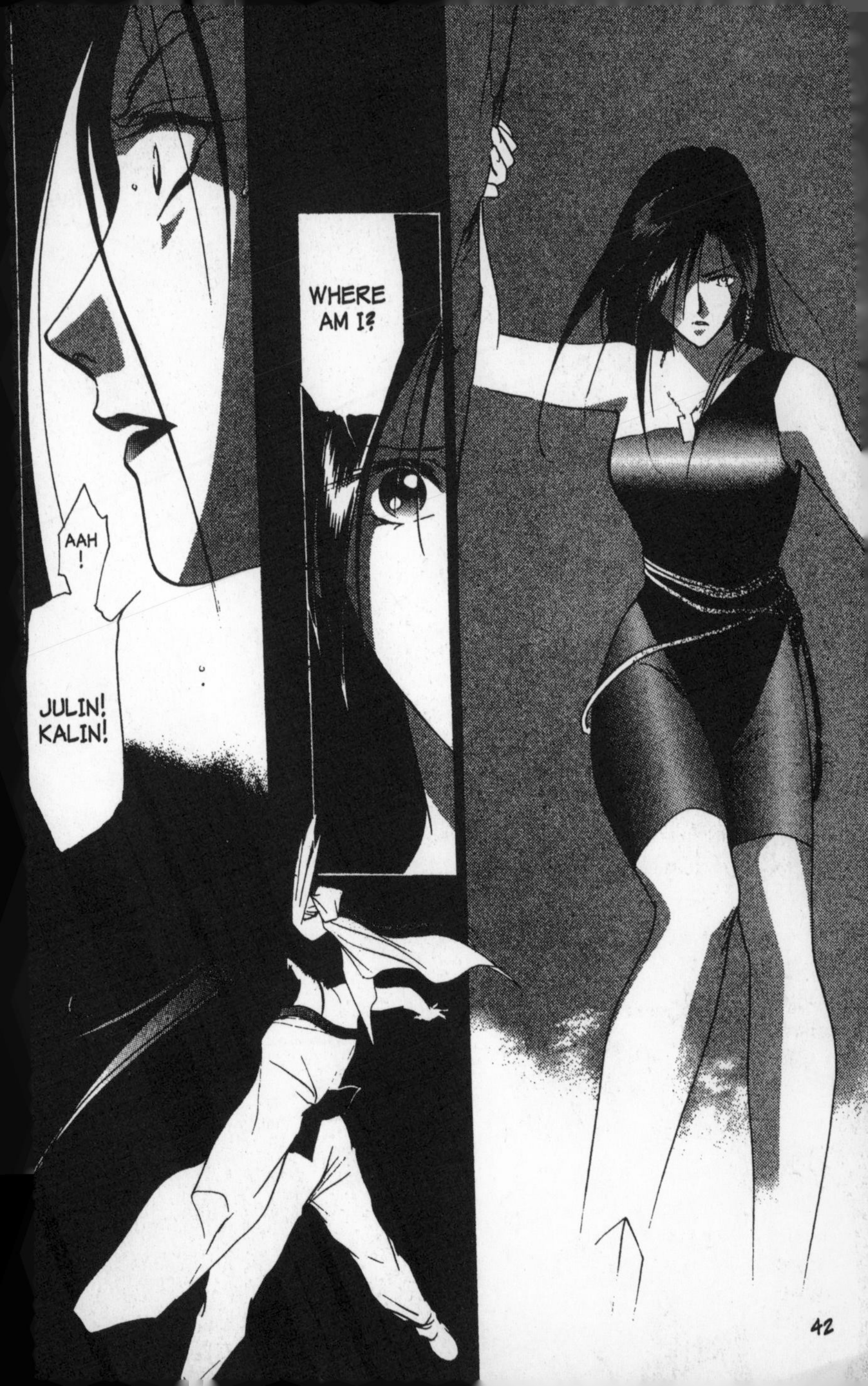
WHERE AM I?
AAH !
JULIN! KALIN!

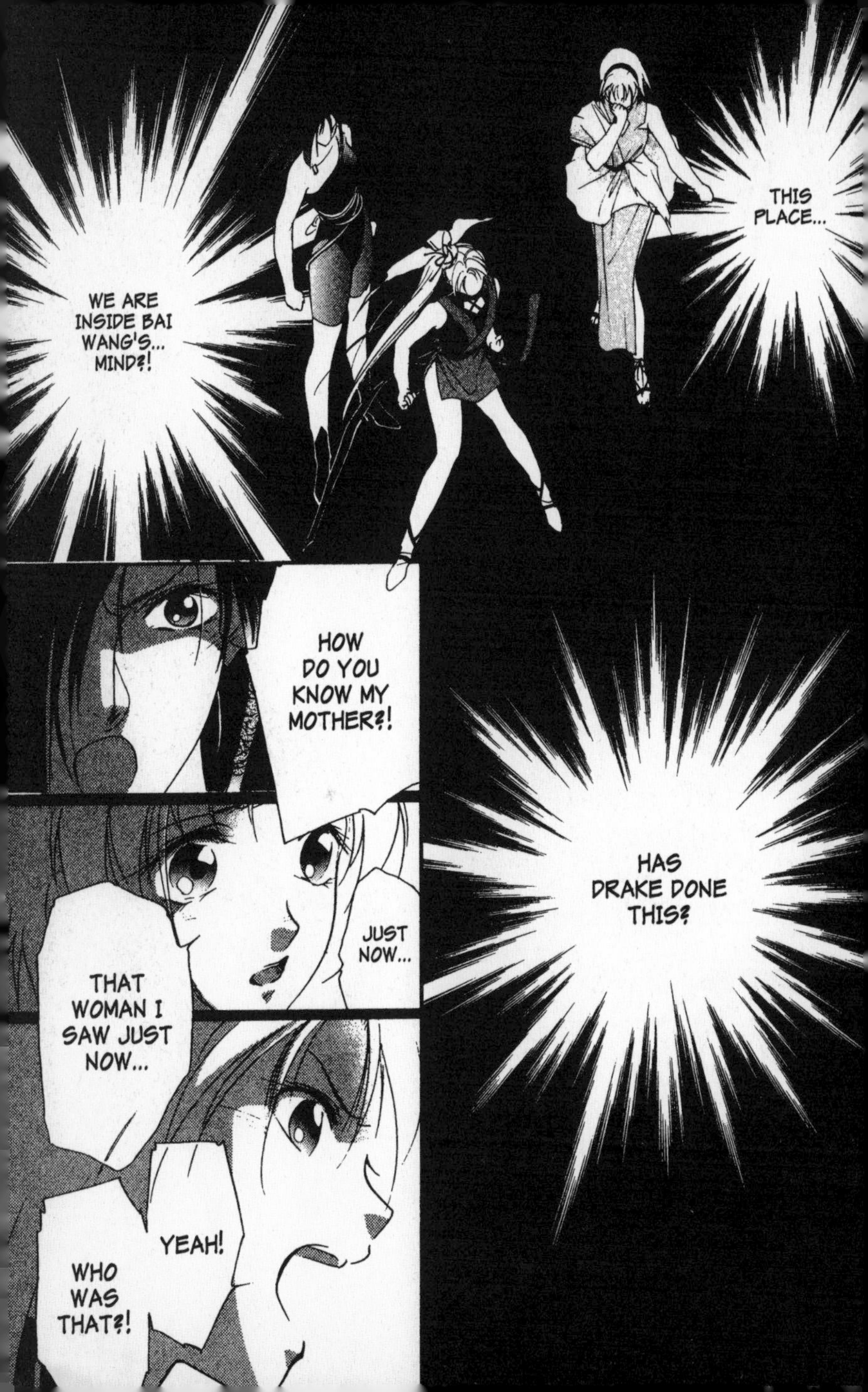
THIS PLACE...
WE ARE INSIDE BAI WANG'S... MIND?!
HAS DRAKE DONE THIS?
HOW DO YOU KNOW MY MOTHER?!
JUST NOW...
THAT WOMAN I SAW JUST NOW...
YEAH!
WHO WAS THAT?!

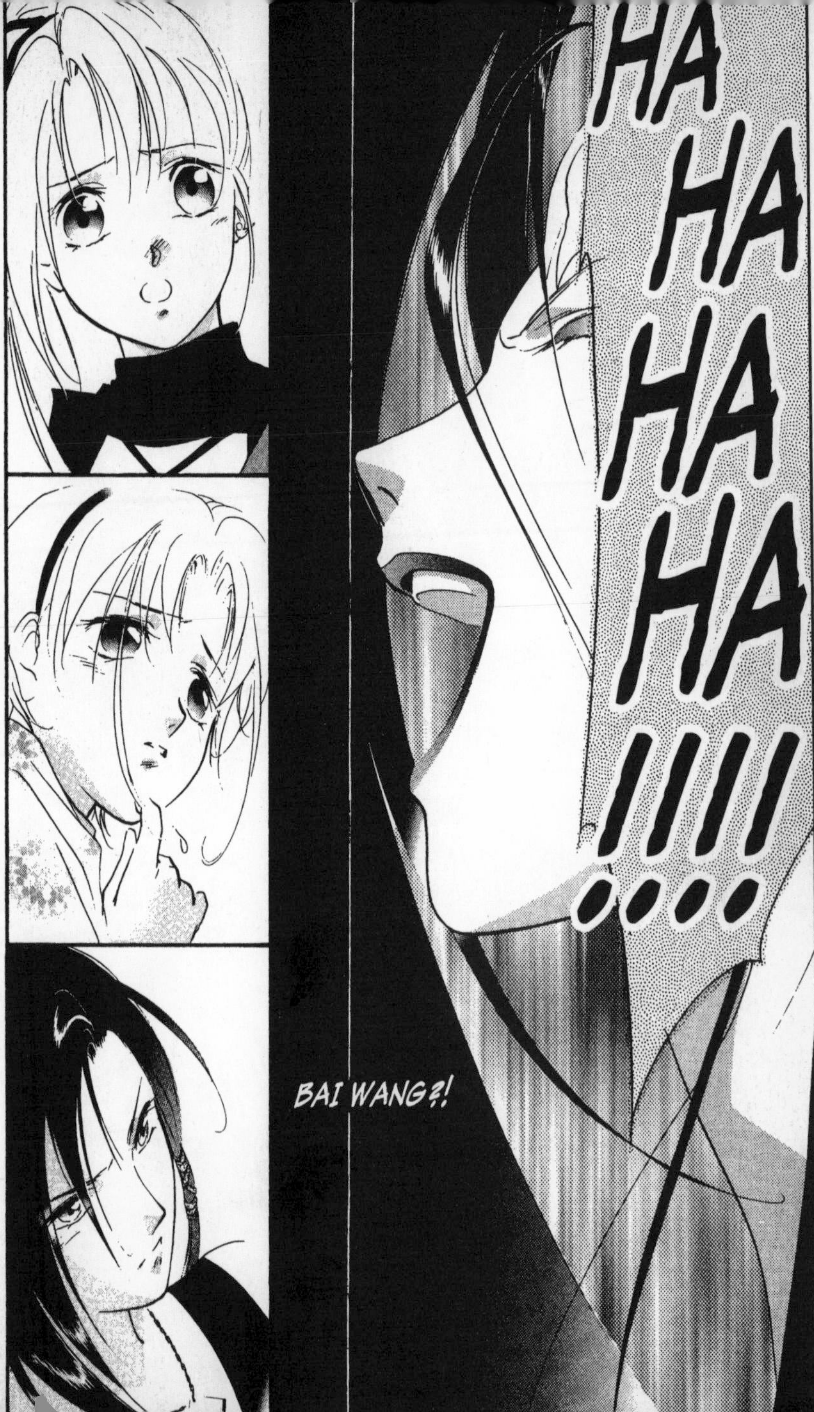
HA HA HA HA HA !!!!....
BAI WANG?!

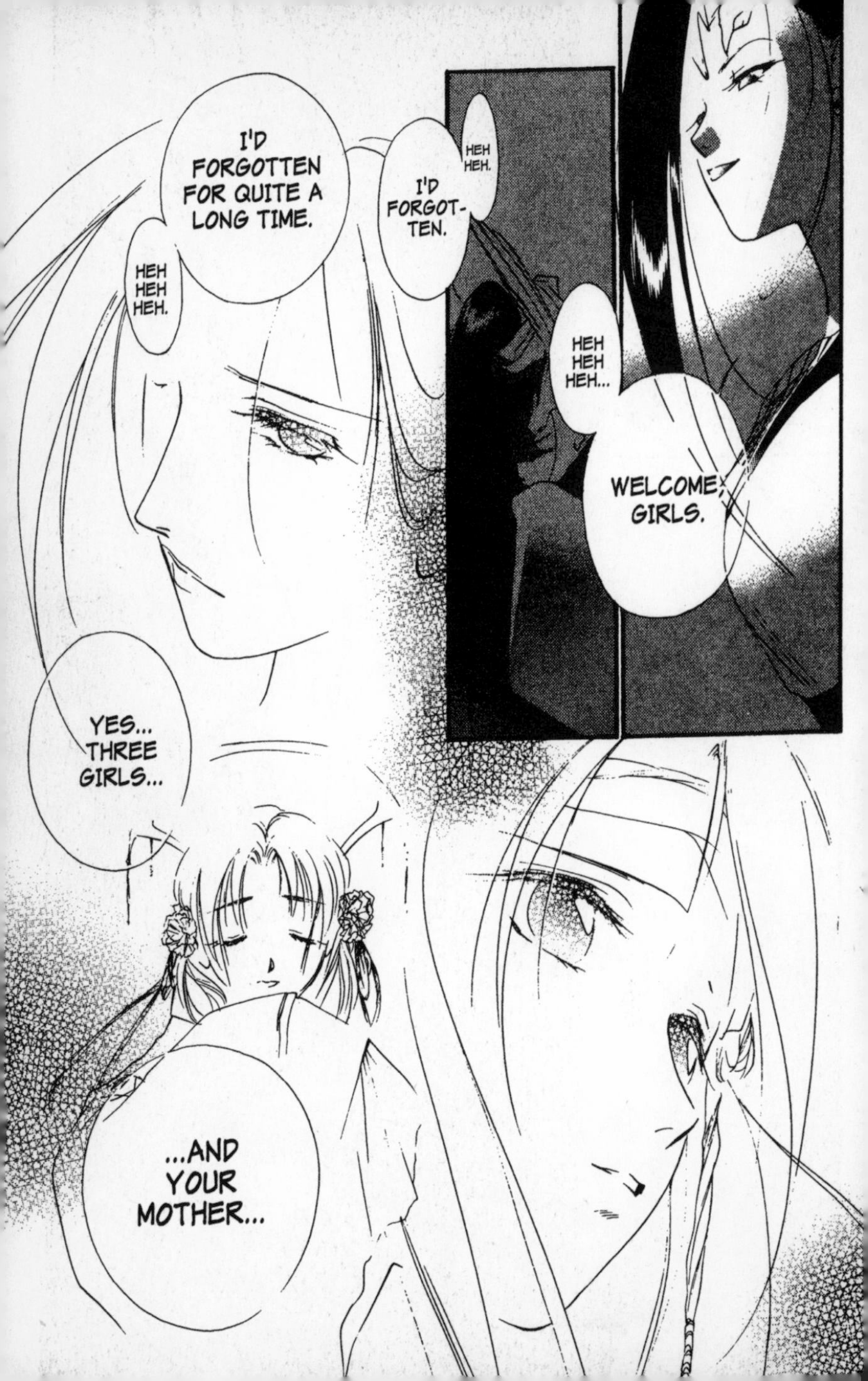
HEH HEH HEH...
WELCOME, GIRLS.
HEH HEH.
I'D FORGOT-TEN.
I'D FORGOTTEN FOR QUITE A LONG TIME.
HEH HEH HEH.
YES... THREE GIRLS...
...AND YOUR MOTHER...

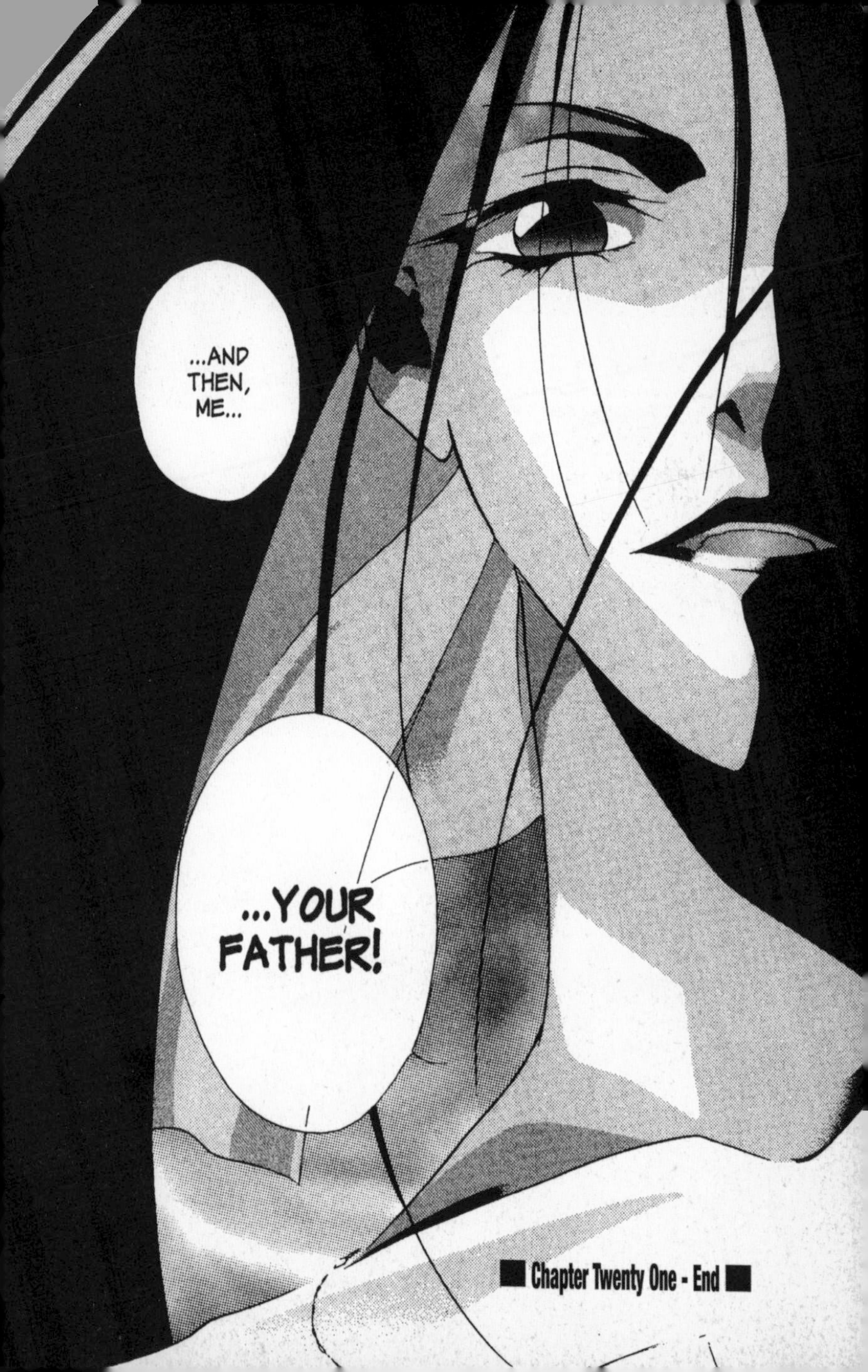
...AND THEN, ME...
...YOUR FATHER!
Chapter Twenty One - End

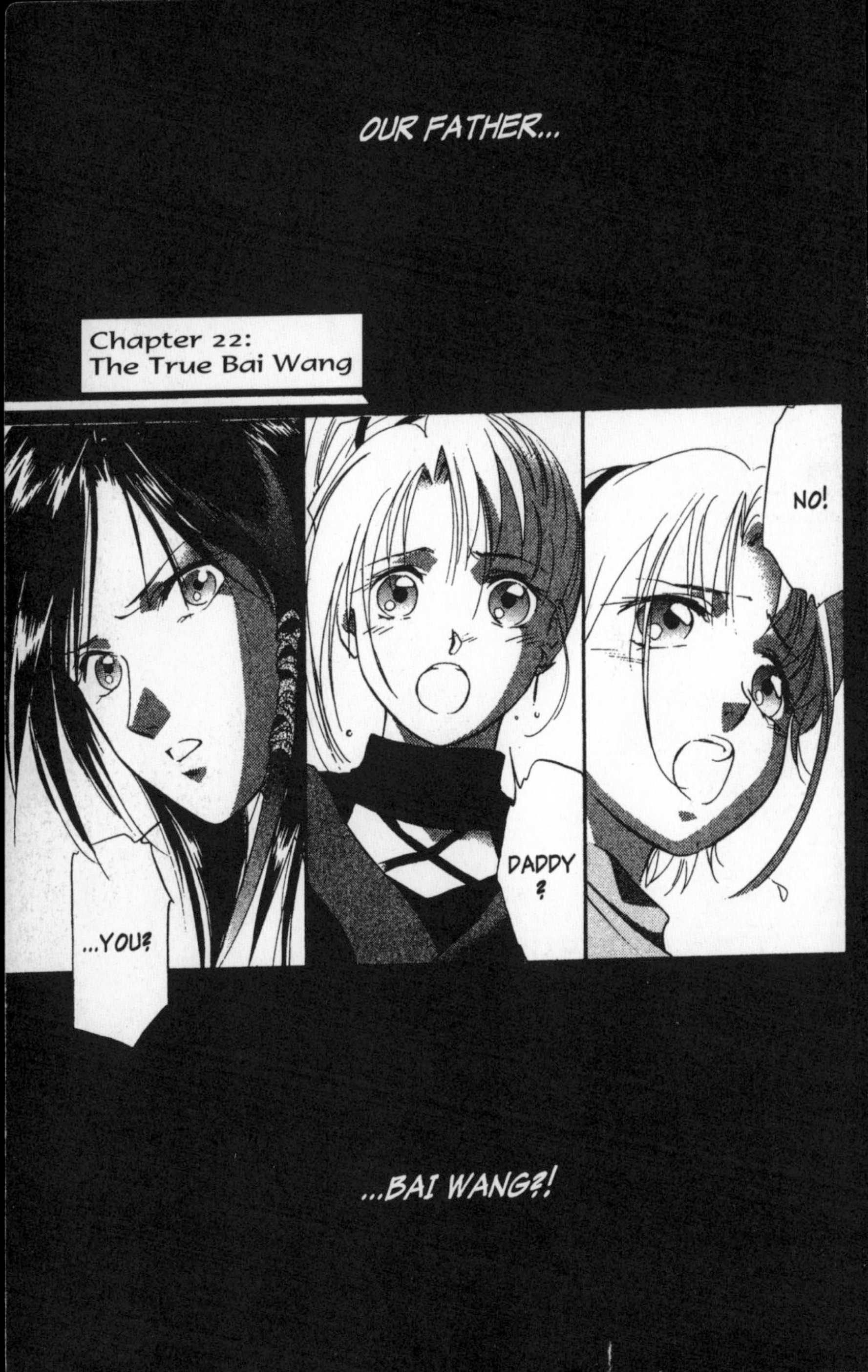
OUR FATHER...
Chapter 22:
The True Bai Wang
NO!
DADDY?
...YOU?
...BAI WANG?!

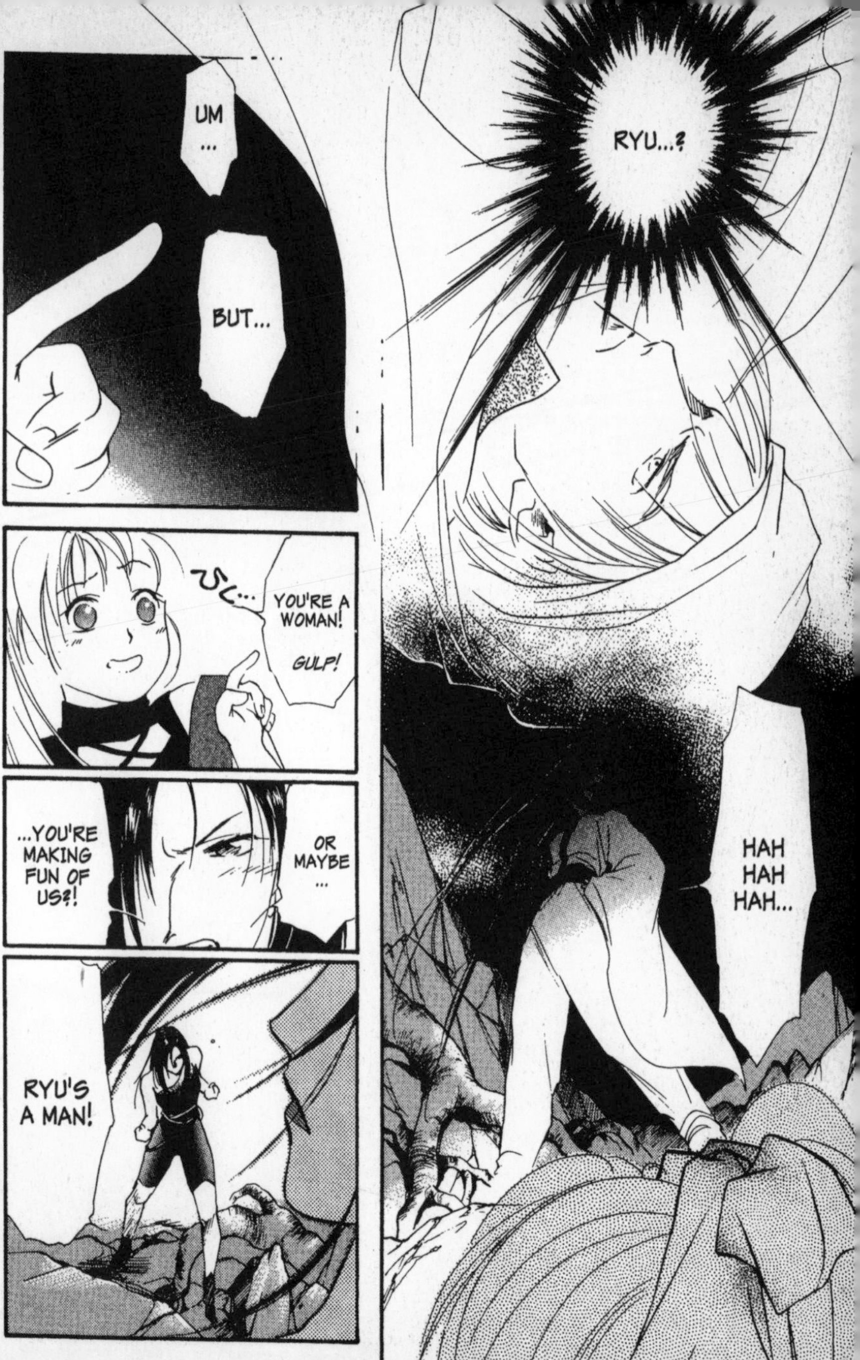
RYU...?
HAH HAH HAH...
UM ...
BUT...
YOU'RE A WOMAN!
GULP!
OR MAYBE ...
...YOU'RE MAKING FUN OF US?!
RYU'S A MAN!

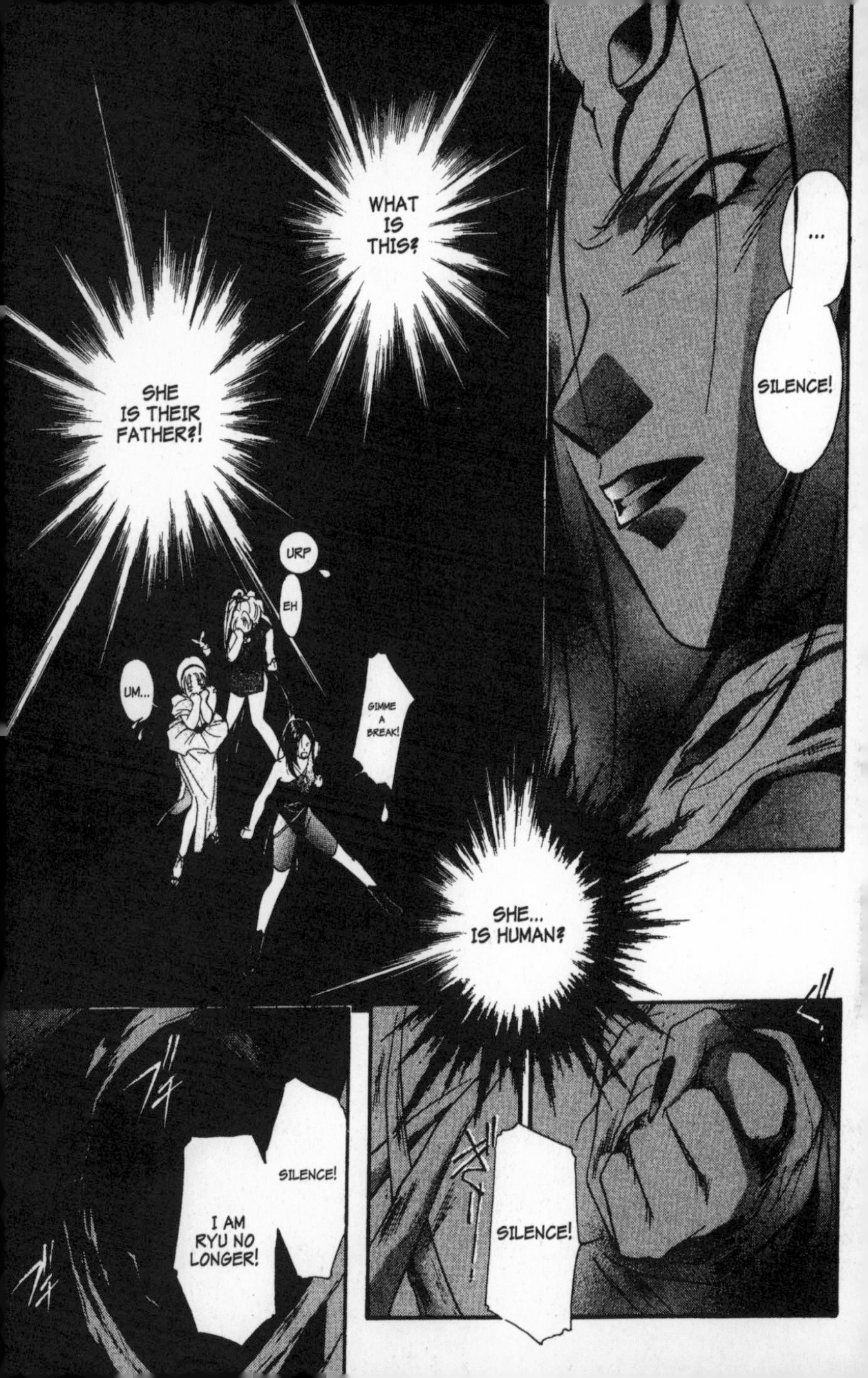
...
SILENCE!
WHAT IS THIS?
SHE IS THEIR FATHER?!
GIMME A BREAK!
URP
EH
UM...
SHE... IS HUMAN?
SILENCE!
SILENCE!
I AM RYU NO LONGER!

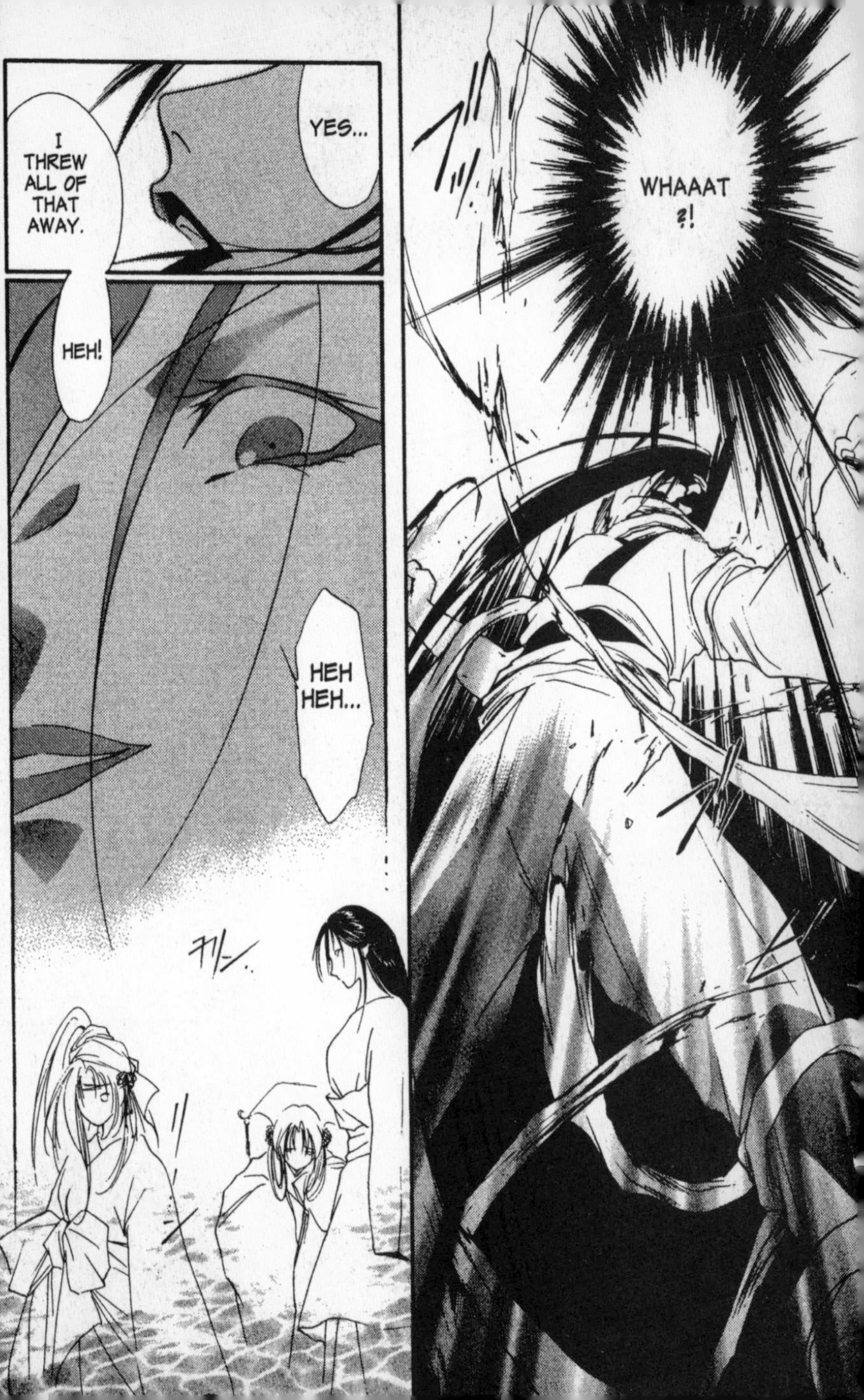
WHAAAT ?!
YES...
I THREW ALL OF THAT AWAY.
HEH!
HEH HEH...

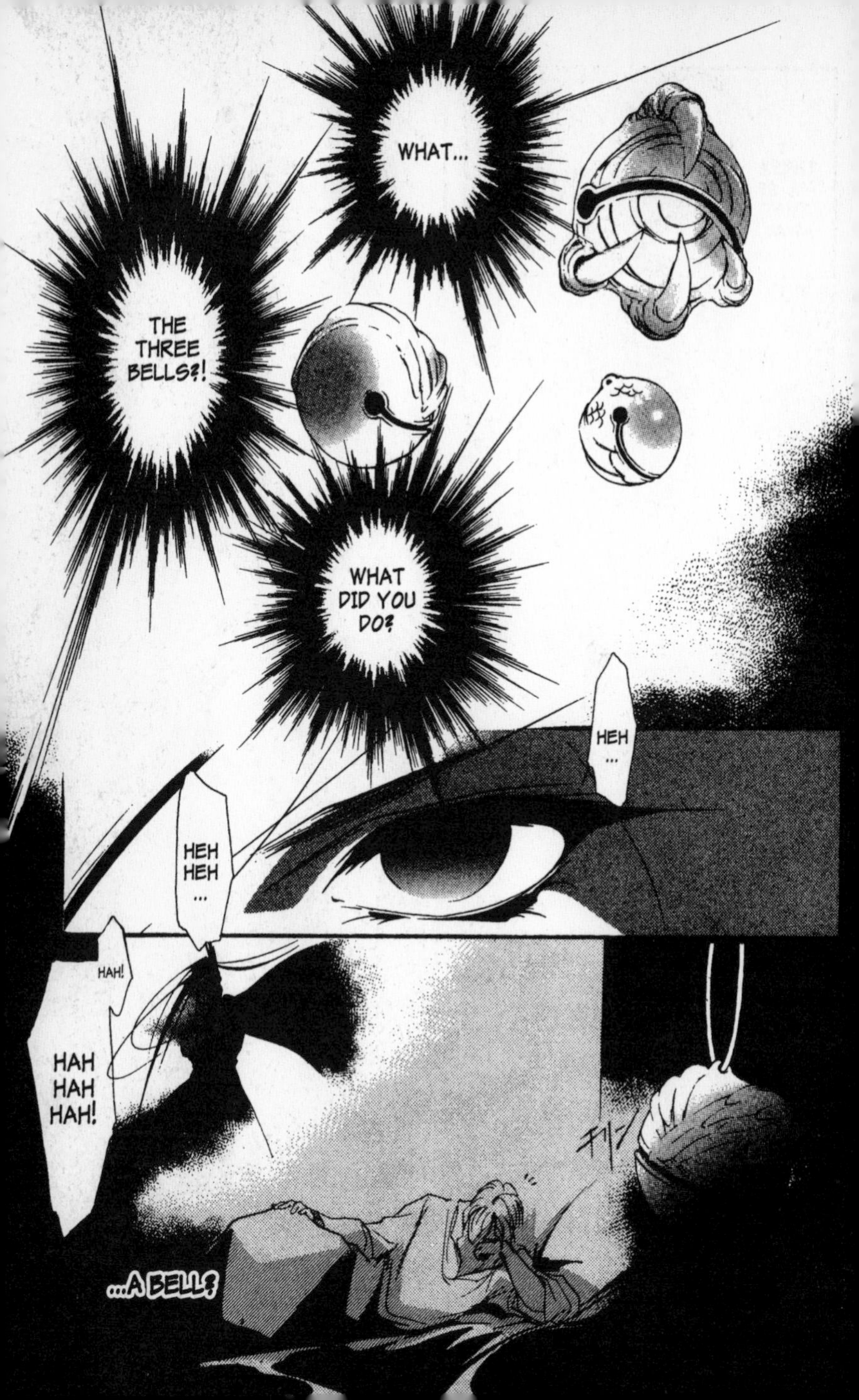
WHAT...
THE THREE BELLS?!
WHAT DID YOU DO?
HEH ...
HEH HEH ...
HAH!
HAH HAH HAH!
...A BELL?

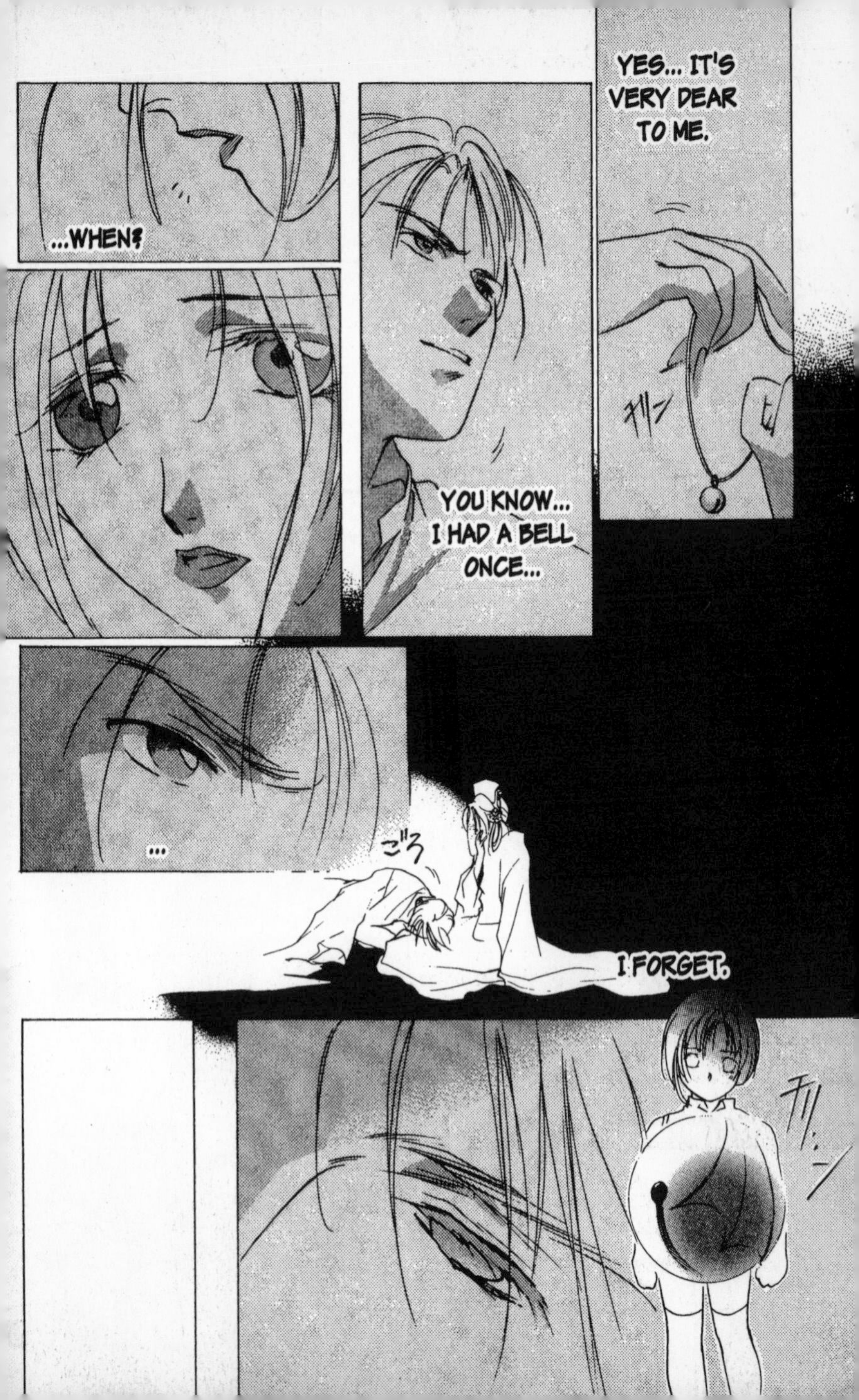
YES... IT'S VERY DEAR TO ME.
チリン
YOU KNOW... I HAD A BELL ONCE...
...WHEN?
...
ごろ
I FORGET.
チリーン

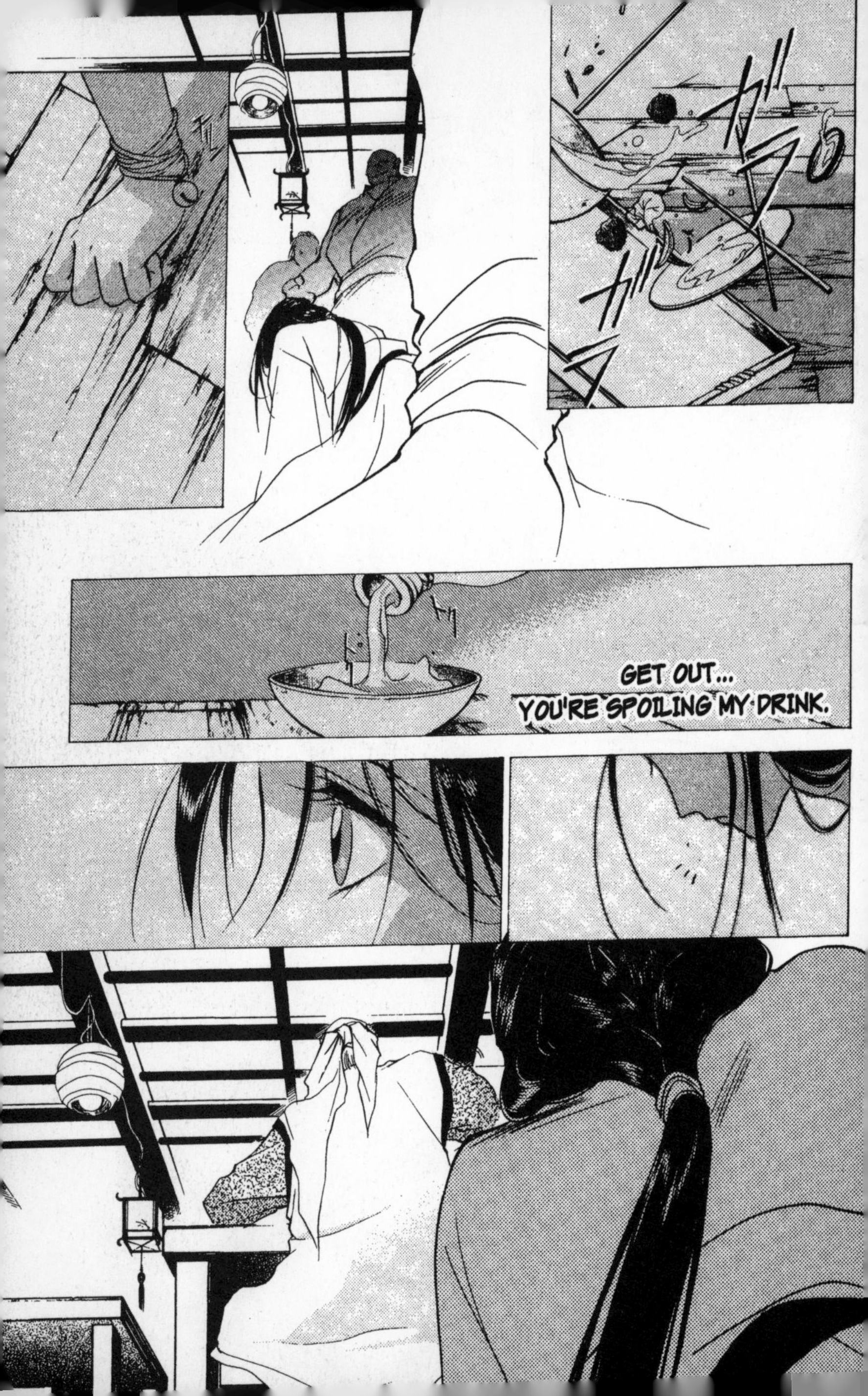
GET OUT...
YOU'RE SPOILING MY DRINK.

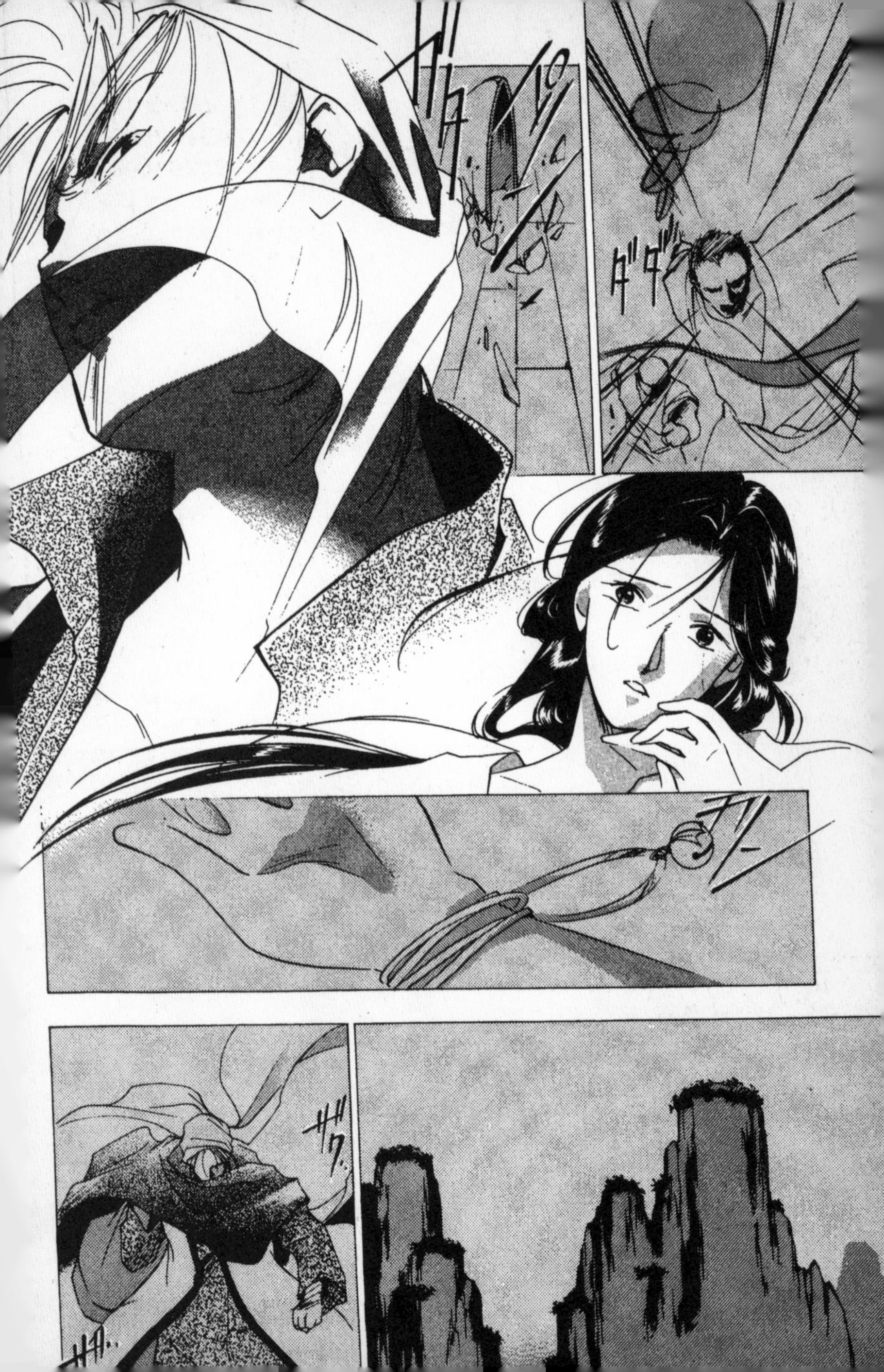
ダダッ
ザク‥

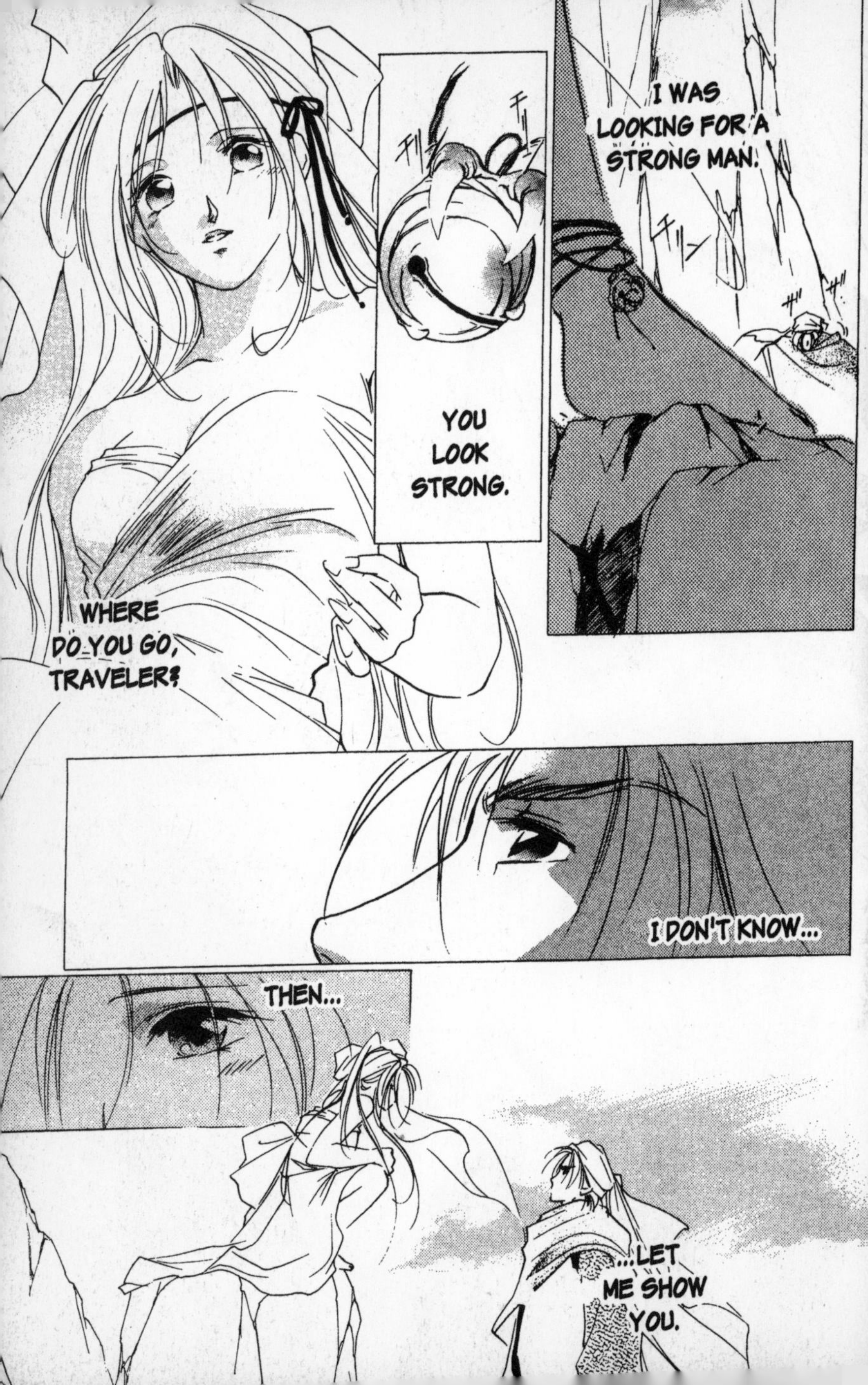
I WAS LOOKING FOR A STRONG MAN.
YOU LOOK STRONG.
WHERE DO YOU GO, TRAVELER?
I DON'T KNOW...
THEN...
...LET ME SHOW YOU.

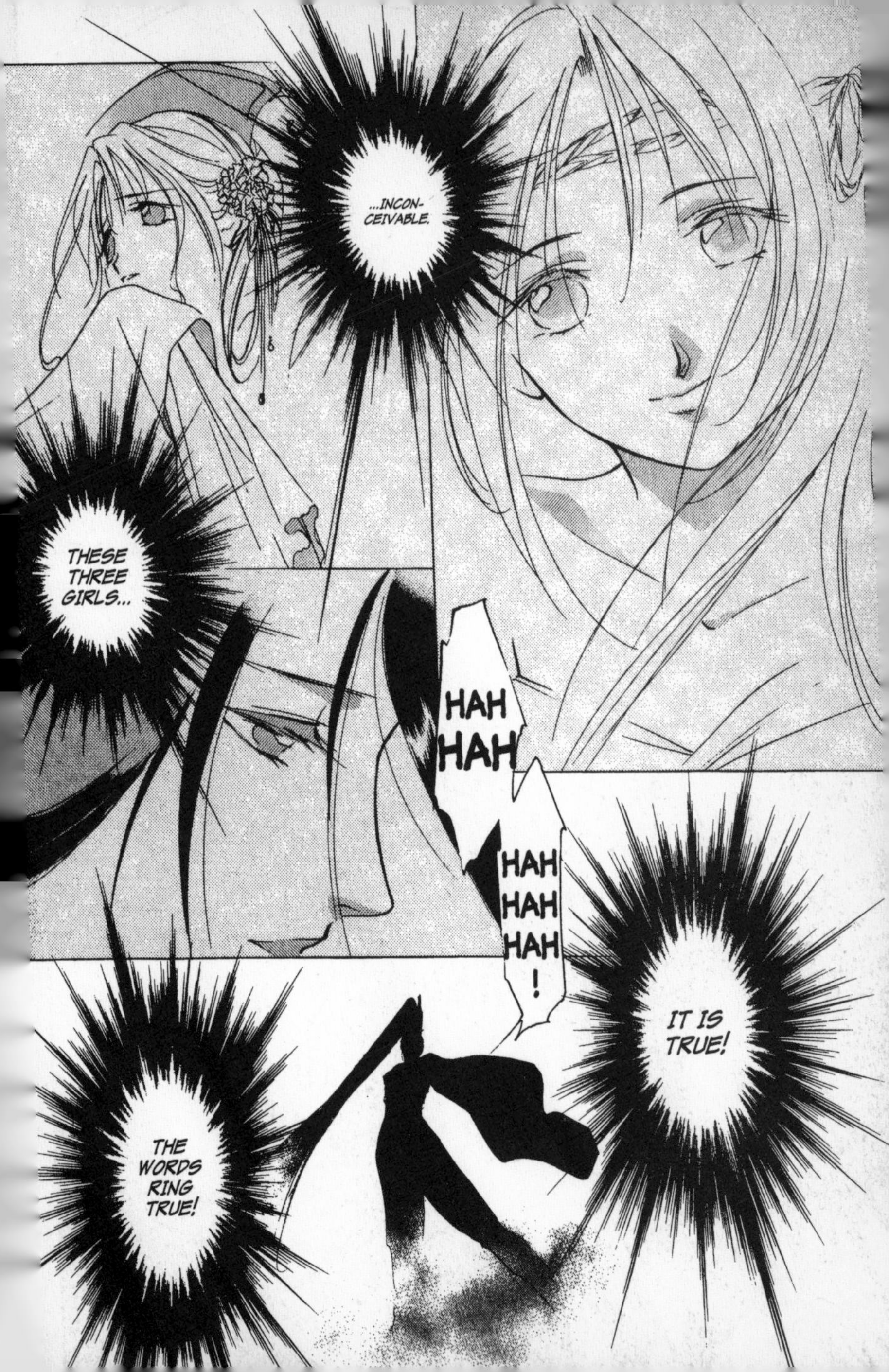
...INCON-CEIVABLE.
THESE THREE GIRLS...
HAH HAH
HAH HAH HAH!
IT IS TRUE!
THE WORDS RING TRUE!

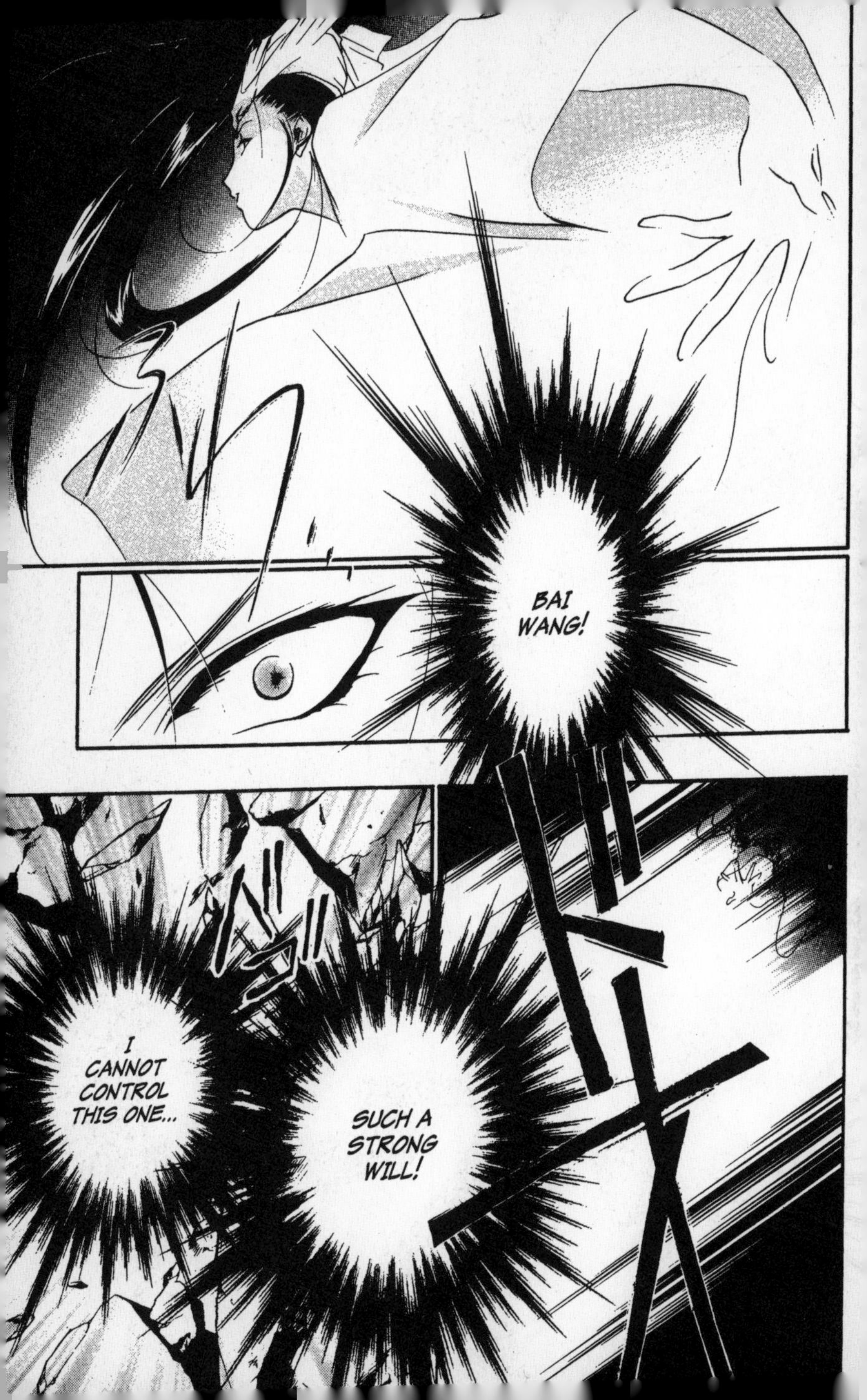
BAI WANG!
SUCH A STRONG WILL!
I CANNOT CONTROL THIS ONE...

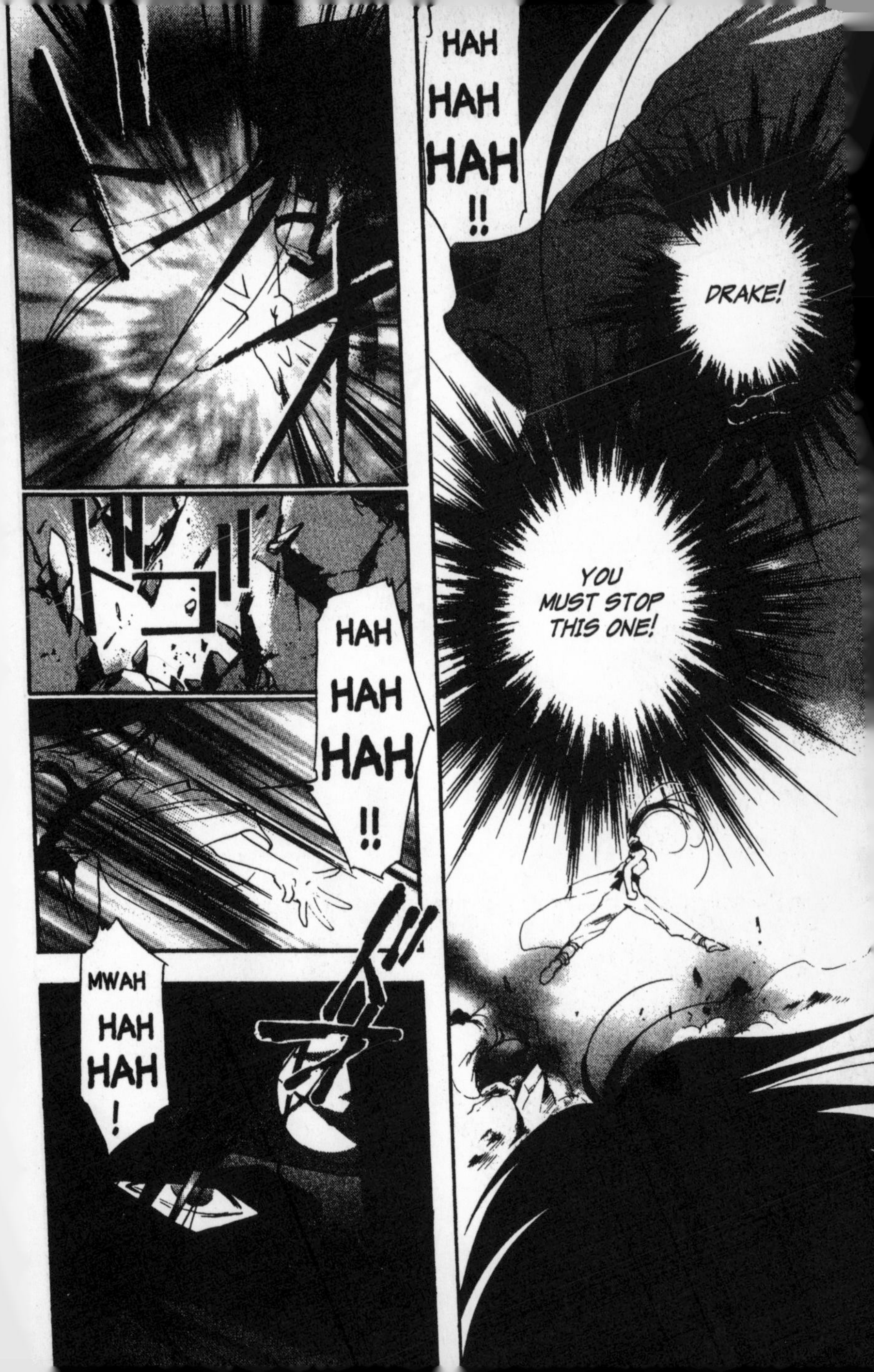
HAH HAH HAH !!
DRAKE!
YOU MUST STOP THIS ONE!
HAH HAH HAH !!
MWAH HAH HAH !

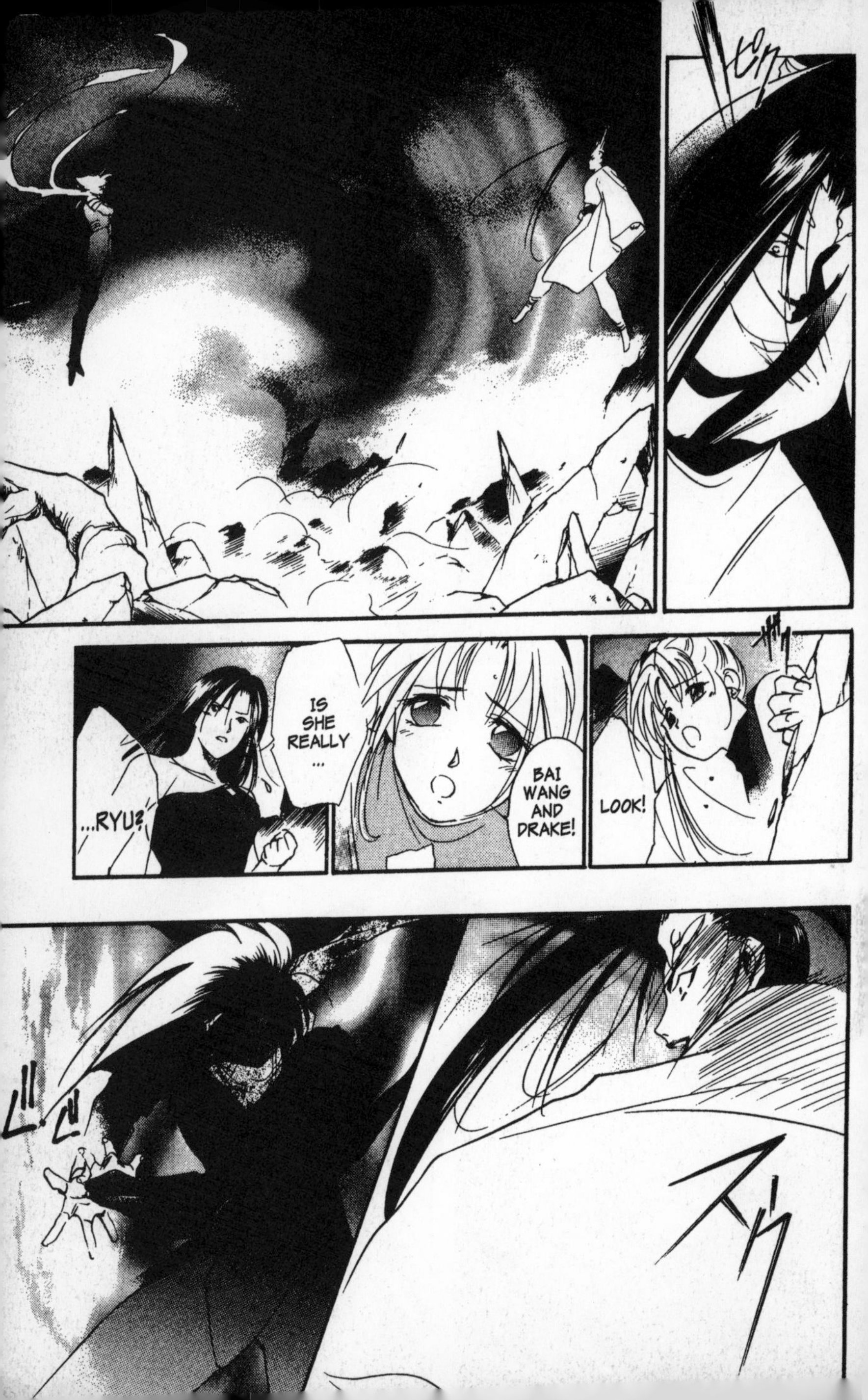
LOOK!
BAI WANG AND DRAKE!
IS SHE REALLY ...
...RYU?

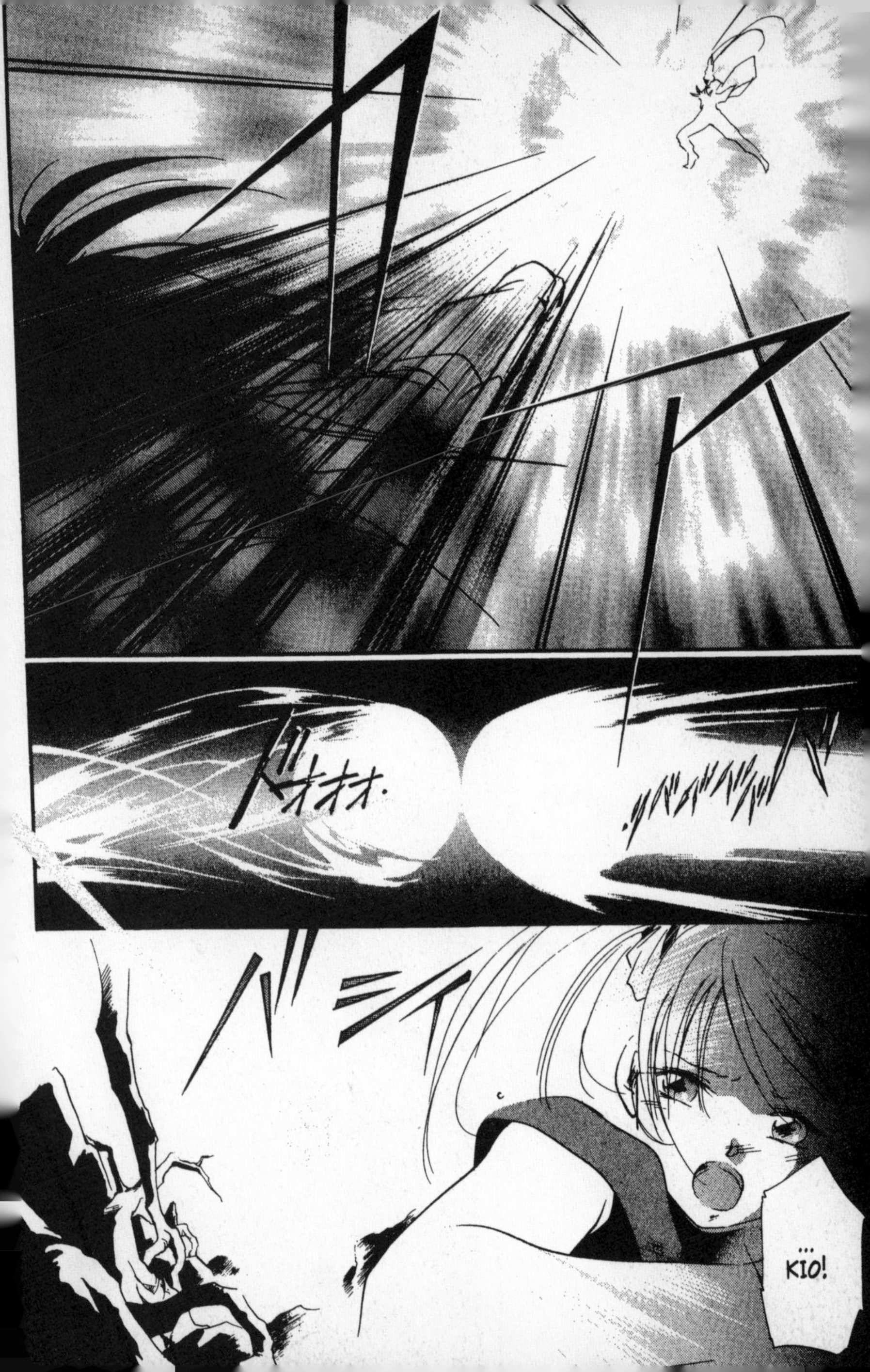
ドオオオ
...KIO!

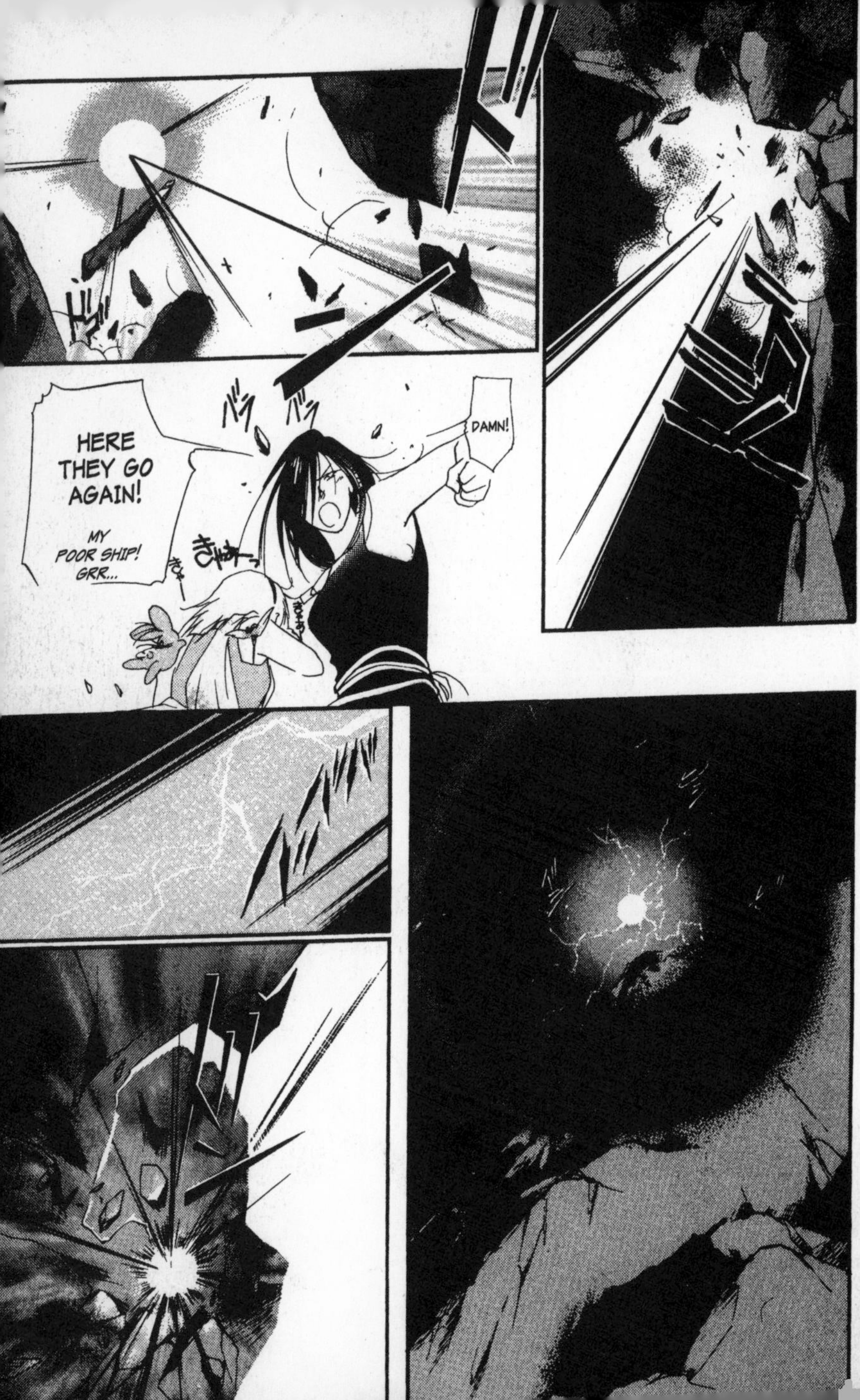
DAMN!
HERE THEY GO AGAIN!
MY POOR SHIP! GRR...

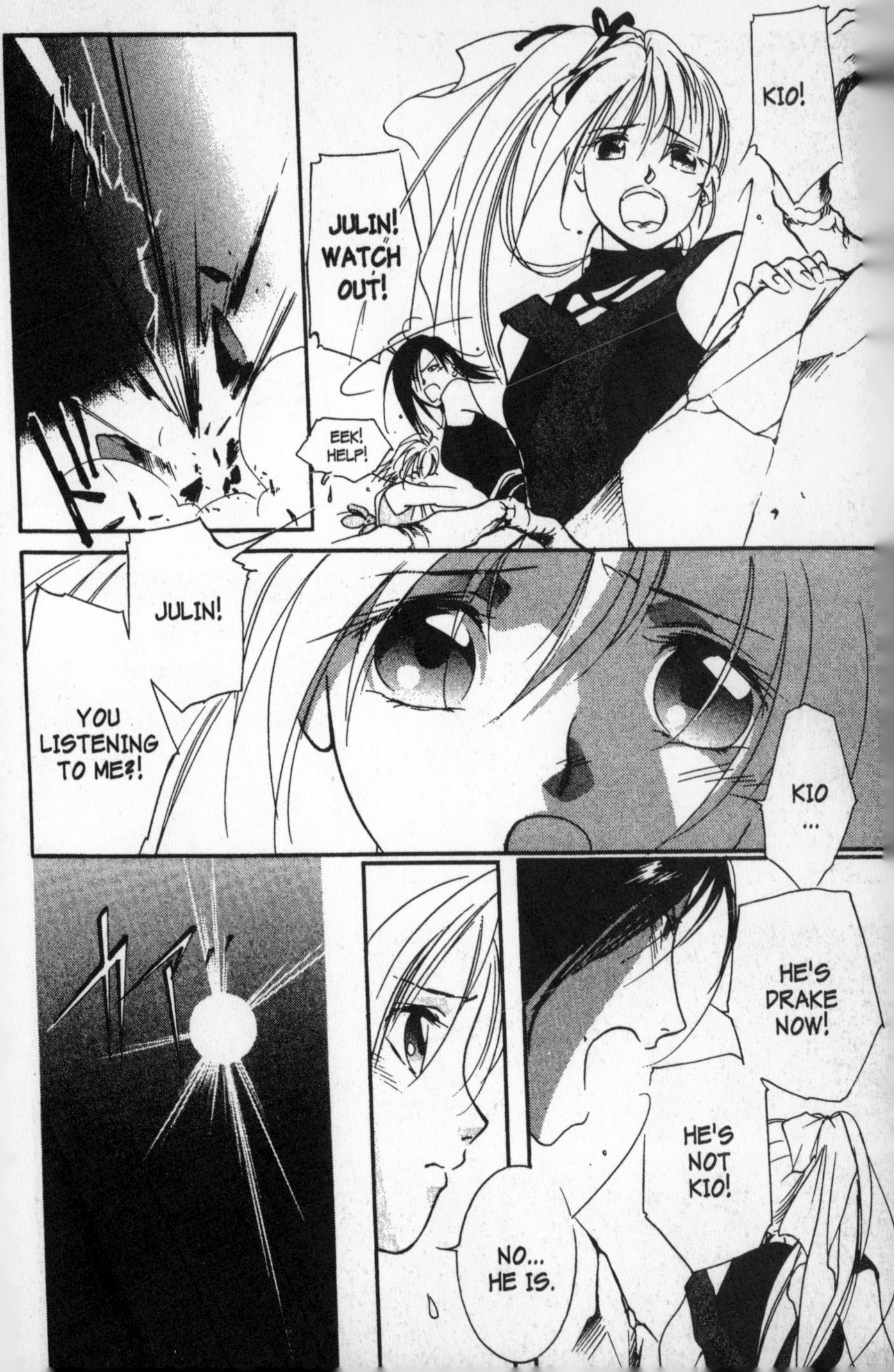
KIO!
JULIN! WATCH OUT!
EEK! HELP!
KIO ...
JULIN!
YOU LISTENING TO ME?!
HE'S DRAKE NOW!
HE'S NOT KIO!
NO... HE IS.

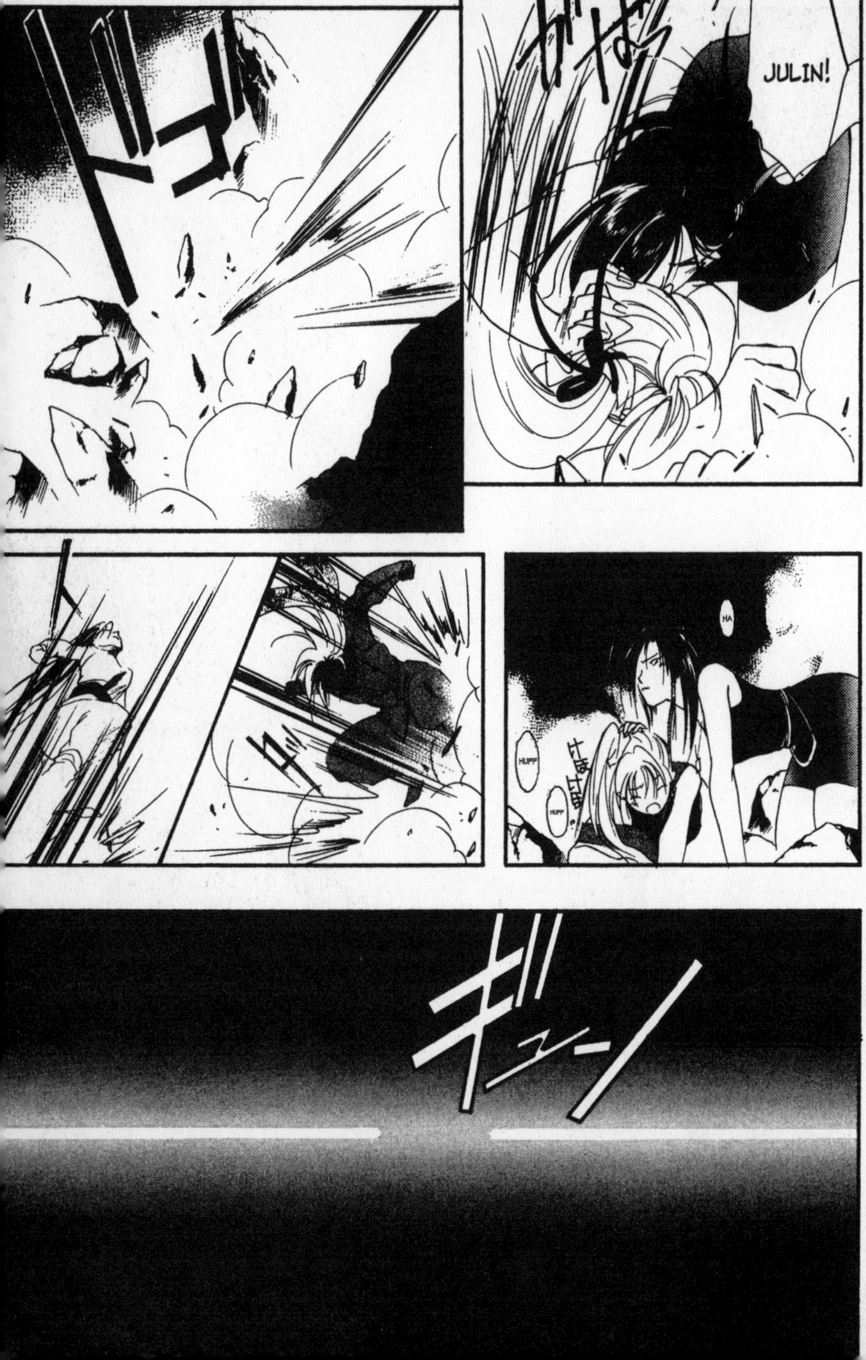
JULIN!
HA
HUFF
HUFF

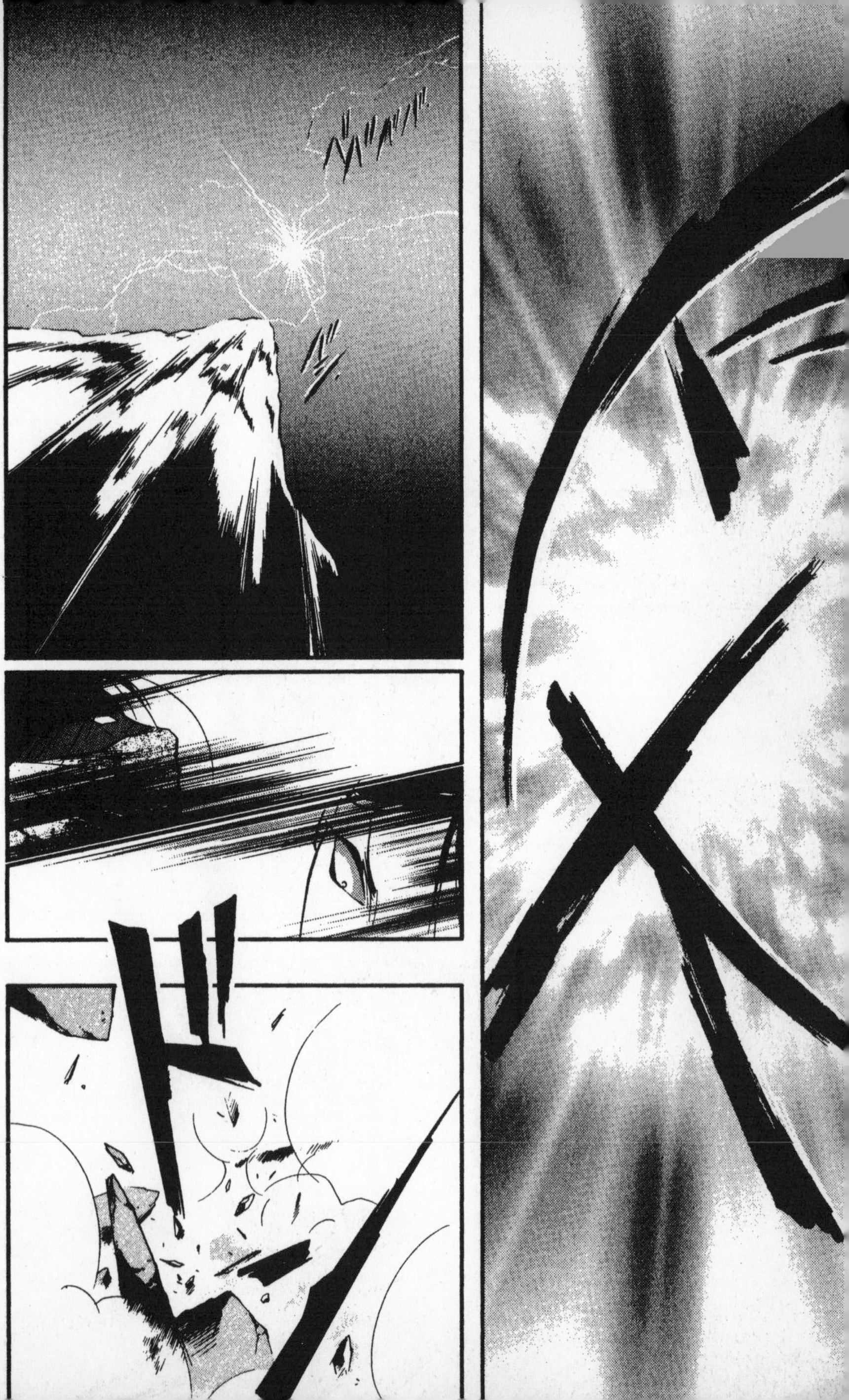

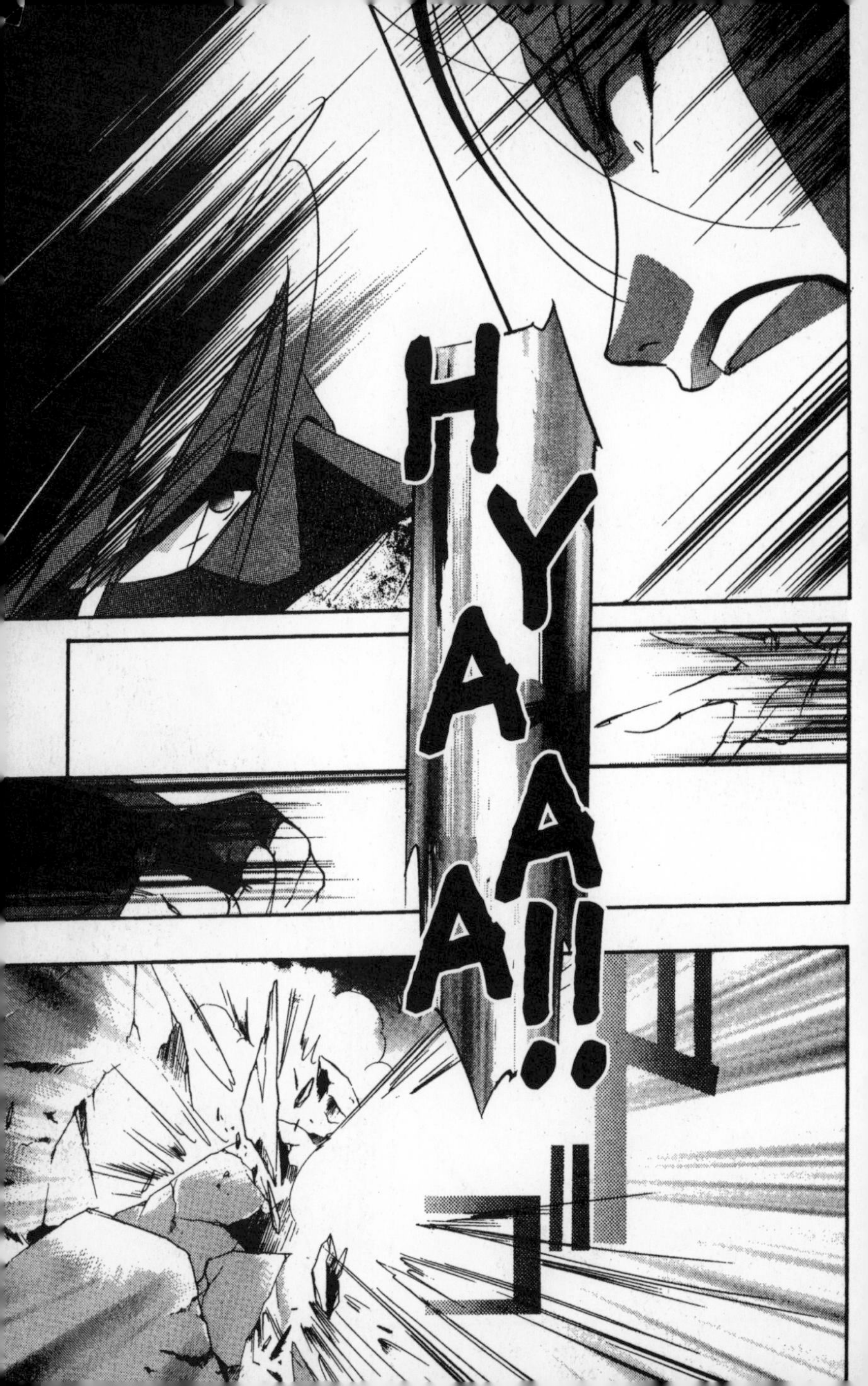
HYAAA!!

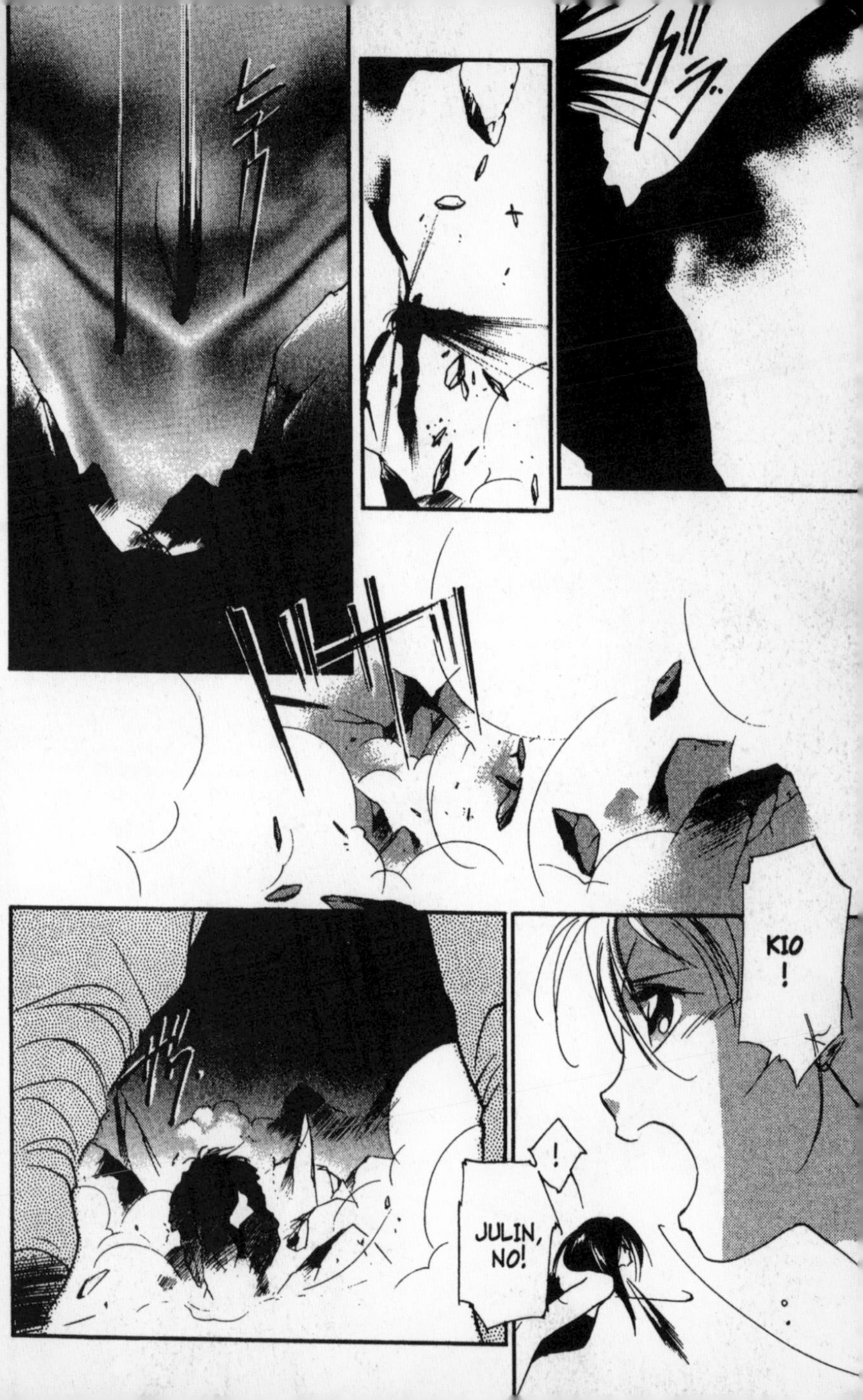
KIO!
!
JULIN, NO!

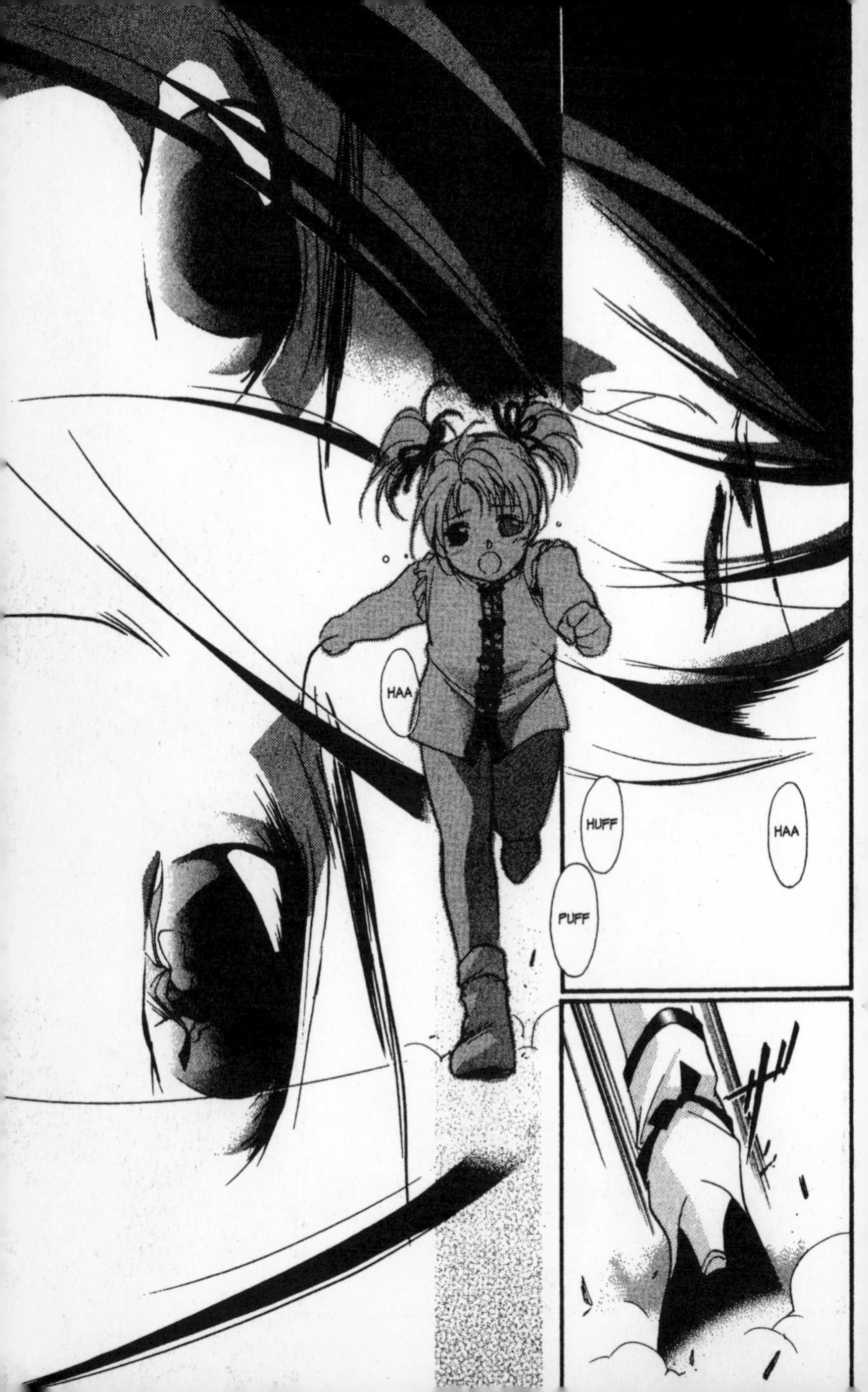
HAA
HAA
HUFF
PUFF

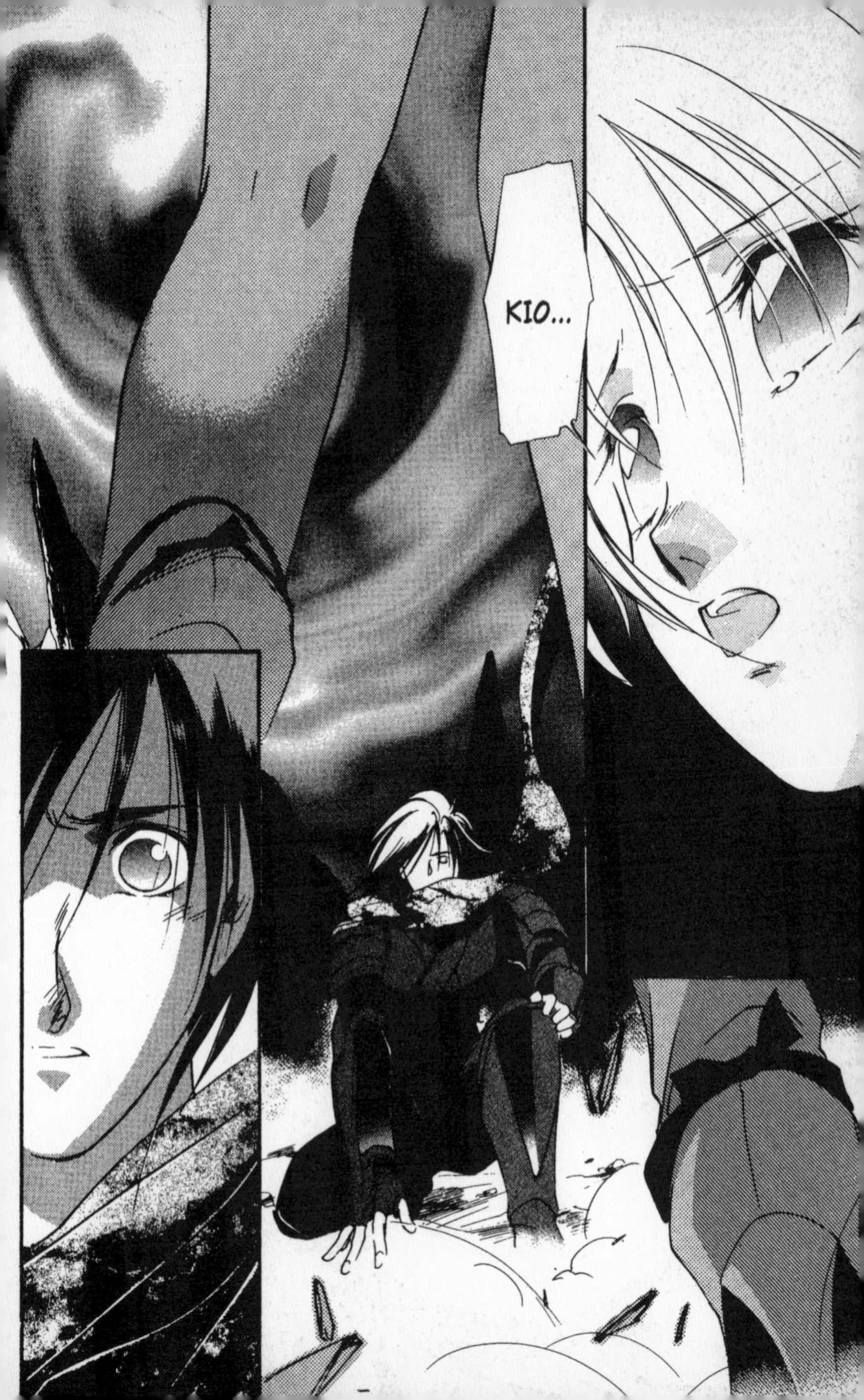
KIO...

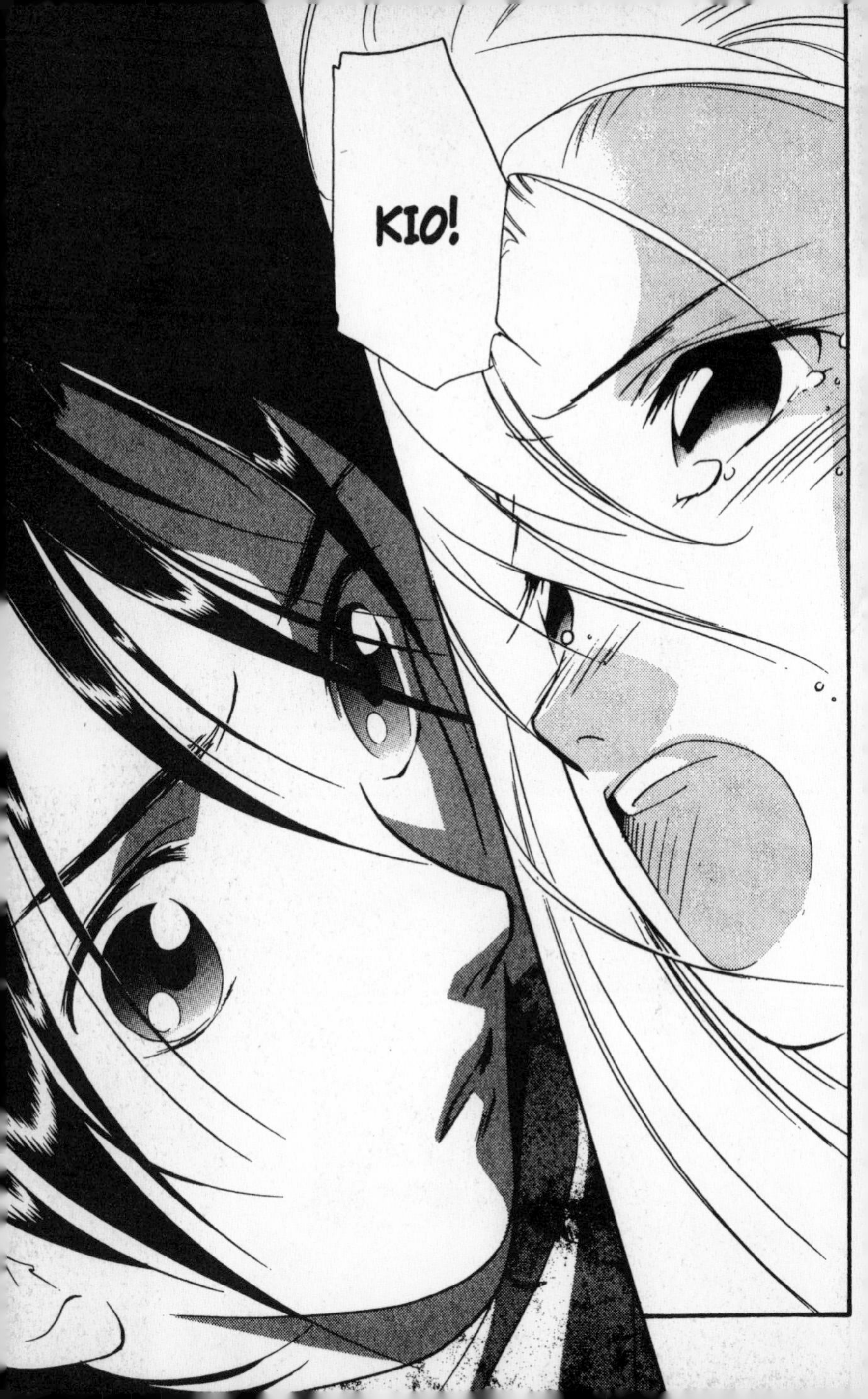
KIO!

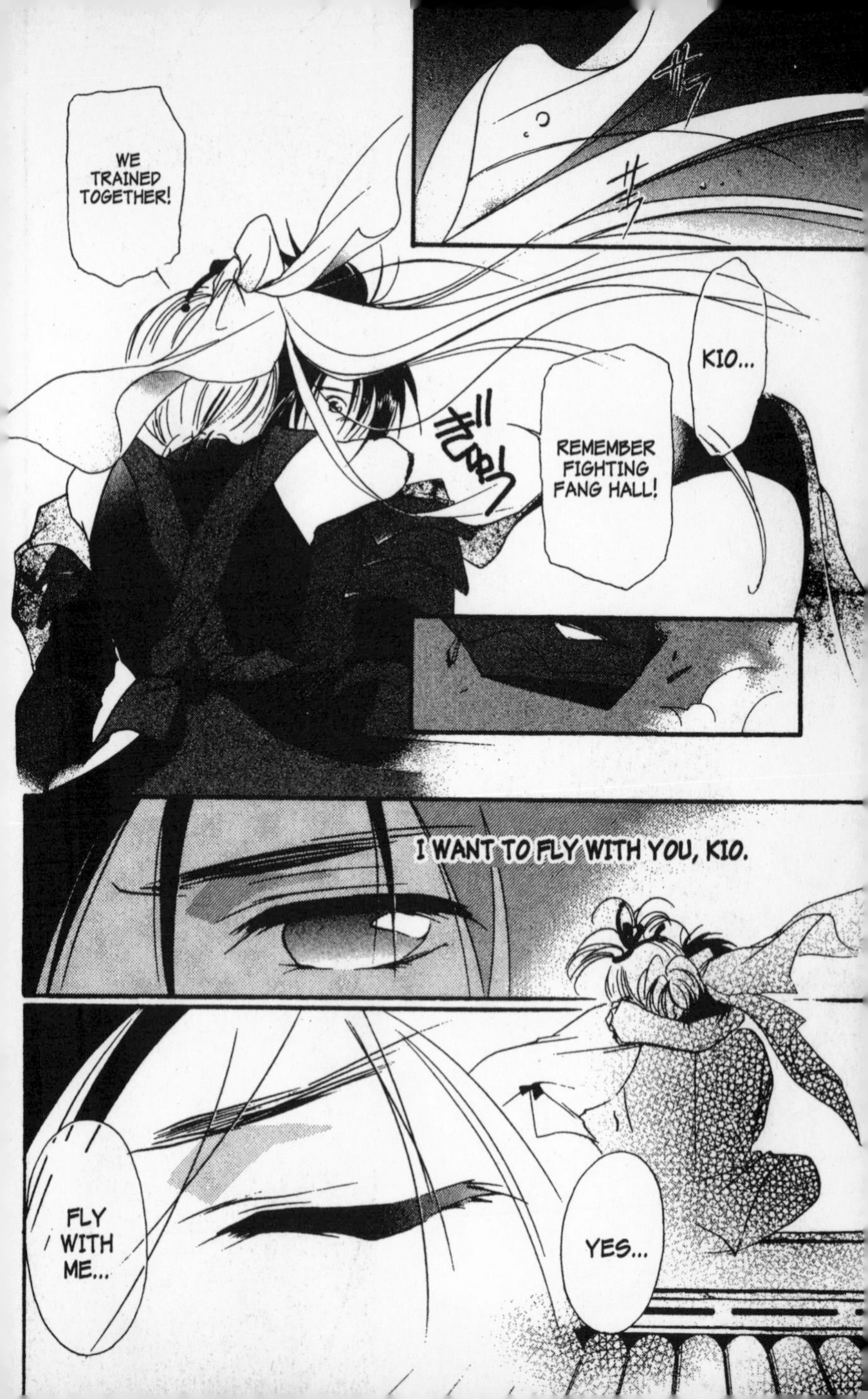
KIO...
REMEMBER FIGHTING FANG HALL!
ぎゅっ
WE TRAINED TOGETHER!
I WANT TO FLY WITH YOU, KIO.
YES...
FLY WITH ME...

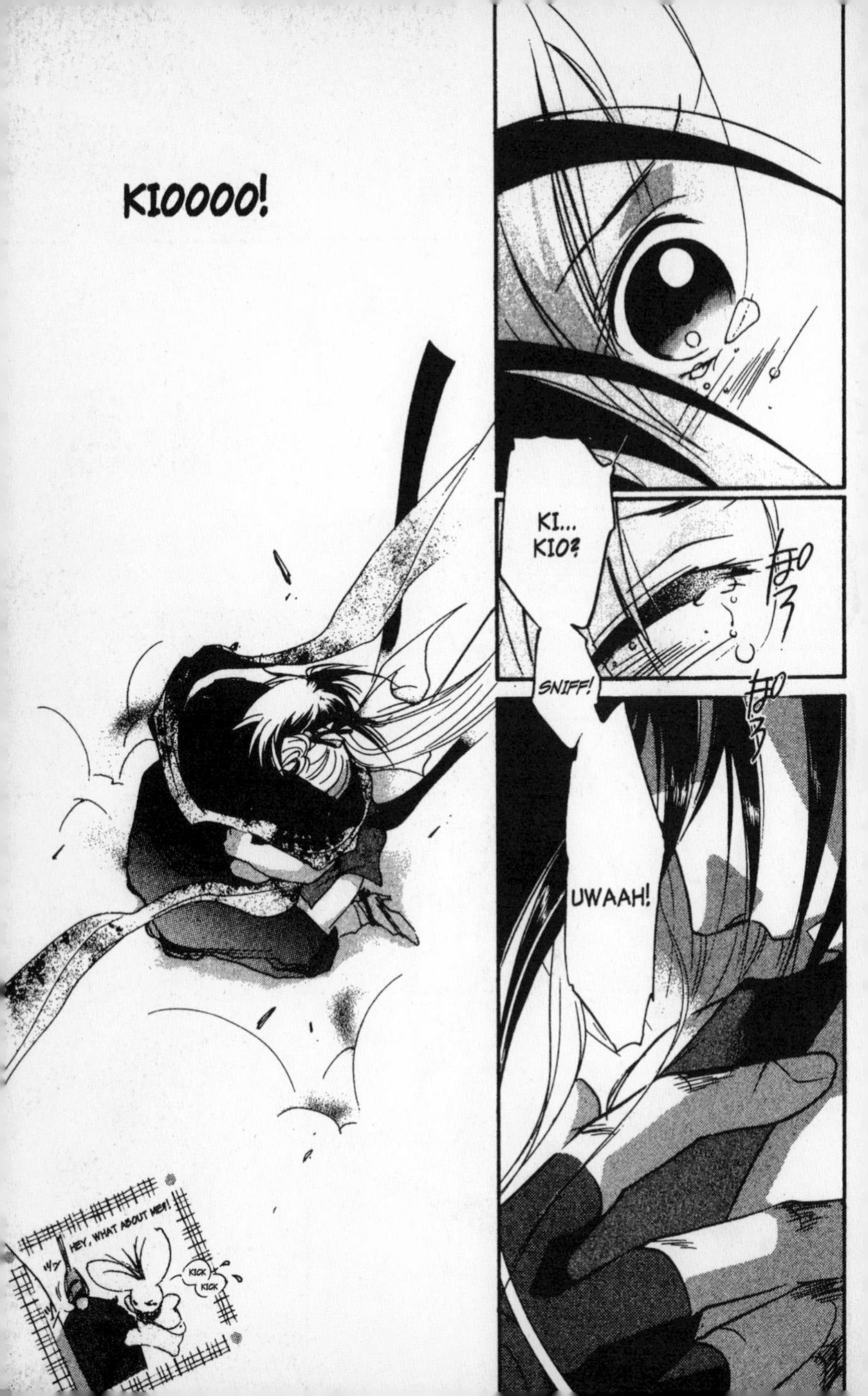
KI... KIO?
ぽろ
ぽろ
SNIFF!
UWAAH!
KIOOOO!
HEY, WHAT ABOUT ME?!
KICK
KICK

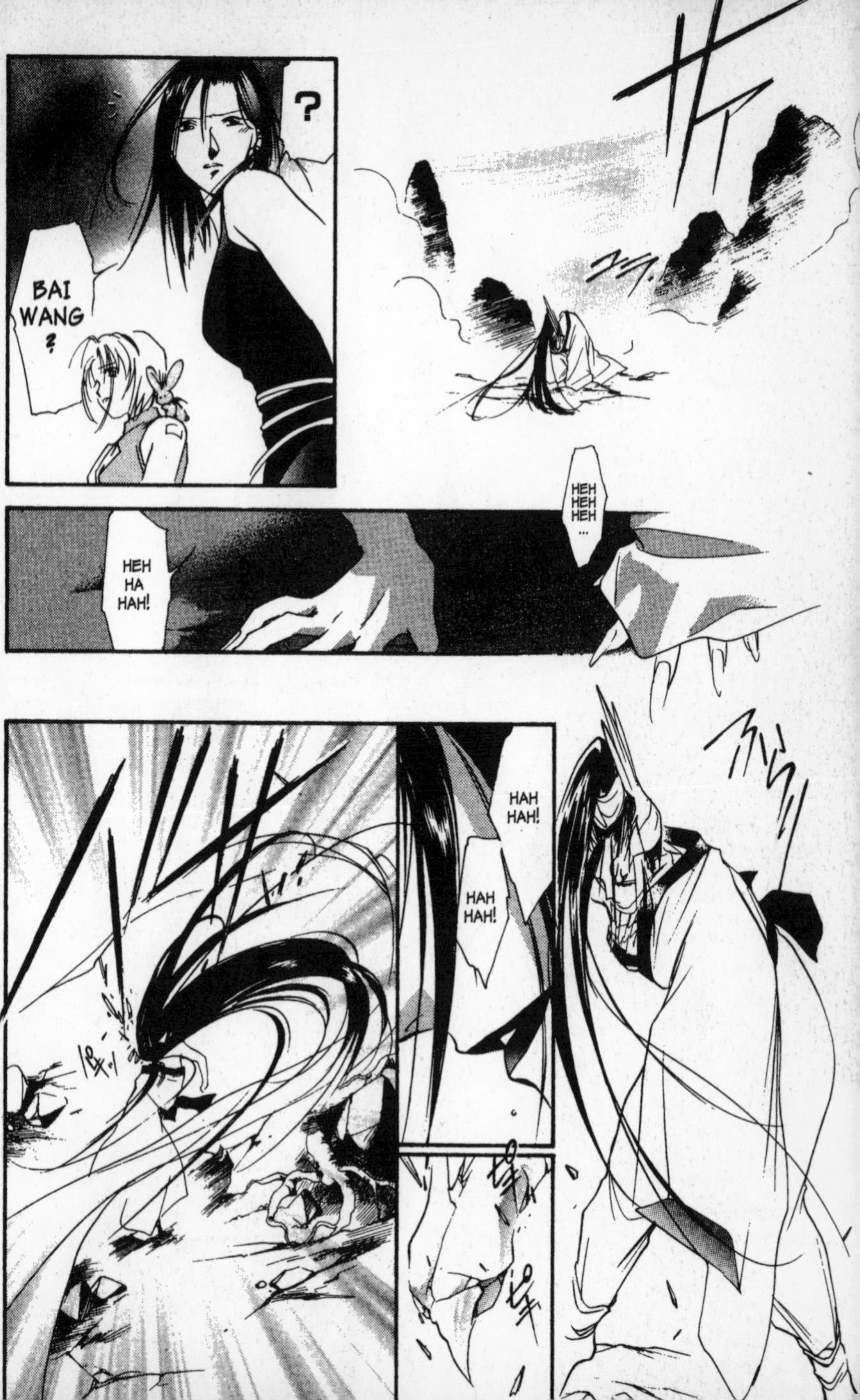
?
BAI WANG?
HEH HEH HEH...
HEH HA HAH!
HAH HAH!
HAH HAH!

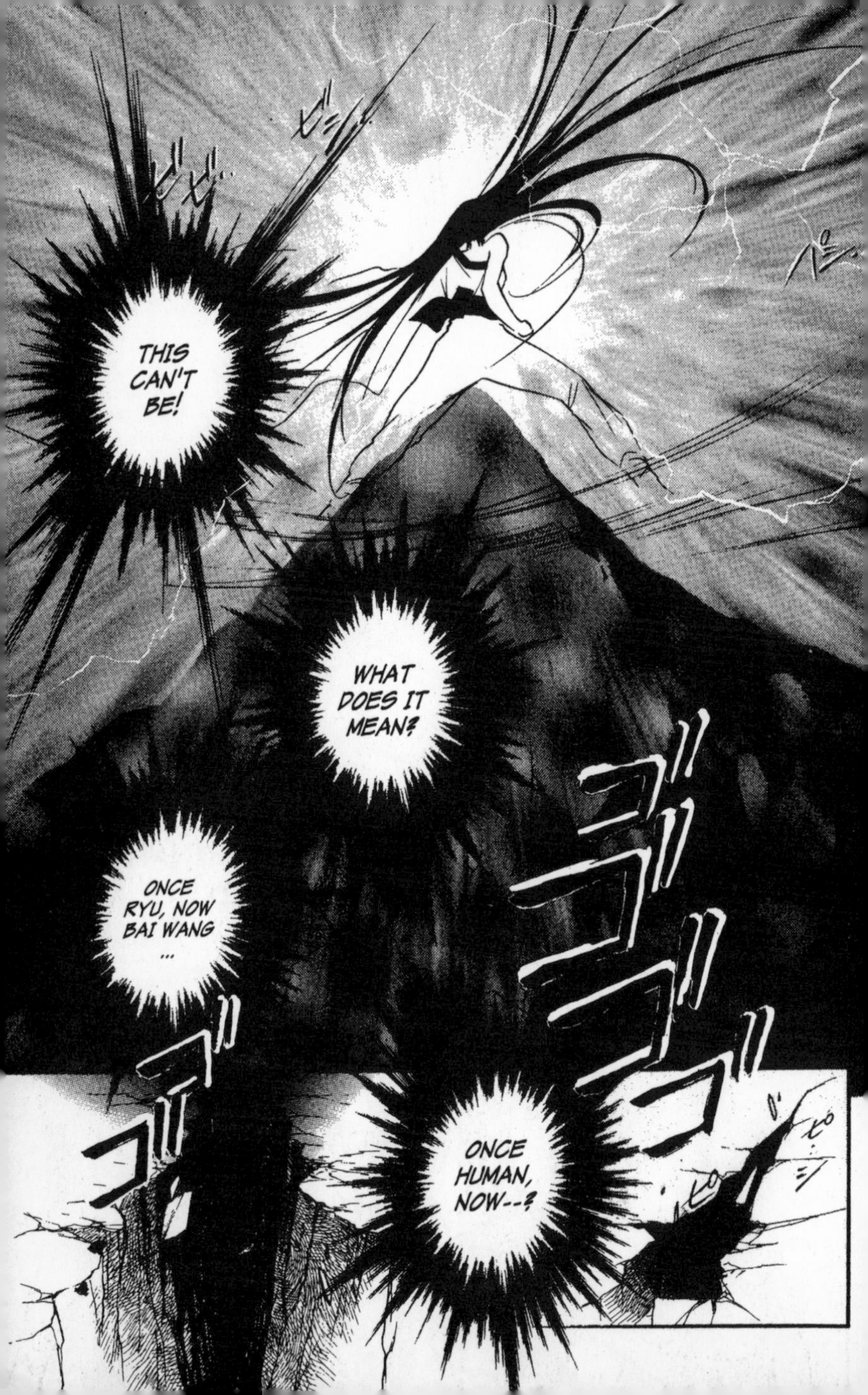
THIS CAN'T BE!
WHAT DOES IT MEAN?
ONCE RYU, NOW BAI WANG ...
ONCE HUMAN, NOW--?

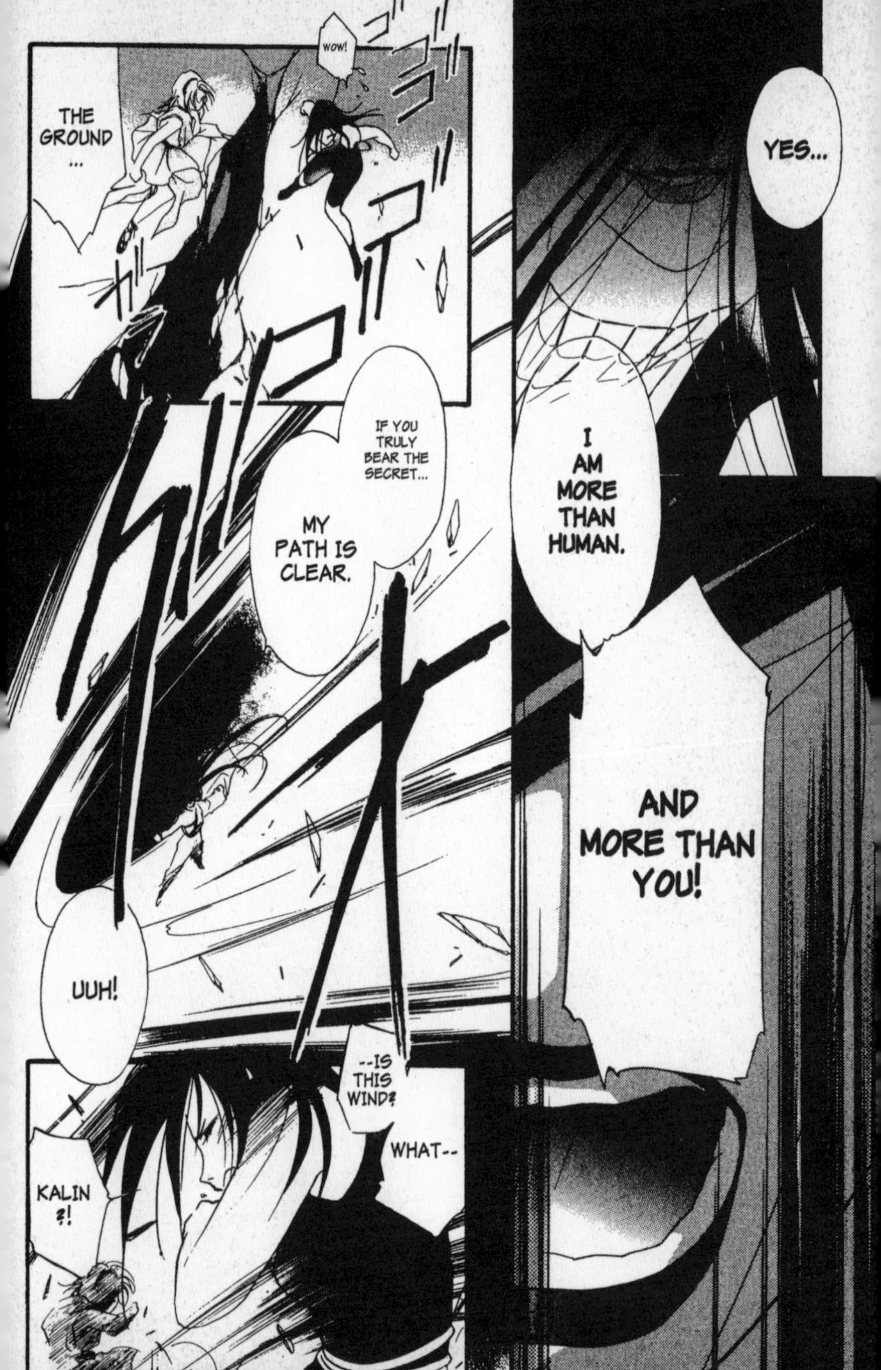
YES...
I AM MORE THAN HUMAN.
AND MORE THAN YOU!
WOW!
THE GROUND ...
IF YOU TRULY BEAR THE SECRET...
MY PATH IS CLEAR.
UUH!
WHAT--
--IS THIS WIND?
KALIN?!

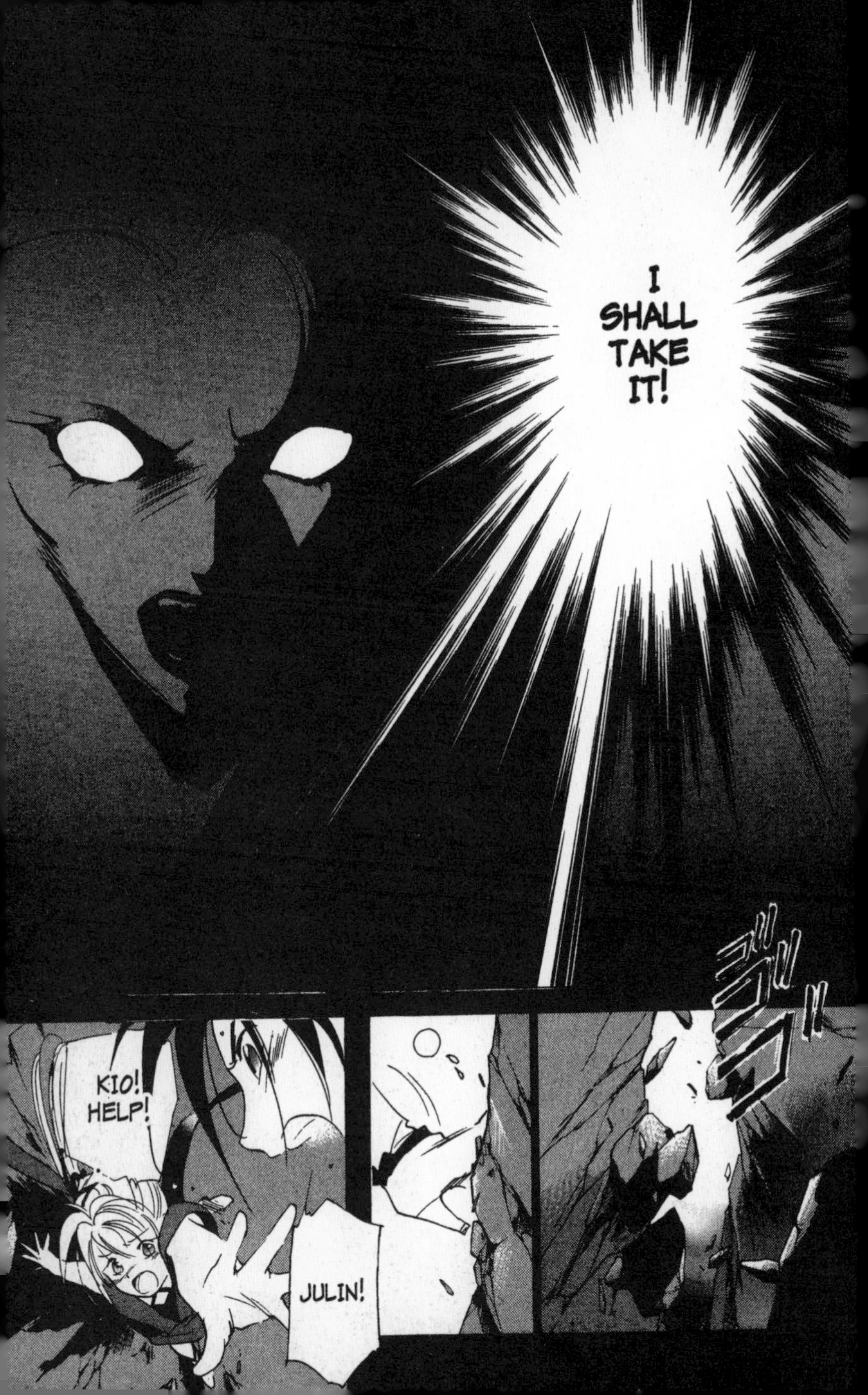
I SHALL TAKE IT!
KIO! HELP!
JULIN!

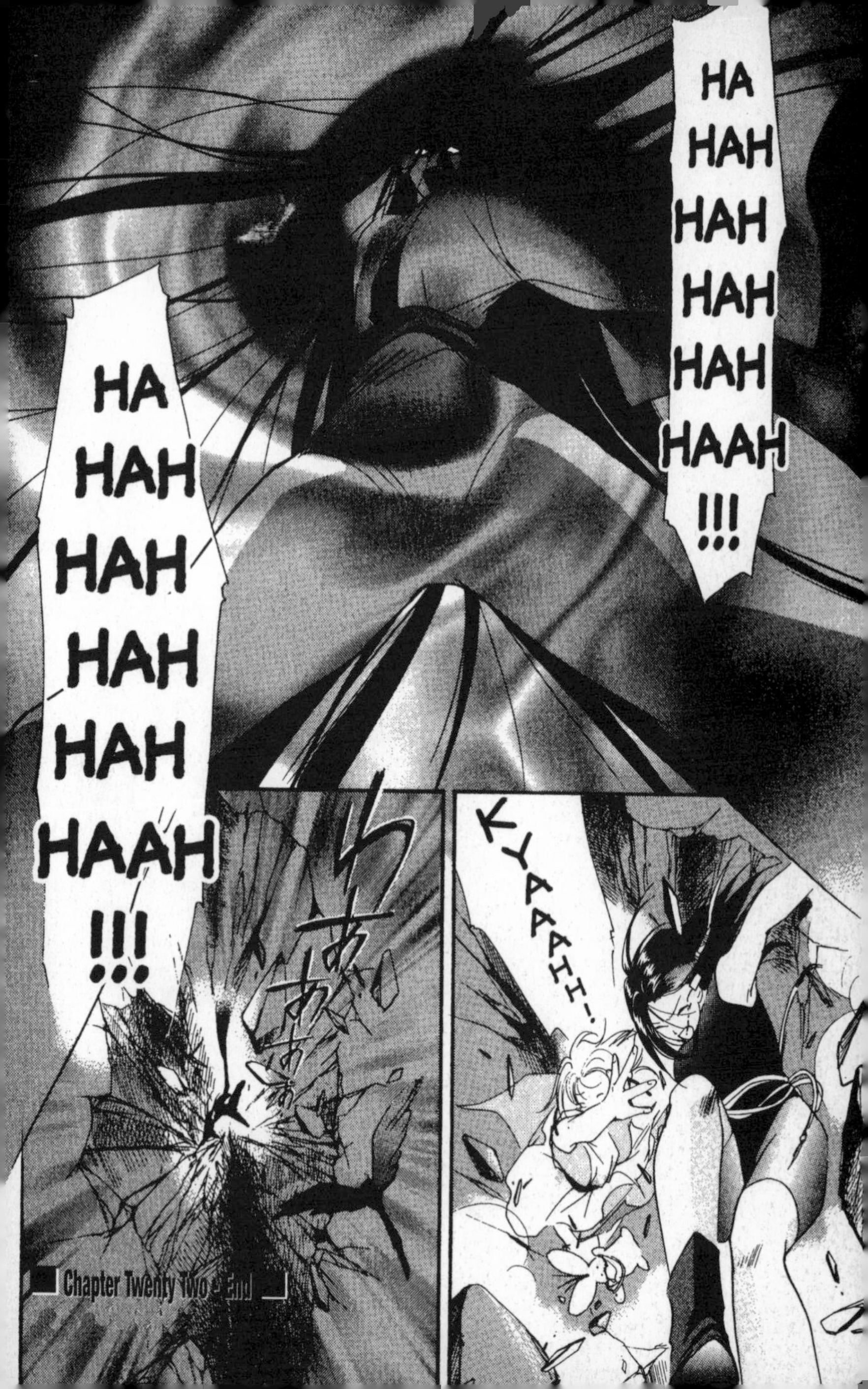
HA HAH HAH HAH HAH HAAH!!!
HA HAH HAH HAH HAH HAAH!!!
KYAAAAHH!
Chapter Twenty Two - End

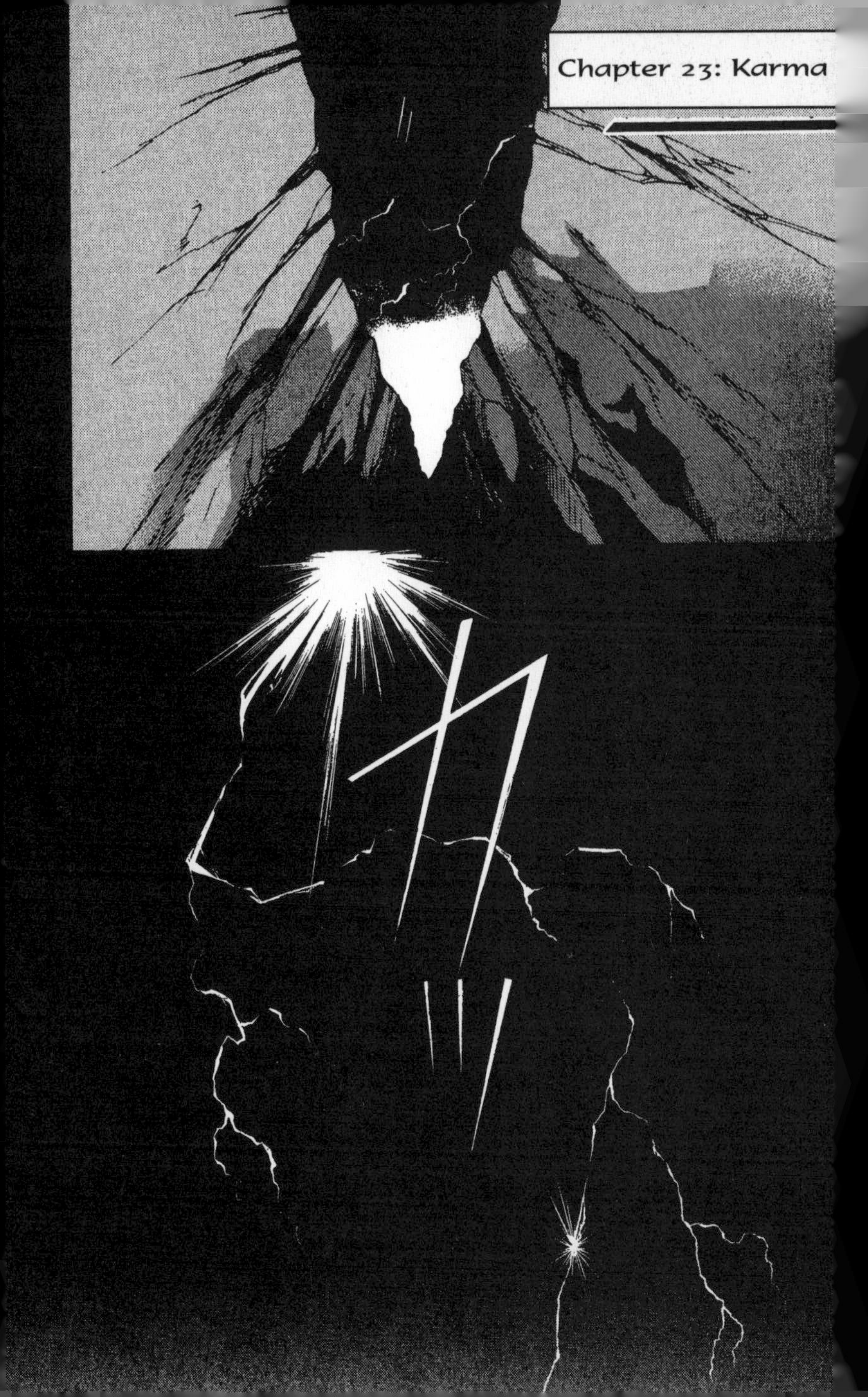
Chapter 23: Karma

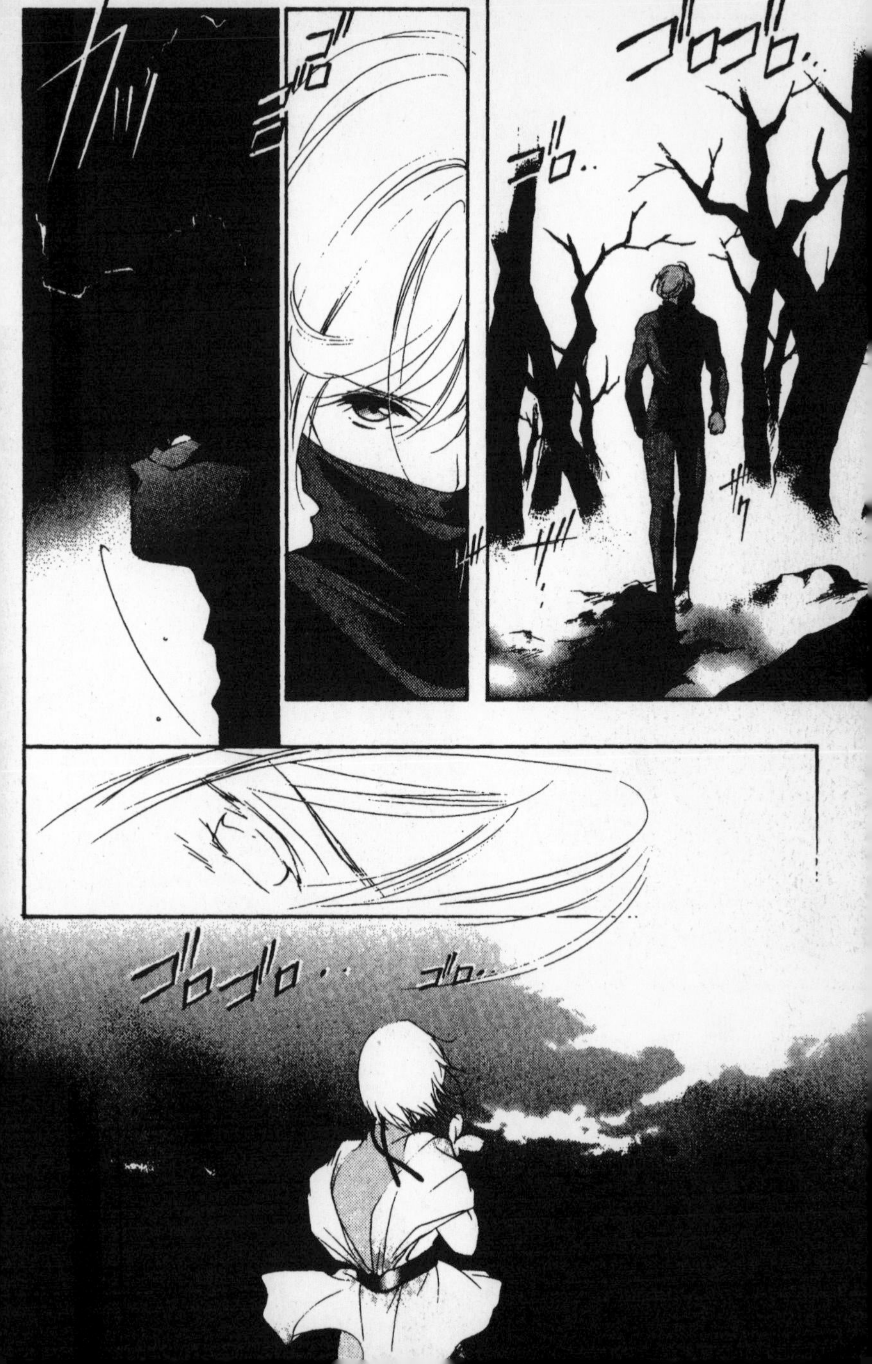
ゴロゴロ…
ゴロ…
ゴロゴロ
カッ
ゴロゴロ・・
ゴロ…

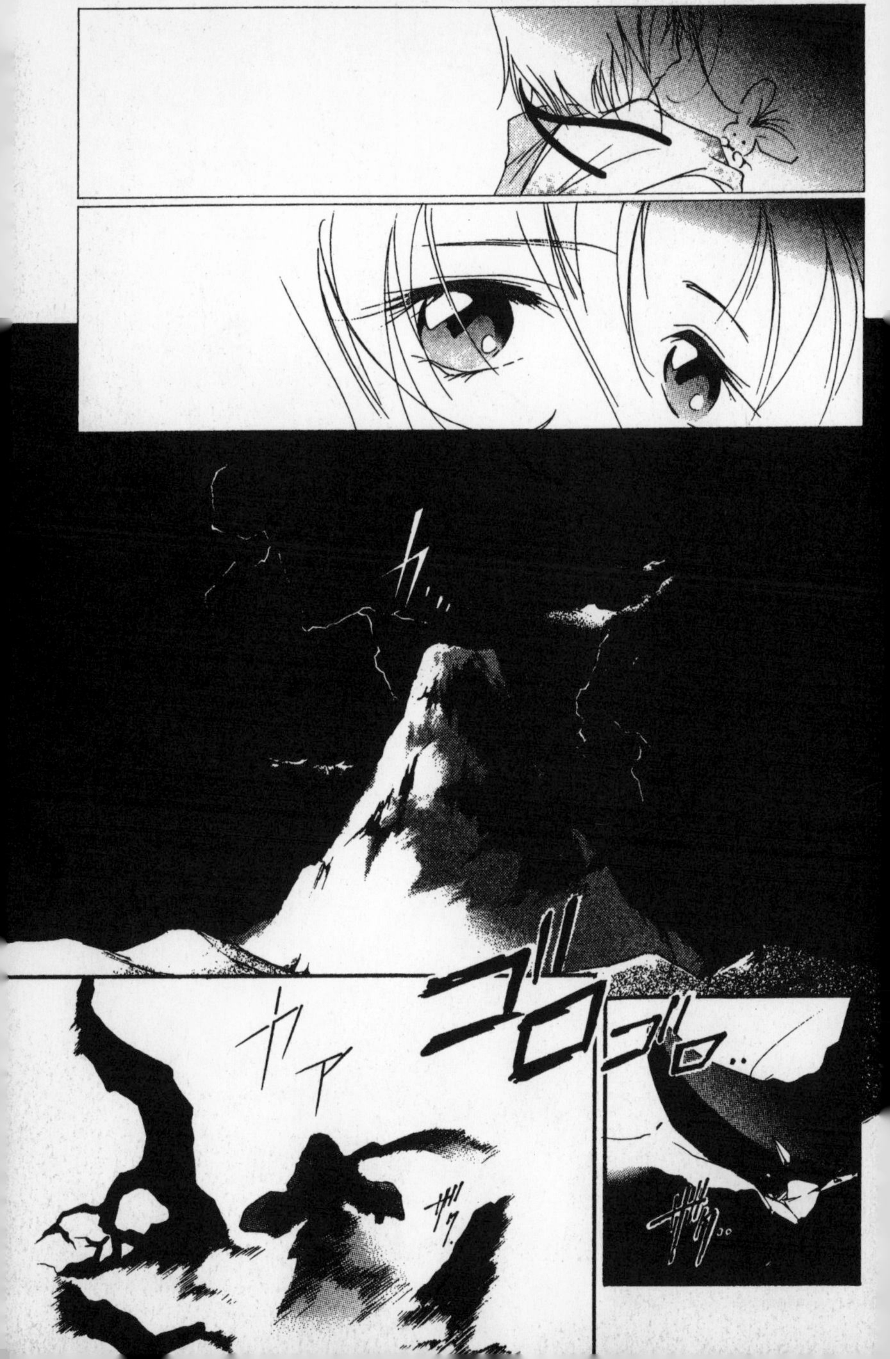
カッ…
ゴロゴロ…
ザザ…
カァ
ザワ.

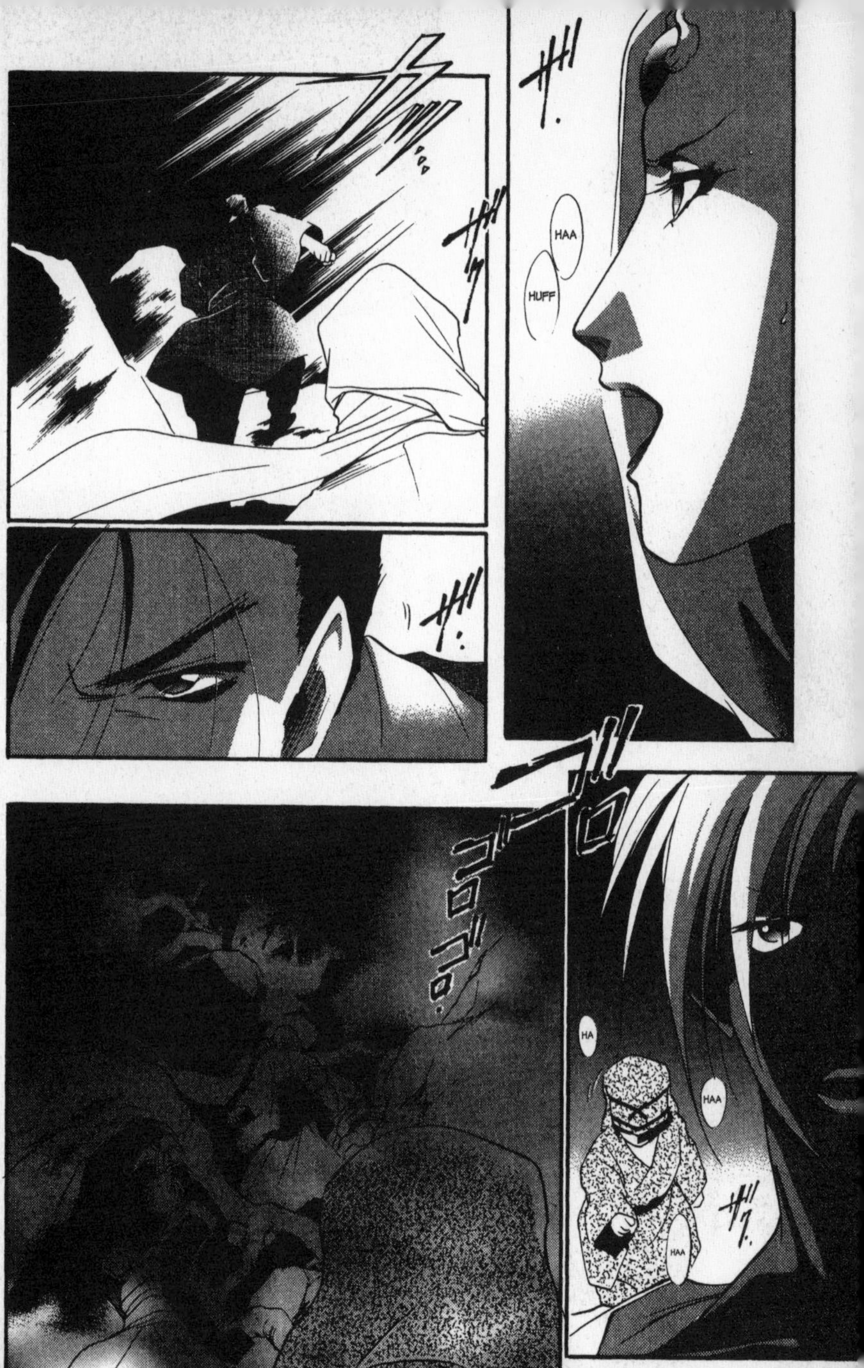
HAA
HUFF
HA
HAA
HAA

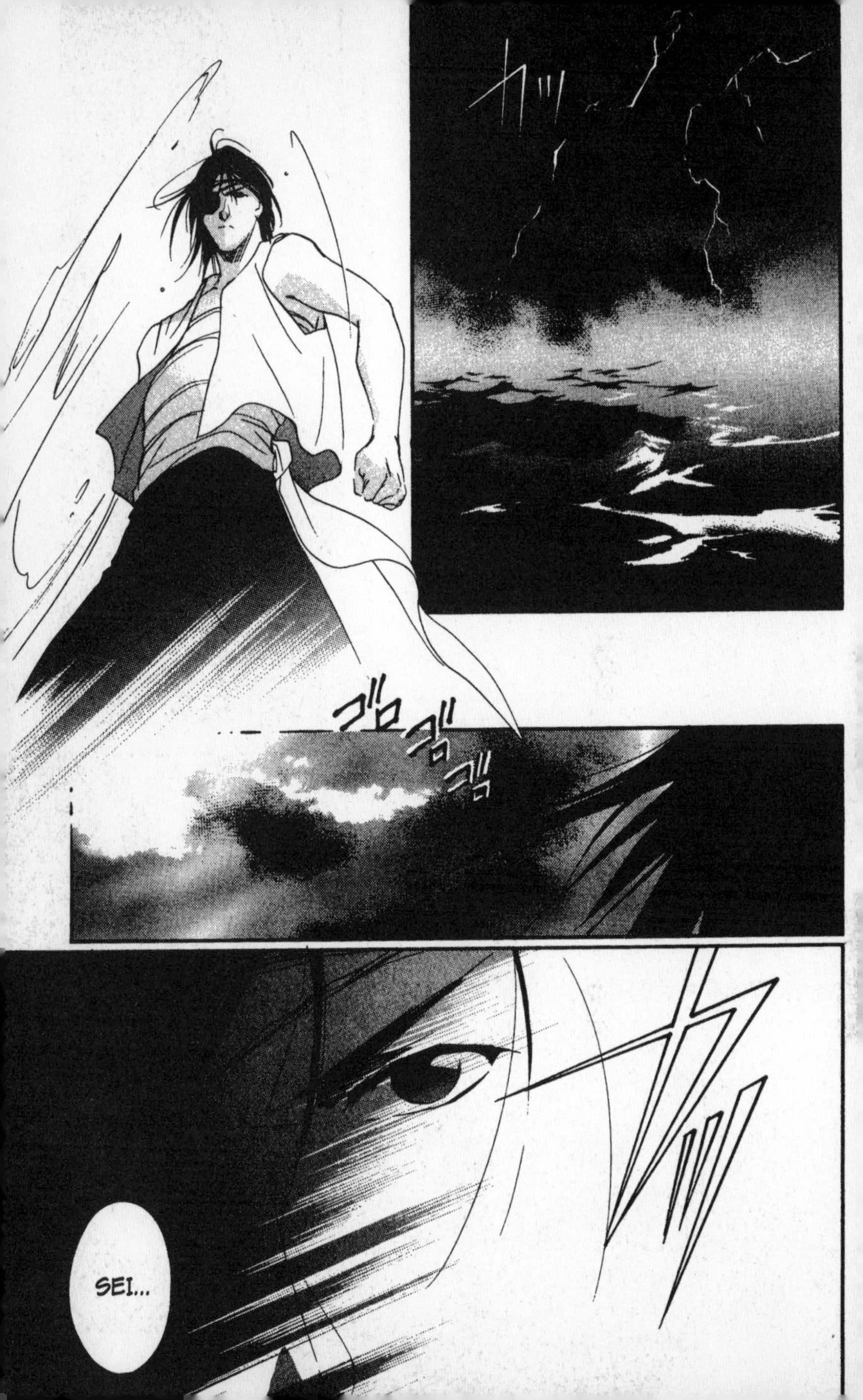
SEI...

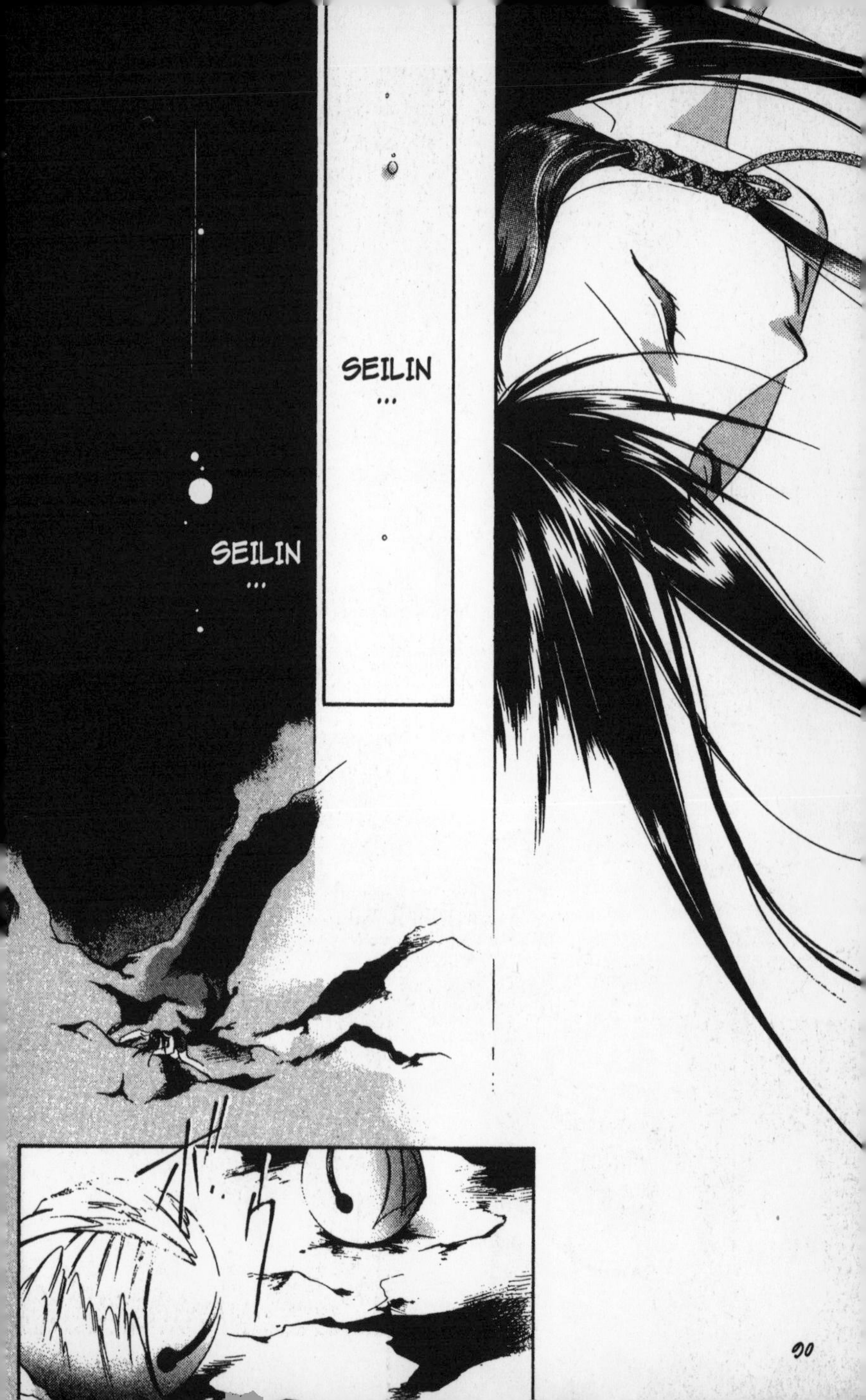
SEILIN ...
SEILIN ...

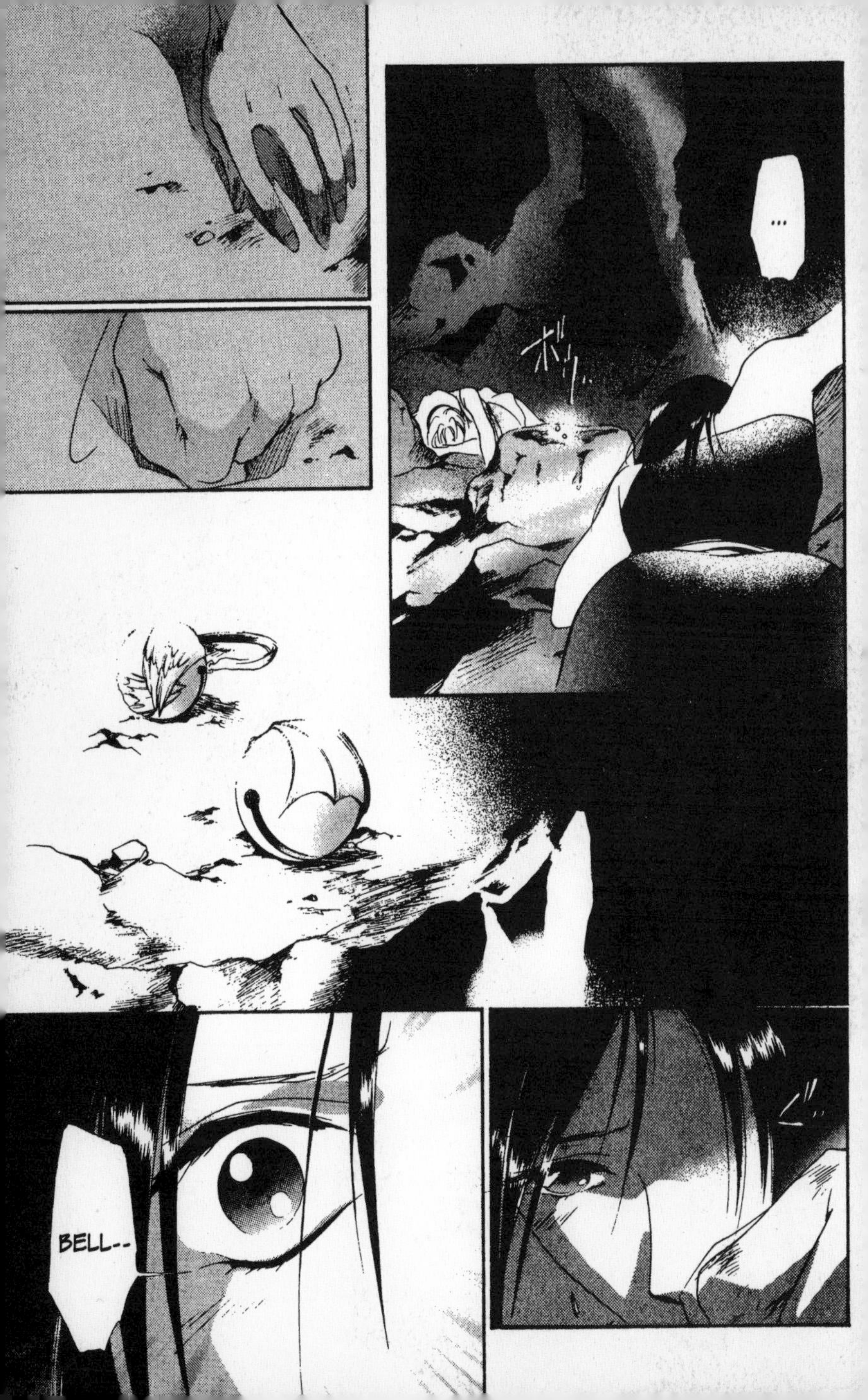
...
BELL--

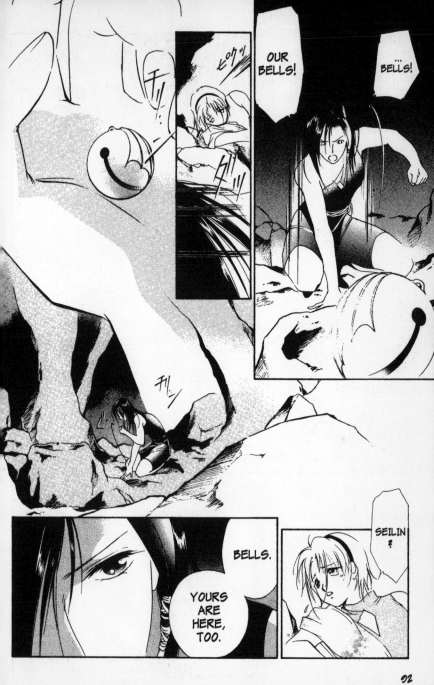

OUR BELLS!

...BELLS!

BELLS.

YOURS ARE HERE, TOO.

SEILIN?

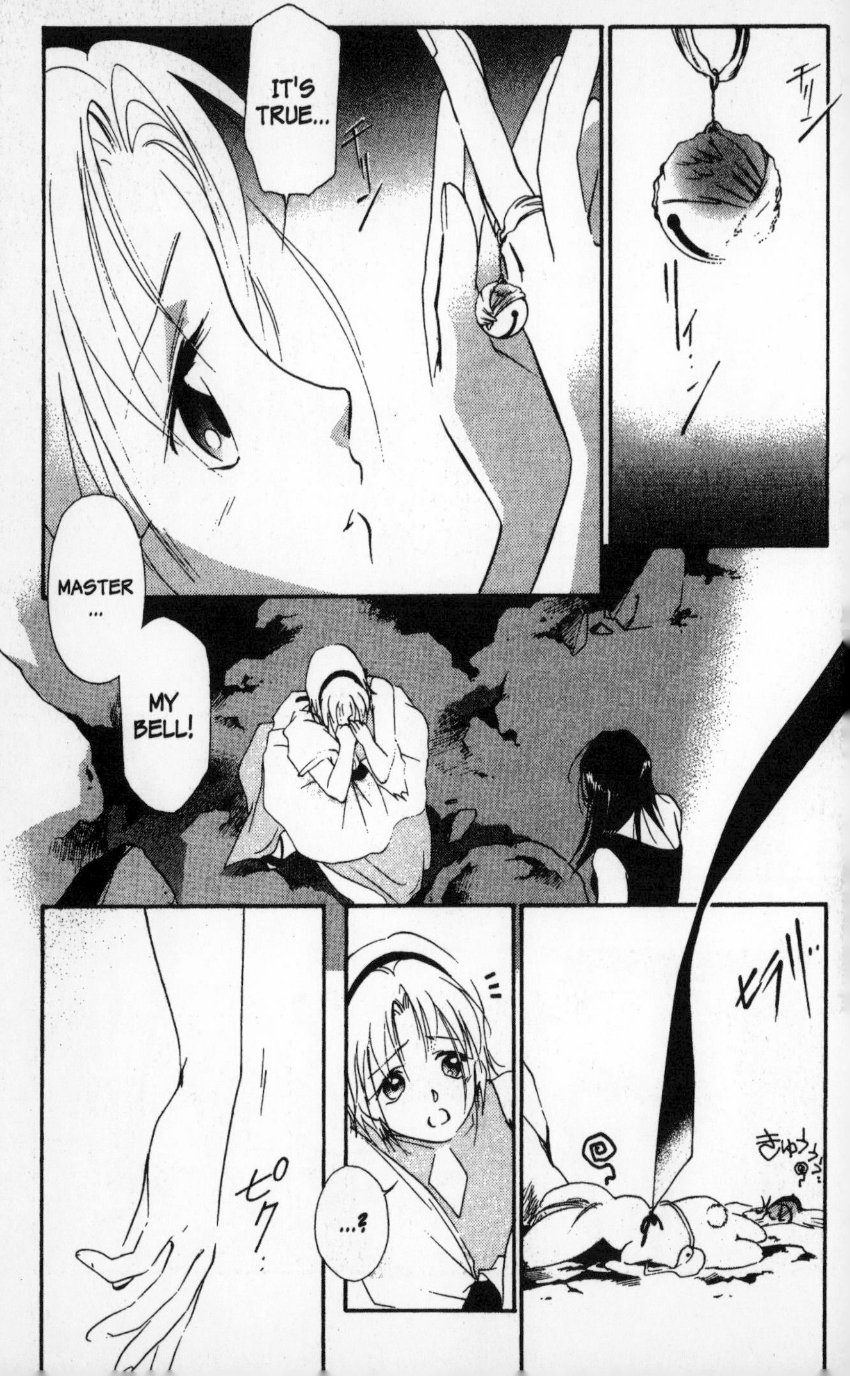
IT'S TRUE...
MASTER ...
MY BELL!
...?

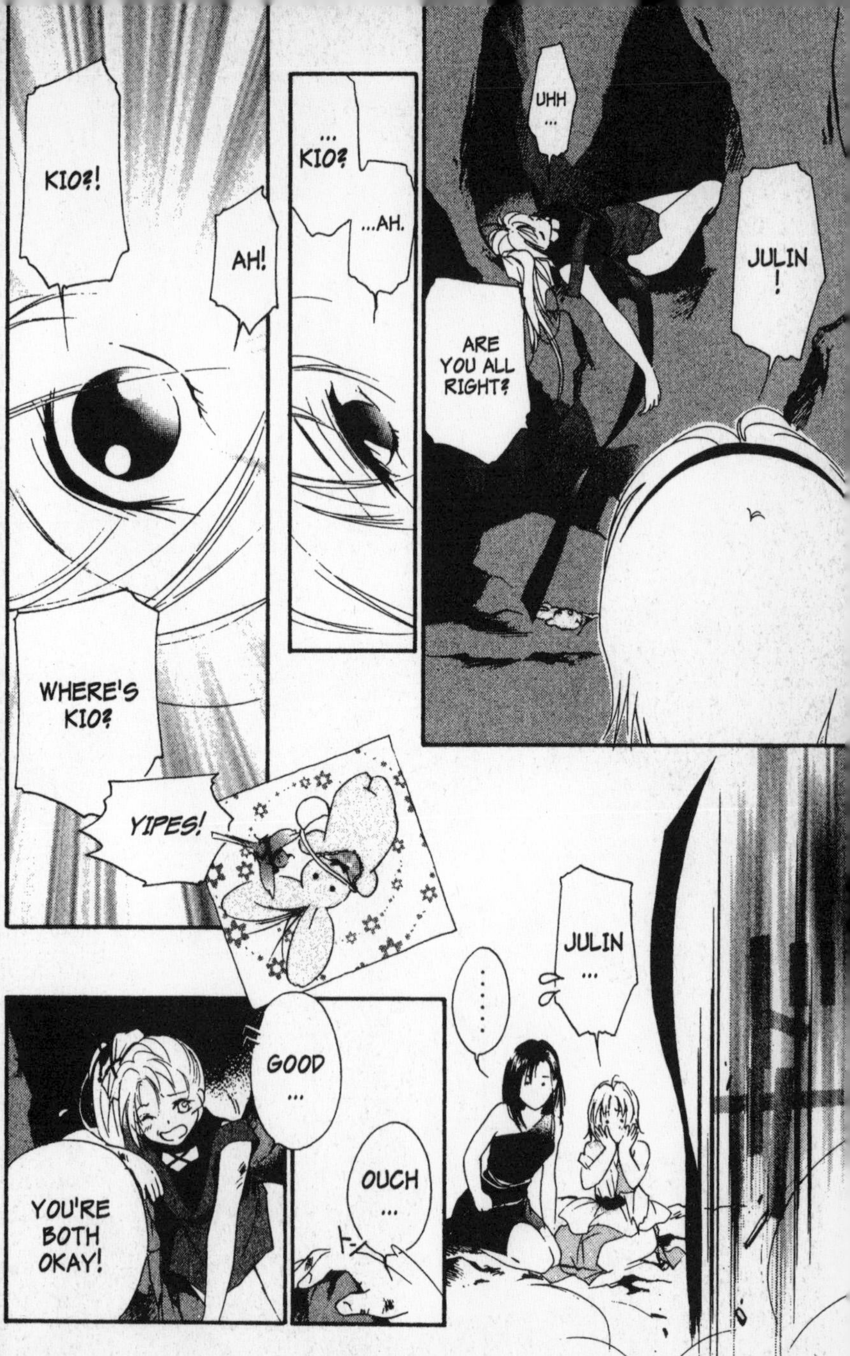
UHH ...
JULIN !
ARE YOU ALL RIGHT?
... KIO?
...AH.
KIO?!
AH!
WHERE'S KIO?
YIPES!
JULIN ...
......
GOOD ...
OUCH ...
YOU'RE BOTH OKAY!

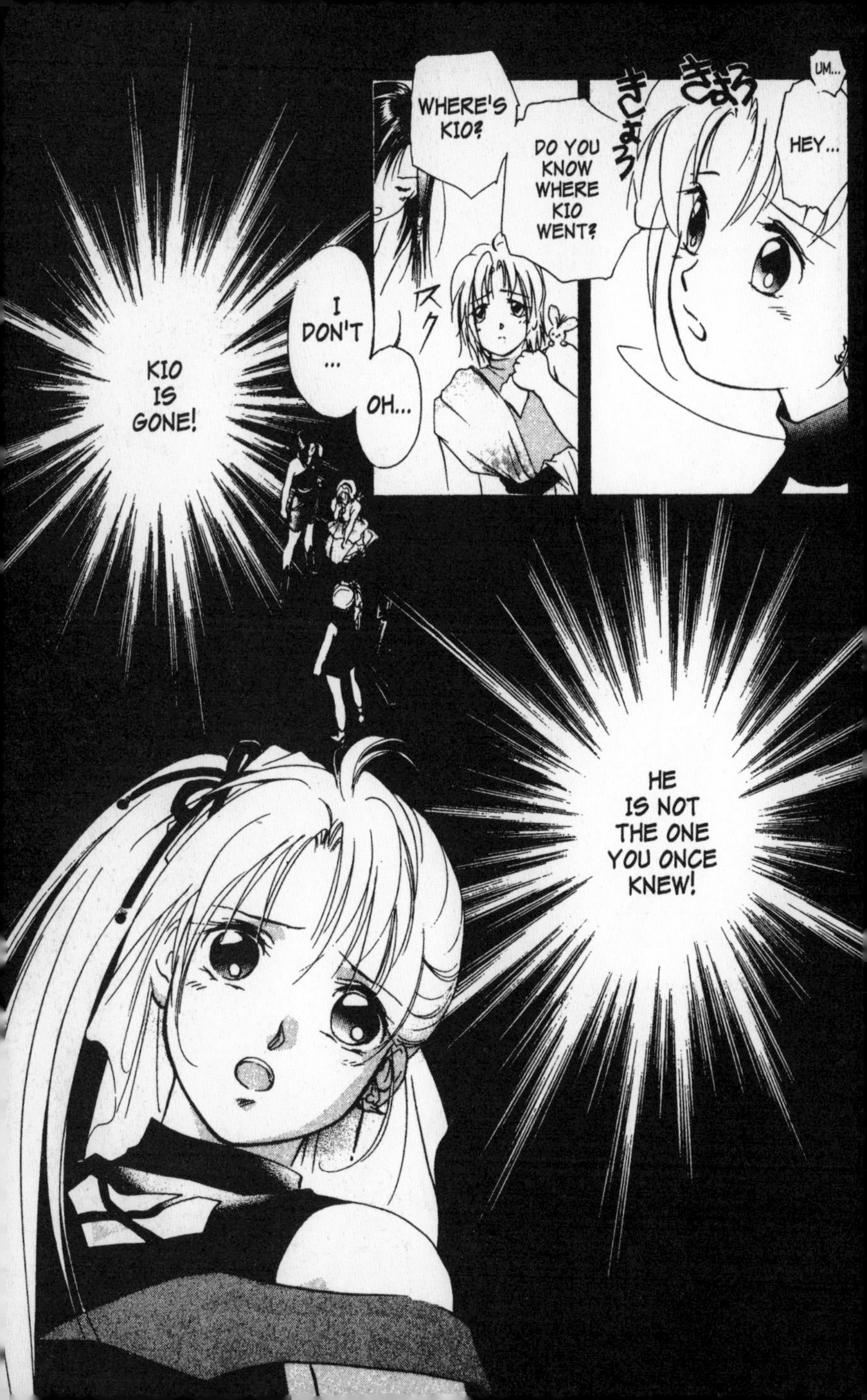
UM...
きょろきょろ
HEY...
WHERE'S KIO?
DO YOU KNOW WHERE KIO WENT?
スク
I DON'T ...
OH...
KIO IS GONE!
HE IS NOT THE ONE YOU ONCE KNEW!

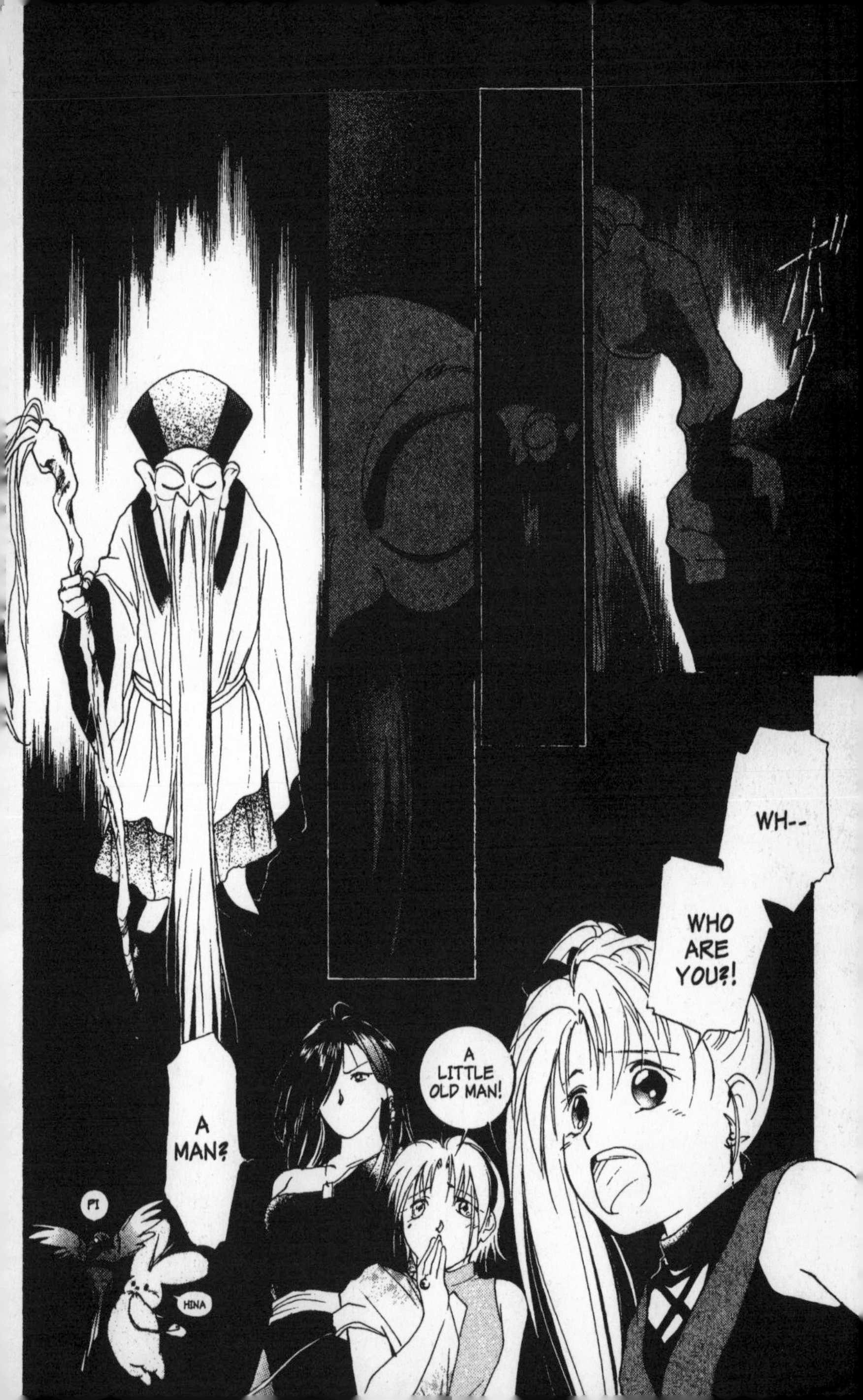
WH--
WHO ARE YOU?!
A LITTLE OLD MAN!
A MAN?
PI
HINA

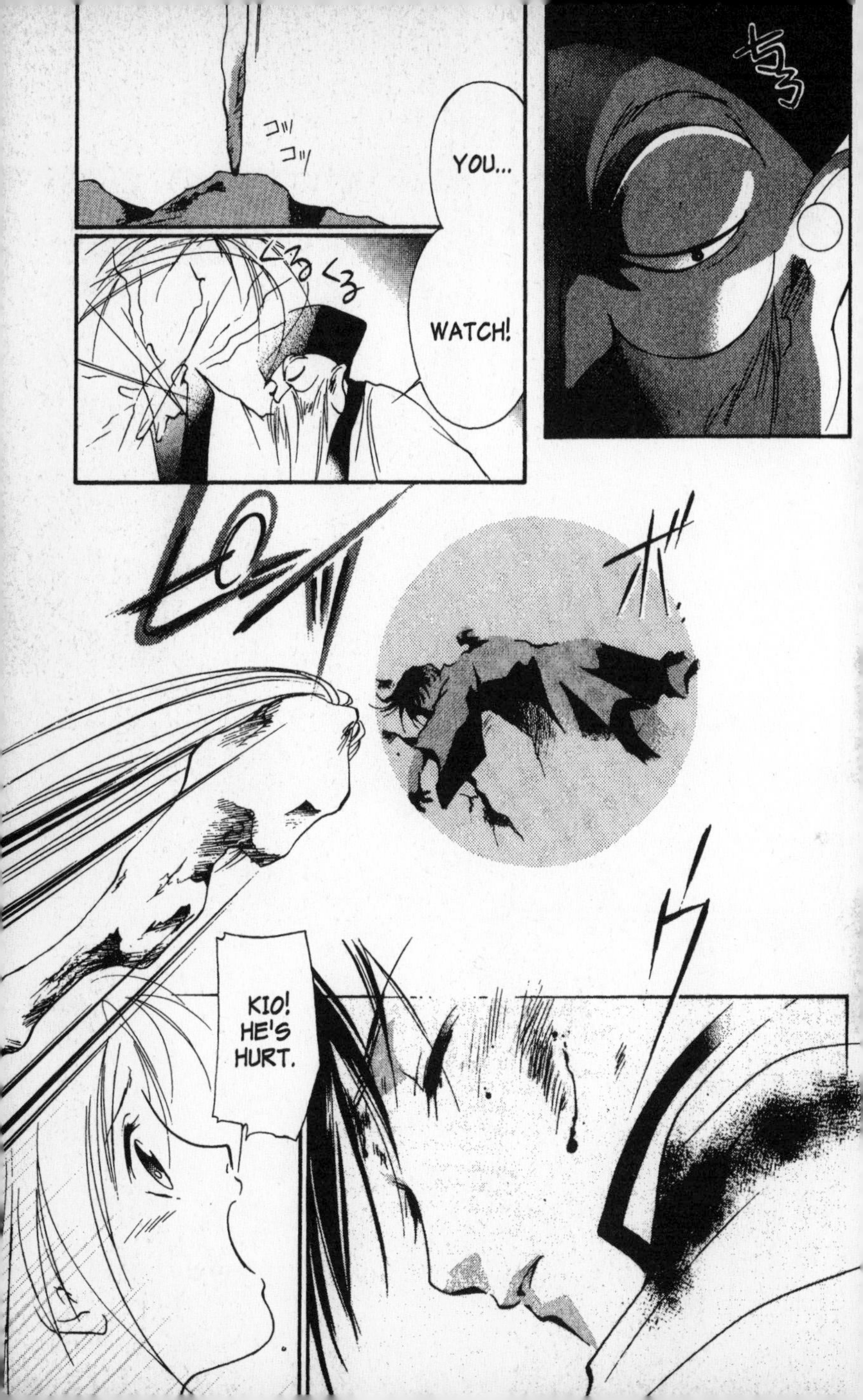
YOU... WATCH!
KIO! HE'S HURT.

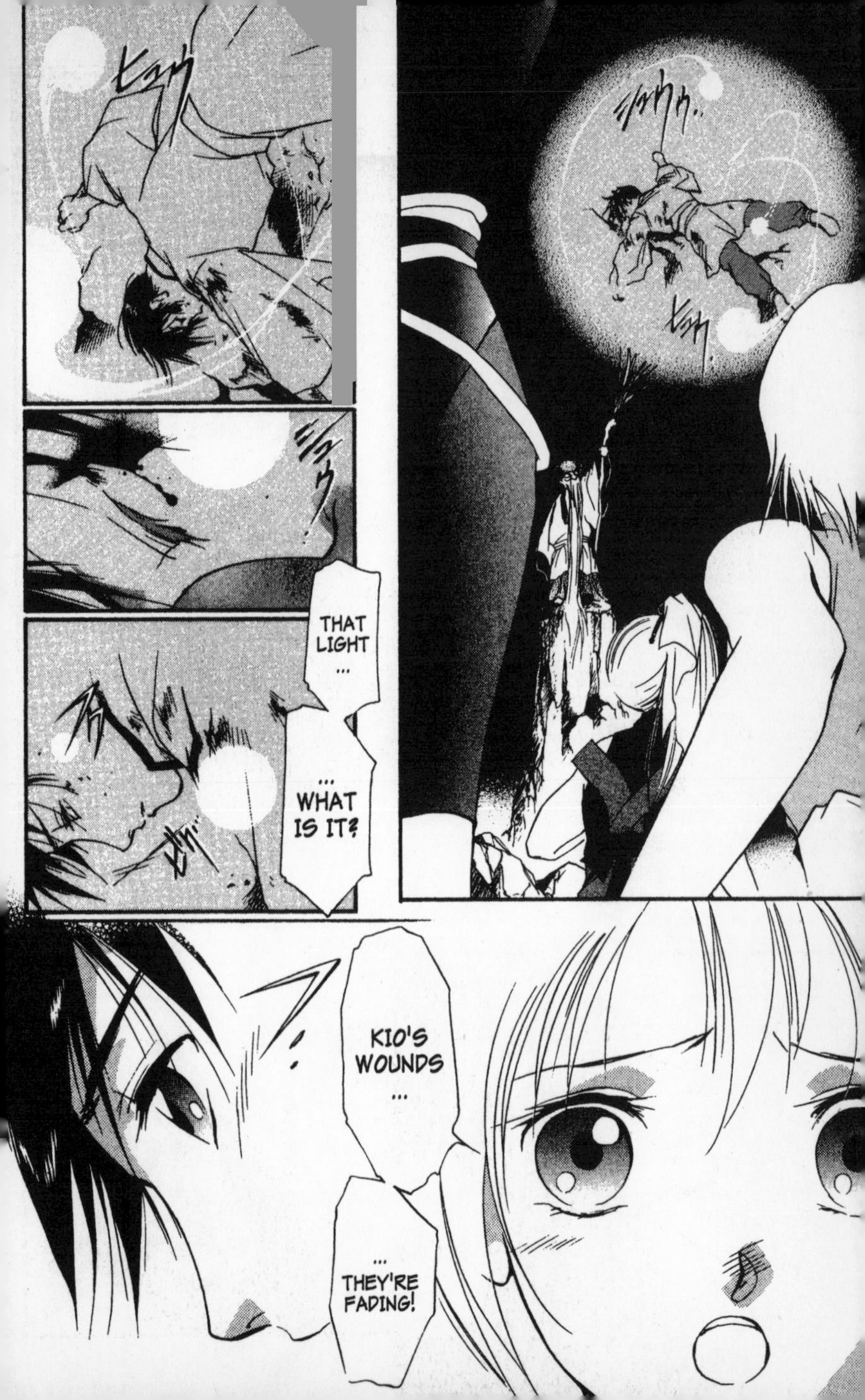
THAT LIGHT ...
... WHAT IS IT?
KIO'S WOUNDS ...
... THEY'RE FADING!

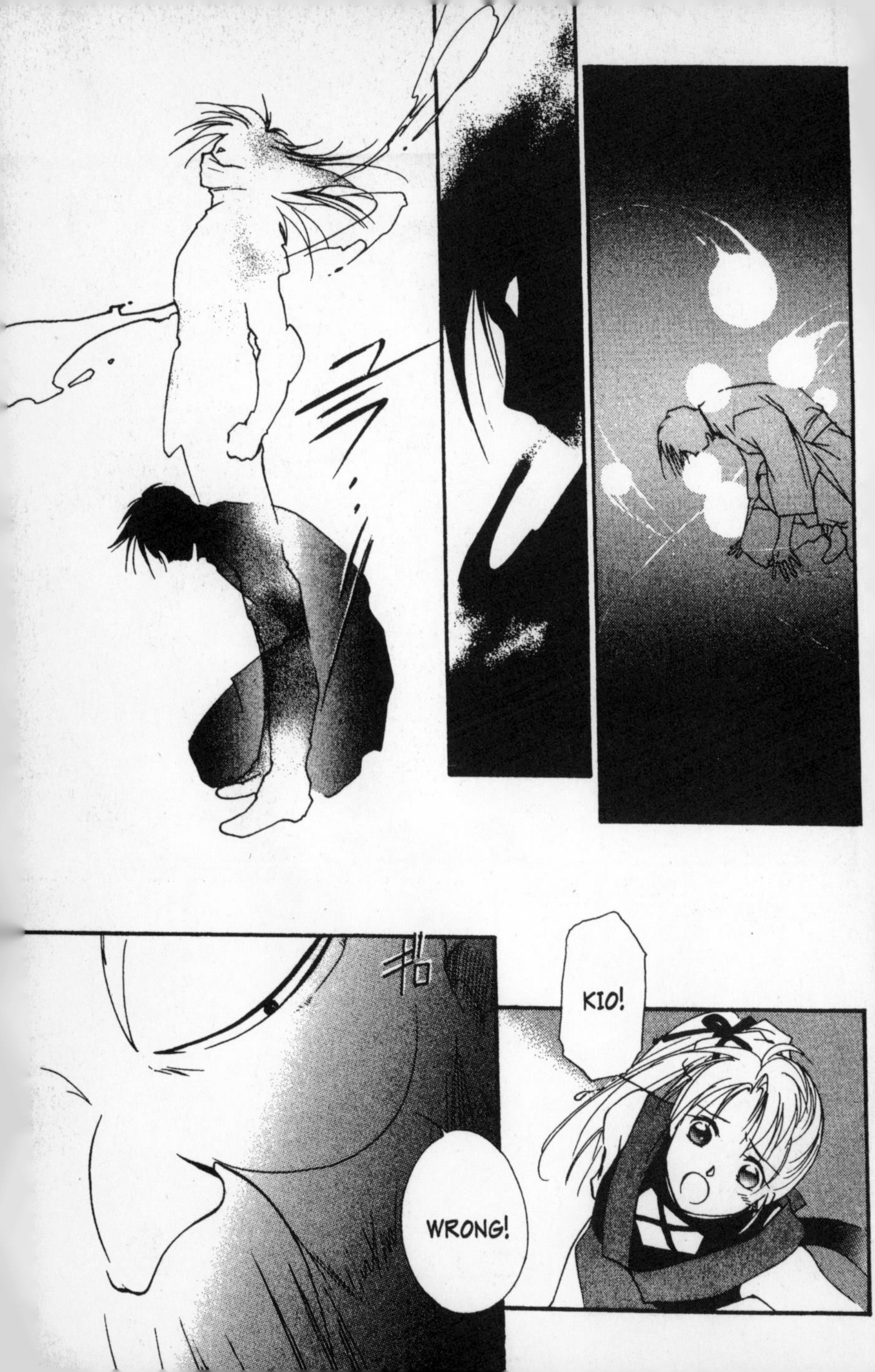
KIO!
WRONG!

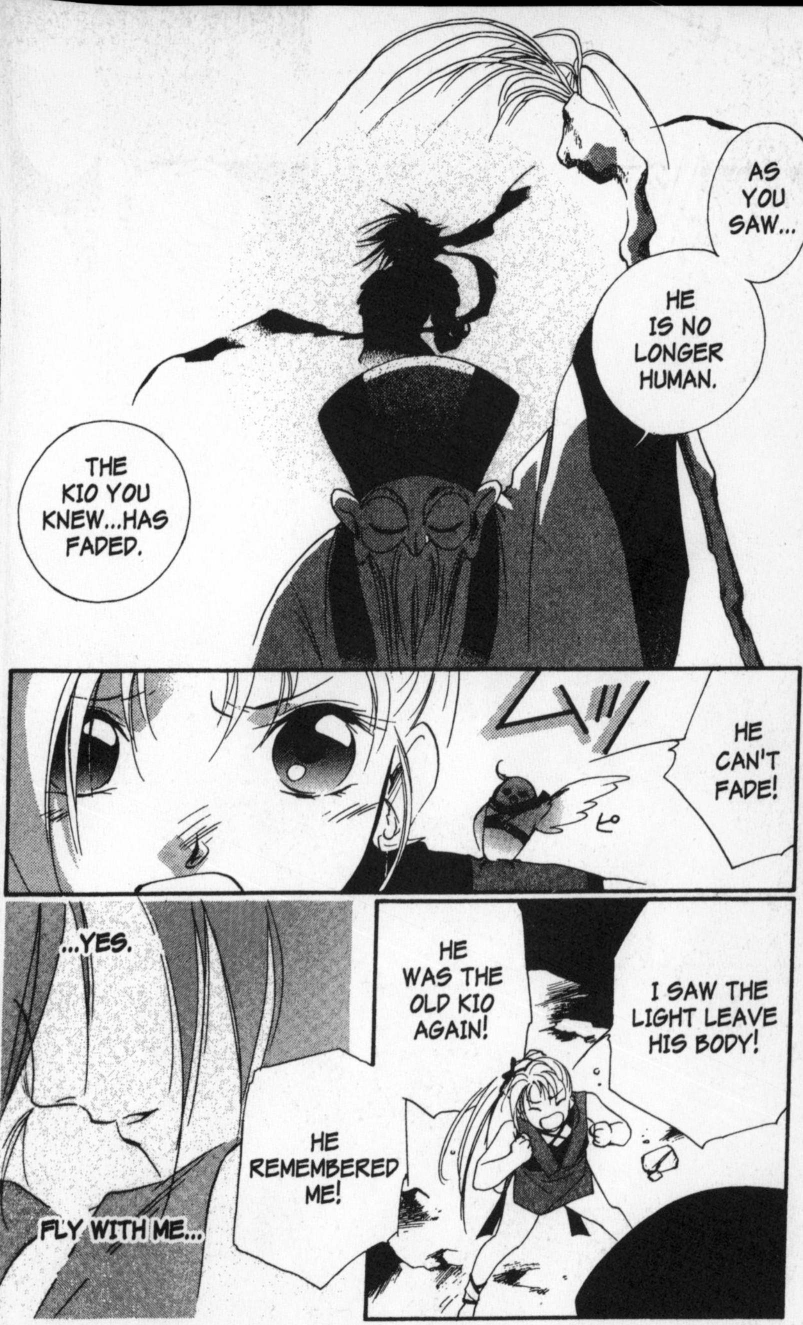

AS YOU SAW...
HE IS NO LONGER HUMAN.
THE KIO YOU KNEW...HAS FADED.
ムッ
HE CAN'T FADE!
ピ
I SAW THE LIGHT LEAVE HIS BODY!
HE WAS THE OLD KIO AGAIN!
HE REMEMBERED ME!
...YES.
FLY WITH ME...

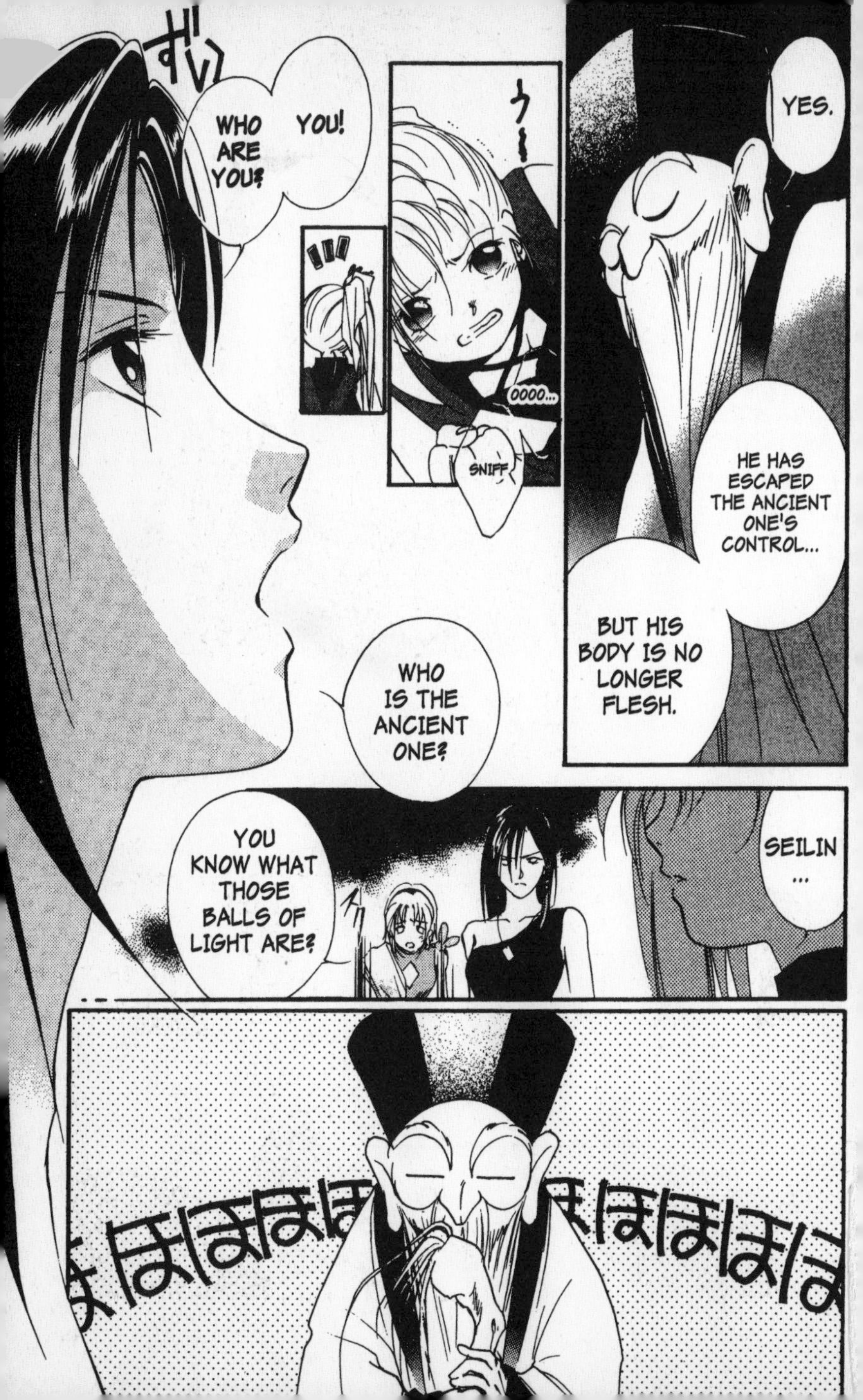
YES.
HE HAS ESCAPED THE ANCIENT ONE'S CONTROL...
BUT HIS BODY IS NO LONGER FLESH.
ウ～
OOOO...
SNIFF
ずい
YOU! WHO ARE YOU?
WHO IS THE ANCIENT ONE?
SEILIN ...
YOU KNOW WHAT THOSE BALLS OF LIGHT ARE?
ほほほほほ
ほほほほほほ

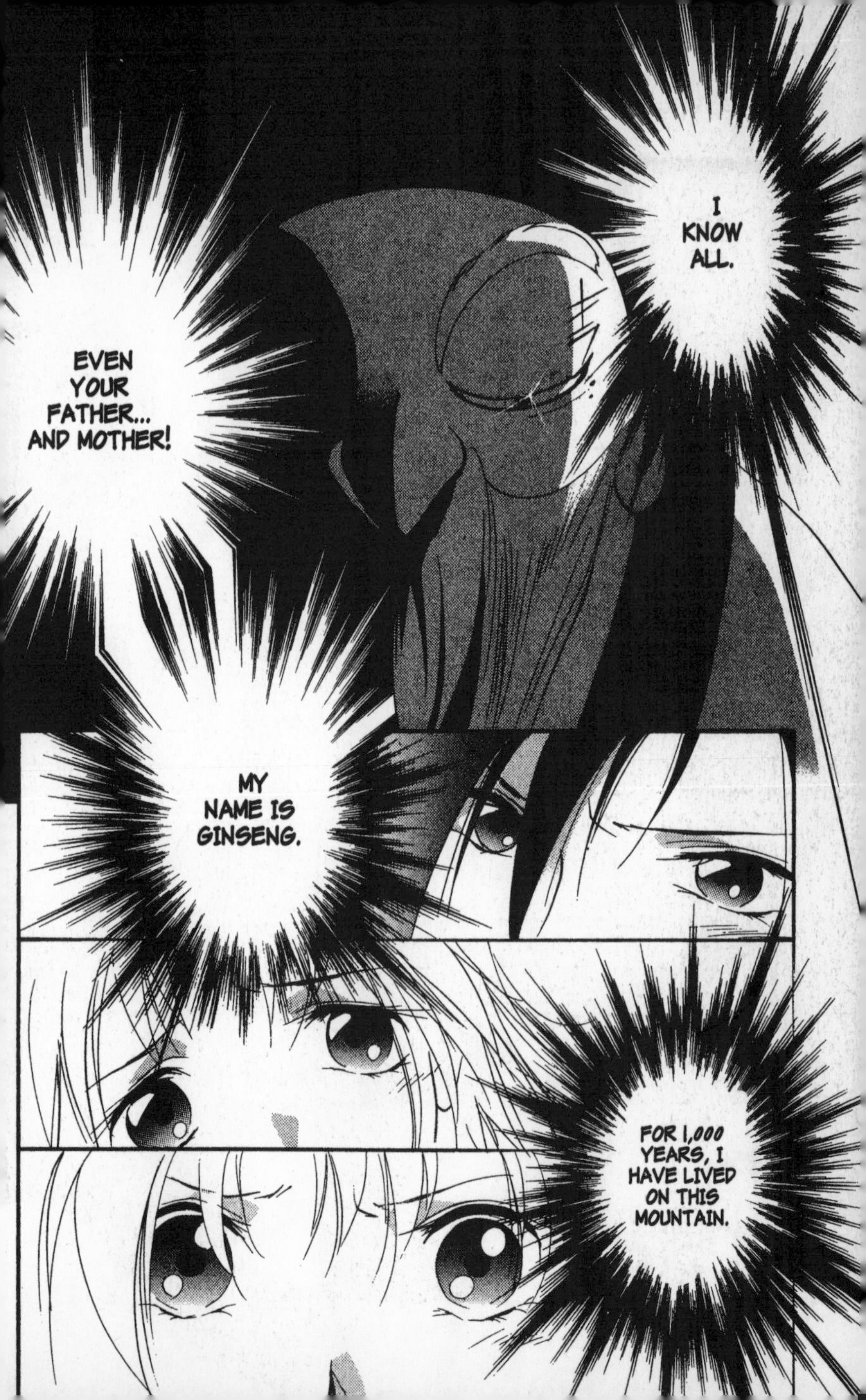
I KNOW ALL.
EVEN YOUR FATHER... AND MOTHER!
MY NAME IS GINSENG.
FOR 1,000 YEARS, I HAVE LIVED ON THIS MOUNTAIN.

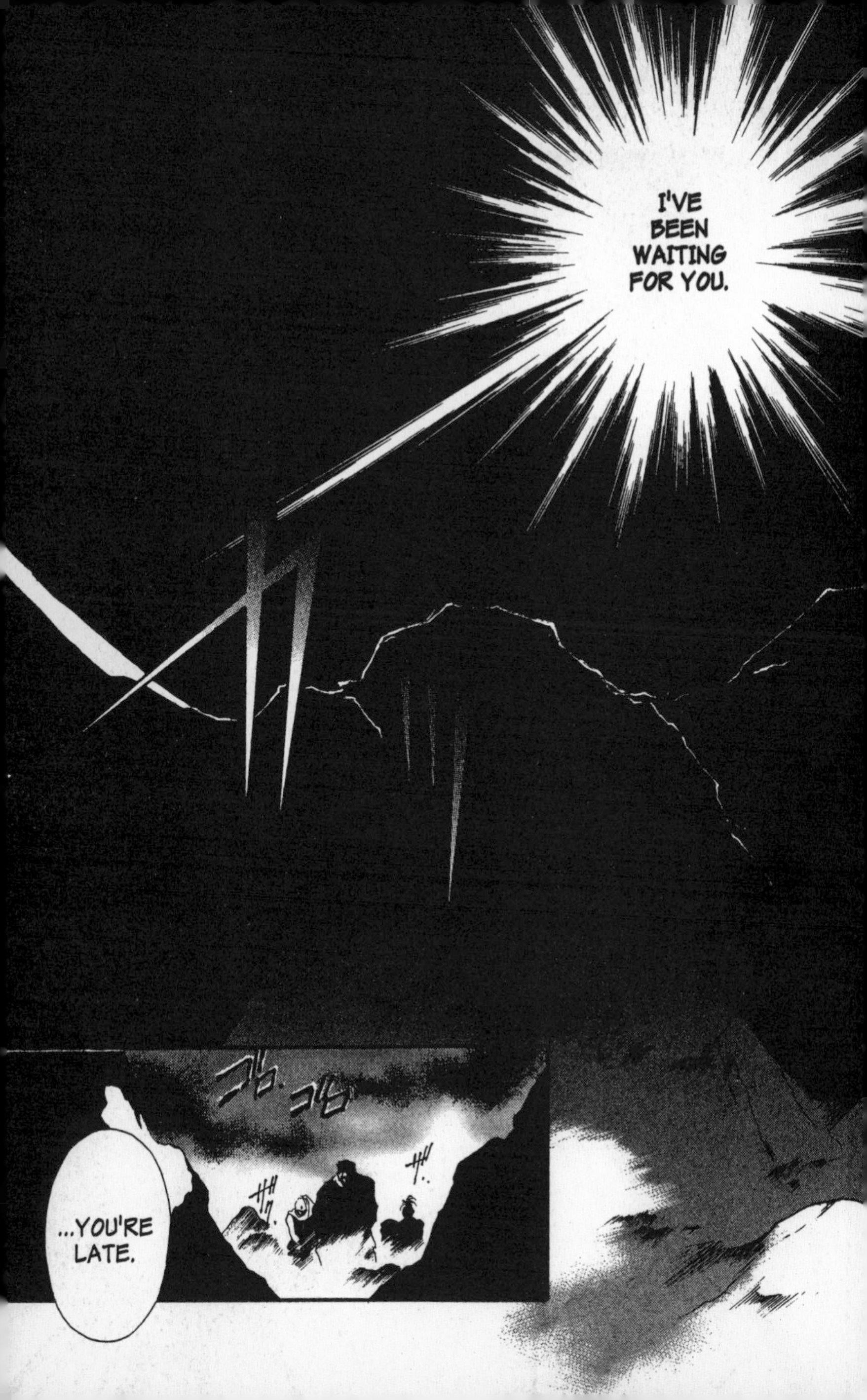
I'VE BEEN WAITING FOR YOU.
...YOU'RE LATE.

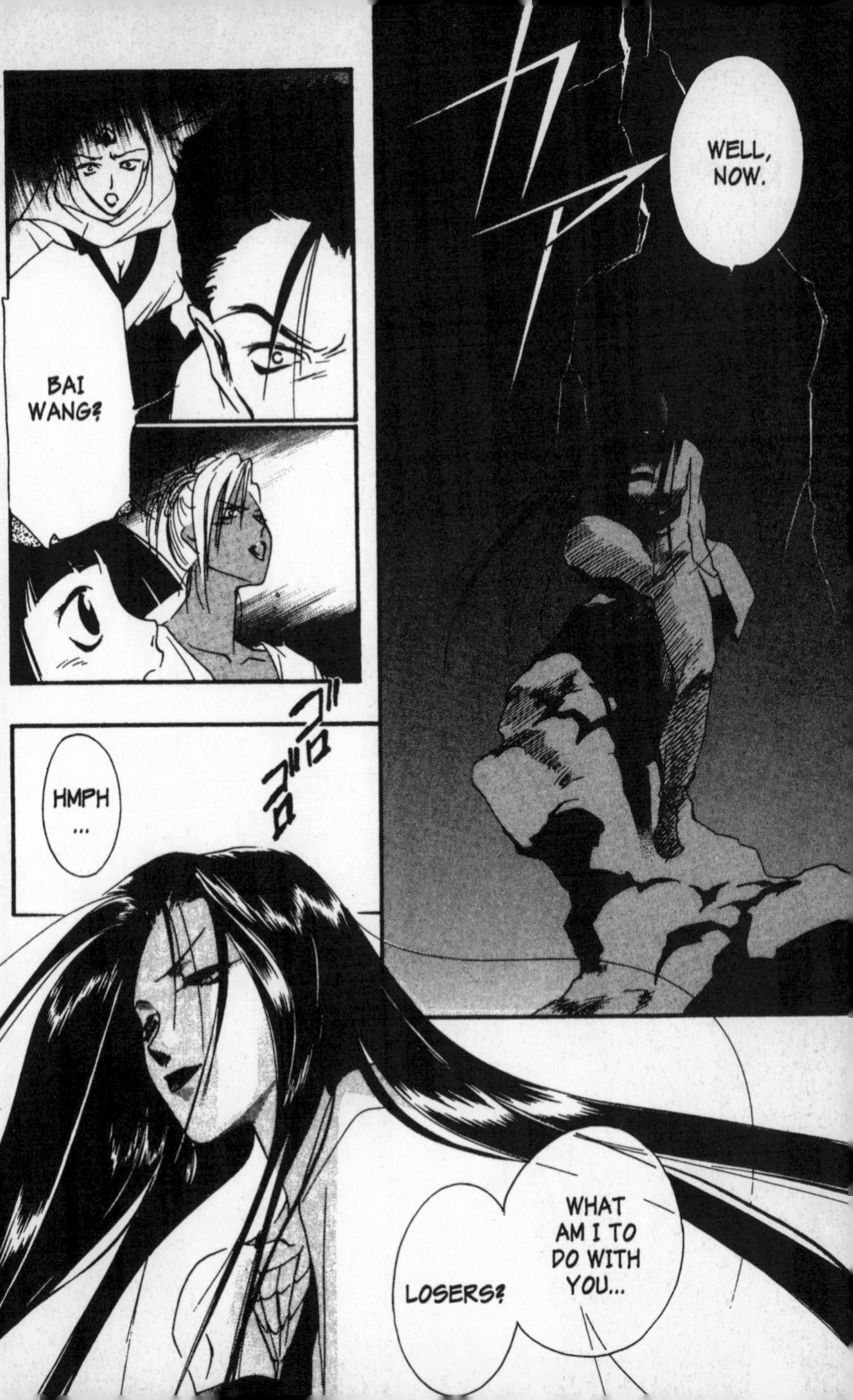
WELL, NOW.
BAI WANG?
ゴロゴロ
HMPH ...
WHAT AM I TO DO WITH YOU...
LOSERS?

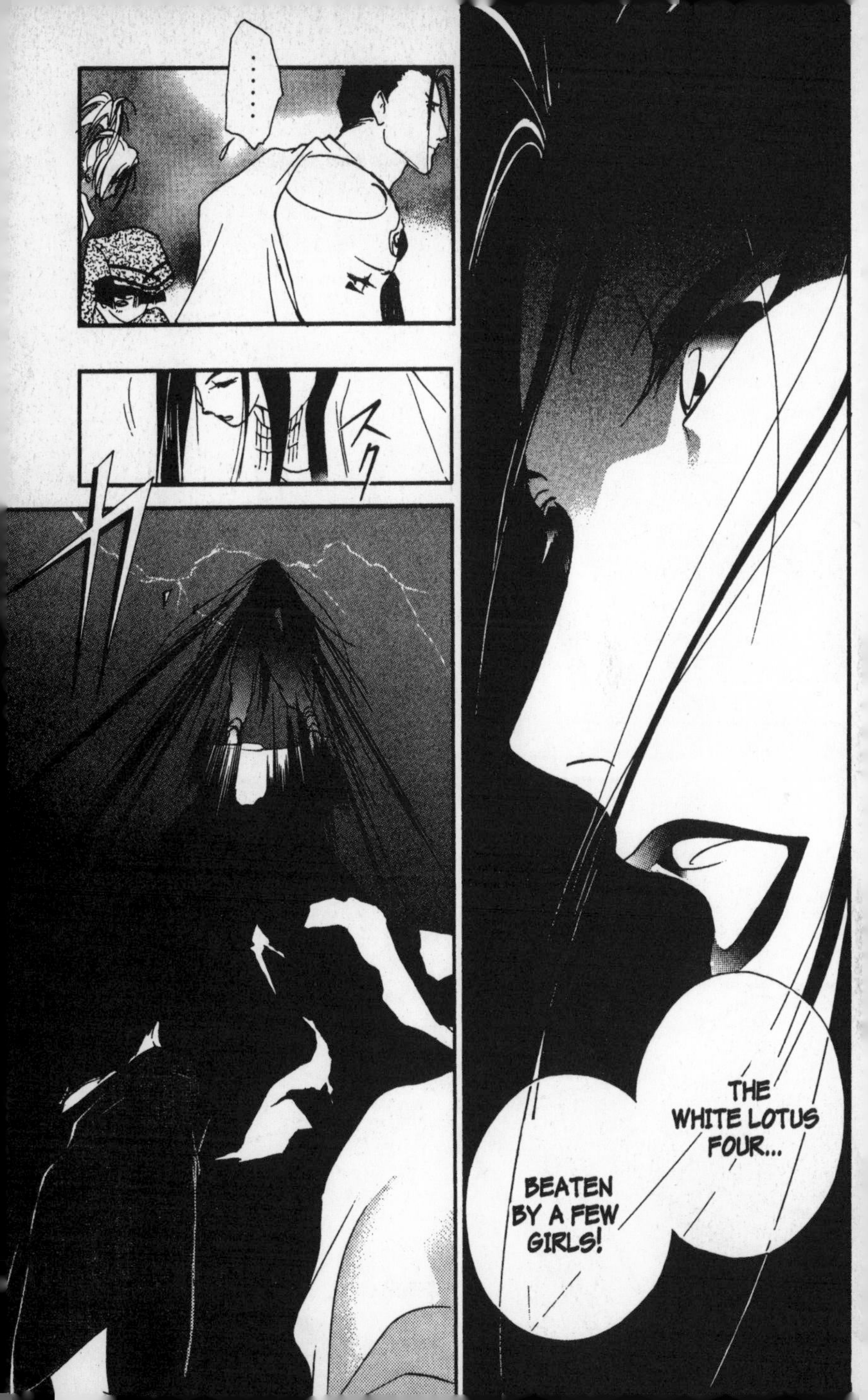
THE WHITE LOTUS FOUR...
BEATEN BY A FEW GIRLS!
......

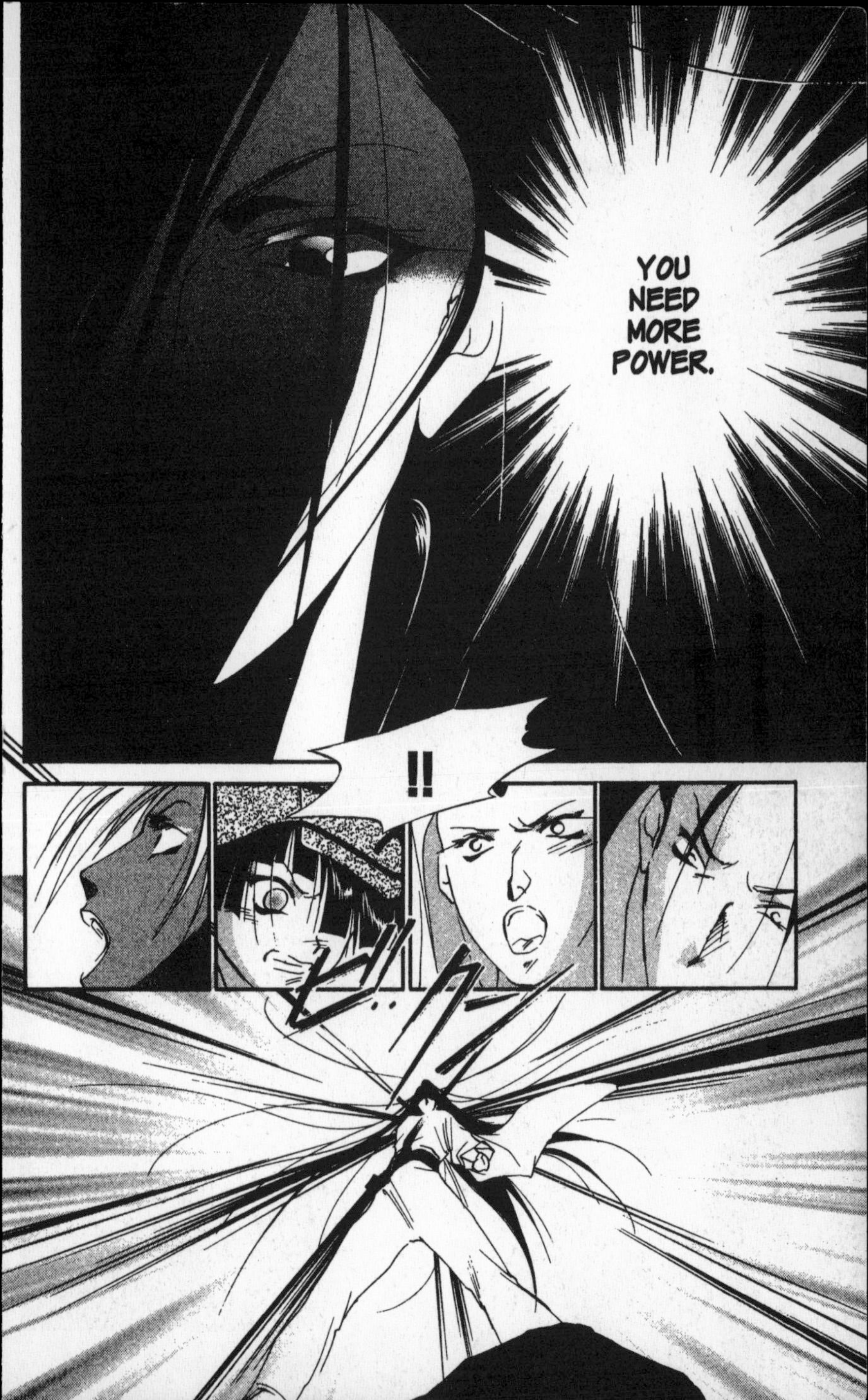
YOU NEED MORE POWER.
!!

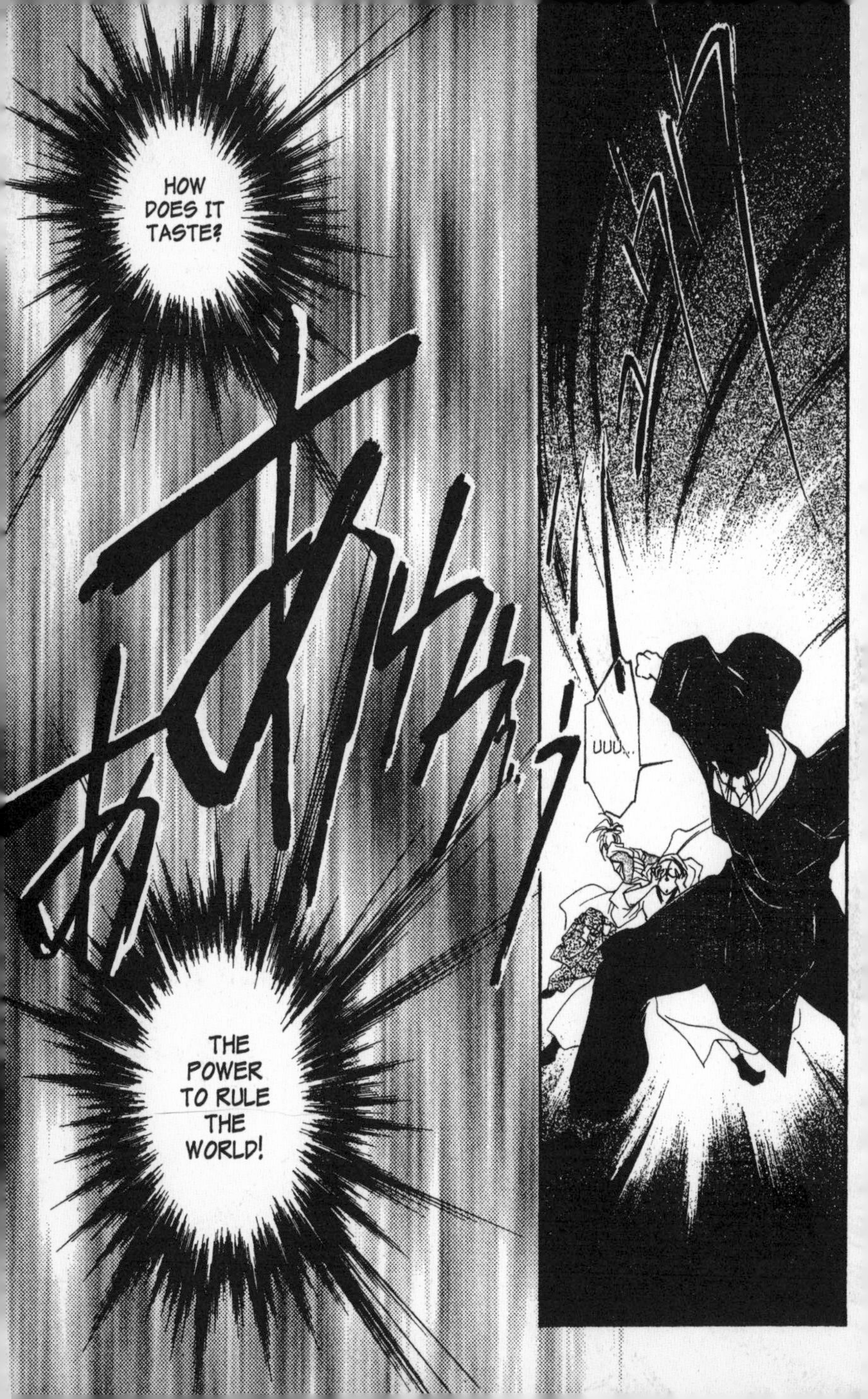
UUU...
HOW DOES IT TASTE?
THE POWER TO RULE THE WORLD!

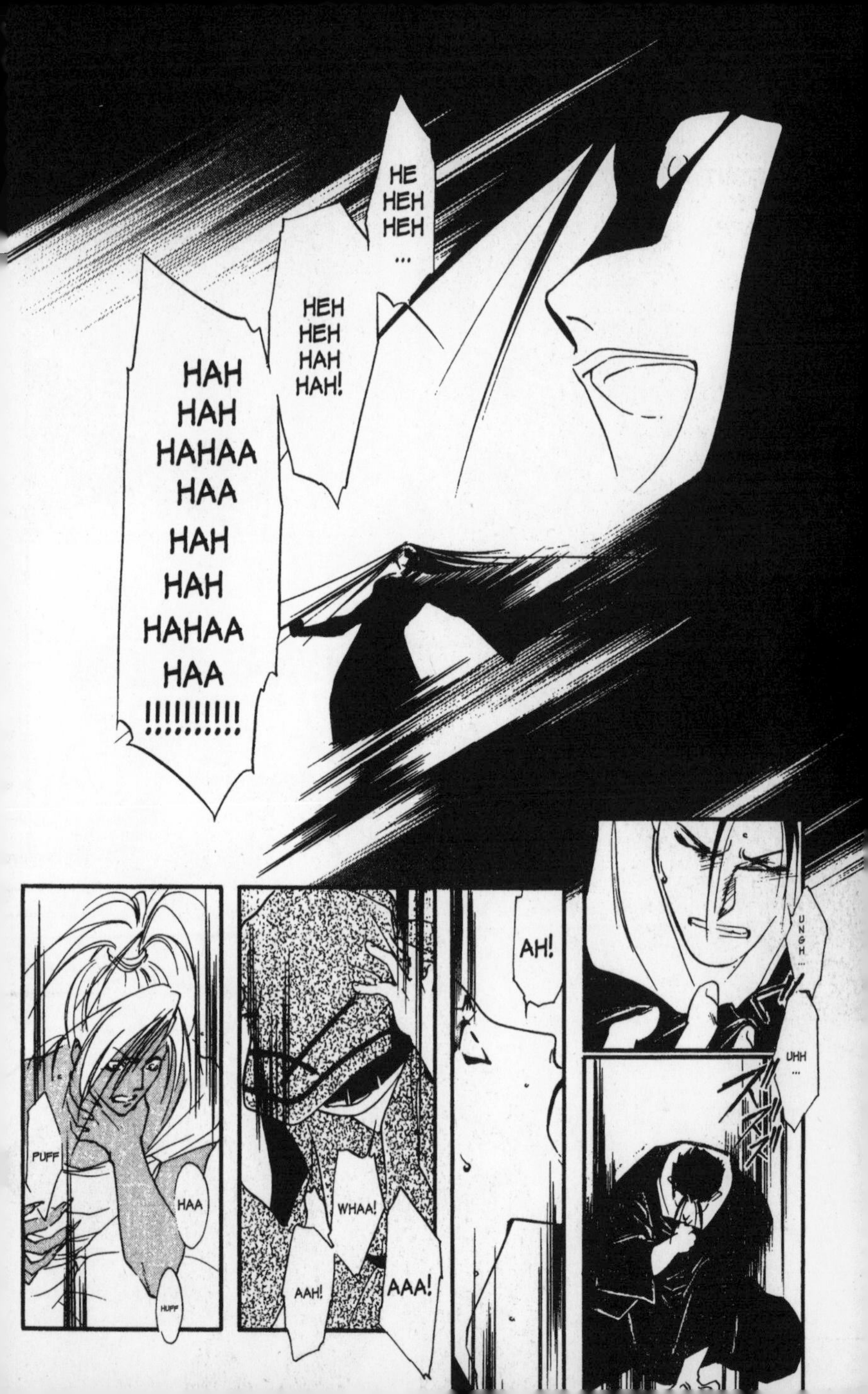
HE HEH HEH ...
HEH HEH HAH HAH!
HAH HAH HAHAA HAA HAH HAH HAHAA HAA !!!!!!!!!!
UNGH ...
UHH ...
AH!
WHAA!
AAA!
AAH!
PUFF
HAA
HUFF

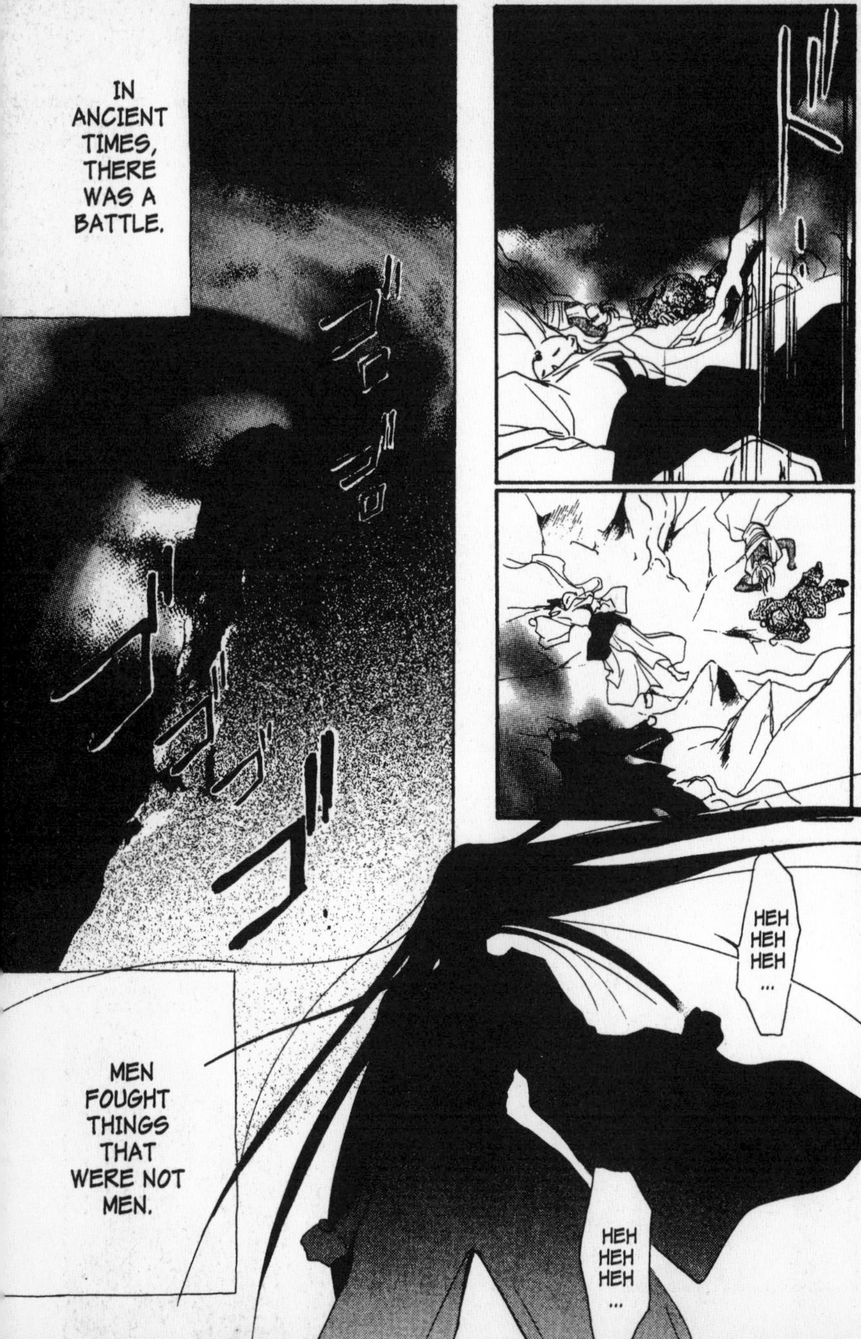
IN ANCIENT TIMES, THERE WAS A BATTLE.
HEH HEH HEH ...
MEN FOUGHT THINGS THAT WERE NOT MEN.
HEH HEH HEH ...

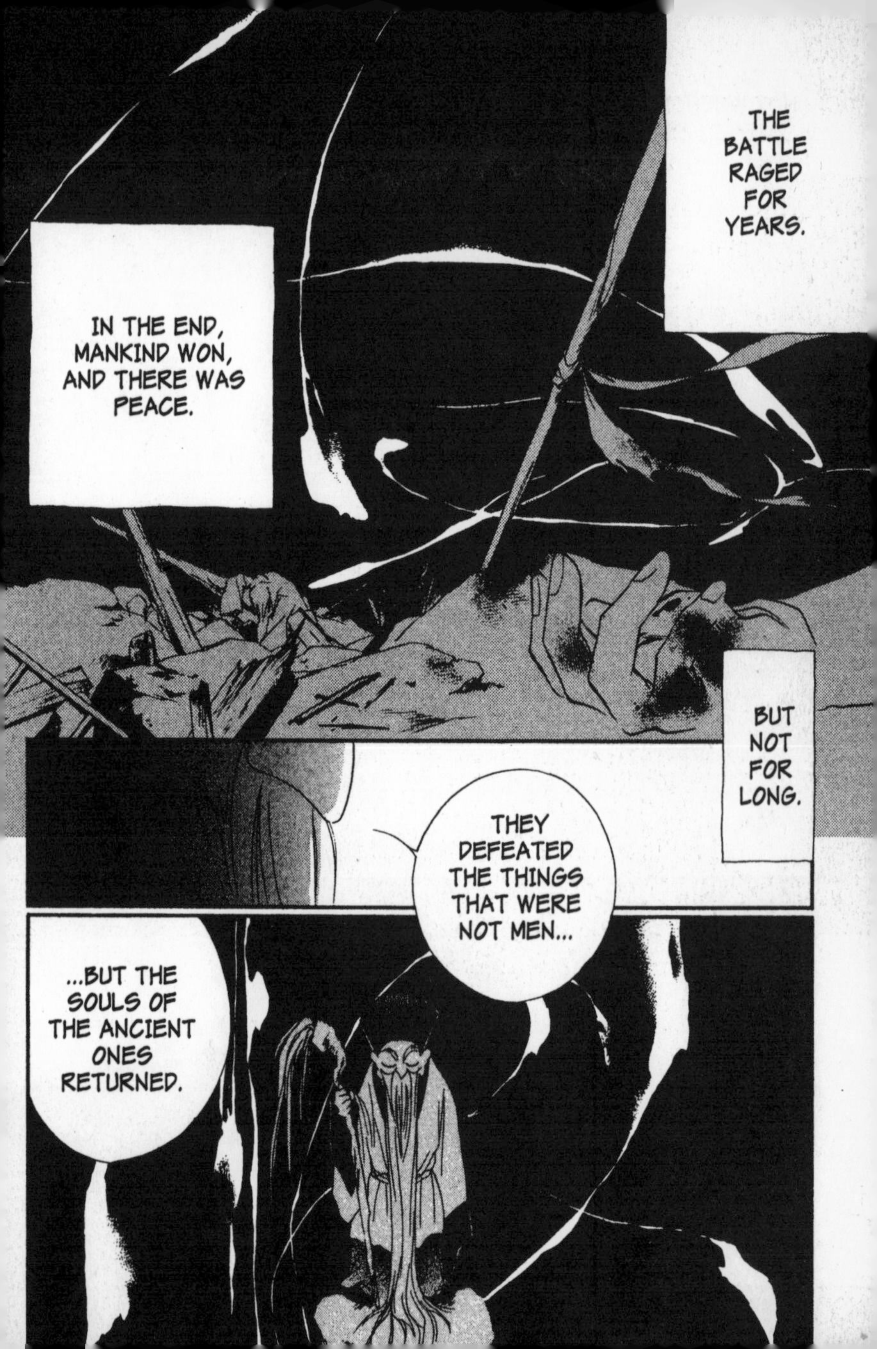
THE BATTLE RAGED FOR YEARS.
IN THE END, MANKIND WON, AND THERE WAS PEACE.
BUT NOT FOR LONG.
THEY DEFEATED THE THINGS THAT WERE NOT MEN...
...BUT THE SOULS OF THE ANCIENT ONES RETURNED.

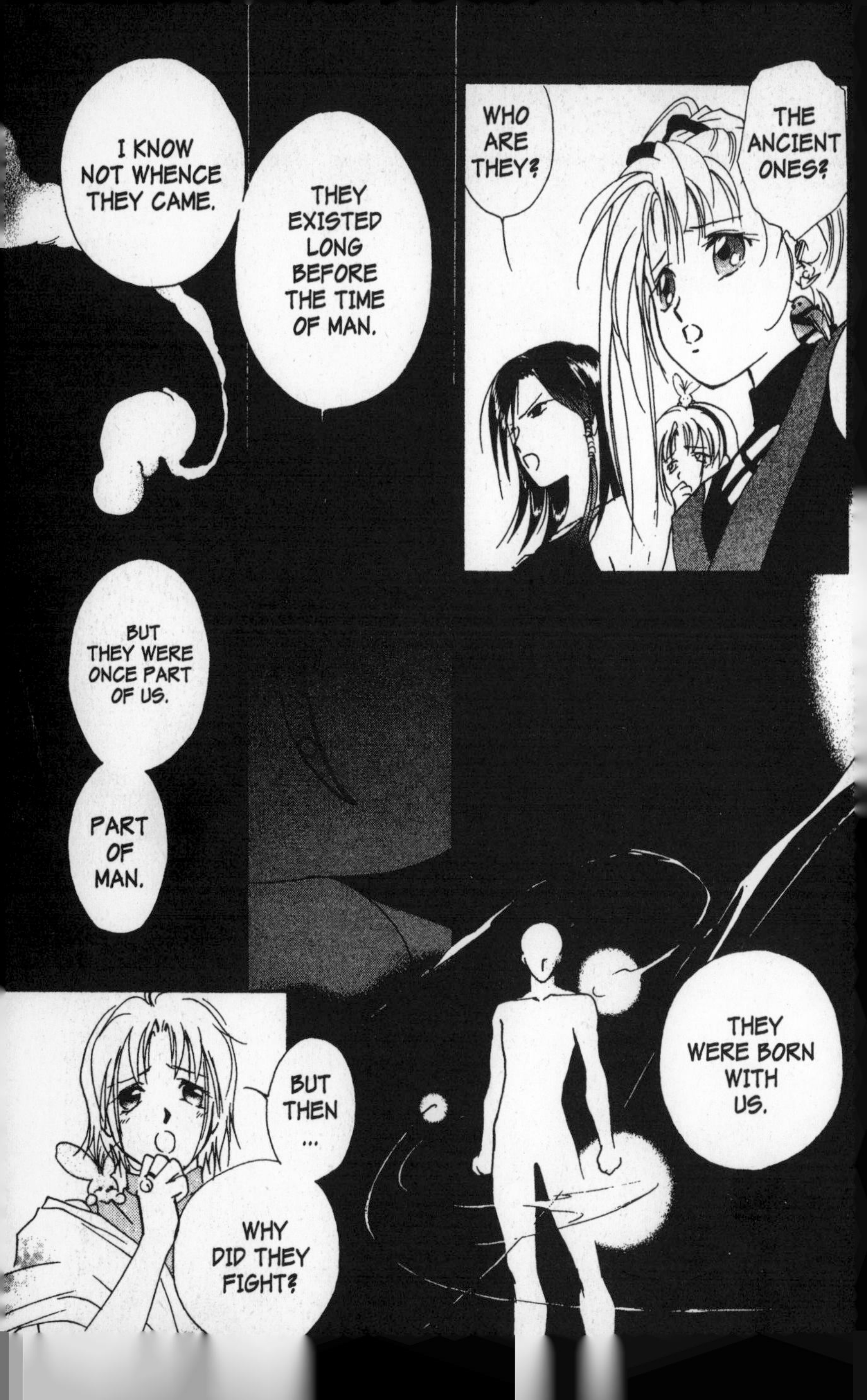
THE ANCIENT ONES?
WHO ARE THEY?
THEY EXISTED LONG BEFORE THE TIME OF MAN.
I KNOW NOT WHENCE THEY CAME.
BUT THEY WERE ONCE PART OF US.
PART OF MAN.
THEY WERE BORN WITH US.
BUT THEN...
WHY DID THEY FIGHT?

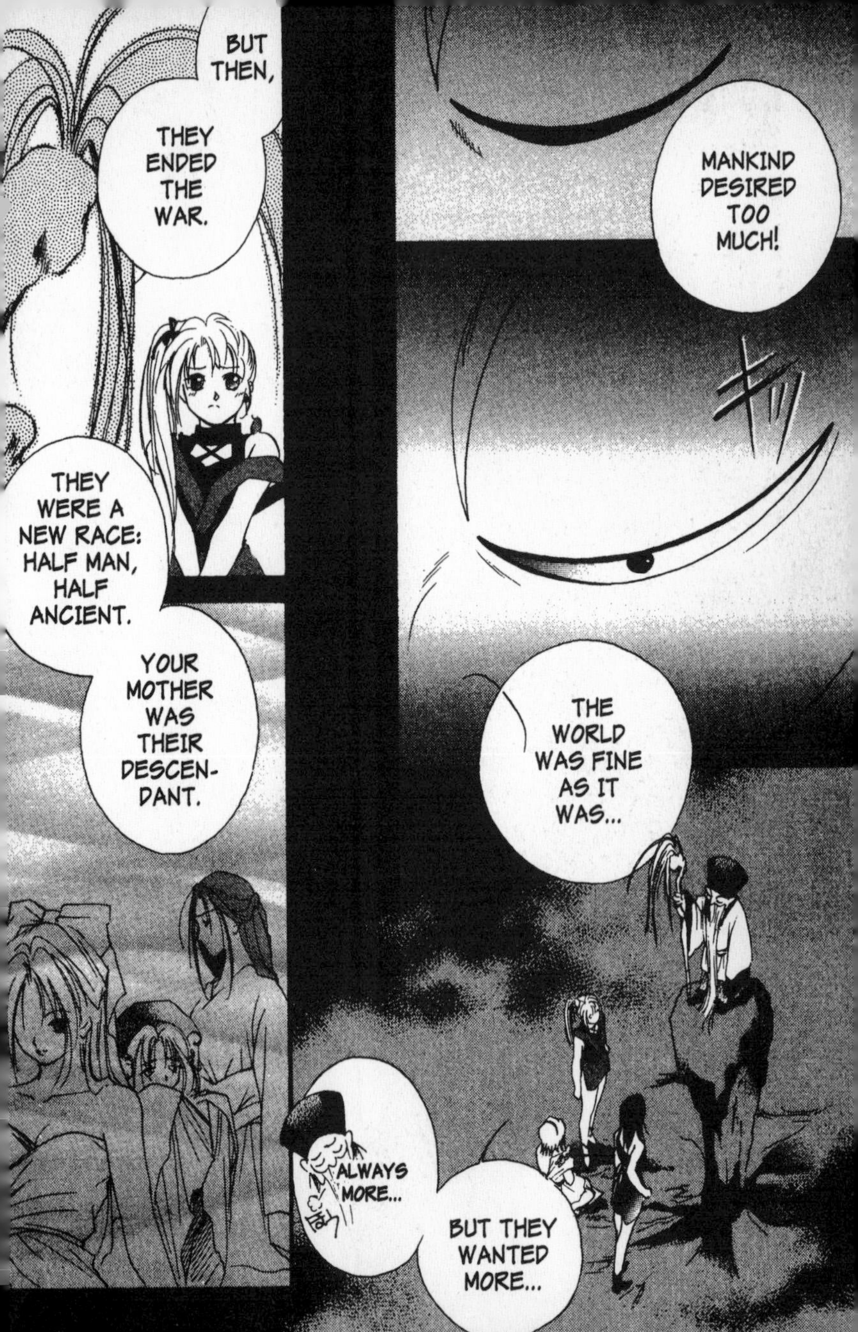
MANKIND DESIRED TOO MUCH!
THE WORLD WAS FINE AS IT WAS...
BUT THEY WANTED MORE...
ALWAYS MORE...
BUT THEN,
THEY ENDED THE WAR.
THEY WERE A NEW RACE: HALF MAN, HALF ANCIENT.
YOUR MOTHER WAS THEIR DESCEN-DANT.

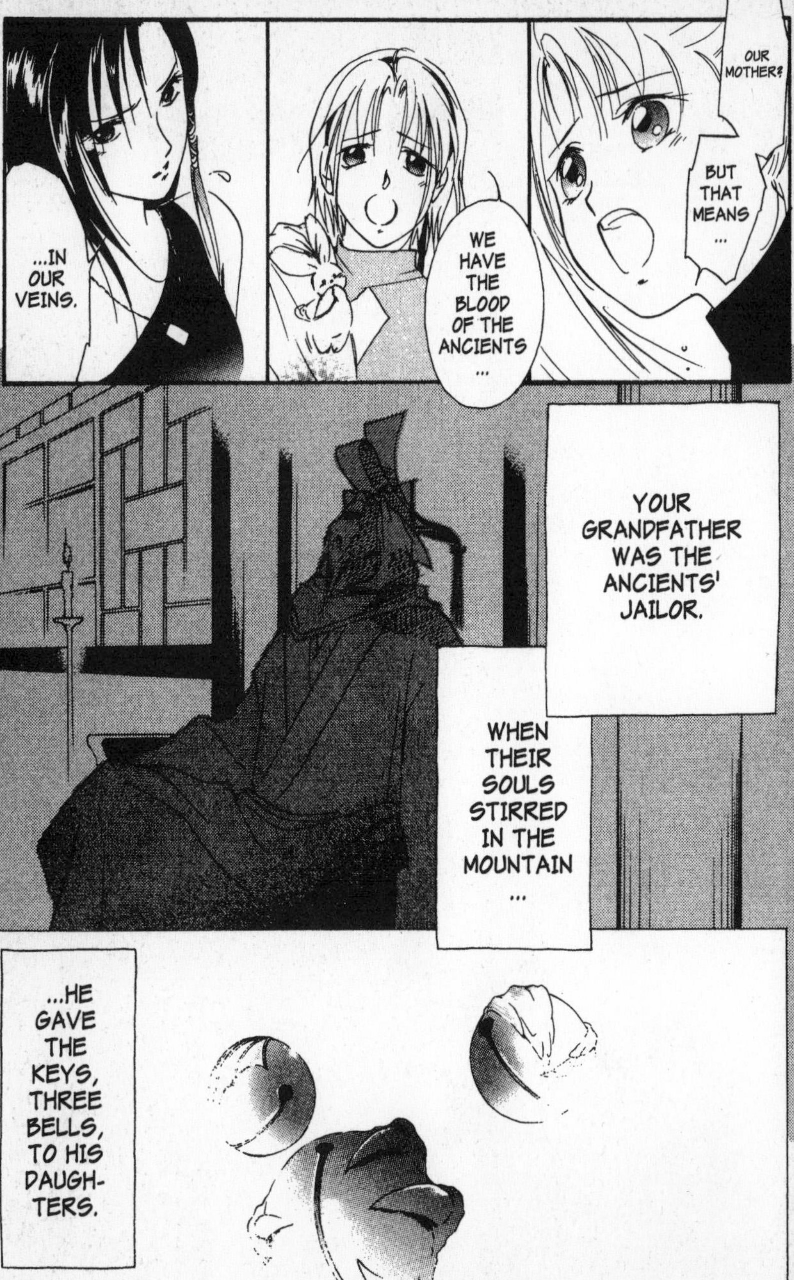
OUR MOTHER?
BUT THAT MEANS ...
WE HAVE THE BLOOD OF THE ANCIENTS ...
...IN OUR VEINS.
YOUR GRANDFATHER WAS THE ANCIENTS' JAILOR.
WHEN THEIR SOULS STIRRED IN THE MOUNTAIN ...
...HE GAVE THE KEYS, THREE BELLS, TO HIS DAUGHTERS.

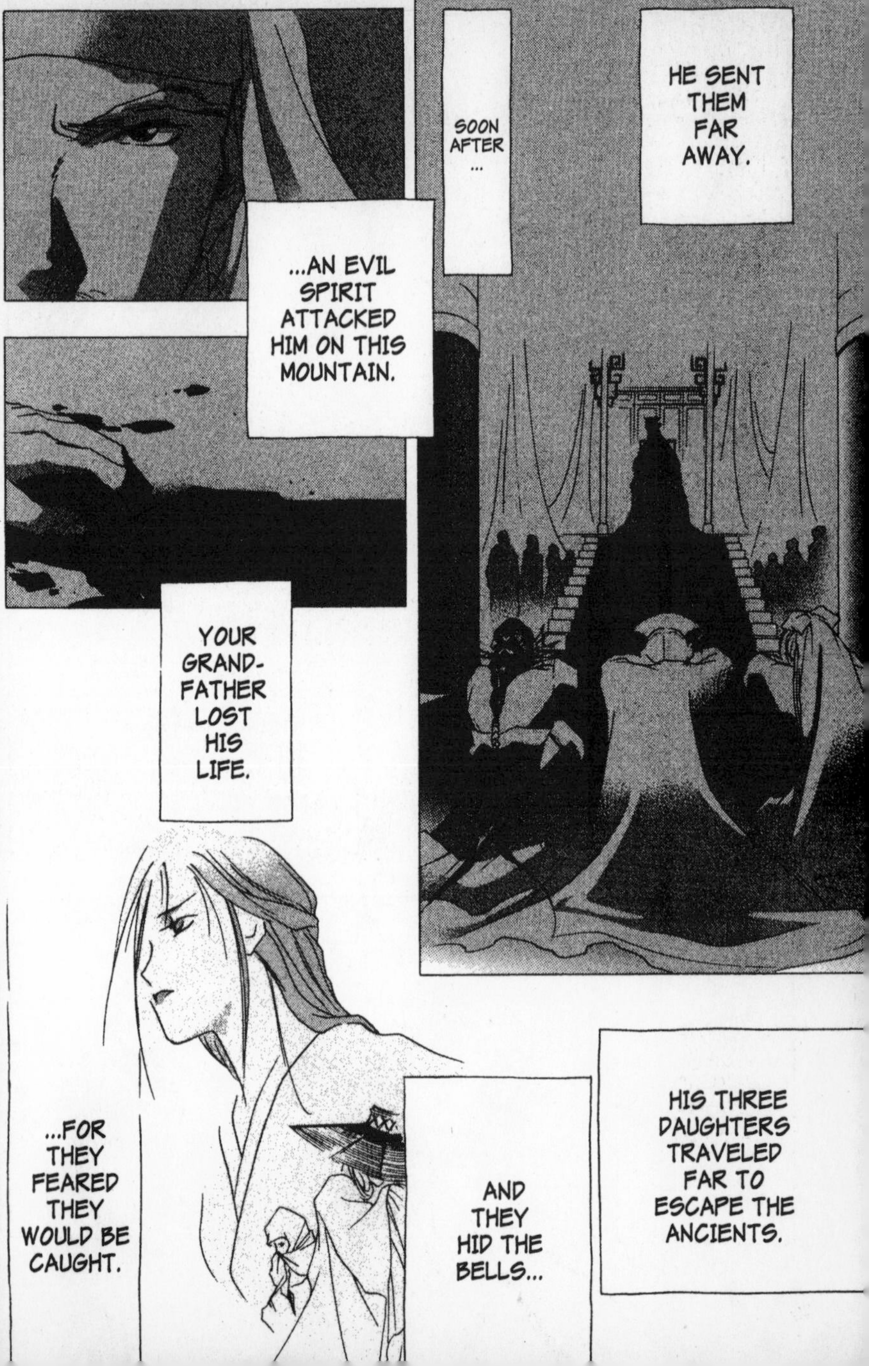
HE SENT THEM FAR AWAY.
SOON AFTER...
...AN EVIL SPIRIT ATTACKED HIM ON THIS MOUNTAIN.
YOUR GRAND-FATHER LOST HIS LIFE.
HIS THREE DAUGHTERS TRAVELED FAR TO ESCAPE THE ANCIENTS.
AND THEY HID THE BELLS...
...FOR THEY FEARED THEY WOULD BE CAUGHT.

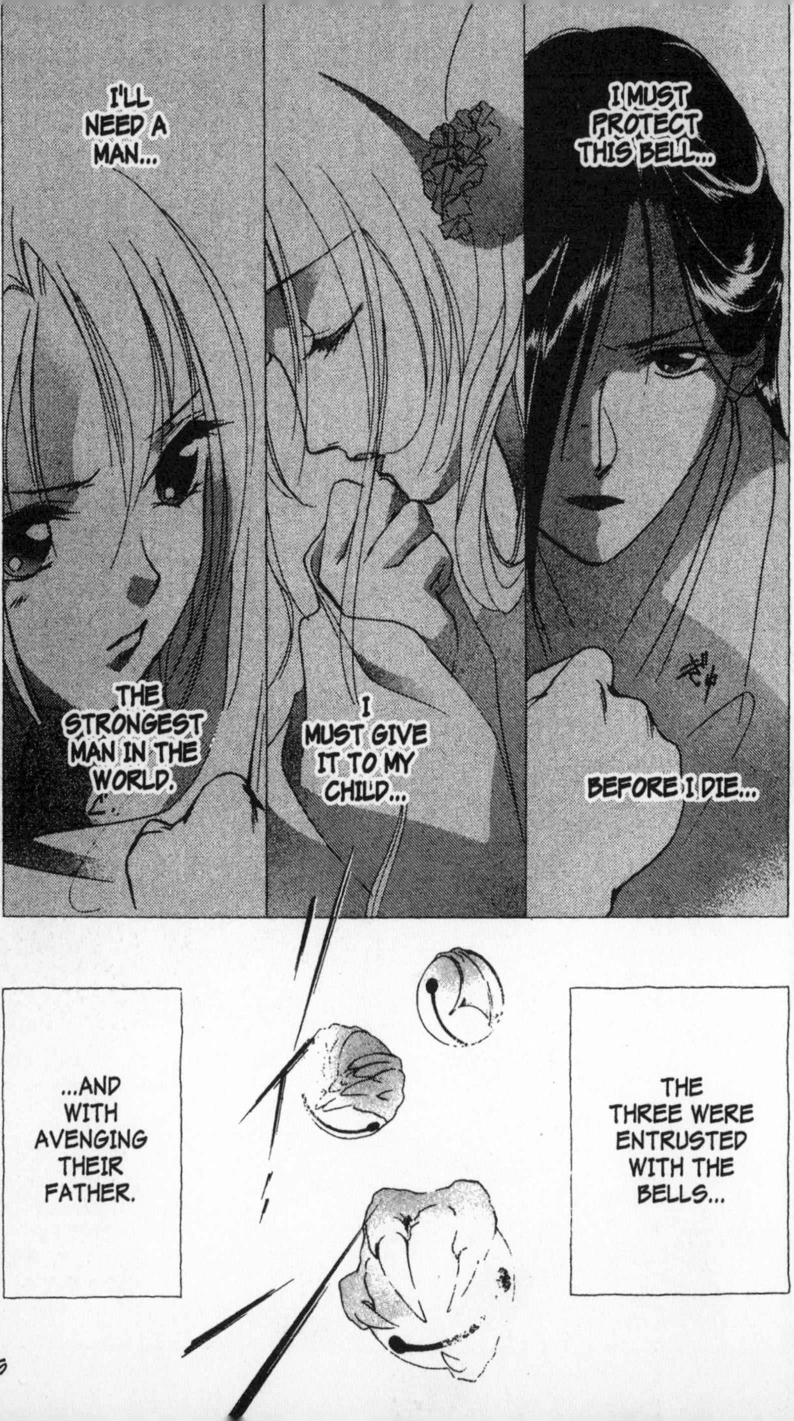
I MUST PROTECT THIS BELL...
BEFORE I DIE...
I MUST GIVE IT TO MY CHILD...
I'LL NEED A MAN...
THE STRONGEST MAN IN THE WORLD.
THE THREE WERE ENTRUSTED WITH THE BELLS...
...AND WITH AVENGING THEIR FATHER.

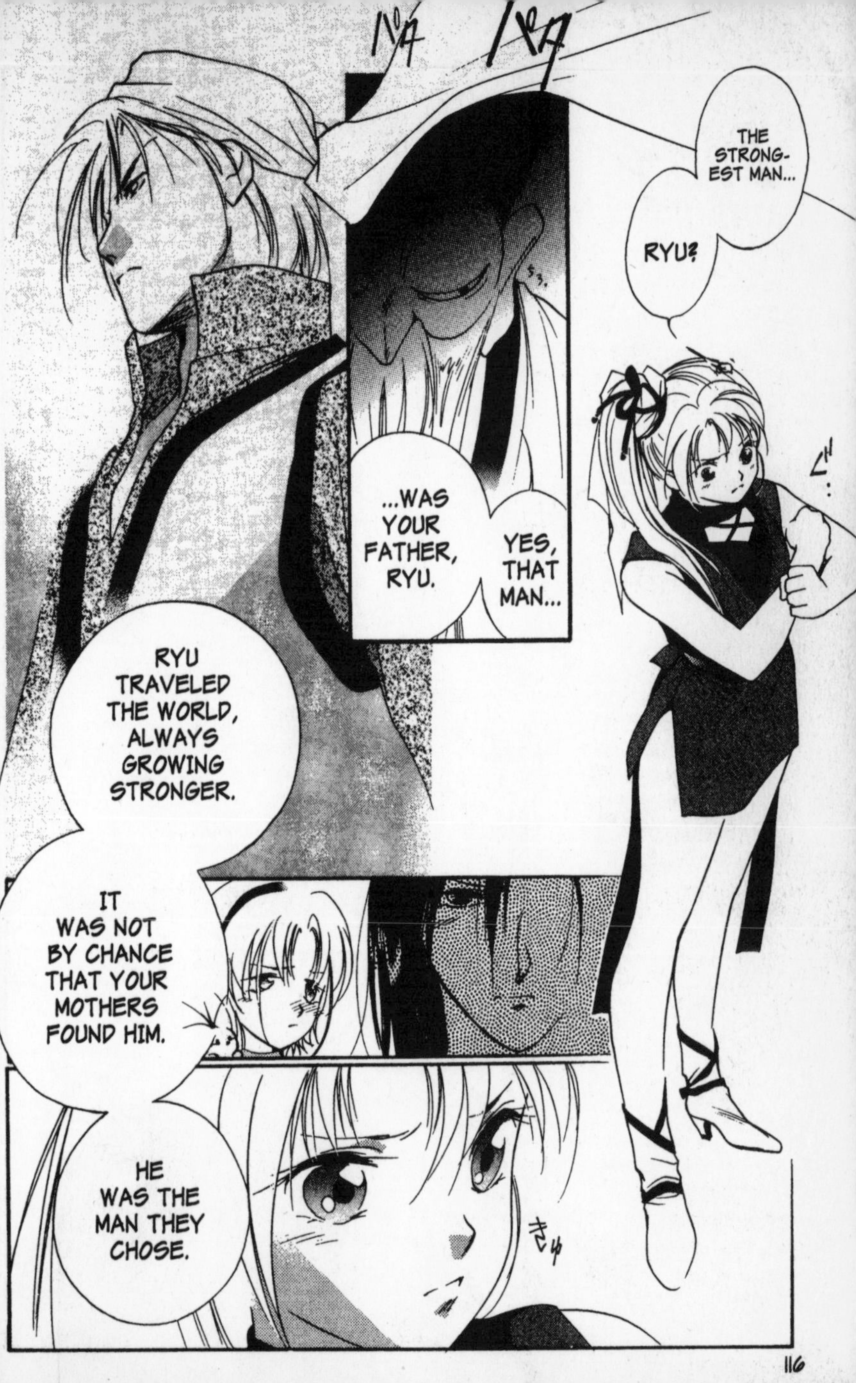
パタ パタ
THE STRONG-EST MAN...
RYU?
ぐ
YES, THAT MAN...
...WAS YOUR FATHER, RYU.
RYU TRAVELED THE WORLD, ALWAYS GROWING STRONGER.
IT WAS NOT BY CHANCE THAT YOUR MOTHERS FOUND HIM.
HE WAS THE MAN THEY CHOSE.
きゅ

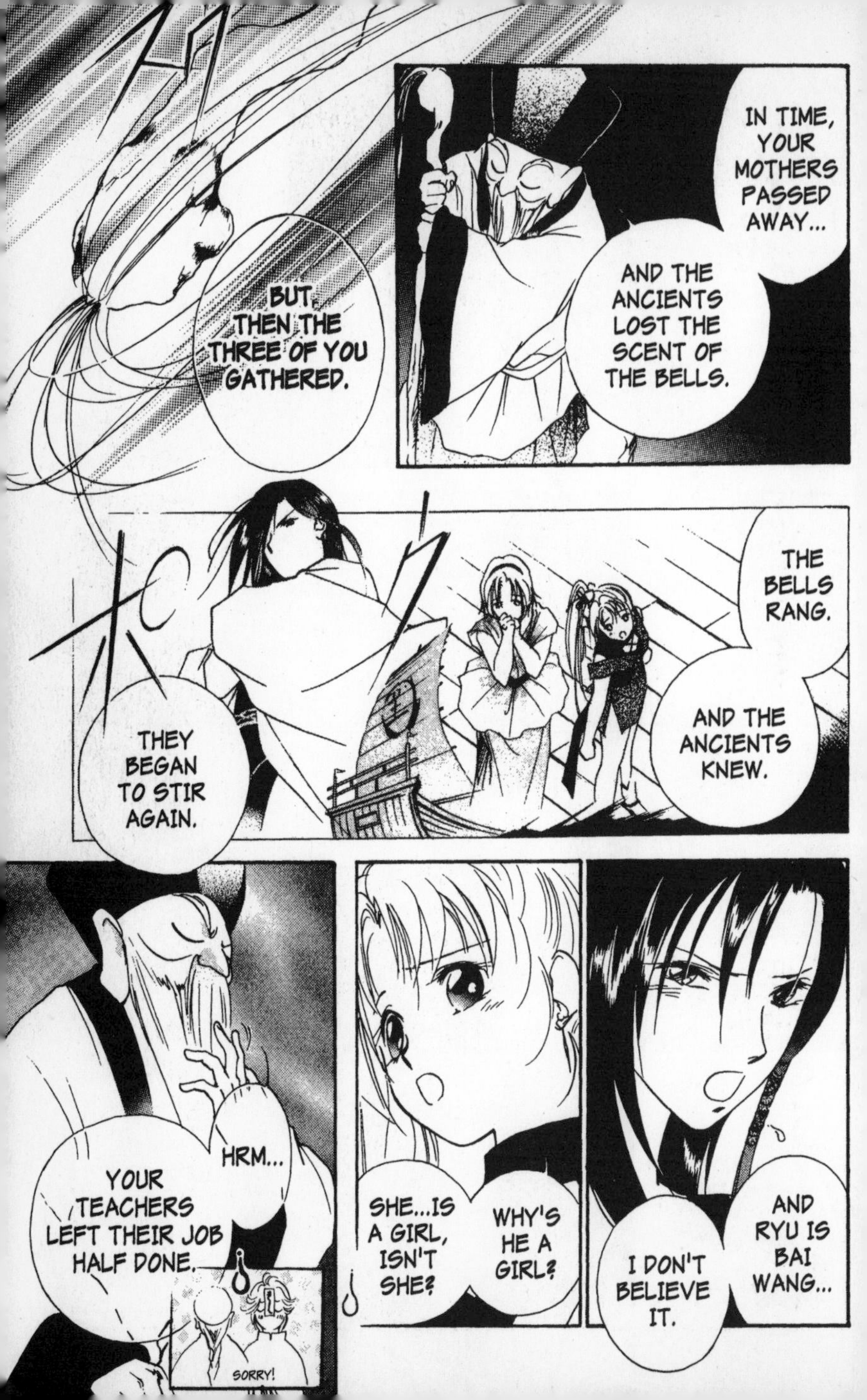
IN TIME, YOUR MOTHERS PASSED AWAY...
AND THE ANCIENTS LOST THE SCENT OF THE BELLS.
BUT THEN THE THREE OF YOU GATHERED.
THE BELLS RANG.
AND THE ANCIENTS KNEW.
THEY BEGAN TO STIR AGAIN.
AND RYU IS BAI WANG...
I DON'T BELIEVE IT.
WHY'S HE A GIRL?
SHE...IS A GIRL, ISN'T SHE?
HRM...
YOUR TEACHERS LEFT THEIR JOB HALF DONE.
SORRY!

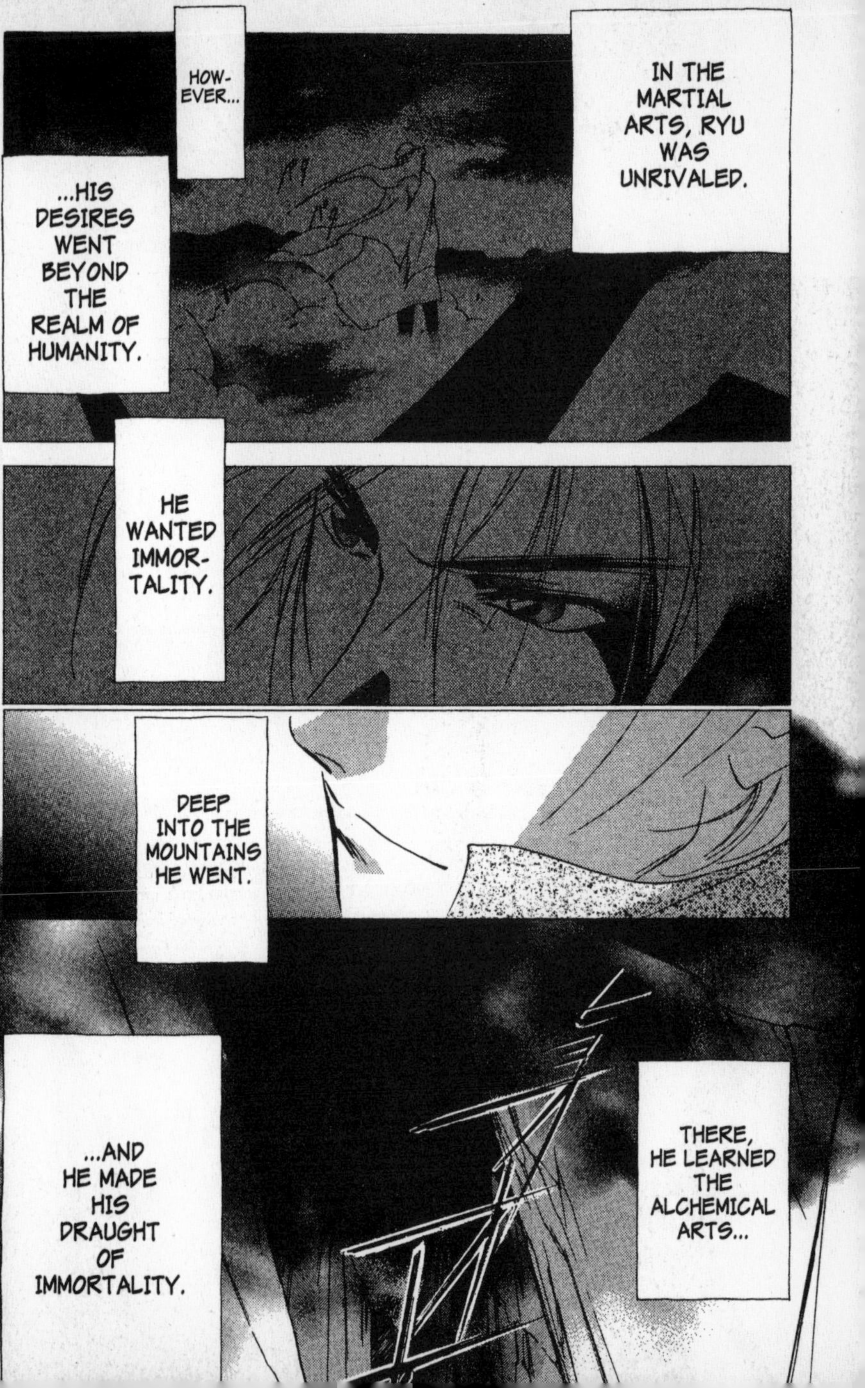
IN THE MARTIAL ARTS, RYU WAS UNRIVALED.
HOW-EVER...
...HIS DESIRES WENT BEYOND THE REALM OF HUMANITY.
HE WANTED IMMOR-TALITY.
DEEP INTO THE MOUNTAINS HE WENT.
THERE, HE LEARNED THE ALCHEMICAL ARTS...
...AND HE MADE HIS DRAUGHT OF IMMORTALITY.

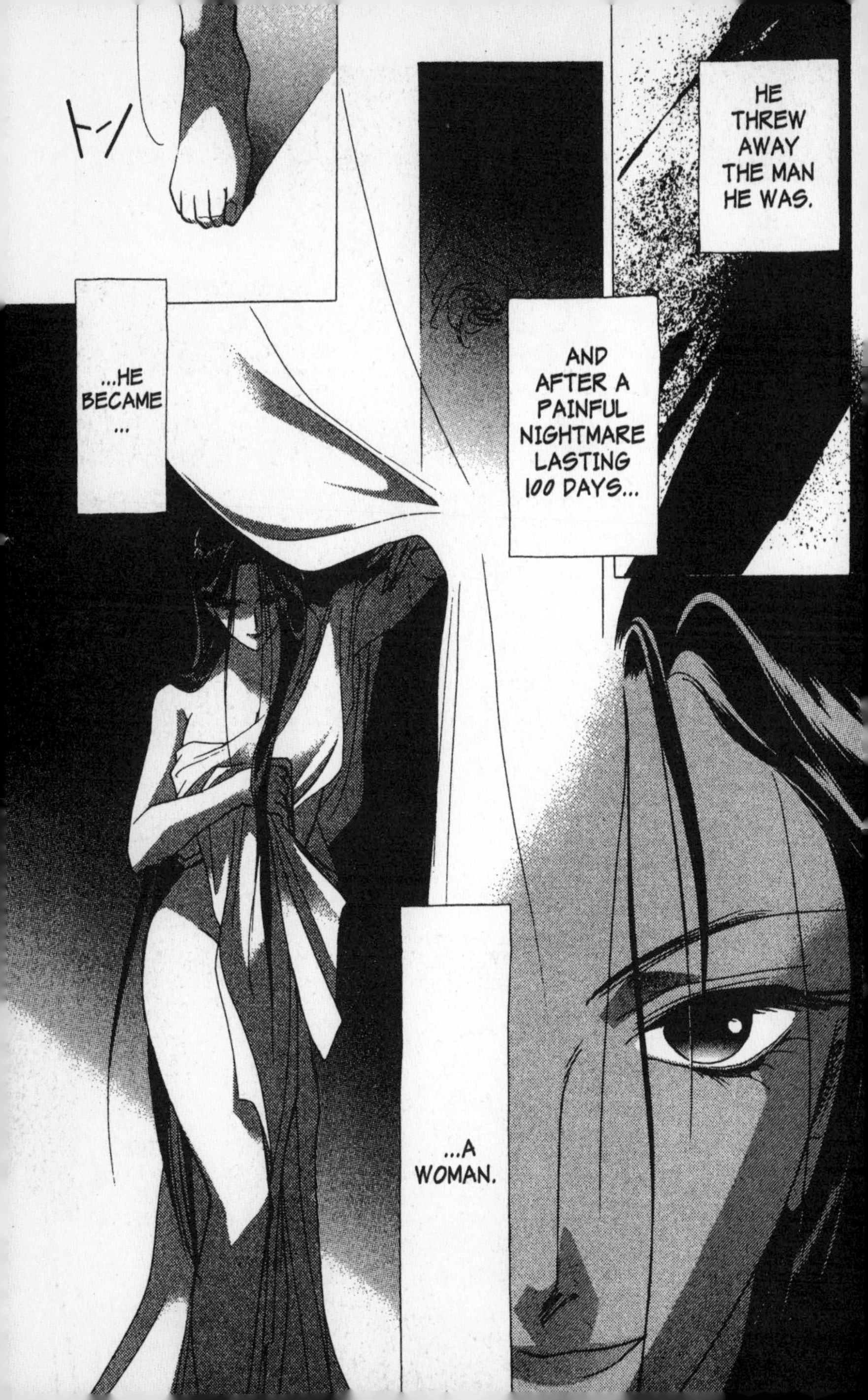
HE THREW AWAY THE MAN HE WAS.
AND AFTER A PAINFUL NIGHTMARE LASTING 100 DAYS...
トン
...HE BECAME ...
...A WOMAN.

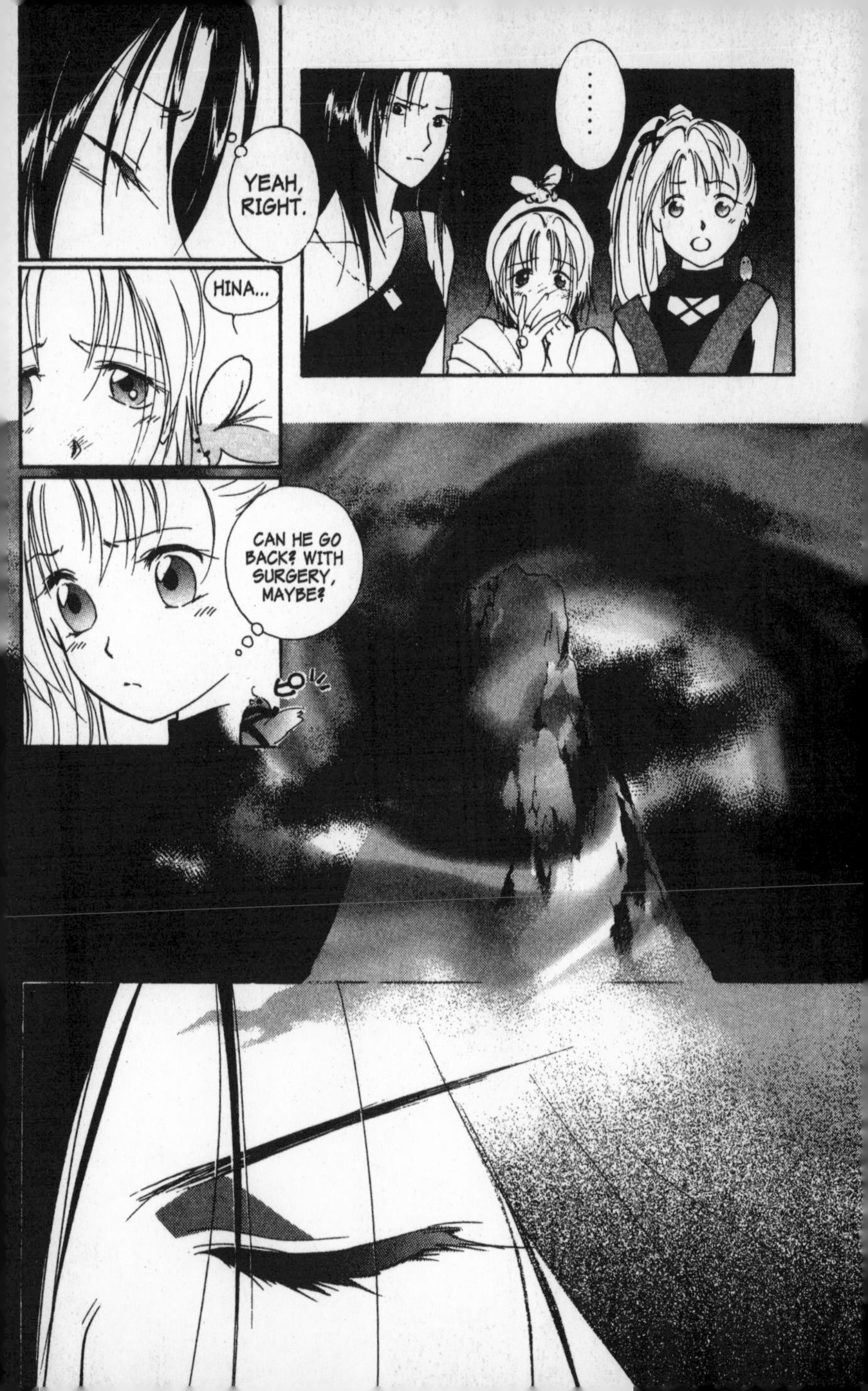

.....
YEAH, RIGHT.
HINA...
CAN HE GO BACK? WITH SURGERY, MAYBE?

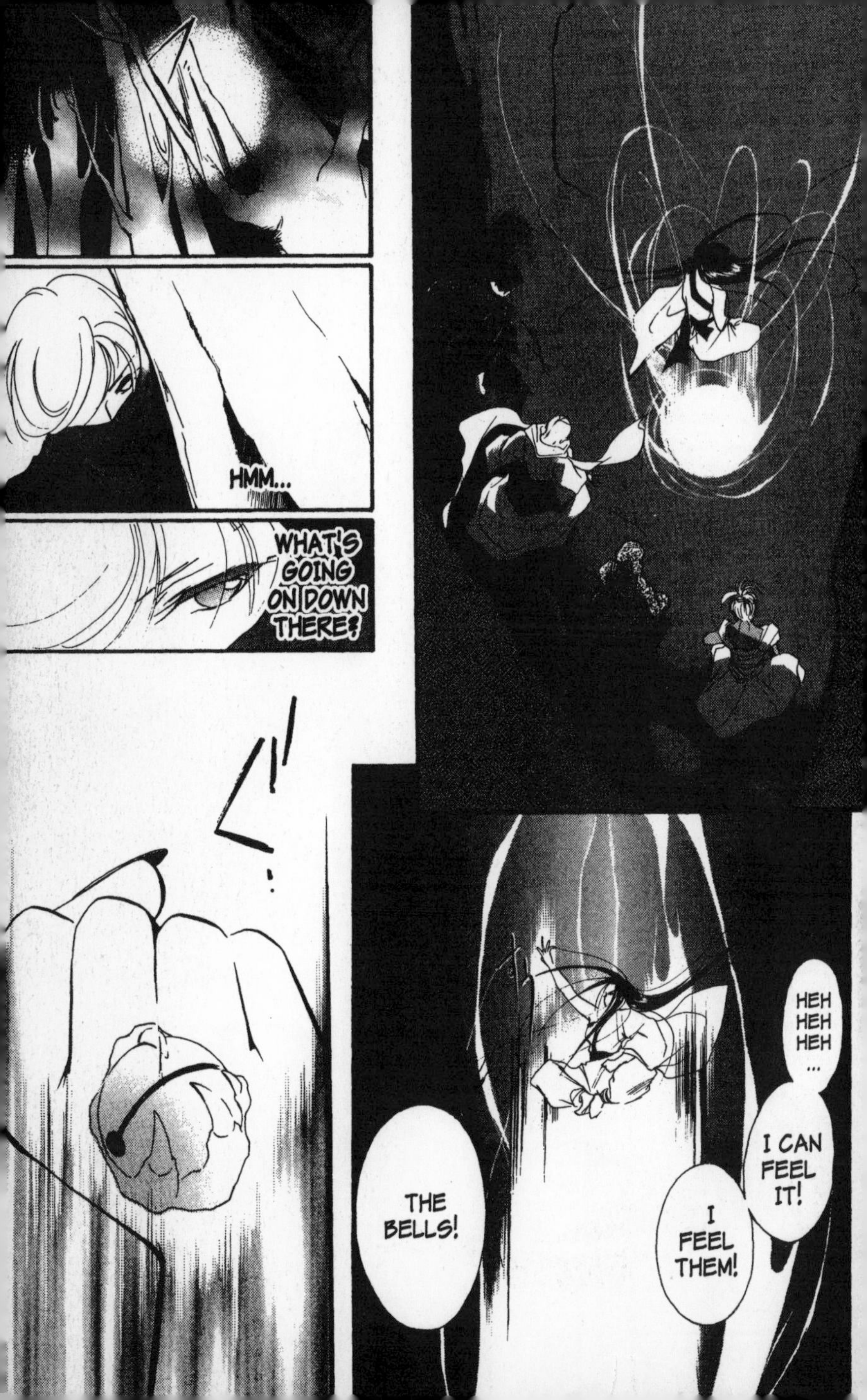
HMM...
WHAT'S GOING ON DOWN THERE?
HEH HEH HEH...
I CAN FEEL IT!
I FEEL THEM!
THE BELLS!

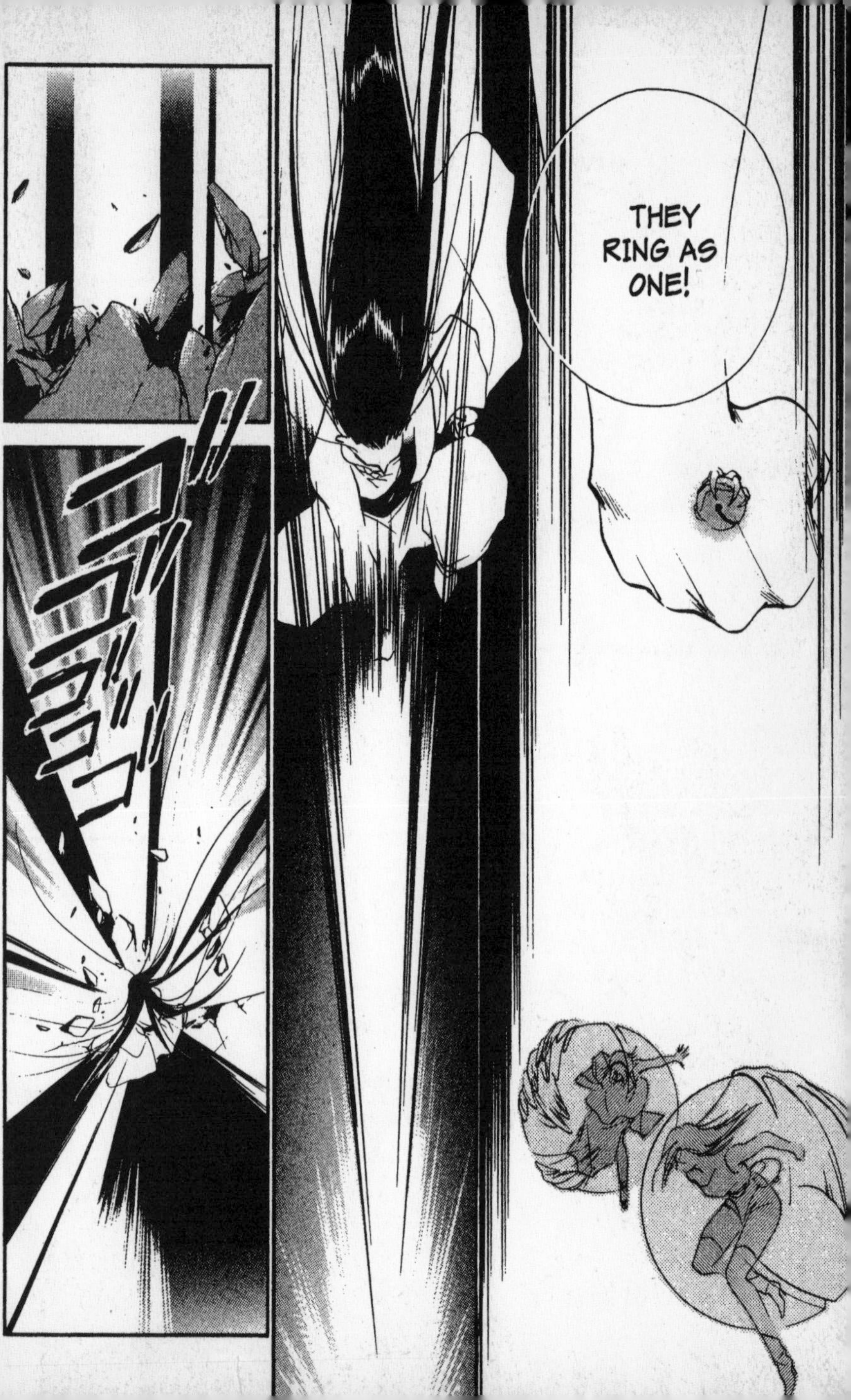
THEY RING AS ONE!

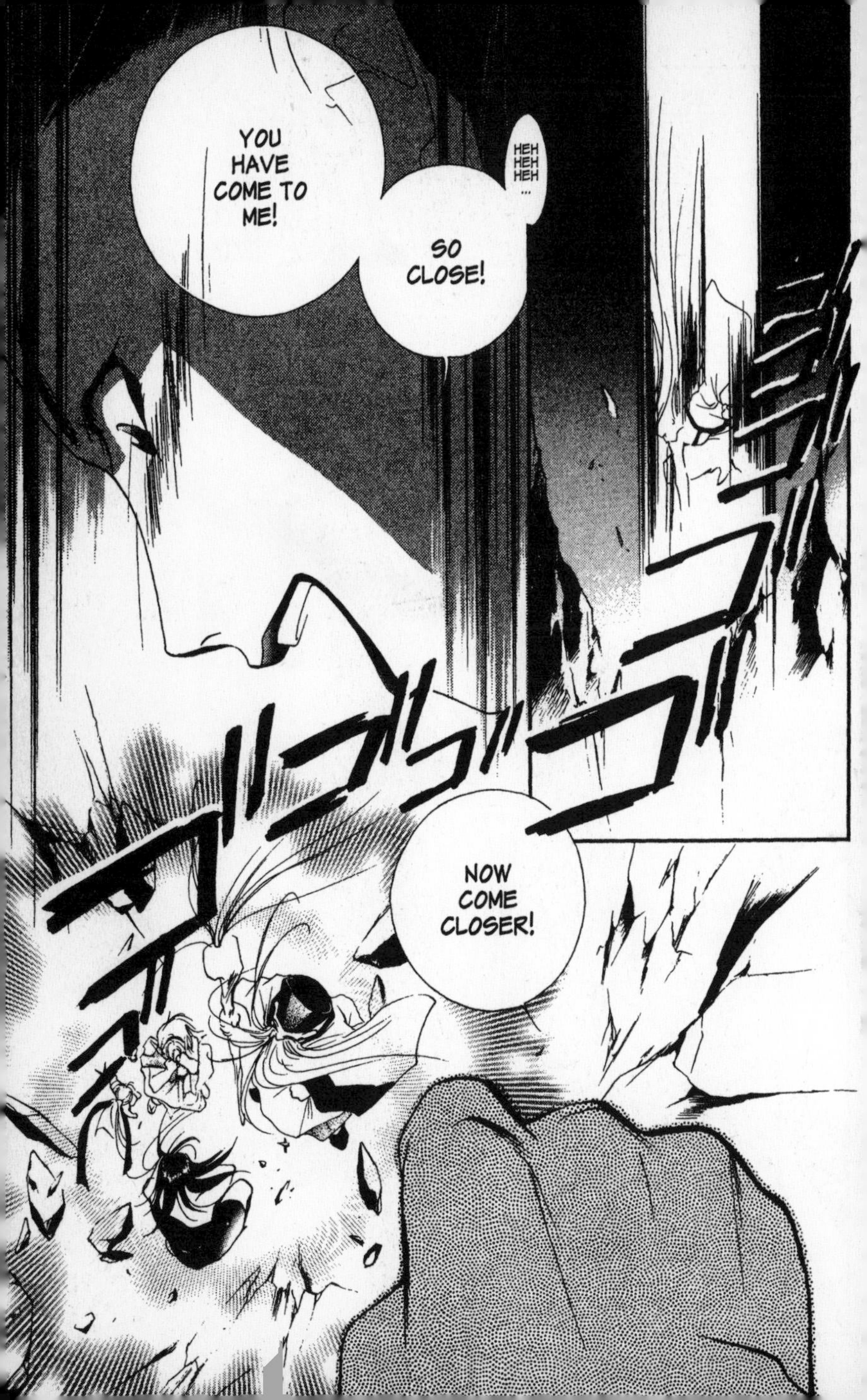
HEH HEH HEH...
YOU HAVE COME TO ME!
SO CLOSE!
NOW COME CLOSER!

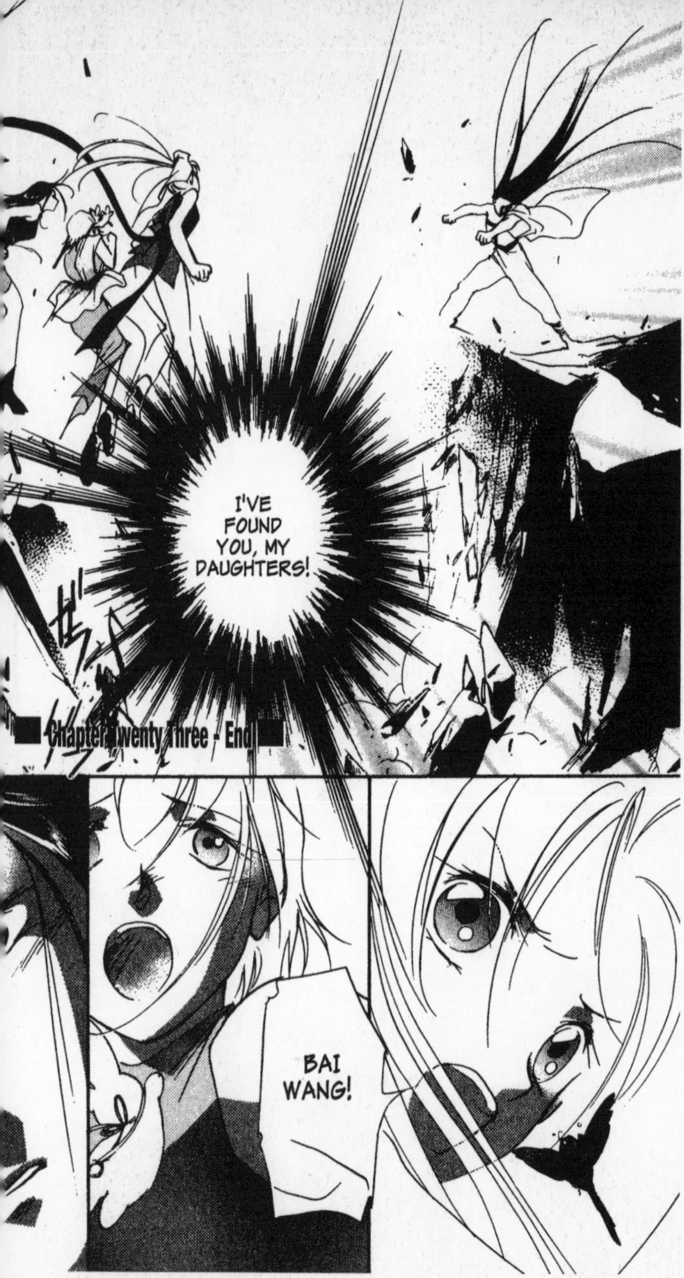
I'VE FOUND YOU, MY DAUGHTERS!
Chapter Twenty Three - End
BAI WANG!

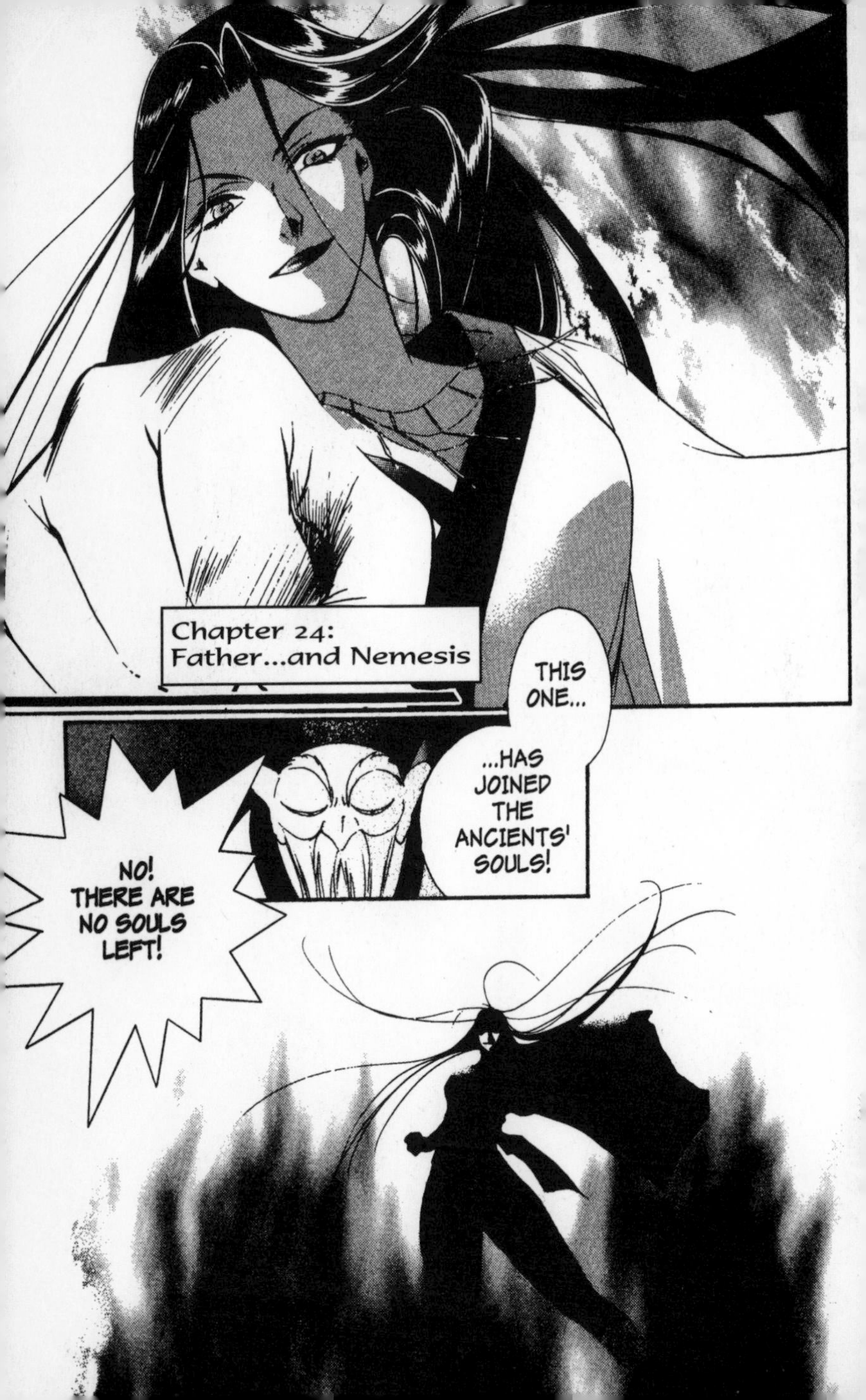
Chapter 24:
Father...and Nemesis
THIS ONE...
...HAS JOINED THE ANCIENTS' SOULS!
NO! THERE ARE NO SOULS LEFT!

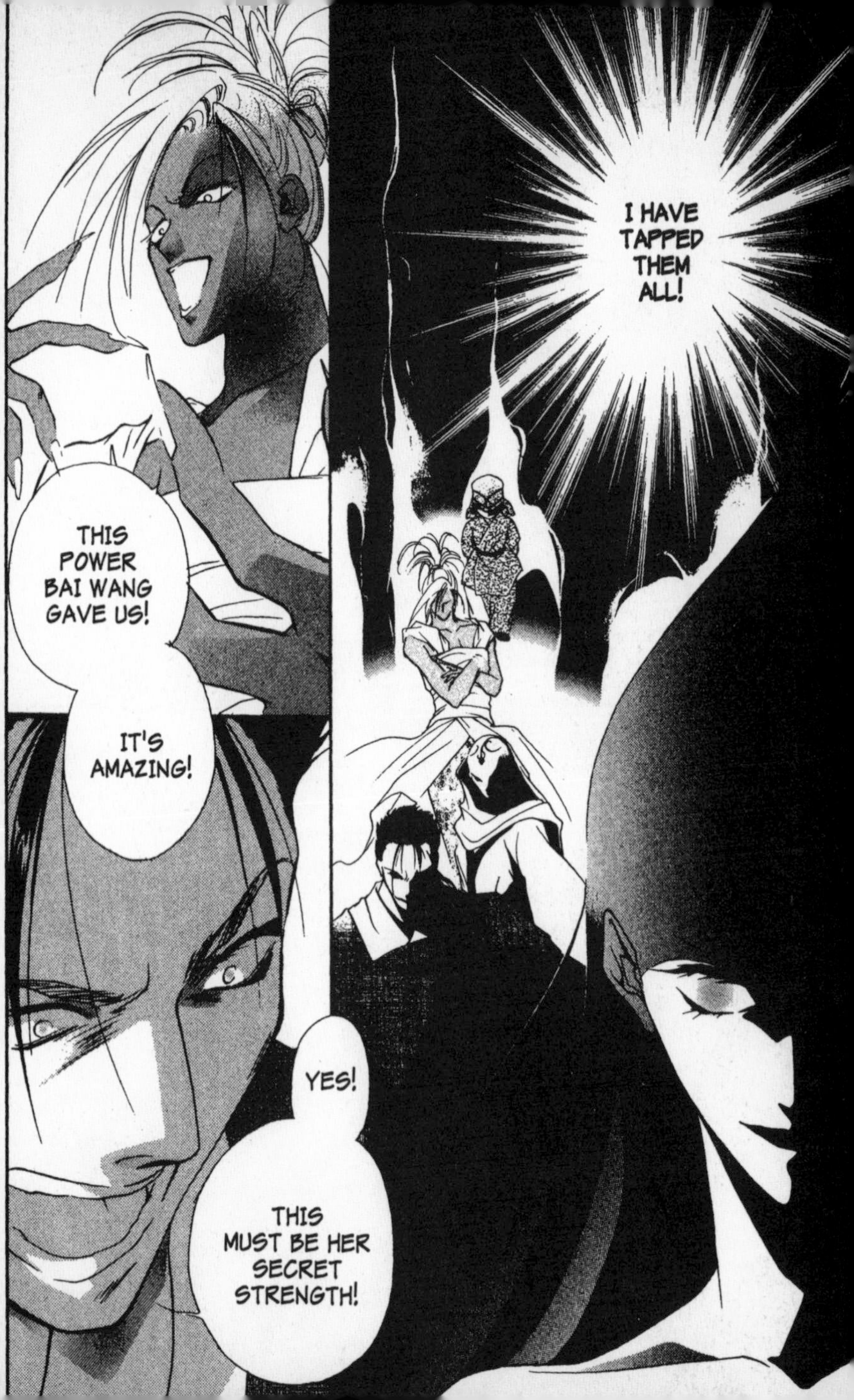
I HAVE TAPPED THEM ALL!
THIS POWER BAI WANG GAVE US!
IT'S AMAZING!
YES!
THIS MUST BE HER SECRET STRENGTH!

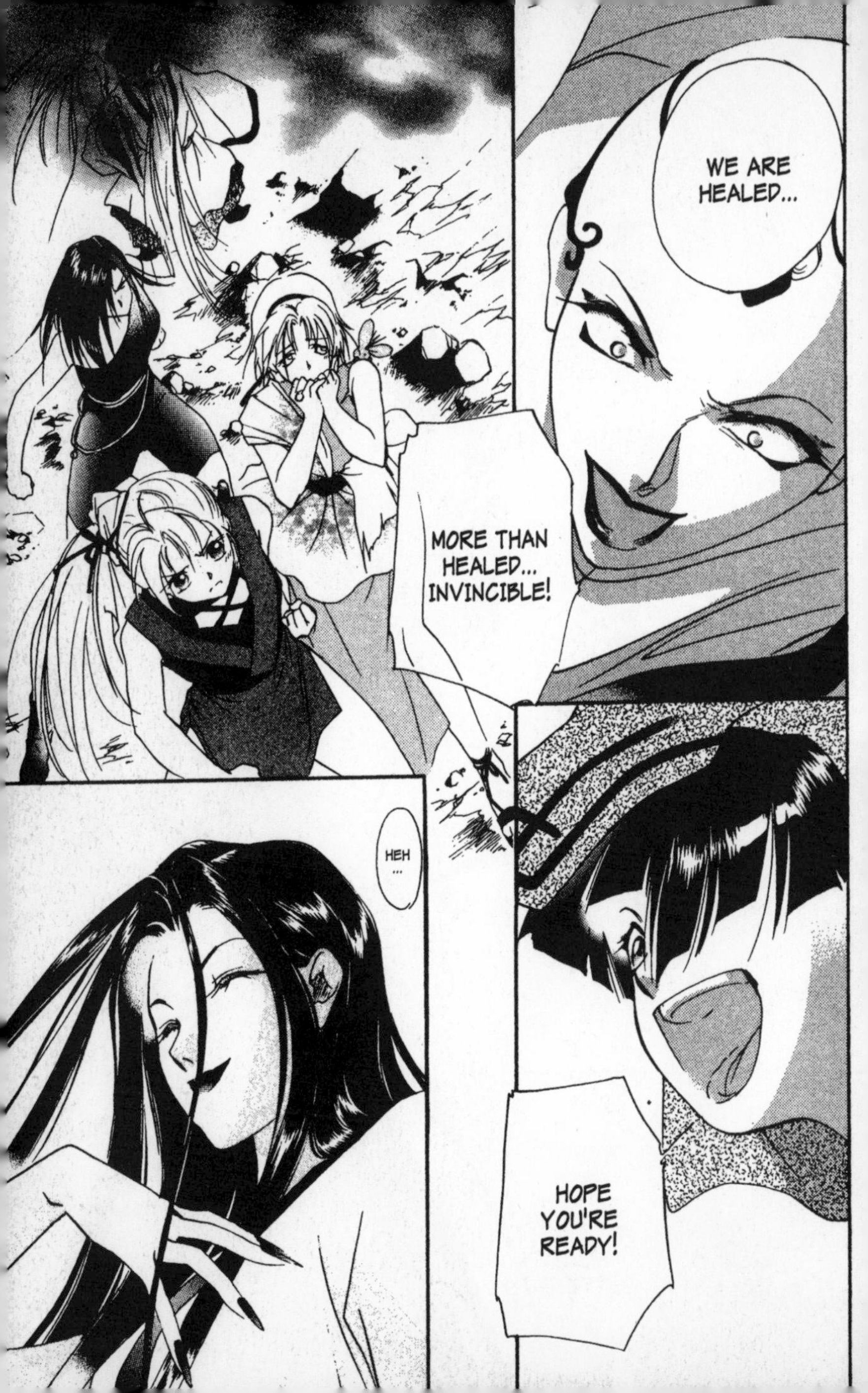
WE ARE HEALED...
MORE THAN HEALED... INVINCIBLE!
HOPE YOU'RE READY!
HEH...

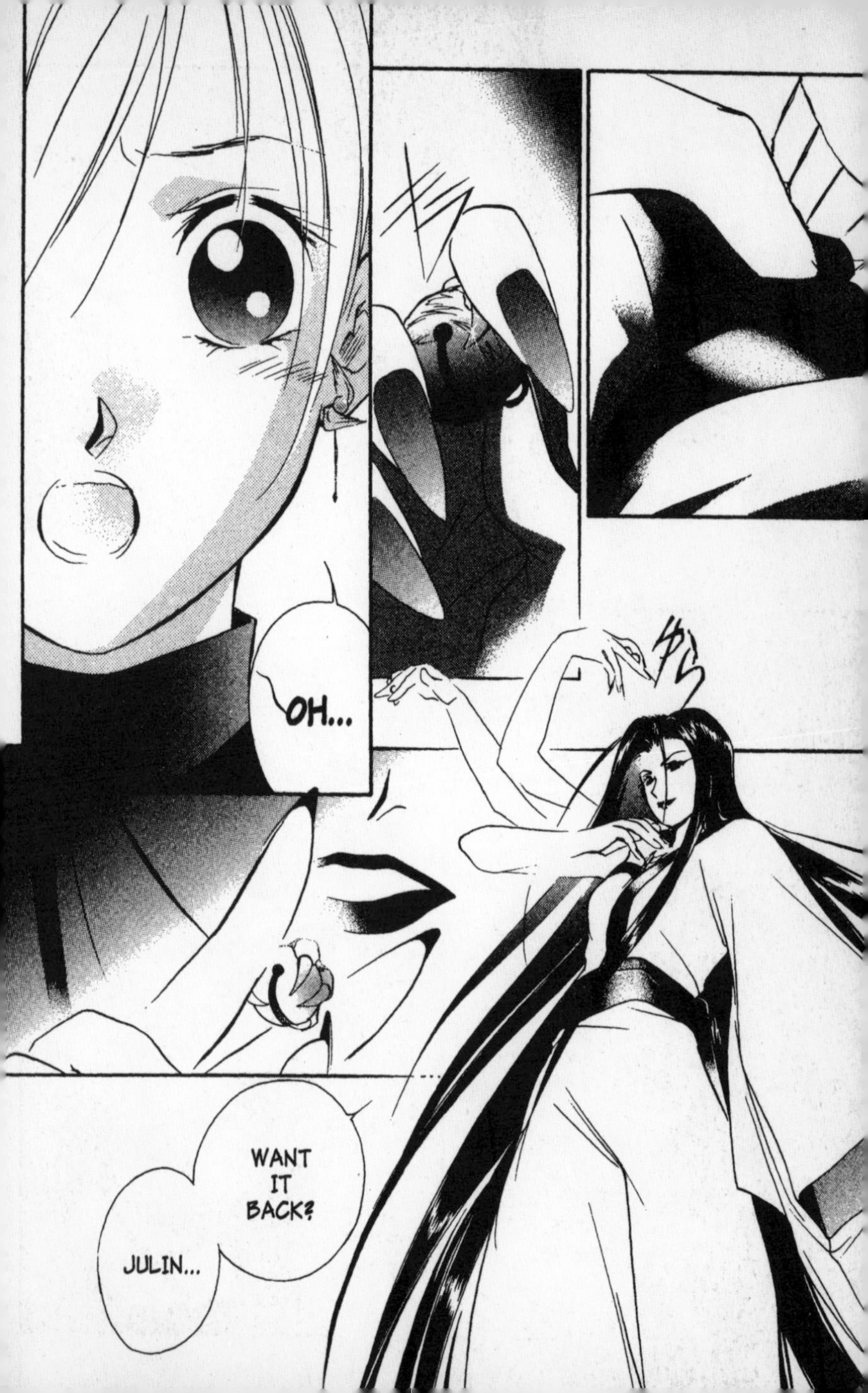
OH...
WANT IT BACK?
JULIN...

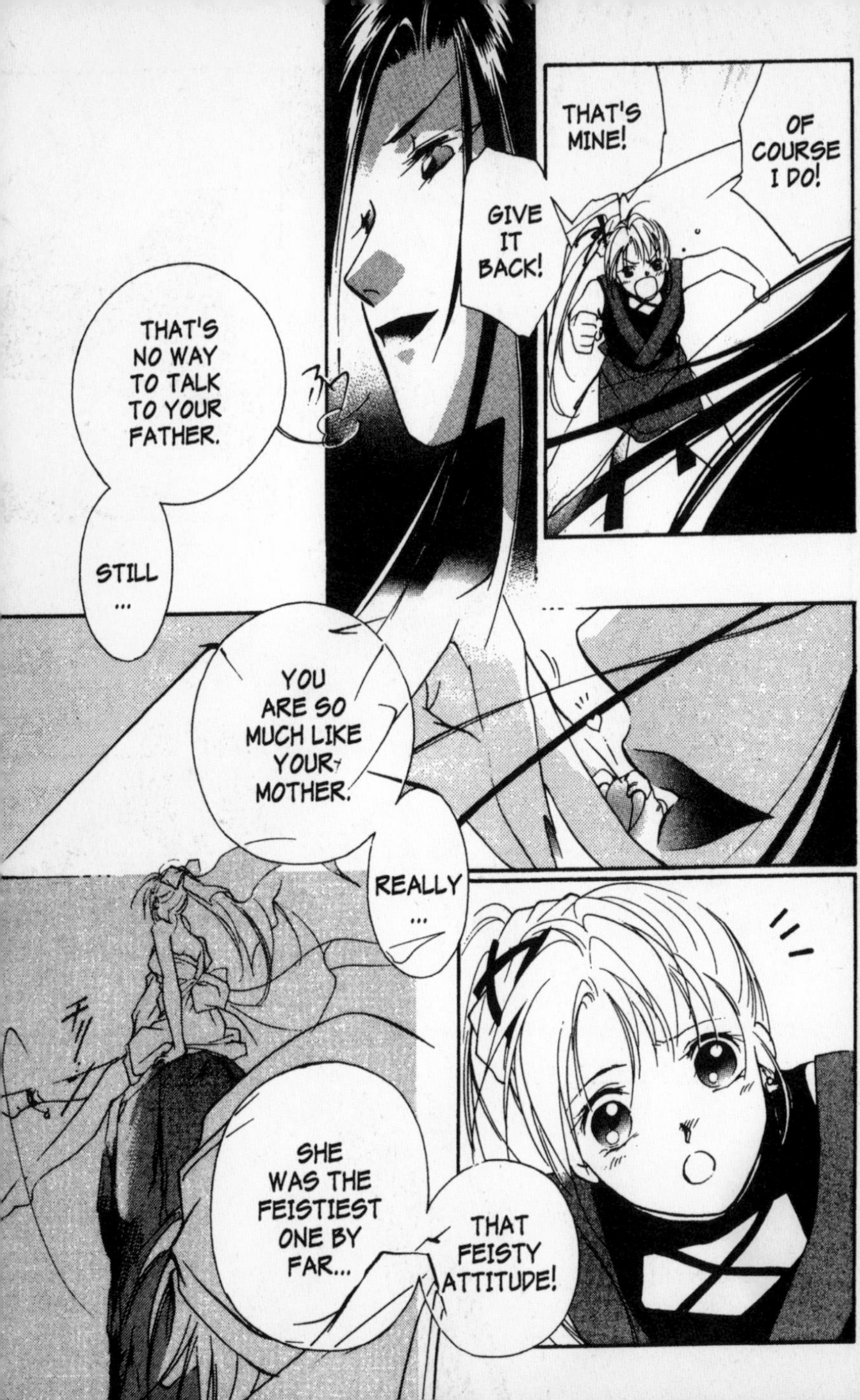
OF COURSE I DO!
THAT'S MINE!
GIVE IT BACK!
THAT'S NO WAY TO TALK TO YOUR FATHER.
STILL ...
YOU ARE SO MUCH LIKE YOUR MOTHER.
REALLY ...
THAT FEISTY ATTITUDE!
SHE WAS THE FEISTIEST ONE BY FAR...

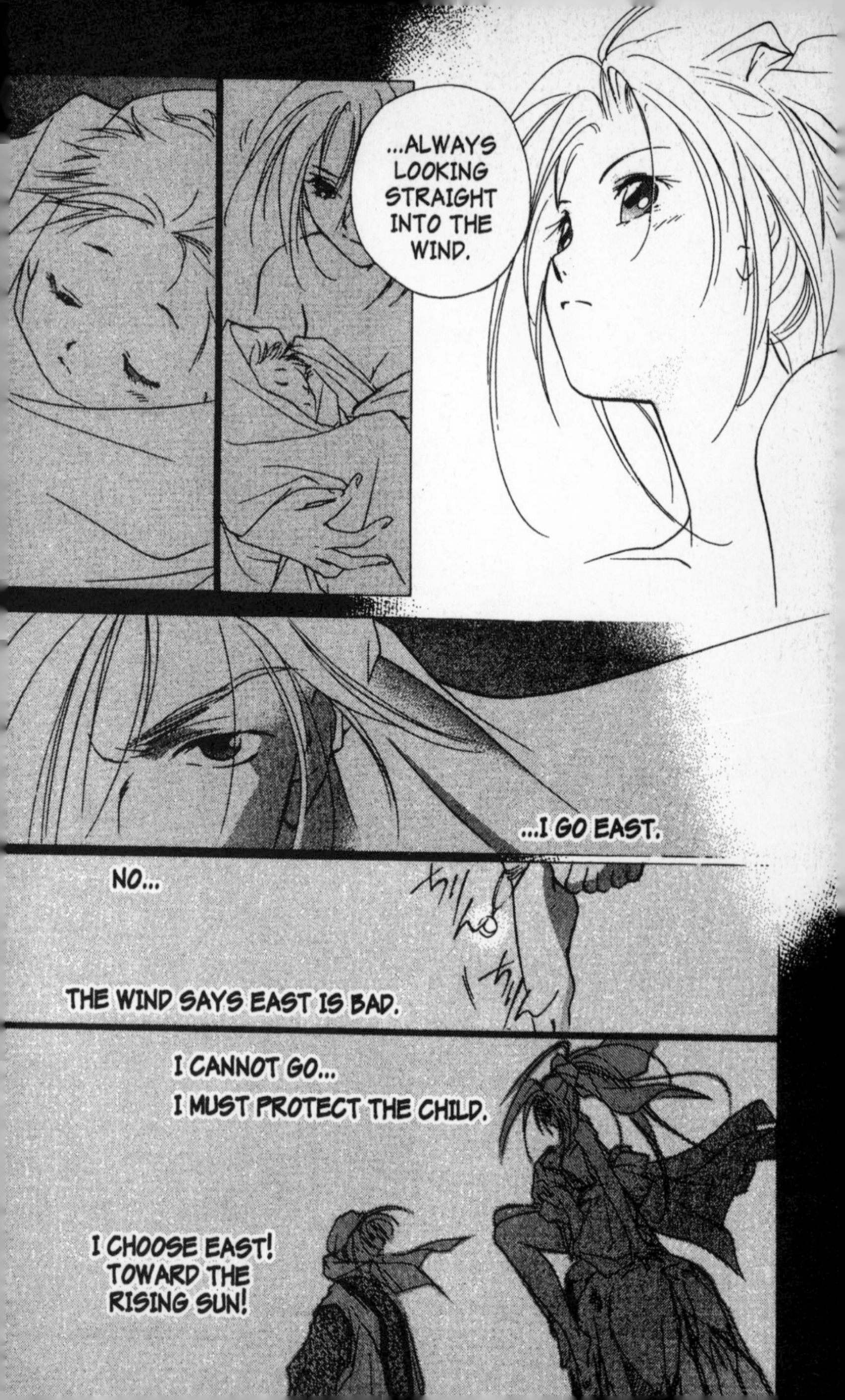
...ALWAYS LOOKING STRAIGHT INTO THE WIND.
...I GO EAST.
NO...
THE WIND SAYS EAST IS BAD.
I CANNOT GO...
I MUST PROTECT THE CHILD.
I CHOOSE EAST! TOWARD THE RISING SUN!

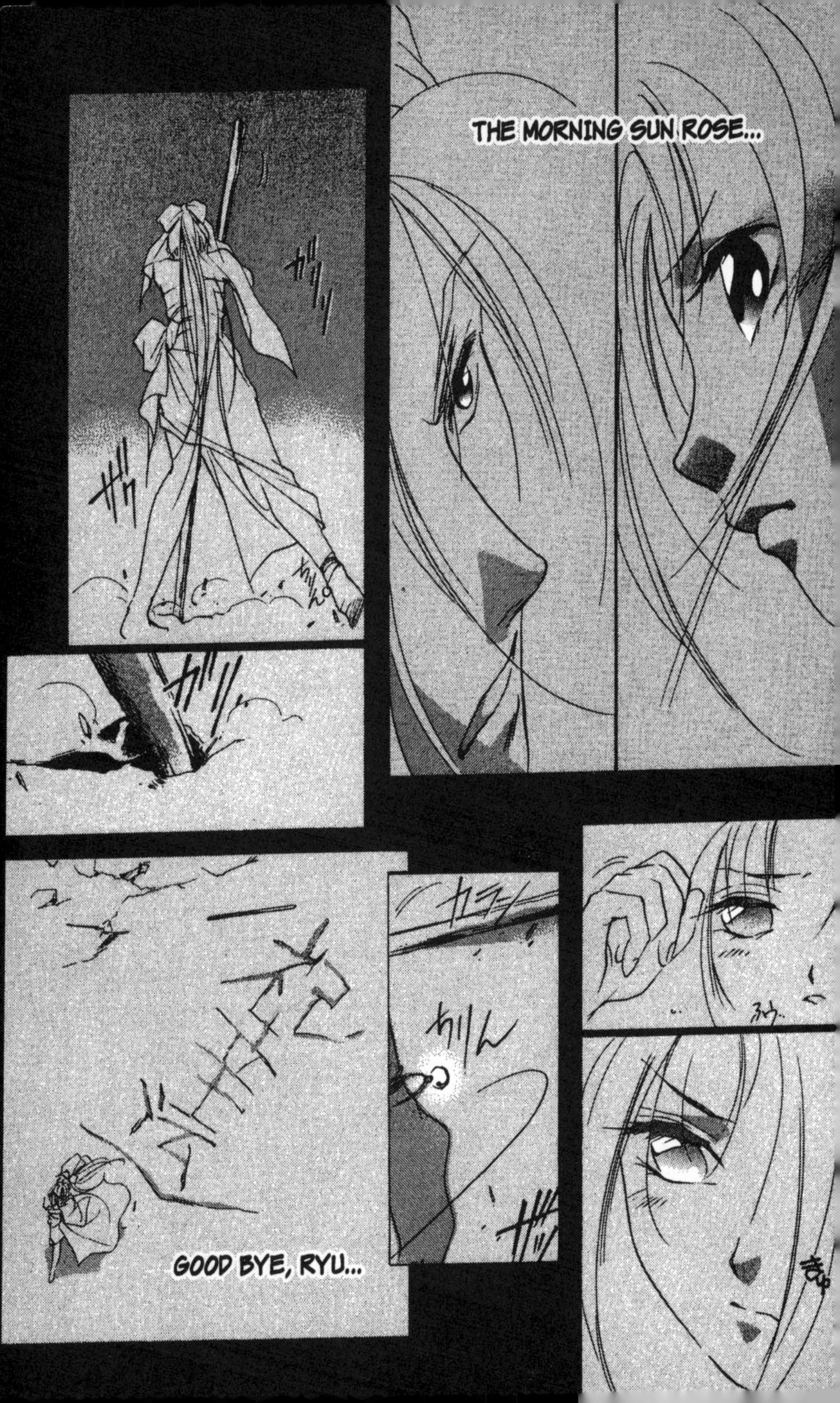
THE MORNING SUN ROSE...
GOOD BYE, RYU...

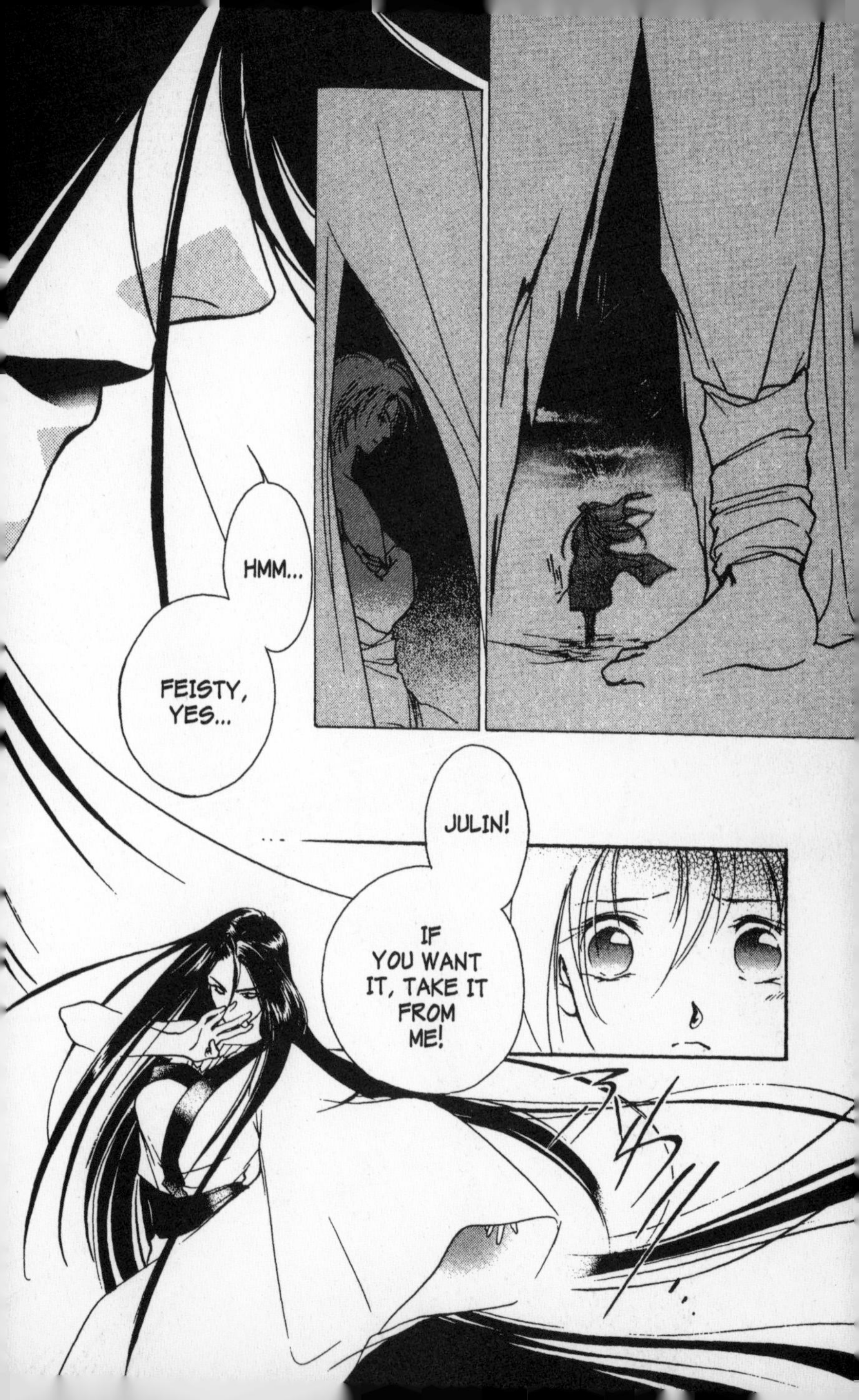
HMM...
FEISTY, YES...
JULIN!
IF YOU WANT IT, TAKE IT FROM ME!

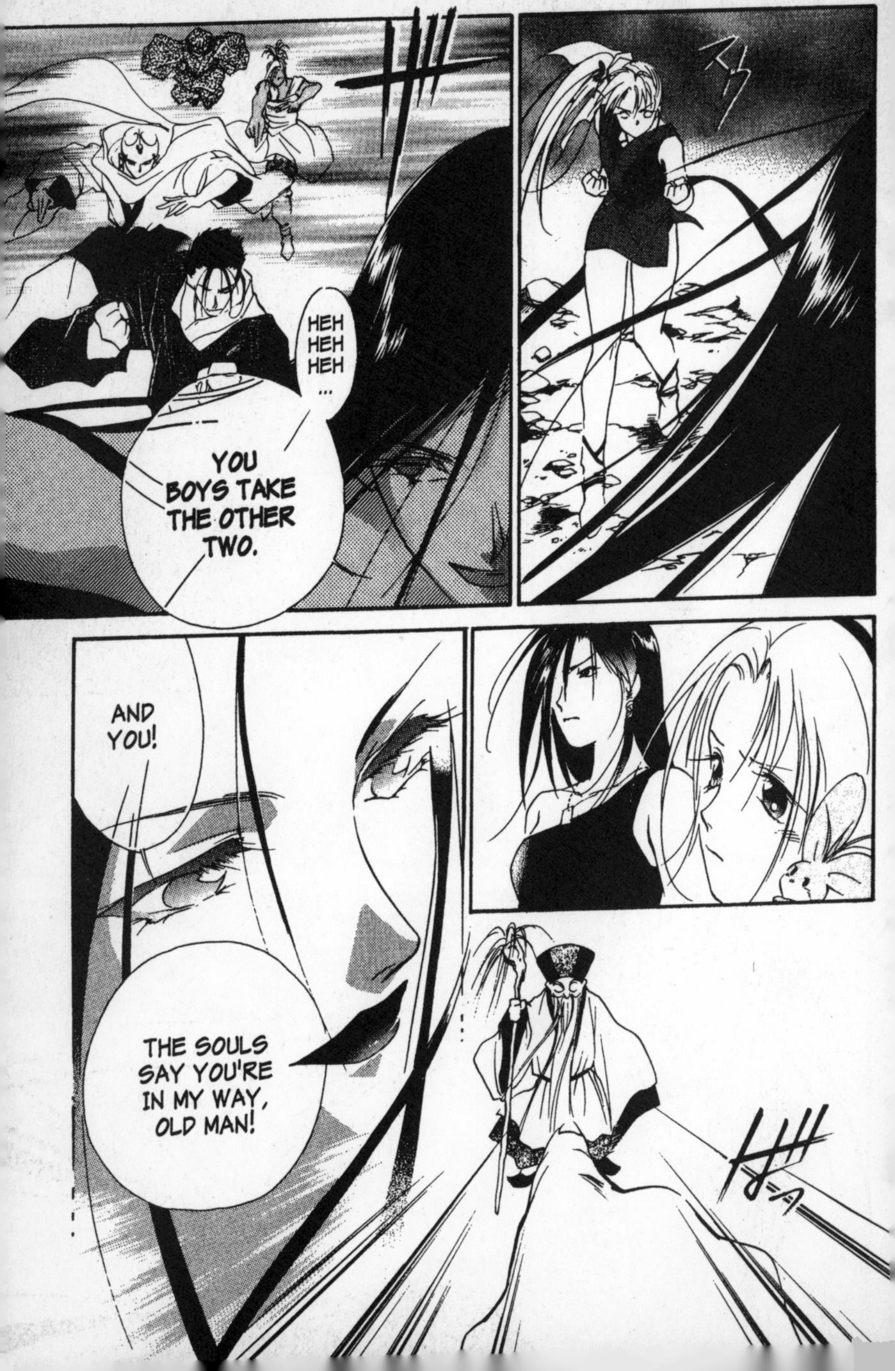
HEH HEH HEH ...
YOU BOYS TAKE THE OTHER TWO.
AND YOU!
THE SOULS SAY YOU'RE IN MY WAY, OLD MAN!

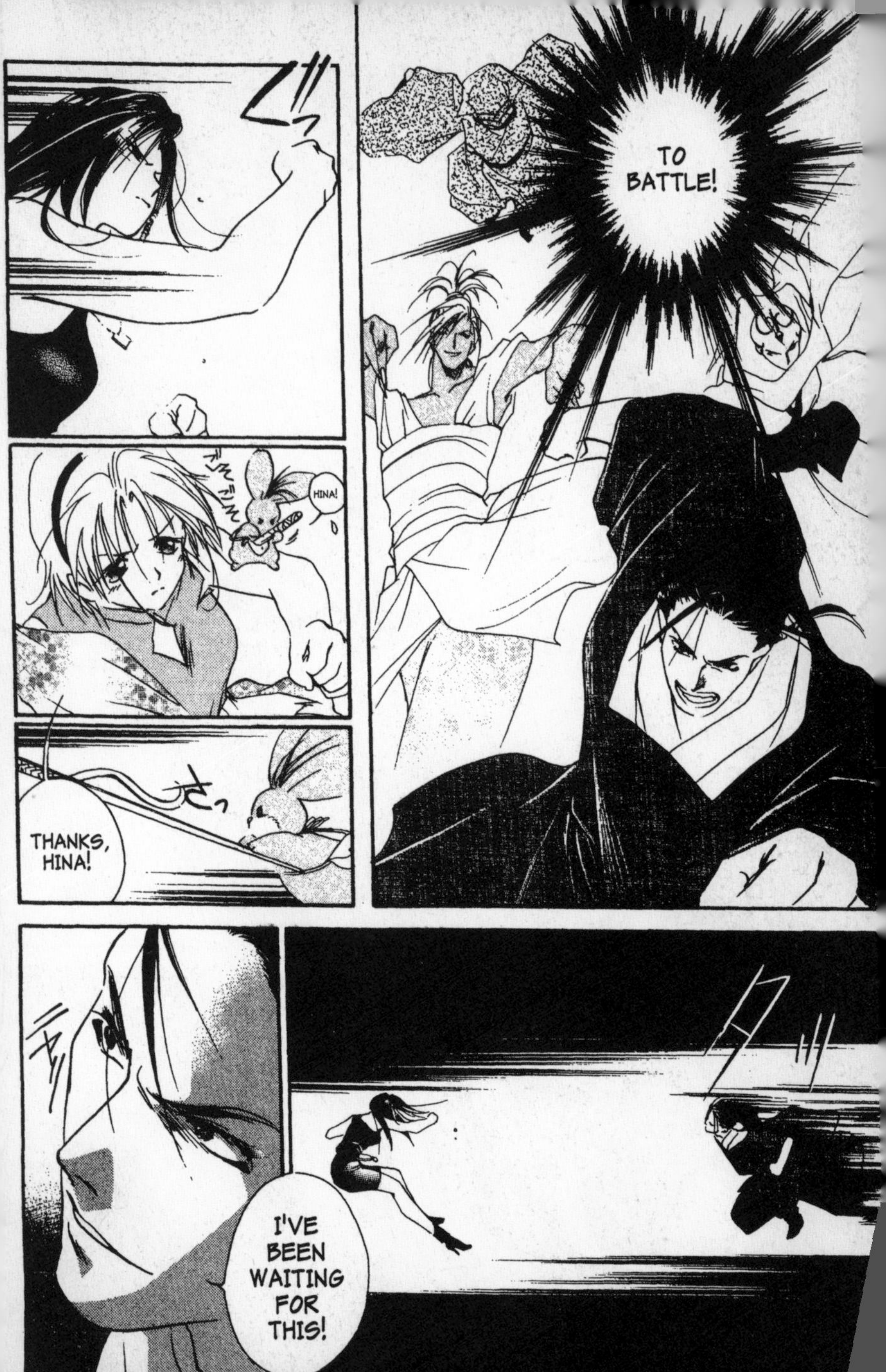
TO BATTLE!
HINA!
THANKS, HINA!
I'VE BEEN WAITING FOR THIS!

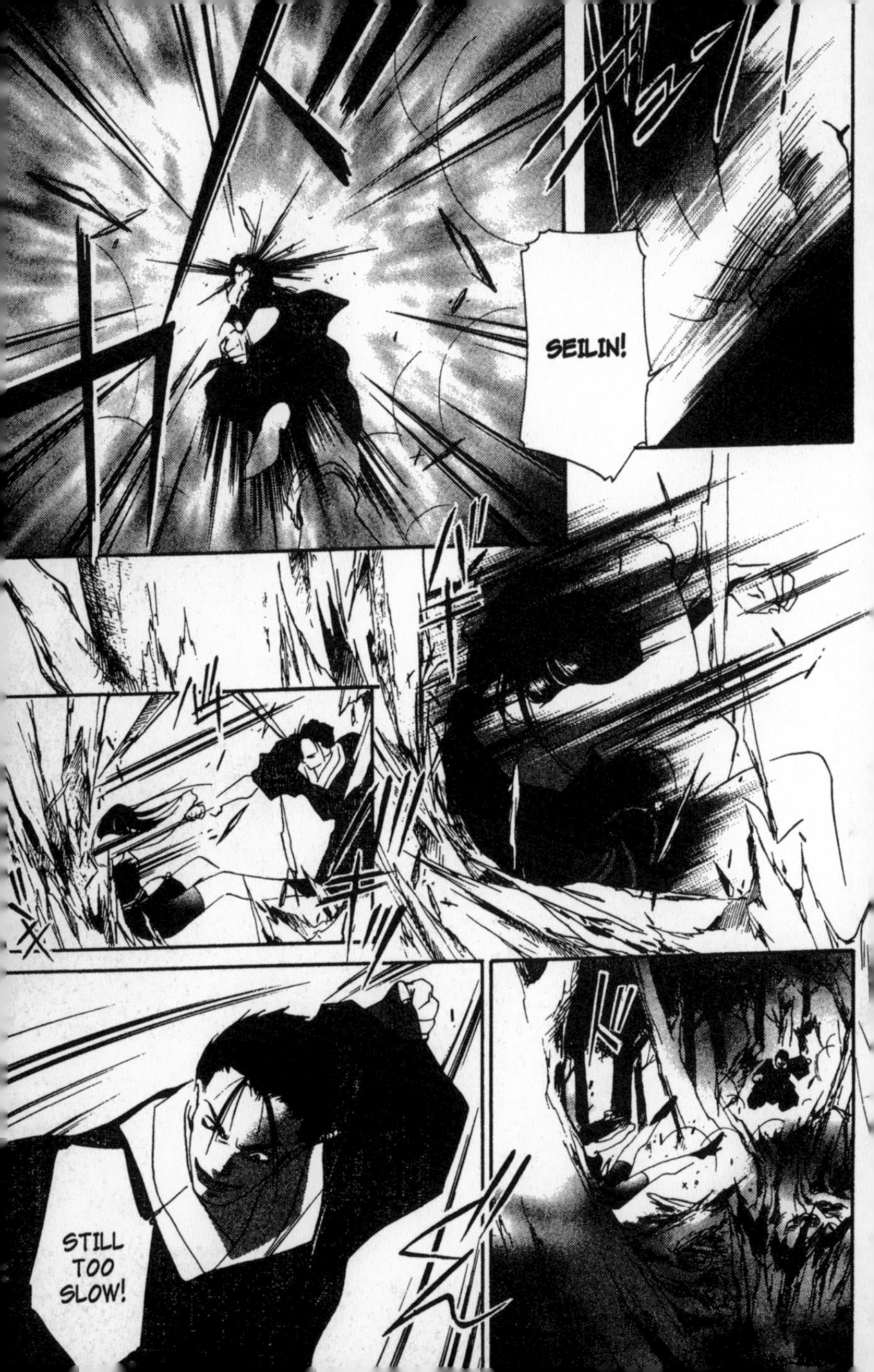
SEILIN!
STILL TOO SLOW!

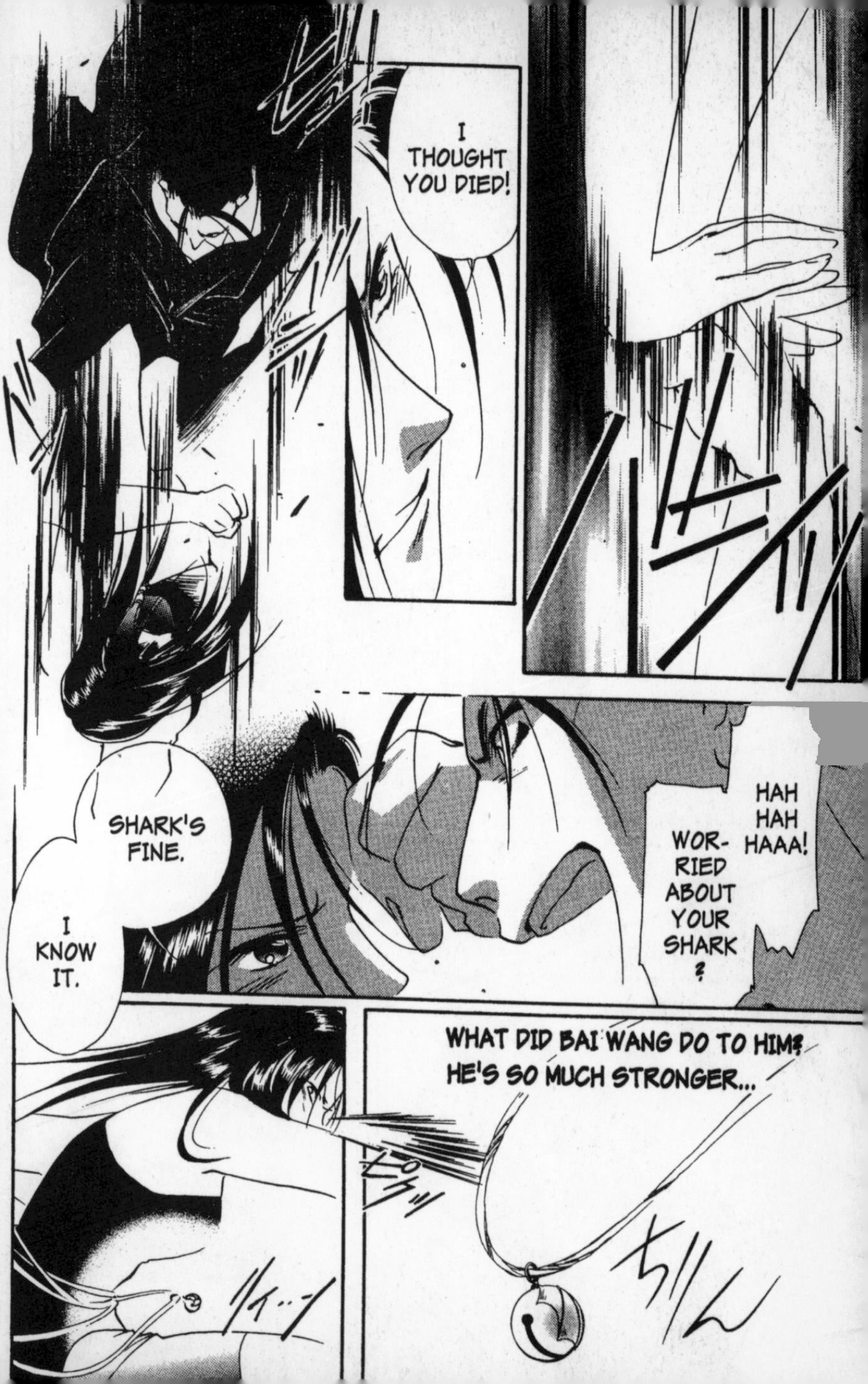
I THOUGHT YOU DIED!
HAH HAH HAAA!
WORRIED ABOUT YOUR SHARK?
SHARK'S FINE.
I KNOW IT.
WHAT DID BAI WANG DO TO HIM? HE'S SO MUCH STRONGER...

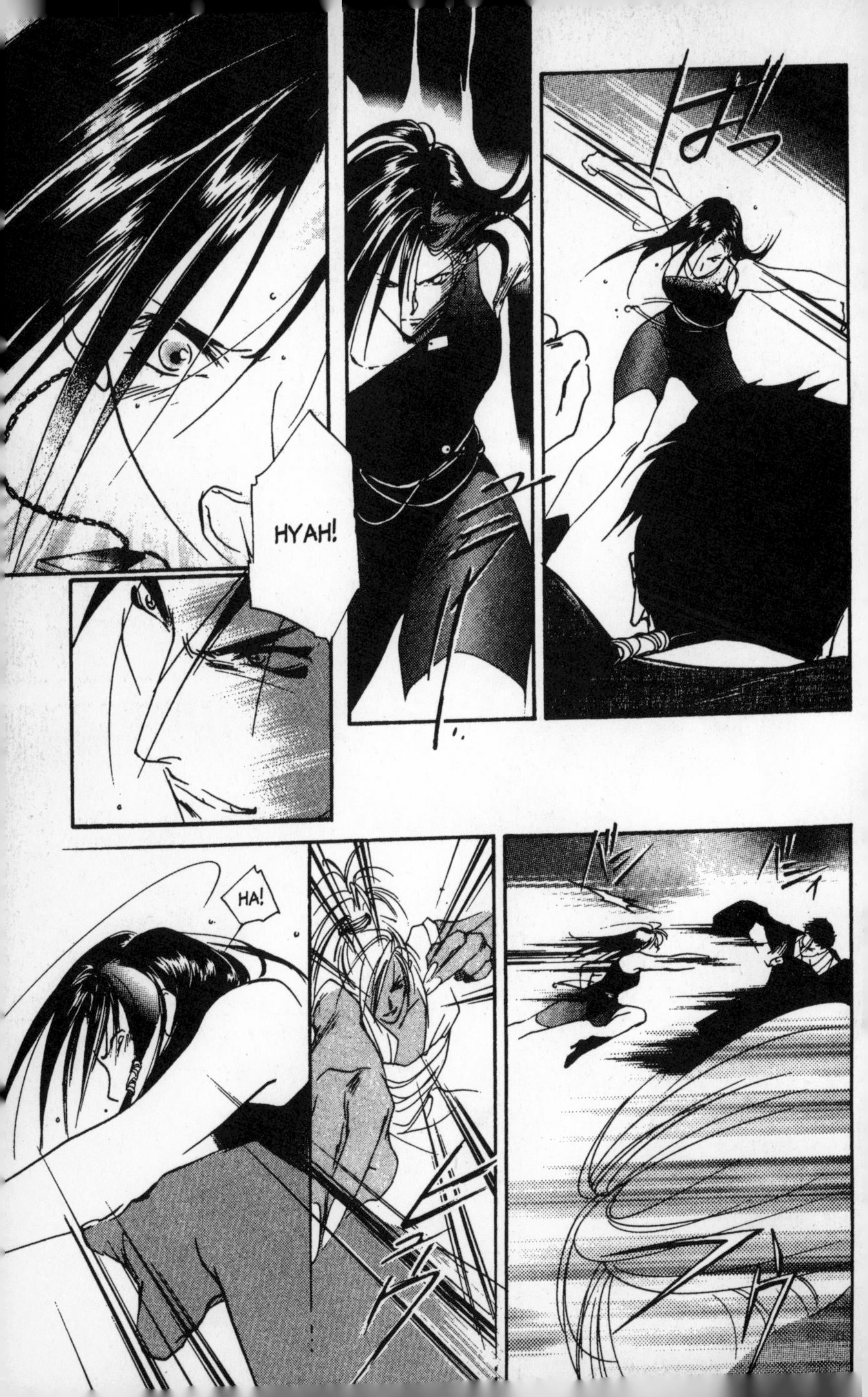
HYAH!
HA!

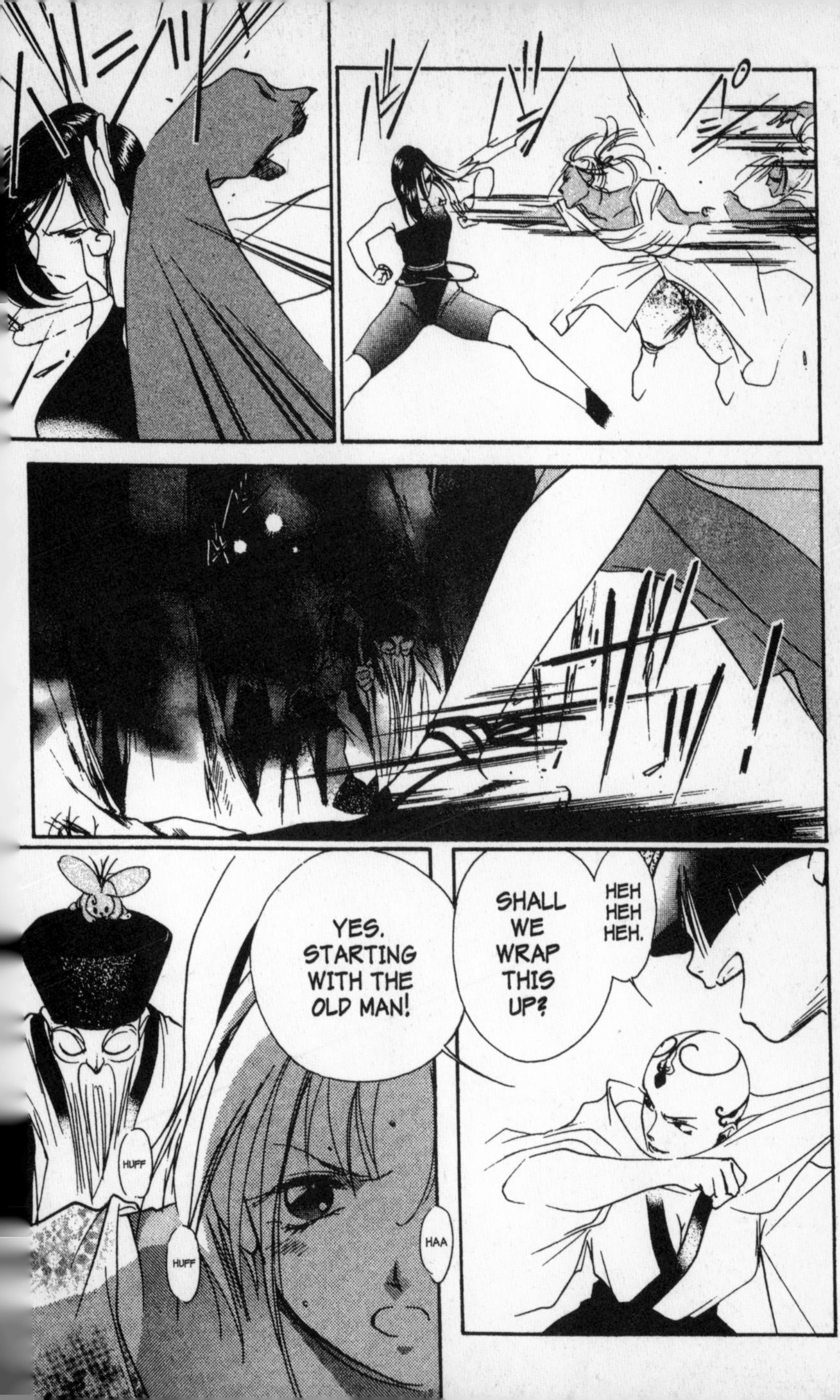
HEH HEH HEH.
SHALL WE WRAP THIS UP?
YES. STARTING WITH THE OLD MAN!
HAA
HUFF
HUFF

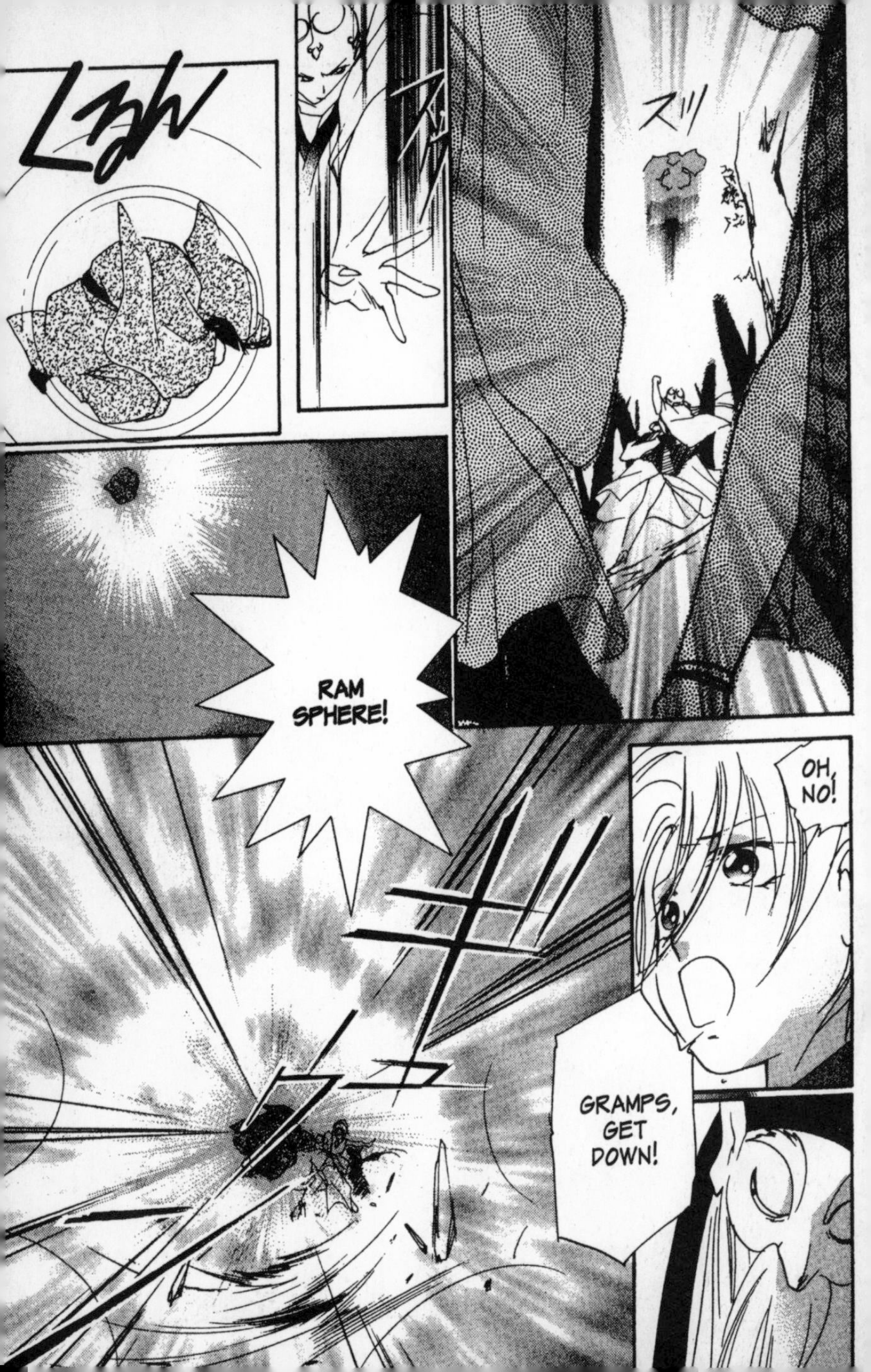
ズリ
くるん
RAM SPHERE!
OH, NO!
GRAMPS, GET DOWN!

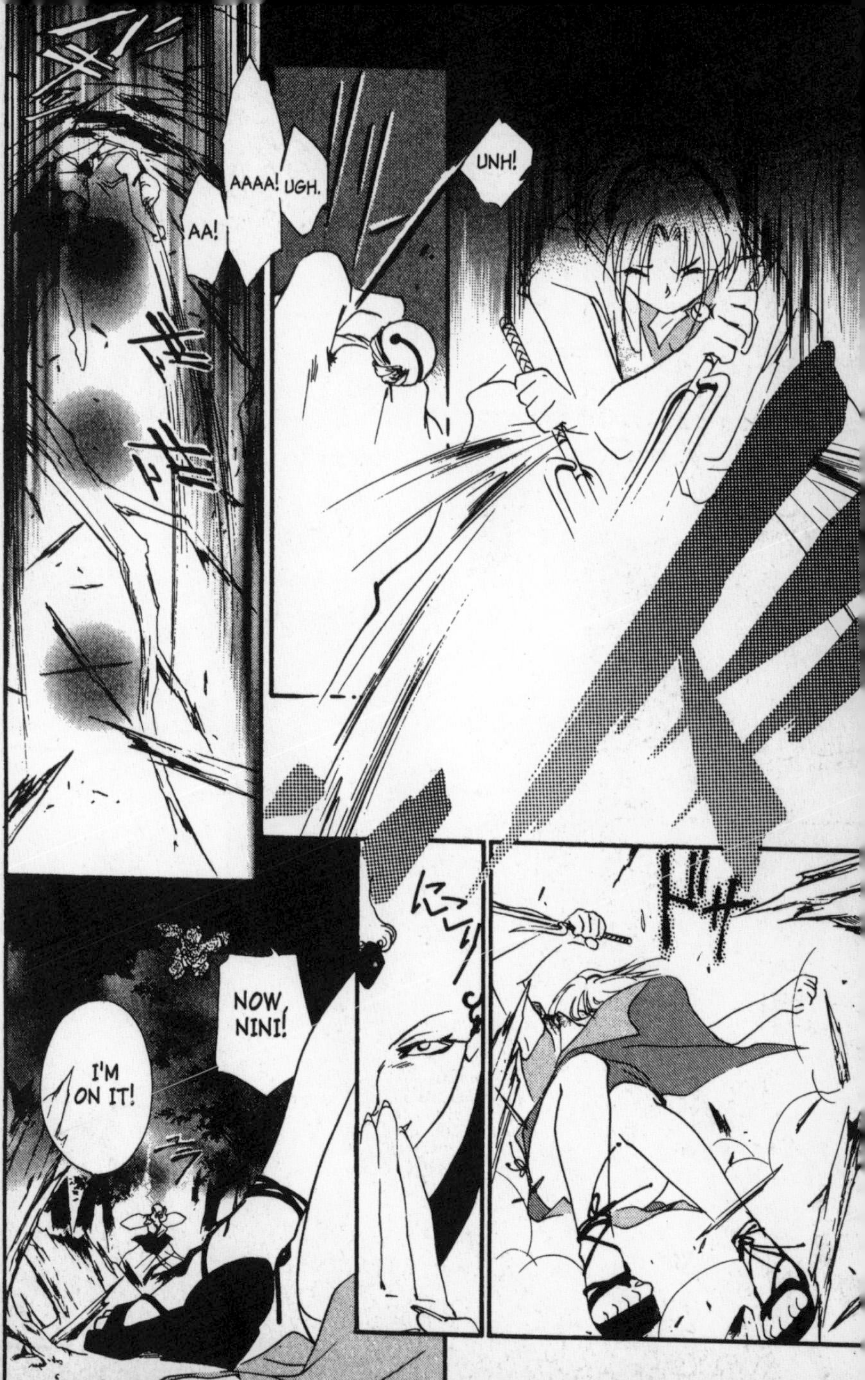
UNH!
UGH.
AAAA!
AA!
NOW NINI!
I'M ON IT!

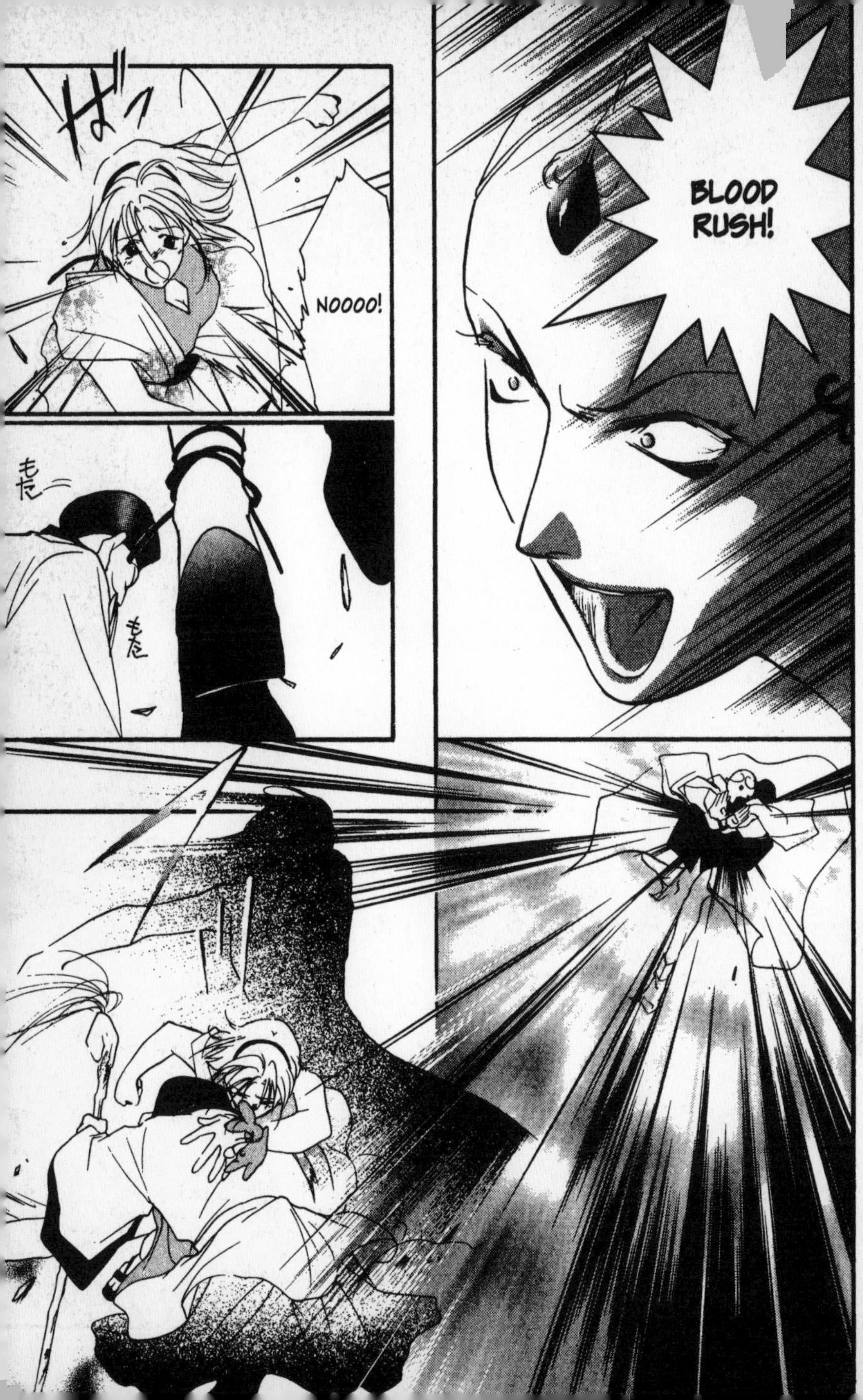
BLOOD RUSH!
ばっ
NOOOO!
もた
もた

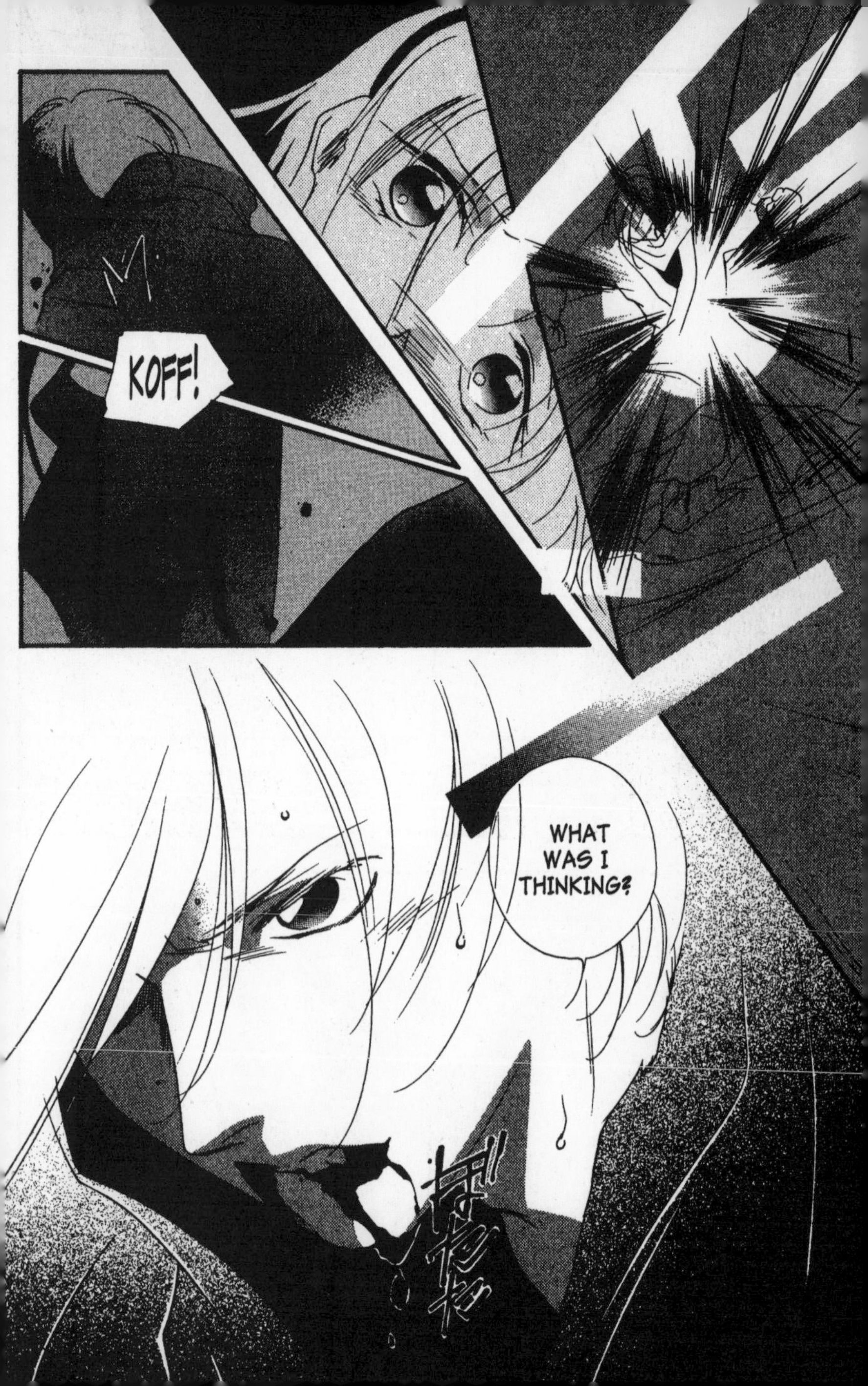
KOFF!
WHAT WAS I THINKING?

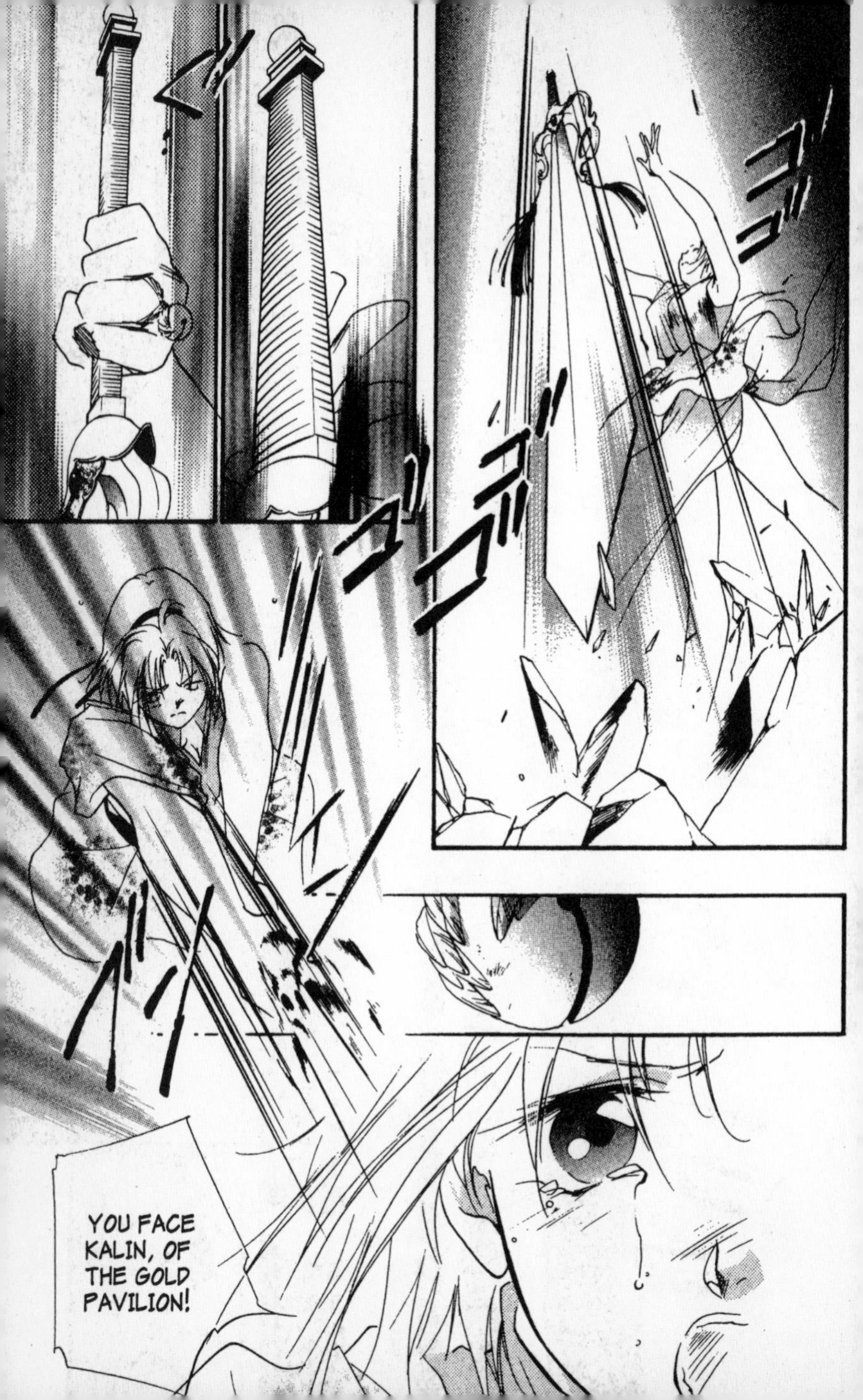
YOU FACE KALIN, OF THE GOLD PAVILION!

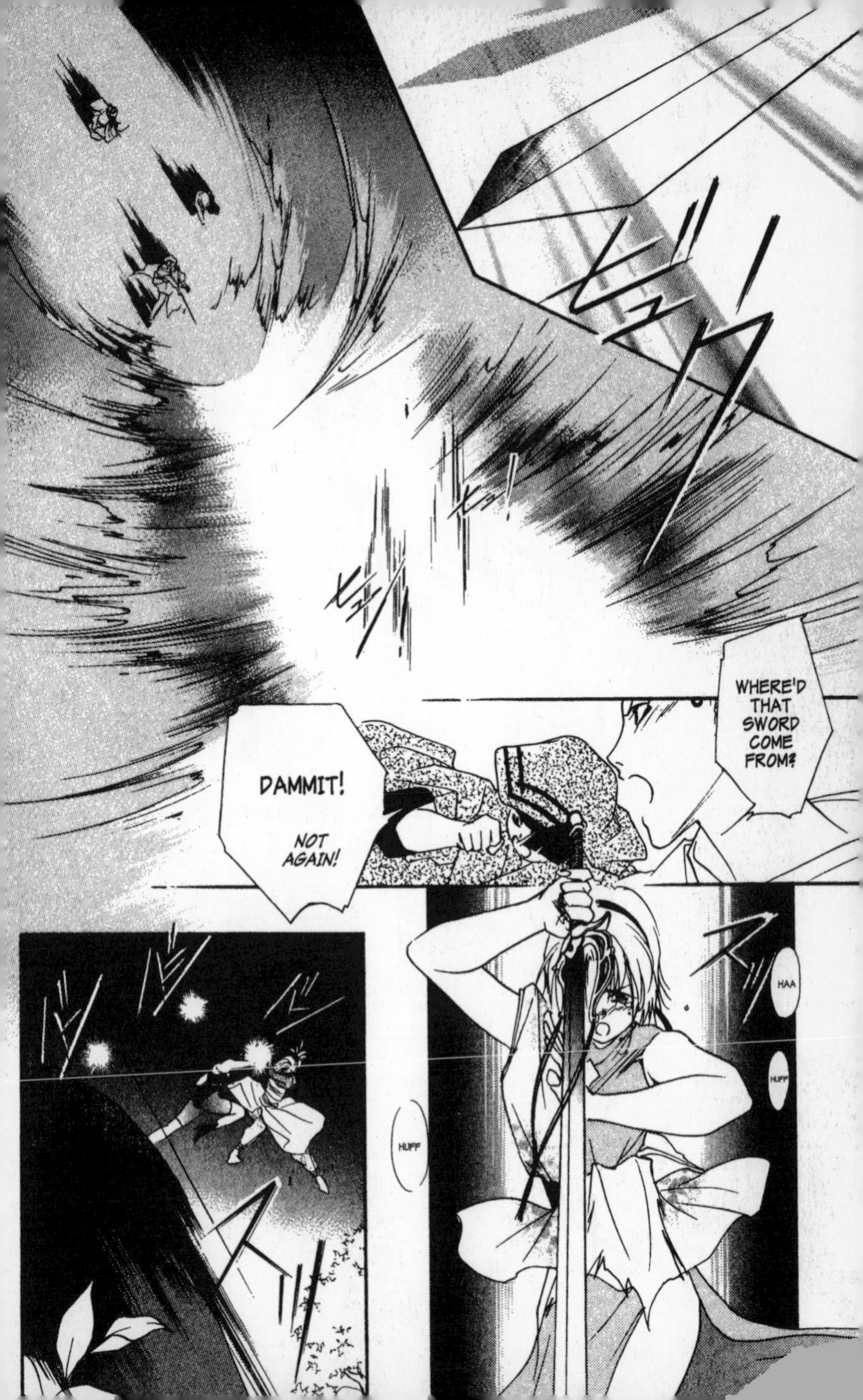
WHERE'D THAT SWORD COME FROM?
DAMMIT!
NOT AGAIN!
HAA
HUFF
HUFF

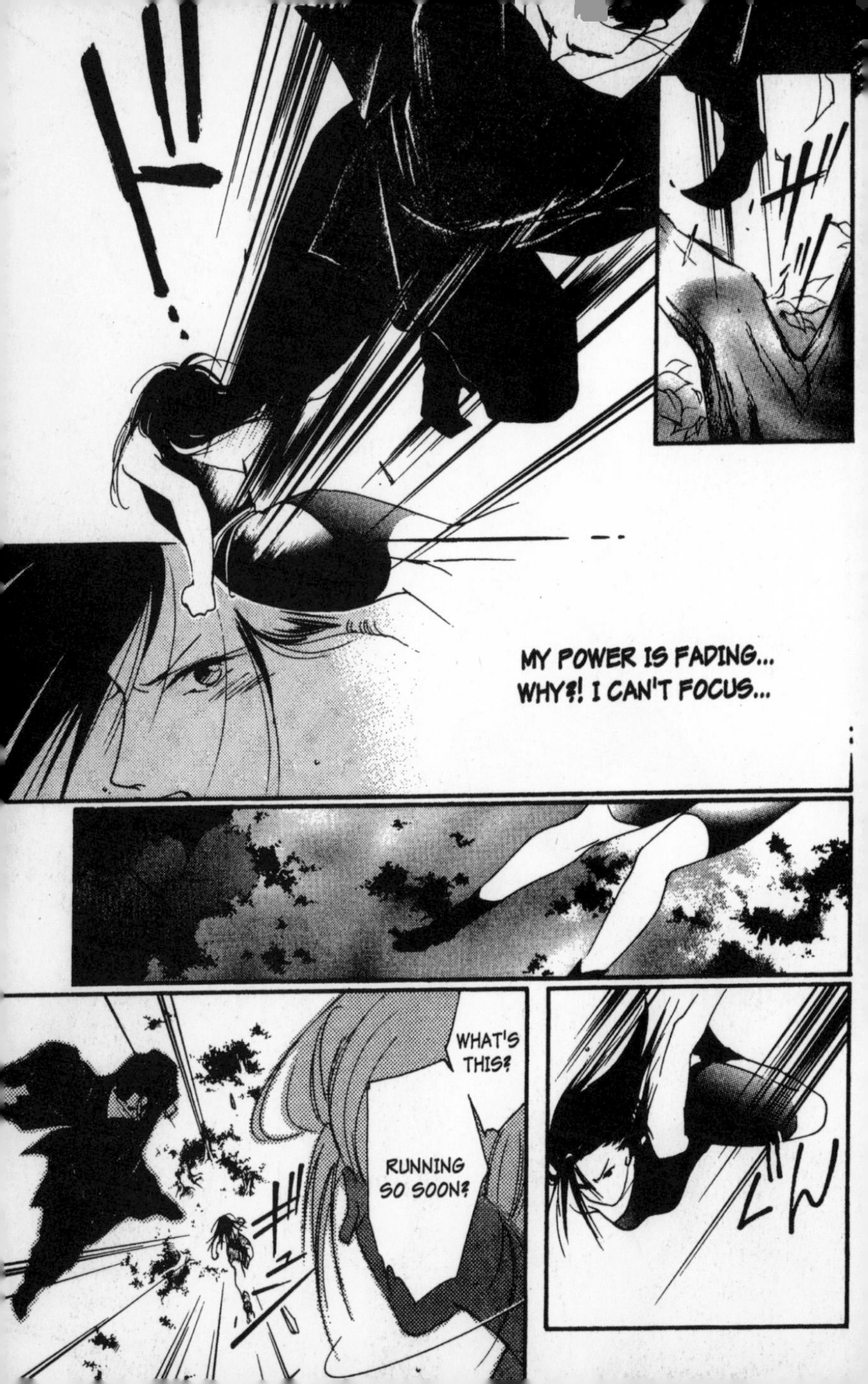
MY POWER IS FADING...
WHY?! I CAN'T FOCUS...
WHAT'S THIS?
RUNNING SO SOON?

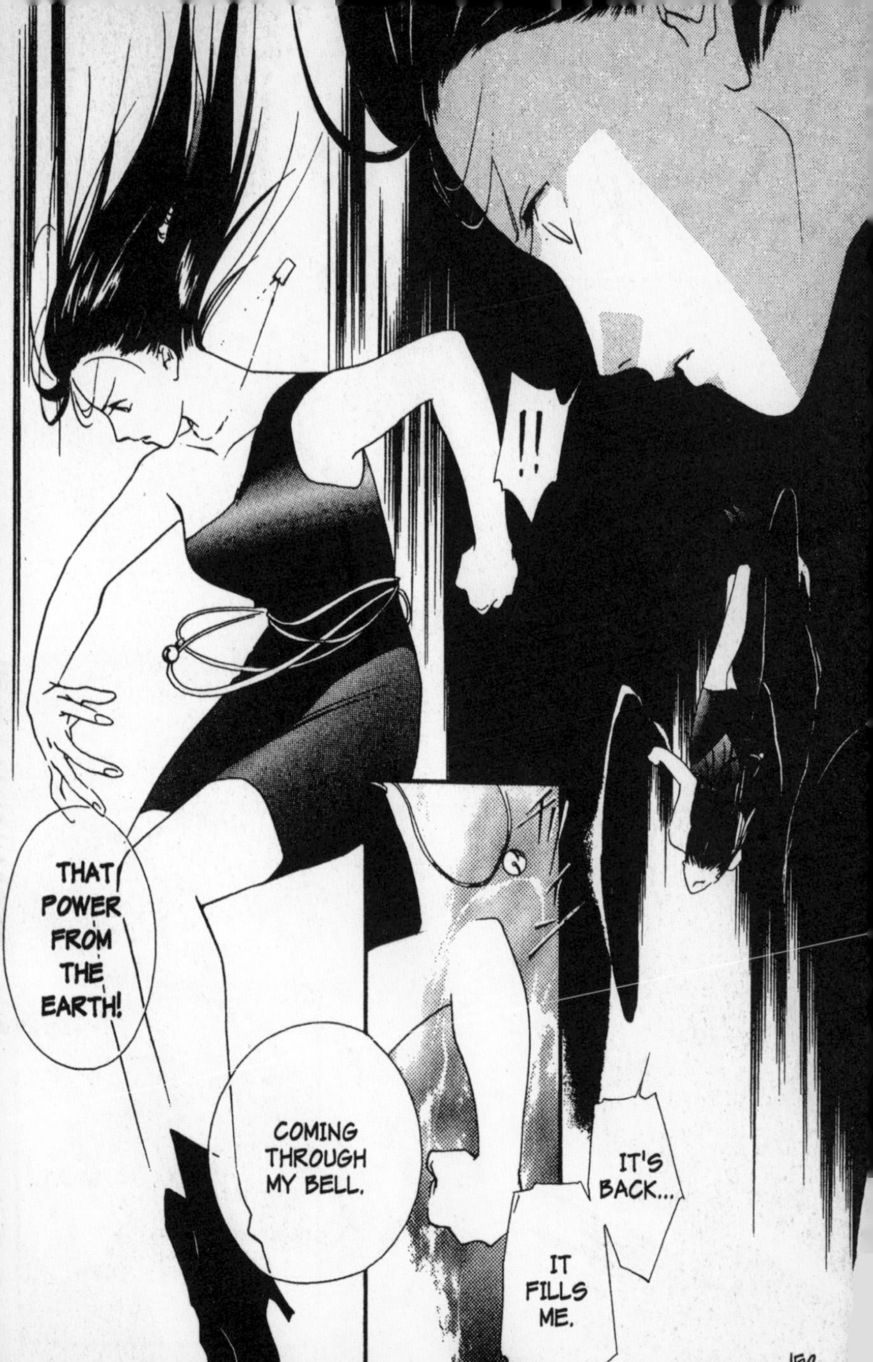
!!
IT'S BACK...
IT FILLS ME.
THAT POWER FROM THE EARTH!
COMING THROUGH MY BELL.

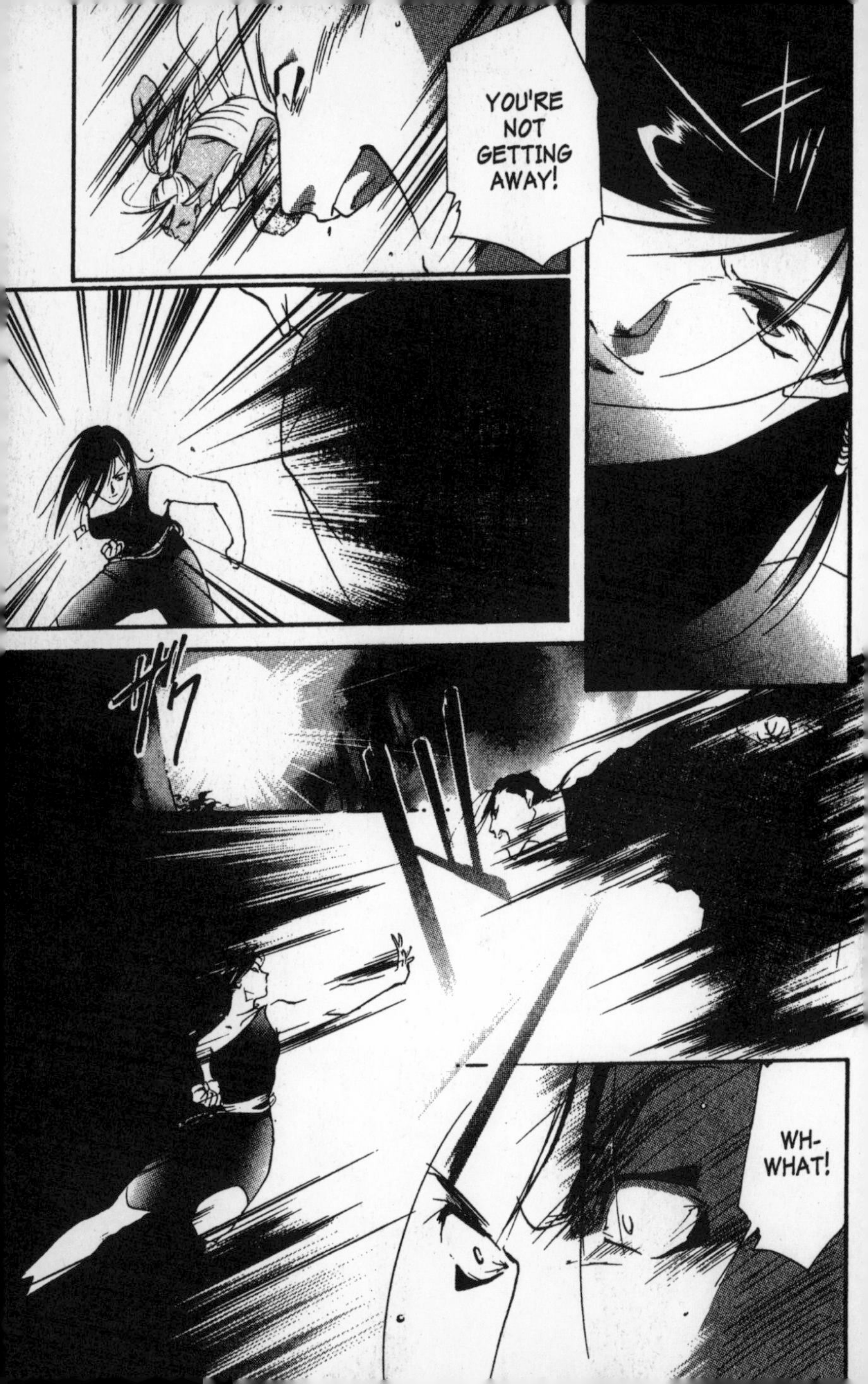
YOU'RE NOT GETTING AWAY!
WH- WHAT!

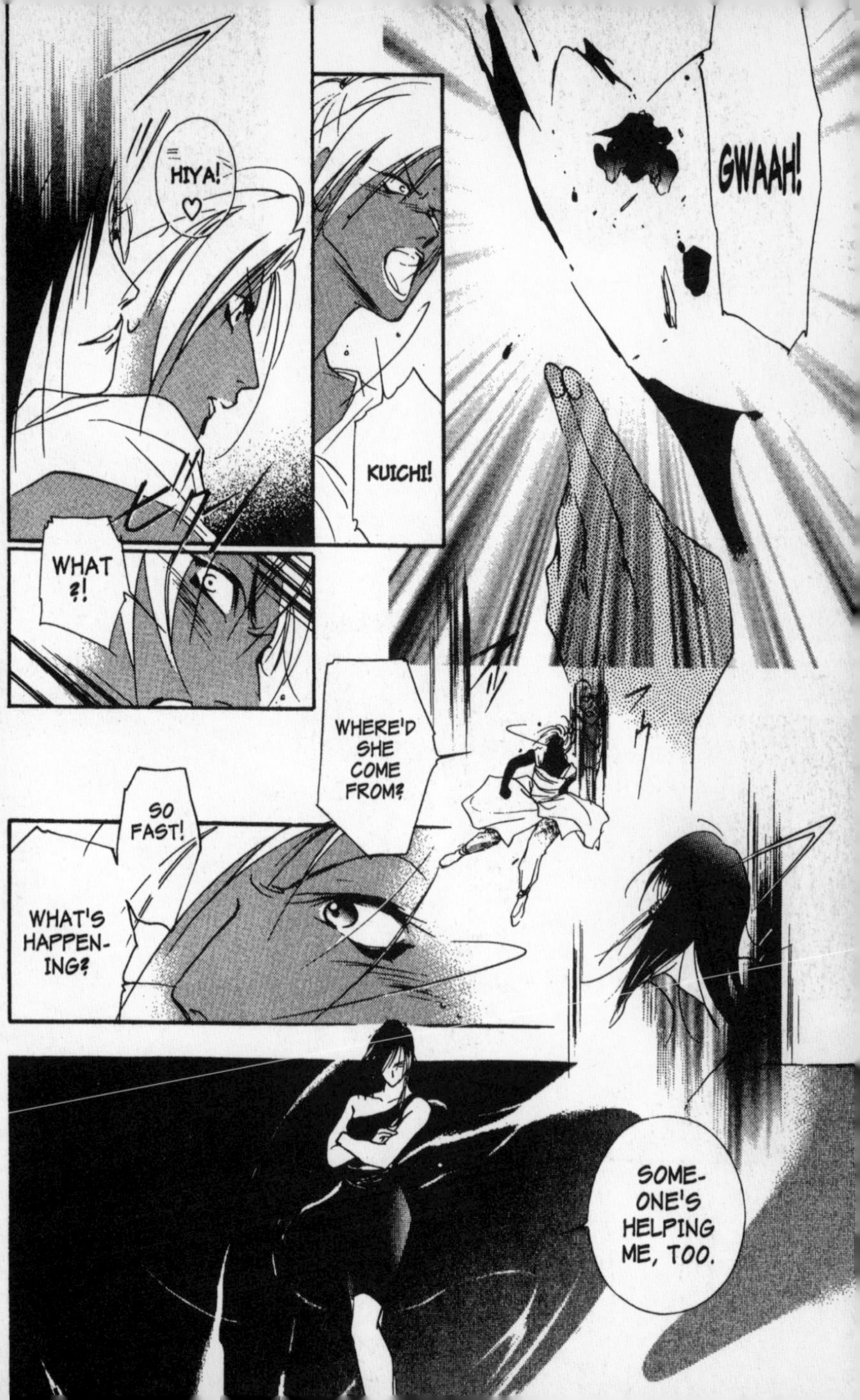
GWAAH!
KUICHI!
HIYA! ♥
WHAT?!
WHERE'D SHE COME FROM?
SO FAST!
WHAT'S HAPPEN-ING?
SOME-ONE'S HELPING ME, TOO.

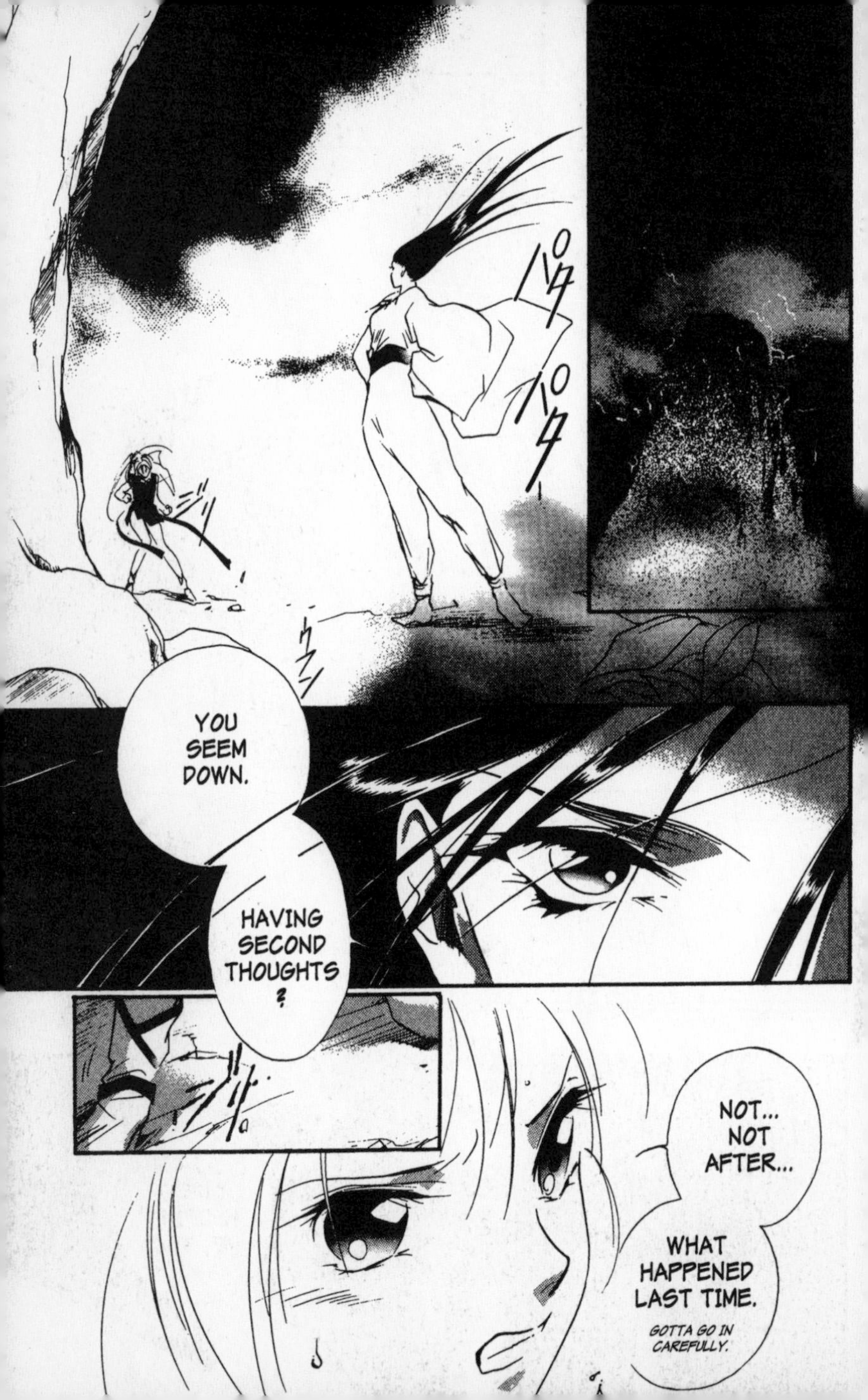
YOU SEEM DOWN.
HAVING SECOND THOUGHTS?
NOT... NOT AFTER...
WHAT HAPPENED LAST TIME.
GOTTA GO IN CAREFULLY.

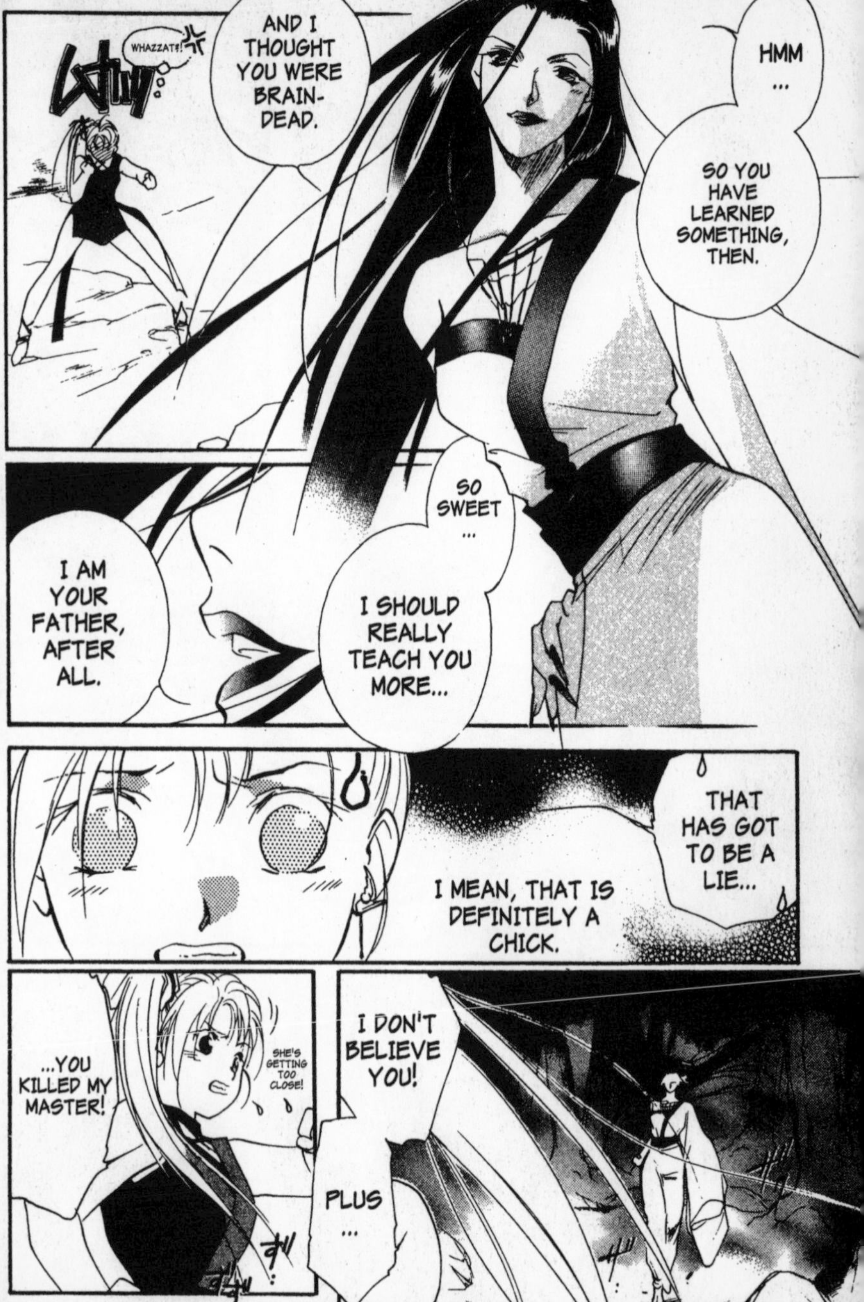
HMM ...
SO YOU HAVE LEARNED SOMETHING, THEN.
AND I THOUGHT YOU WERE BRAIN-DEAD.
WHAZZAT?!
SO SWEET ...
I SHOULD REALLY TEACH YOU MORE...
I AM YOUR FATHER, AFTER ALL.
THAT HAS GOT TO BE A LIE...
I MEAN, THAT IS DEFINITELY A CHICK.
I DON'T BELIEVE YOU!
PLUS ...
...YOU KILLED MY MASTER!
SHE'S GETTING TOO CLOSE!

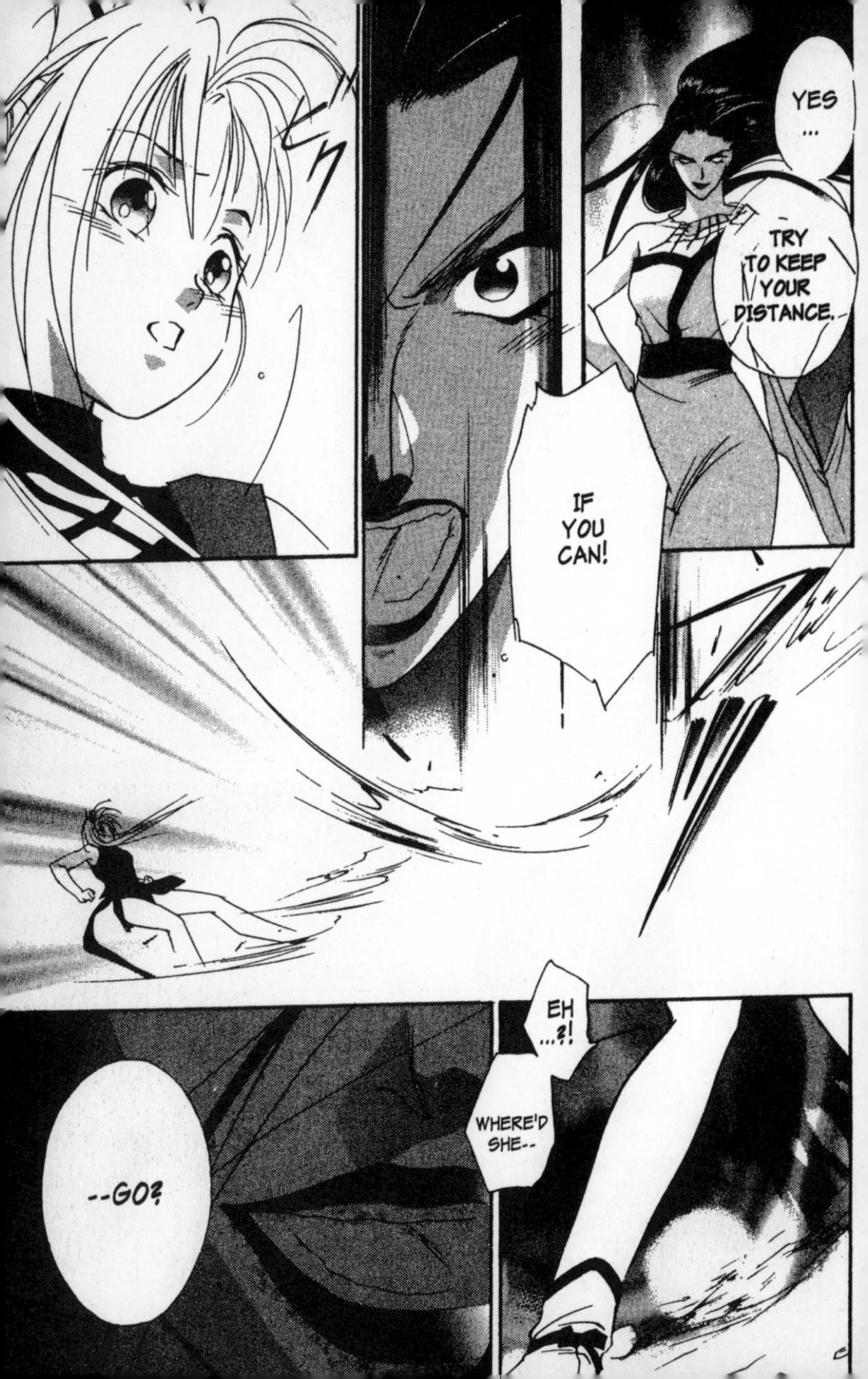
YES ...
TRY TO KEEP YOUR DISTANCE.
IF YOU CAN!
EH ...?!
WHERE'D SHE--
--GO?

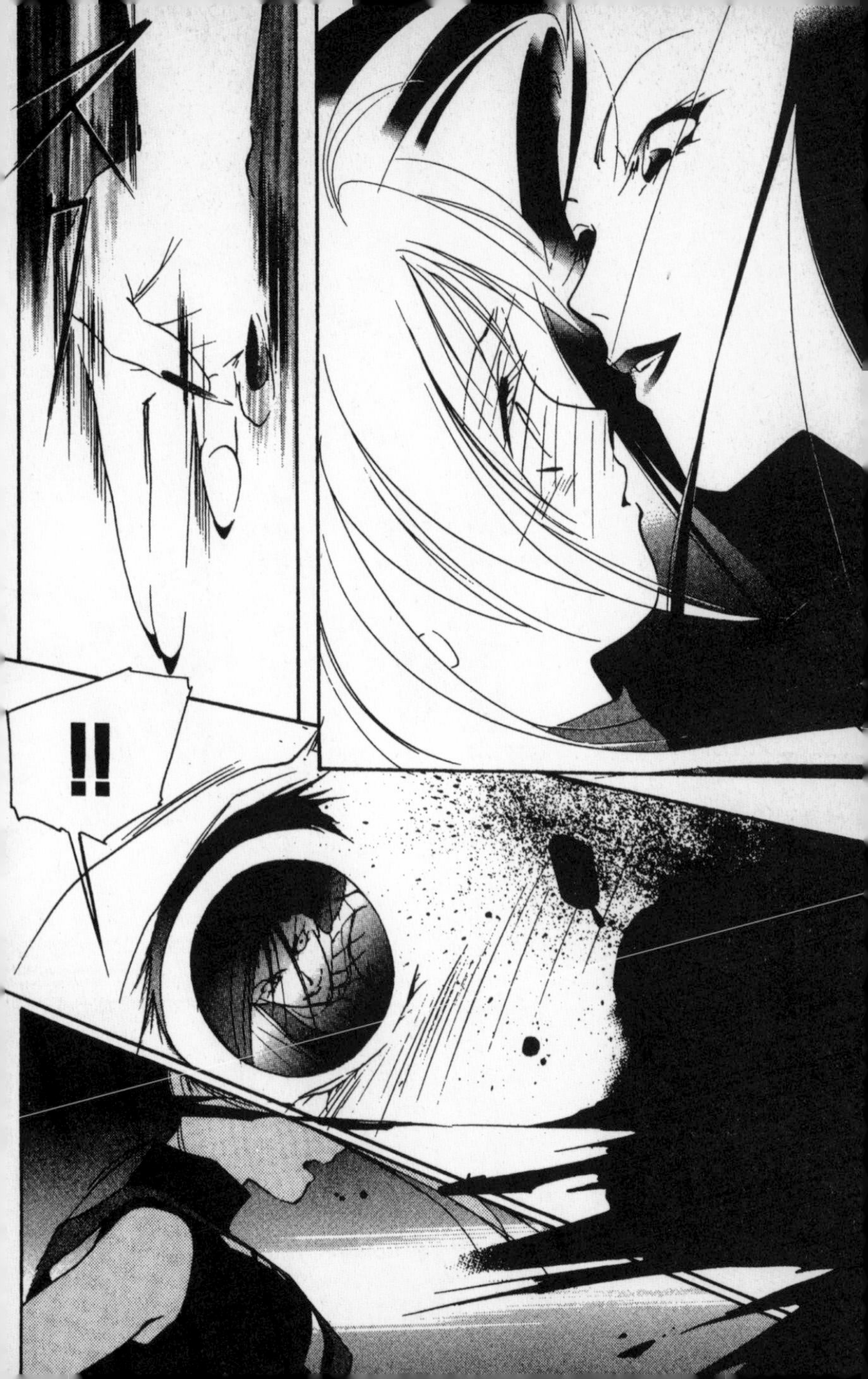
!!

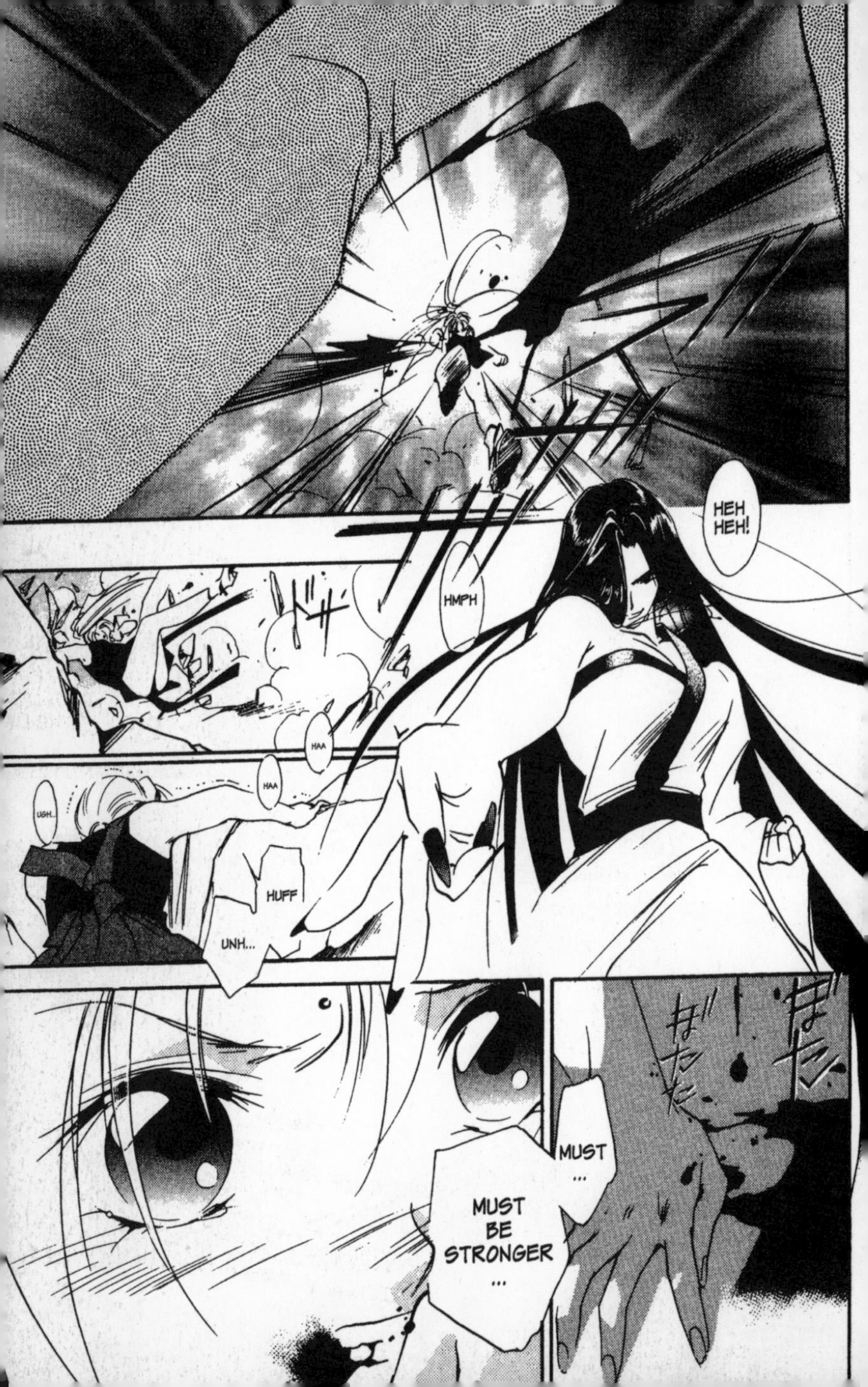

HEH HEH!
HMPH
HAA
HAA
HUFF
UNH...
UGH...
MUST ...
MUST BE STRONGER ...

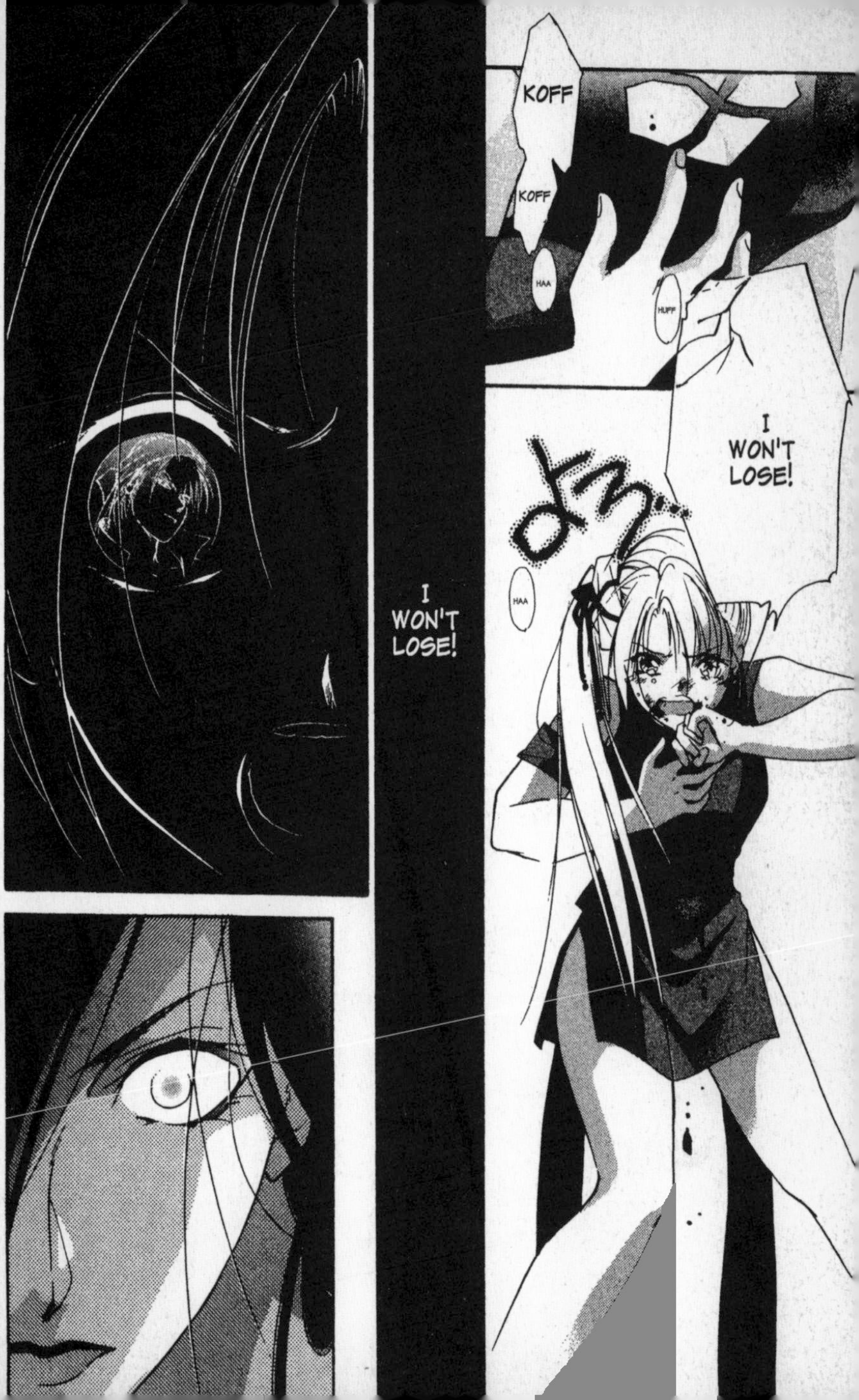
KOFF
KOFF
HUFF
HAA
I WON'T LOSE!
よろ…
HAA
I WON'T LOSE!

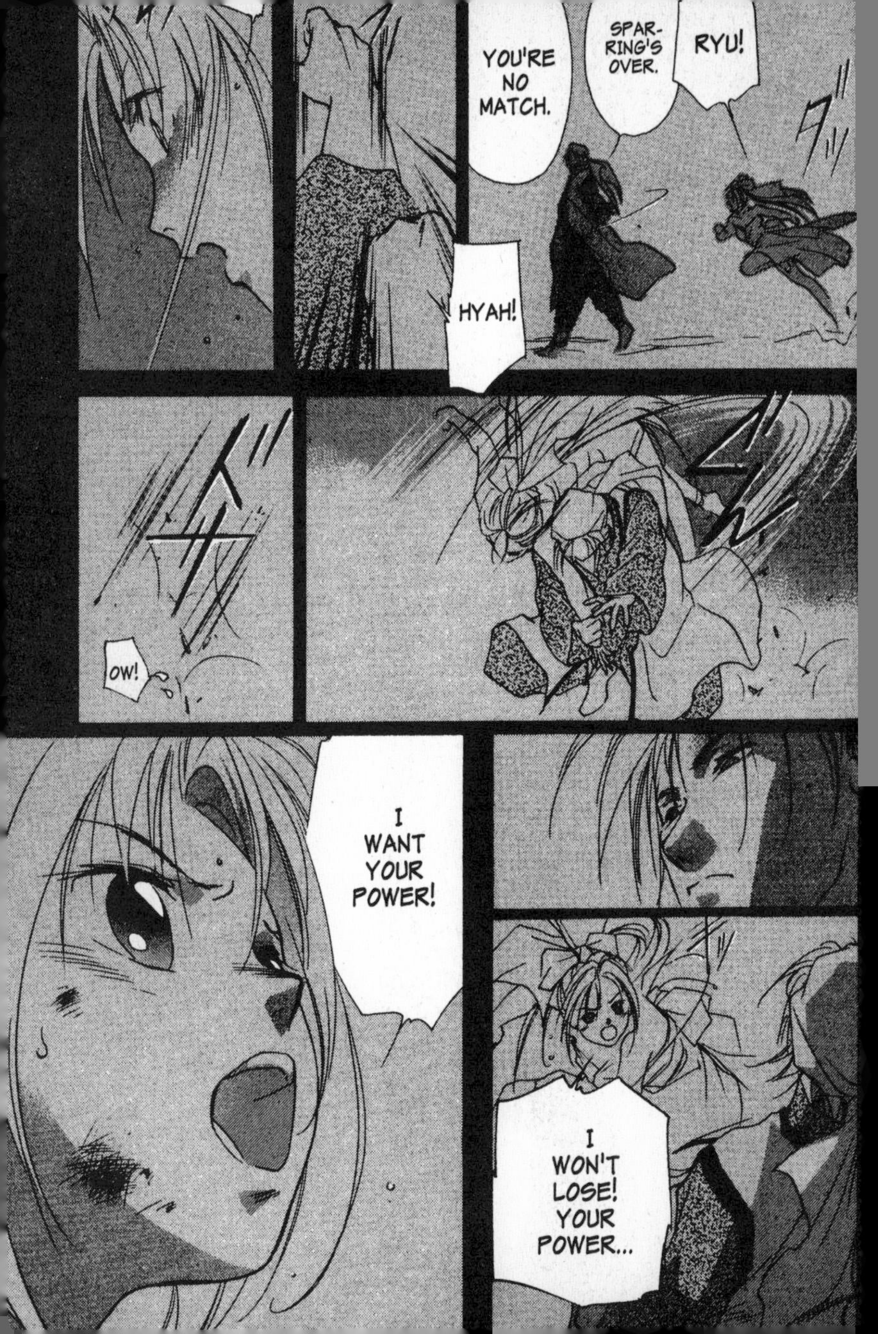
RYU!
SPAR-RING'S OVER.
YOU'RE NO MATCH.
HYAH!
OW!
I WON'T LOSE! YOUR POWER...
I WANT YOUR POWER!

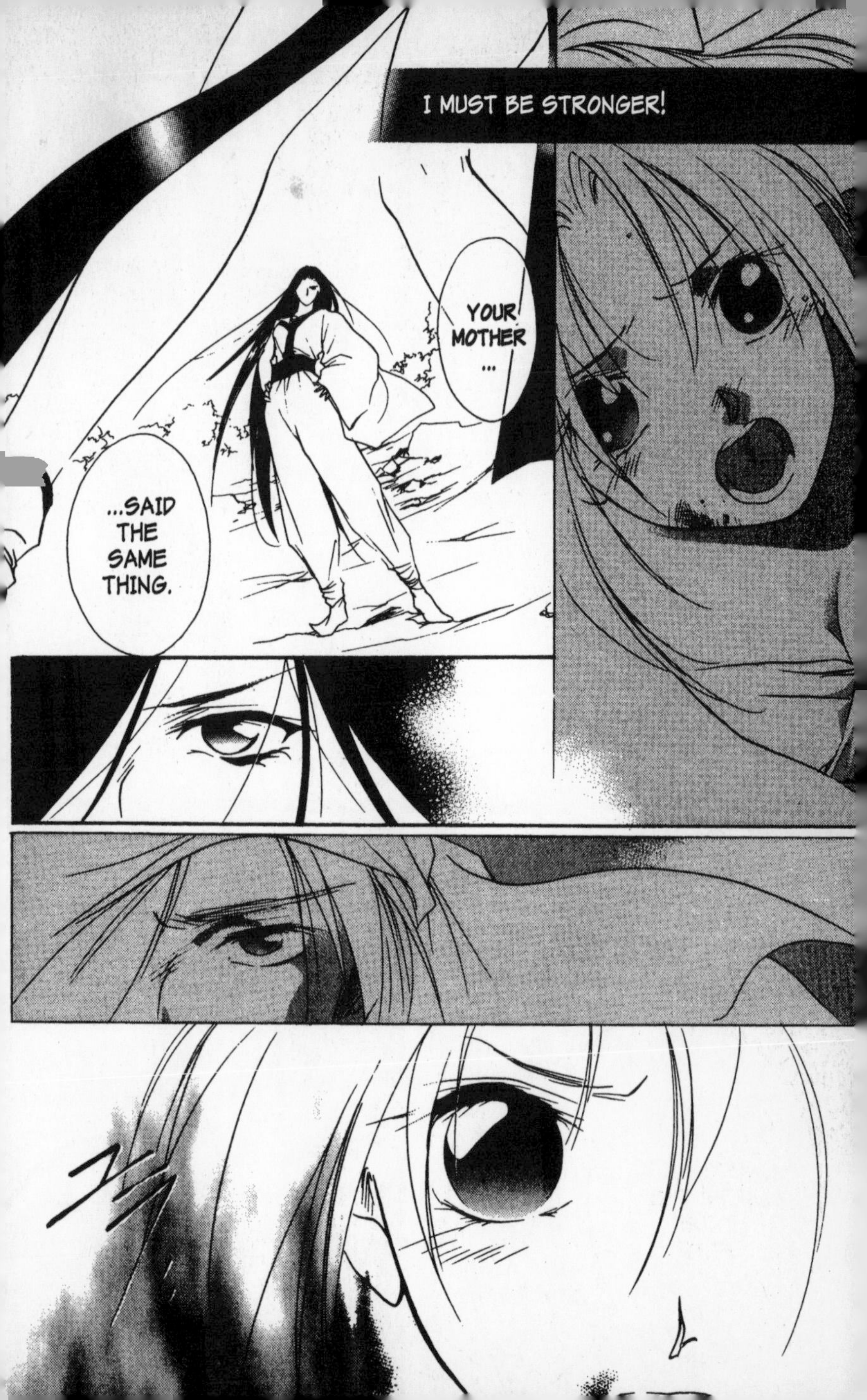
I MUST BE STRONGER!
YOUR MOTHER ...
...SAID THE SAME THING.

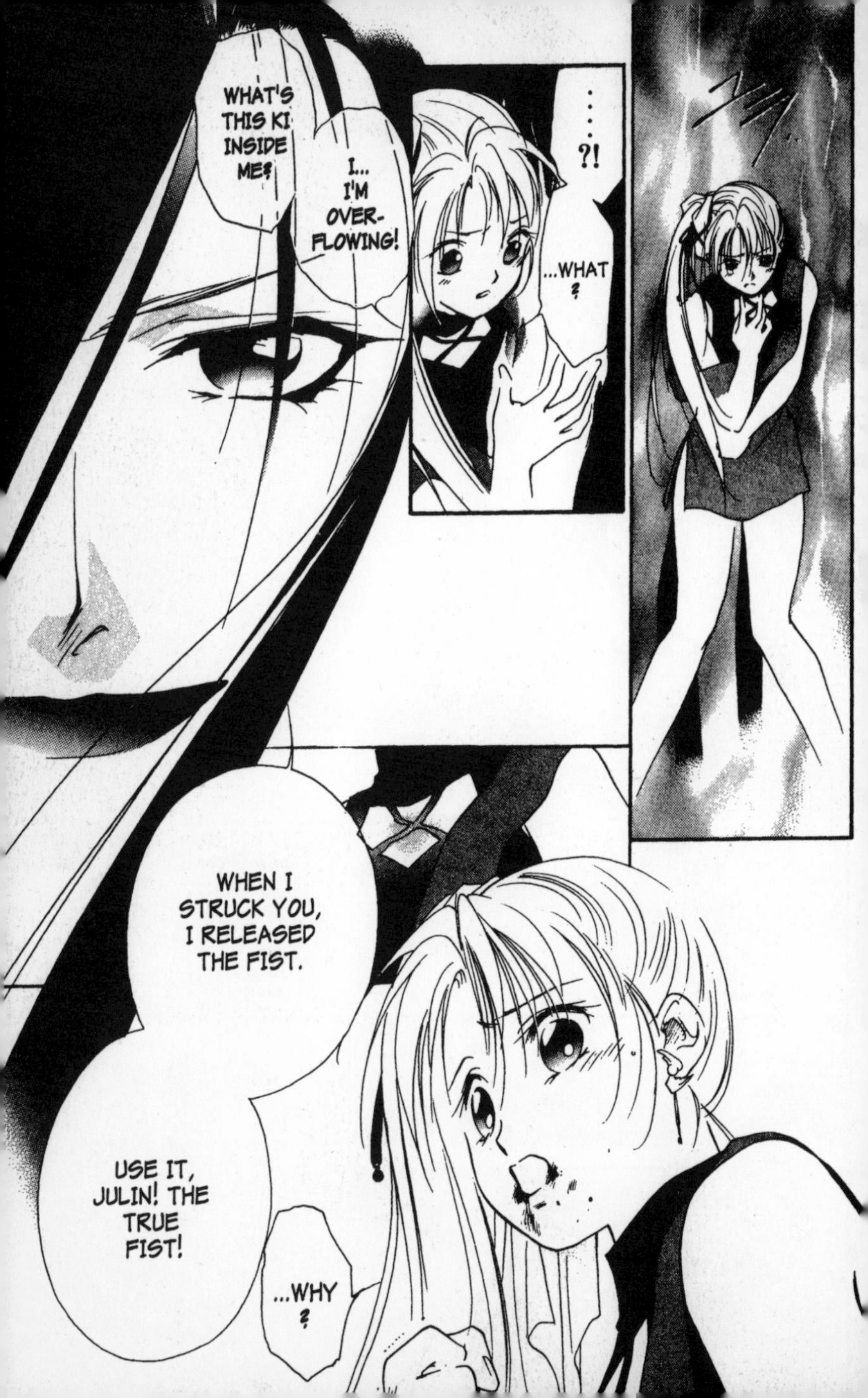

...?!
...WHAT?
WHAT'S THIS KI INSIDE ME?
I... I'M OVER-FLOWING!
WHEN I STRUCK YOU, I RELEASED THE FIST.
USE IT, JULIN! THE TRUE FIST!
...WHY?

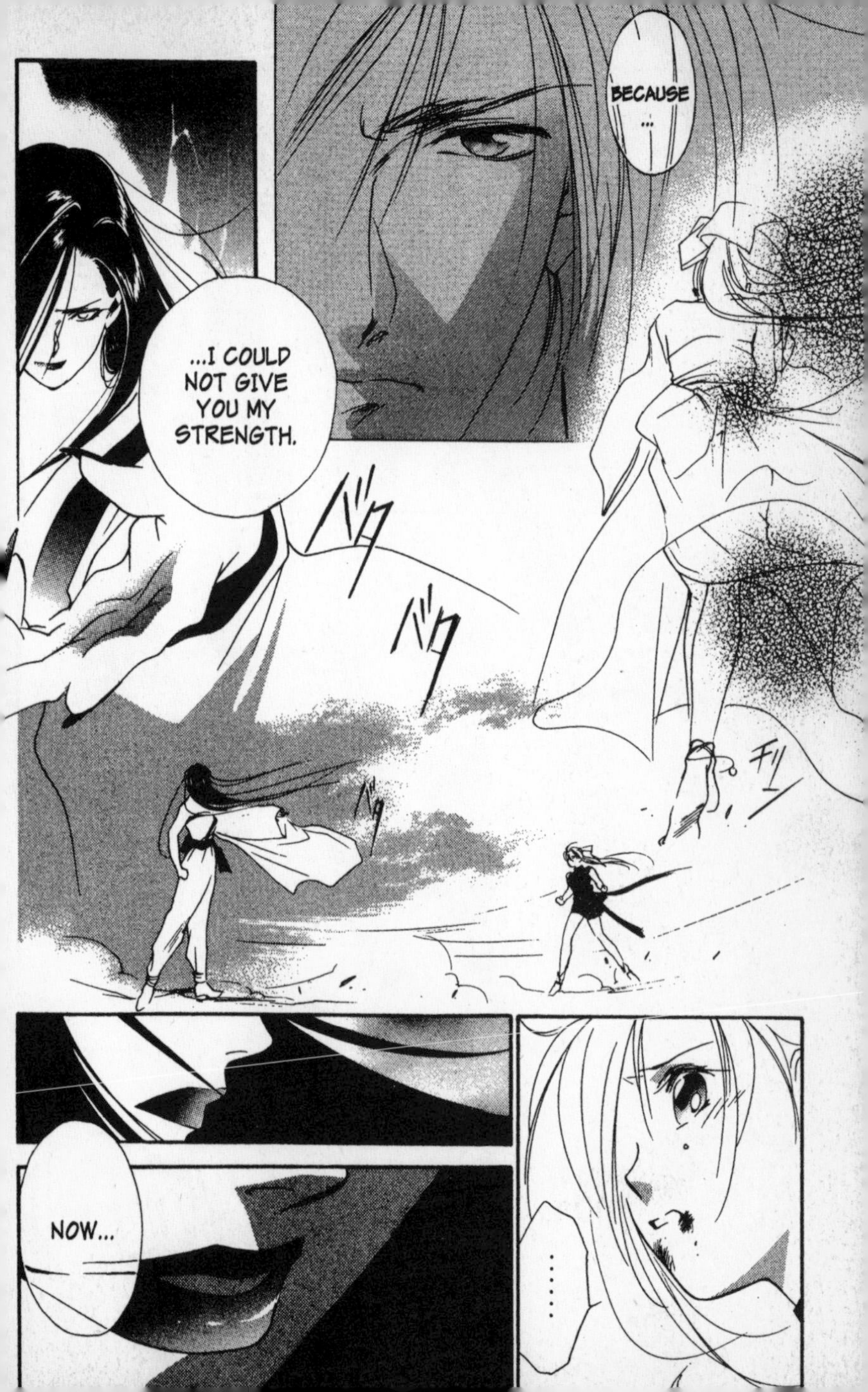
BECAUSE ...
...I COULD NOT GIVE YOU MY STRENGTH.
バタ
バタ
バタ
チリ
......
NOW...

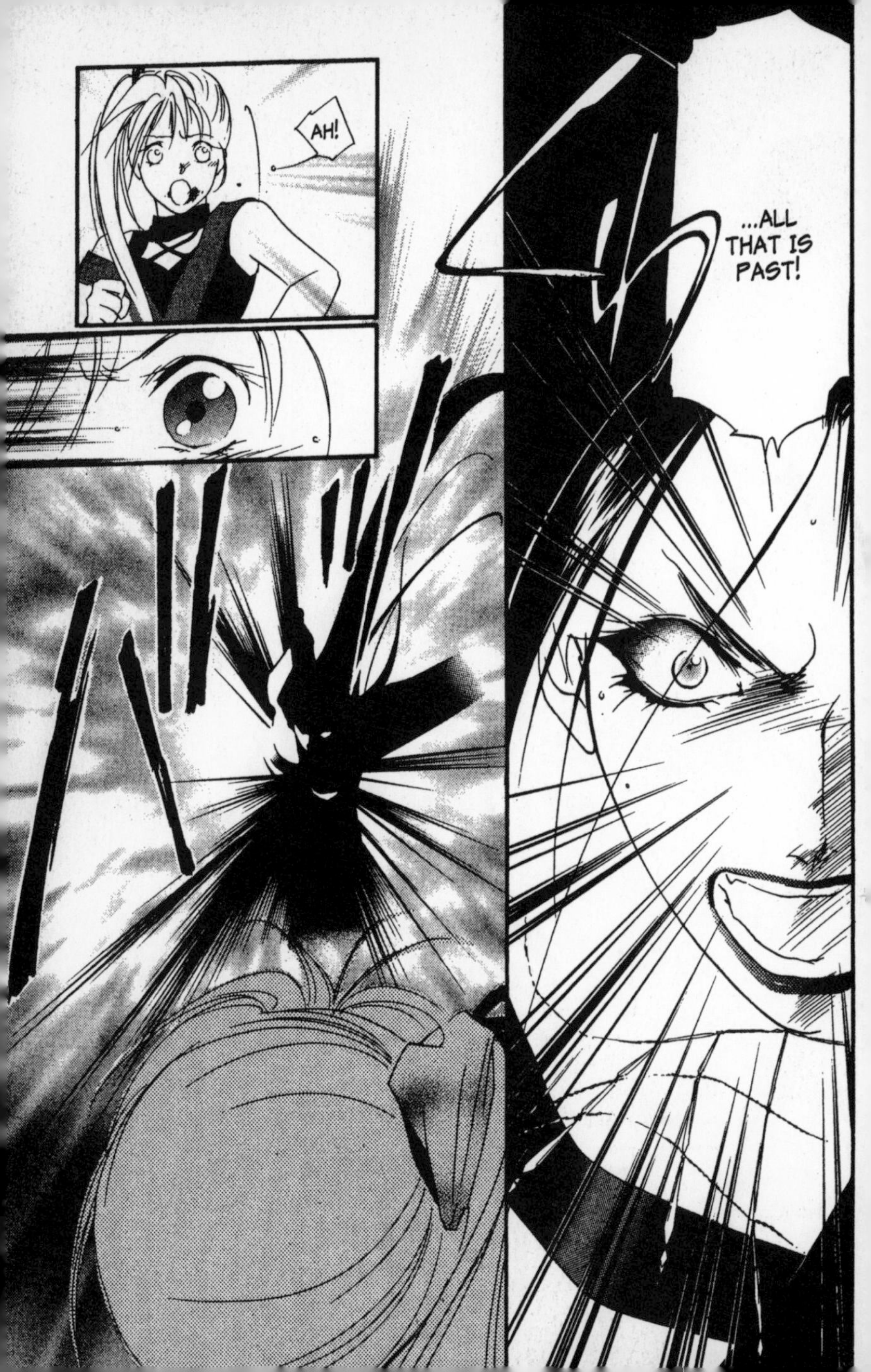
...ALL THAT IS PAST!
AH!

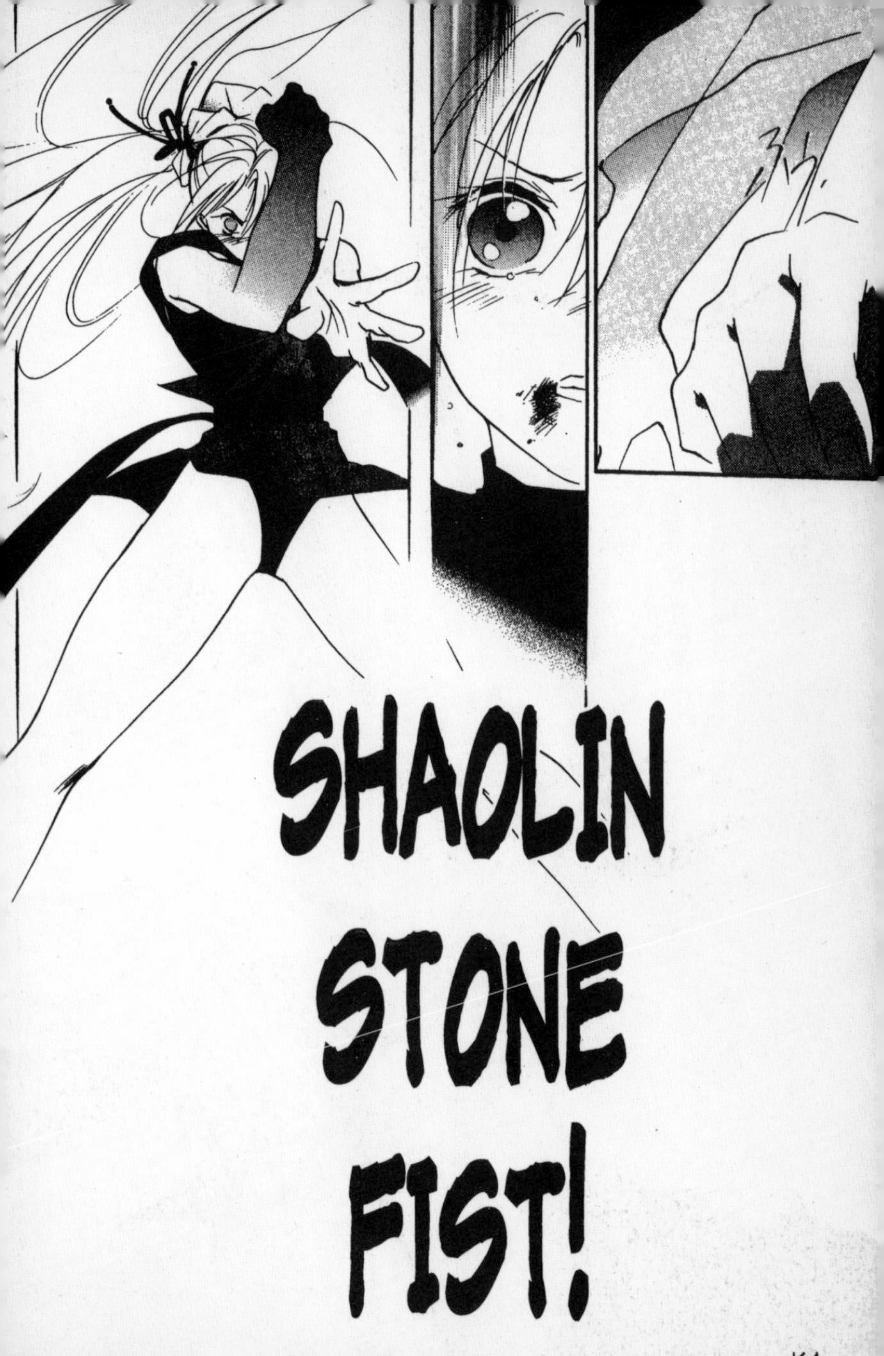
SHAOLIN STONE FIST!

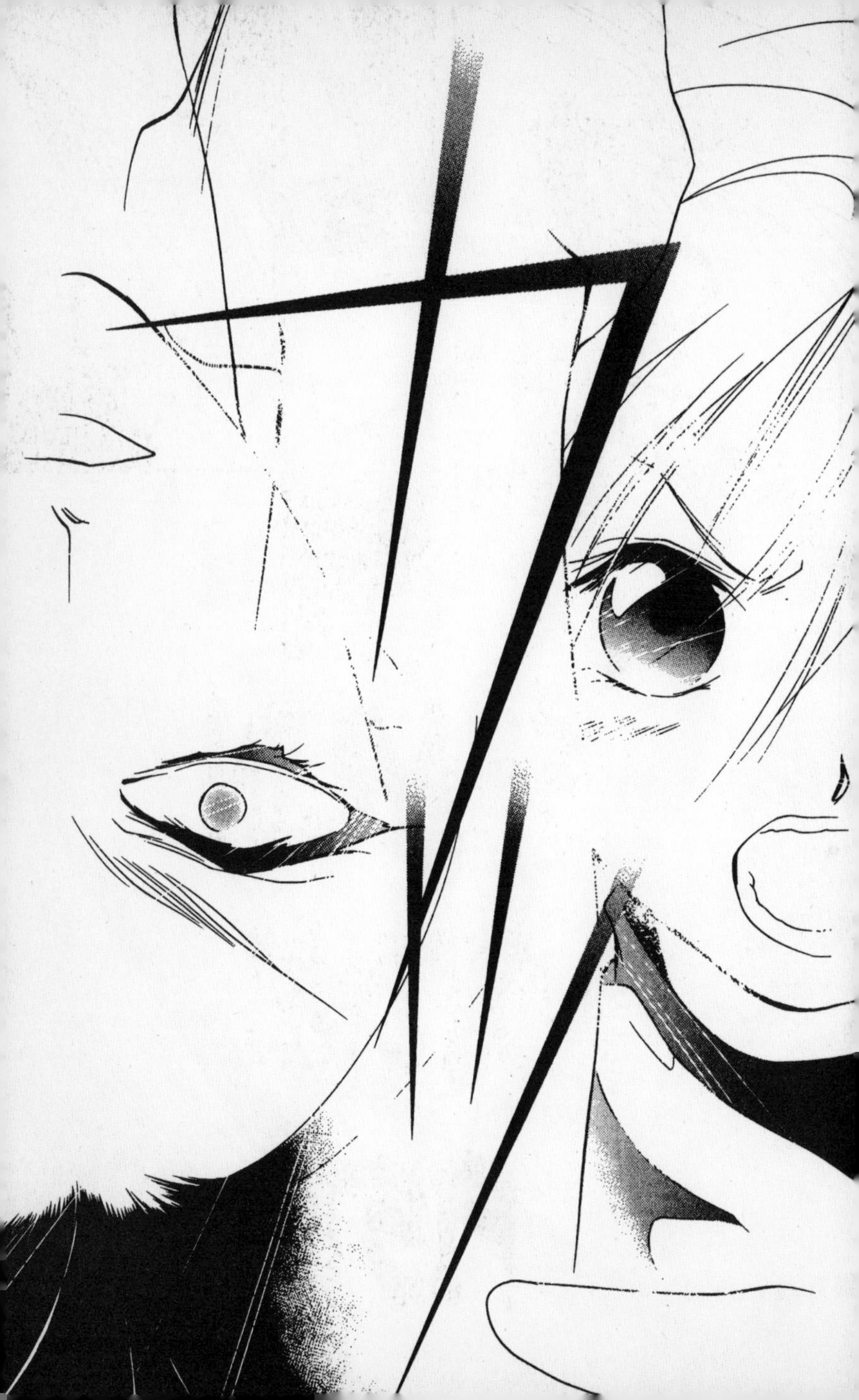

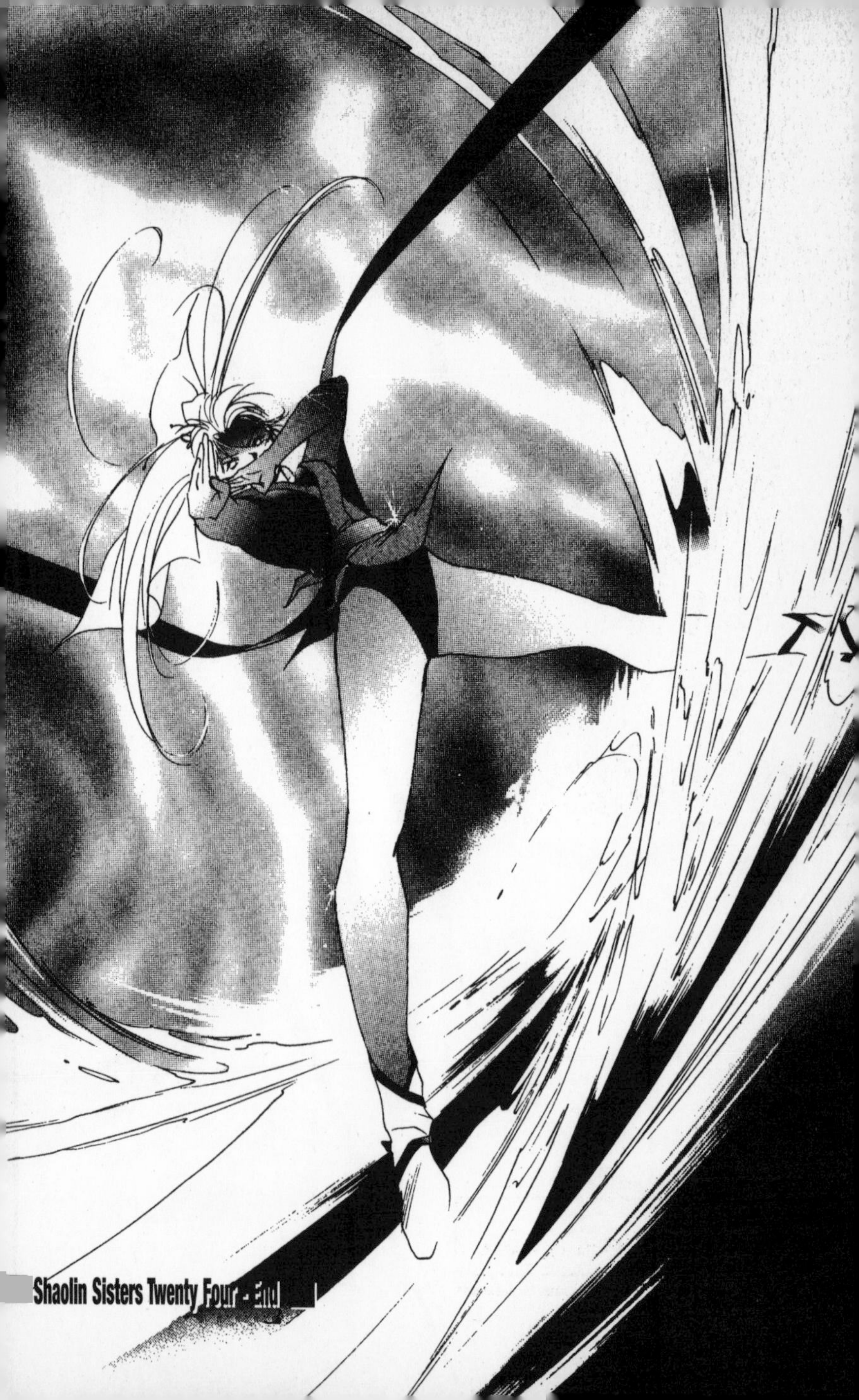
Shaolin Sisters Twenty Four - End

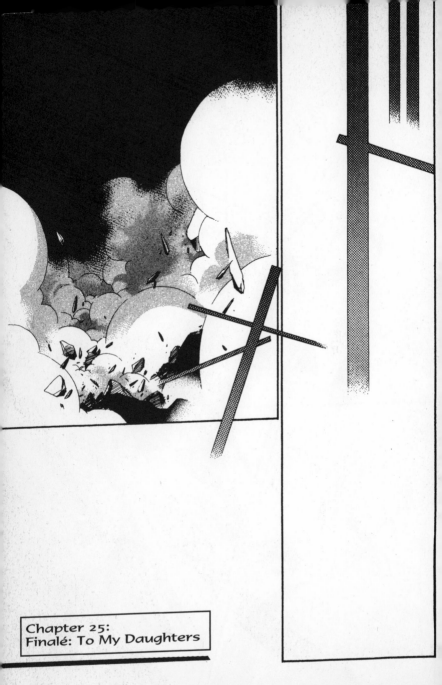

Chapter 25:
Finalé: To My Daughters

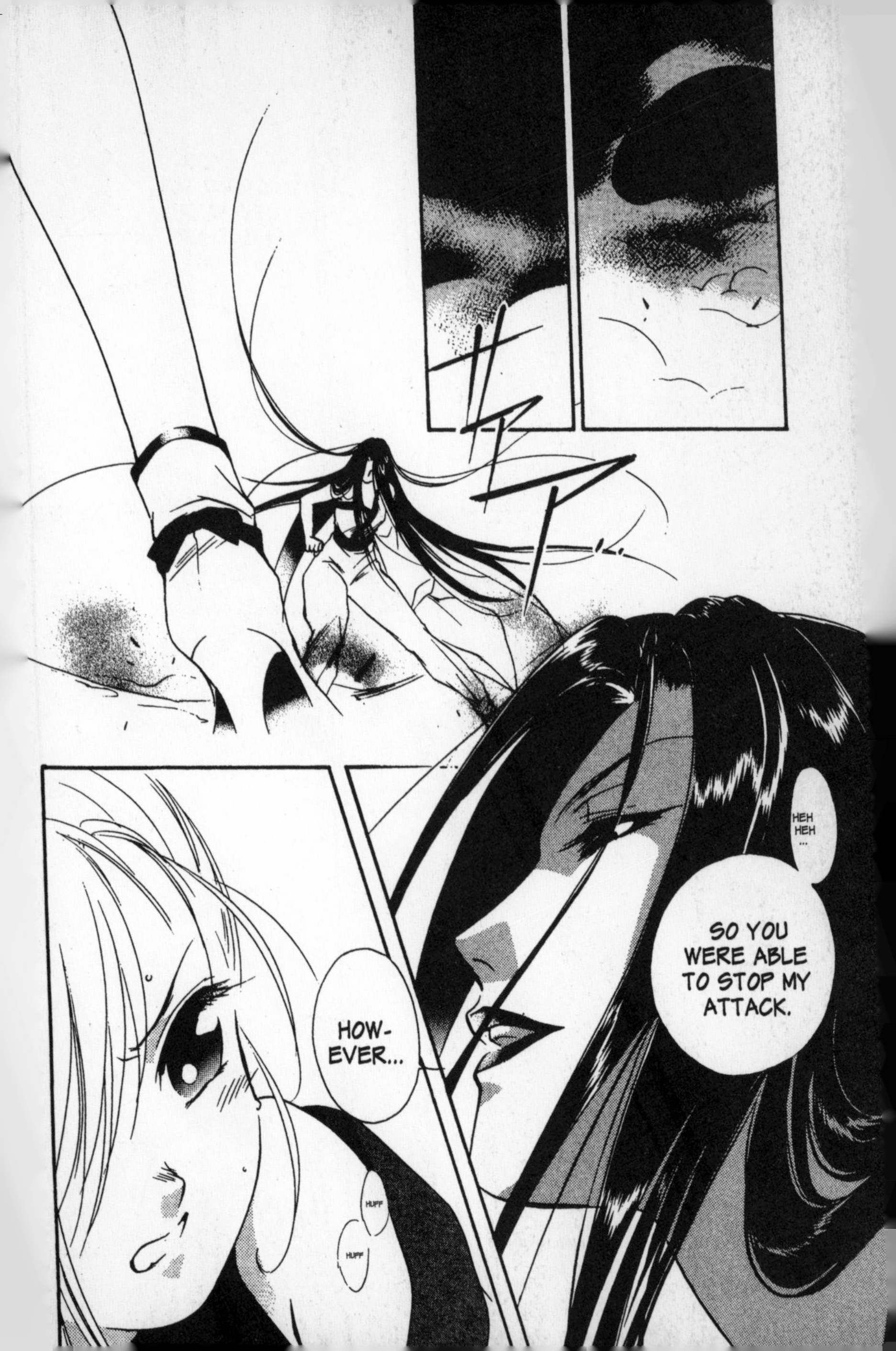
HEH HEH...
SO YOU WERE ABLE TO STOP MY ATTACK.
HOW-EVER...
HUFF
HUFF

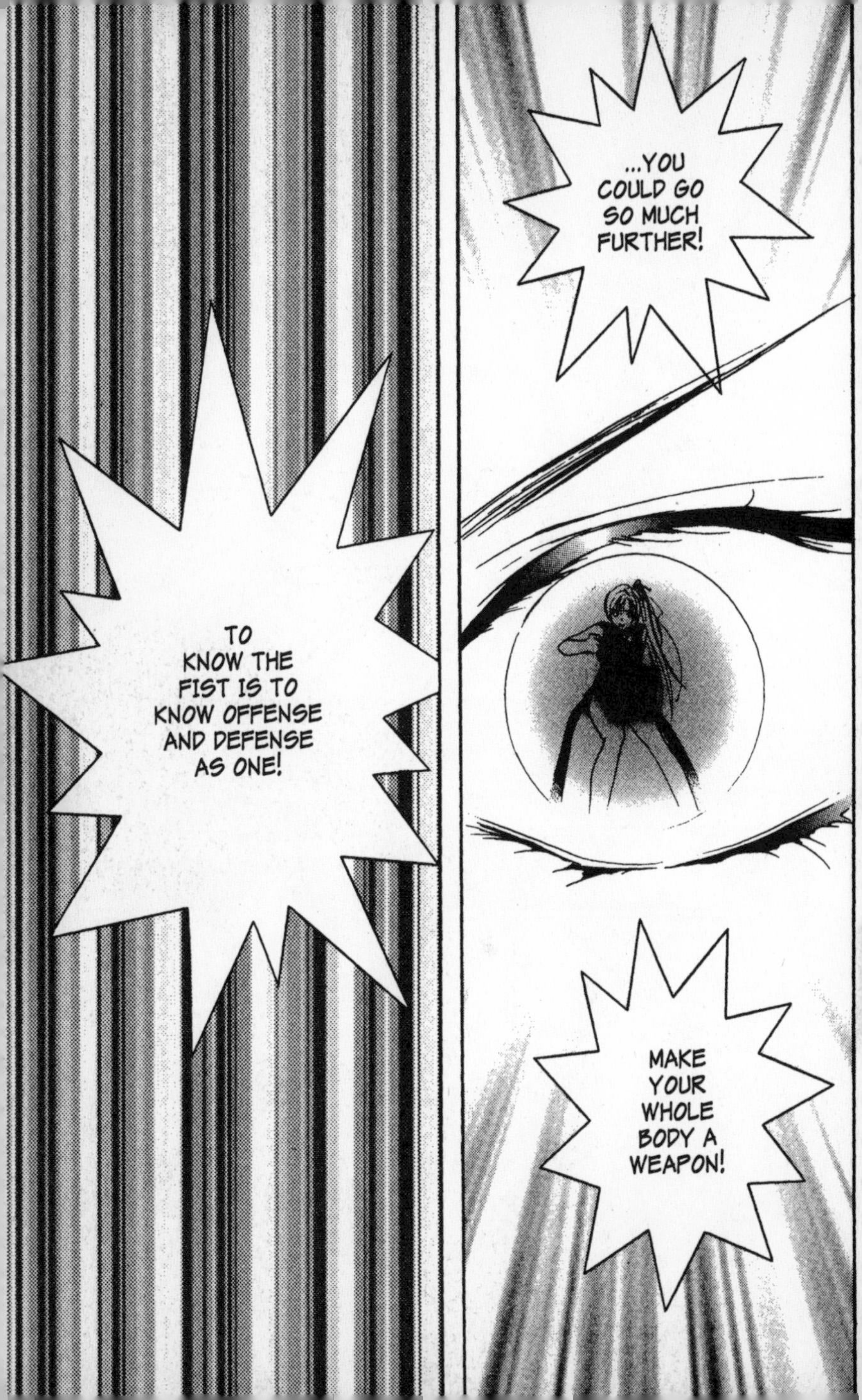
...YOU COULD GO SO MUCH FURTHER!
MAKE YOUR WHOLE BODY A WEAPON!
TO KNOW THE FIST IS TO KNOW OFFENSE AND DEFENSE AS ONE!

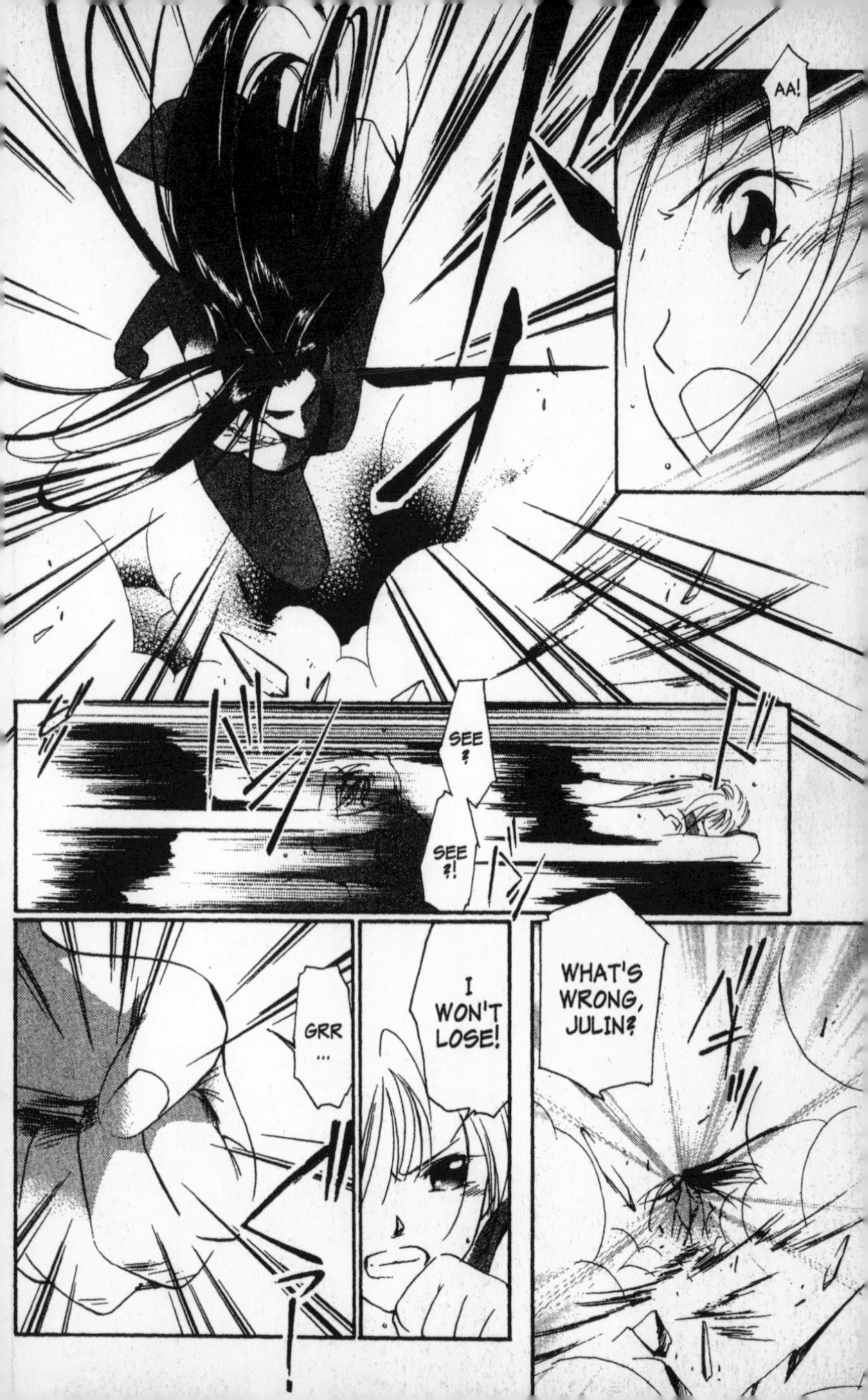
AA!
SEE?
SEE?!
WHAT'S WRONG, JULIN?
I WON'T LOSE!
GRR...

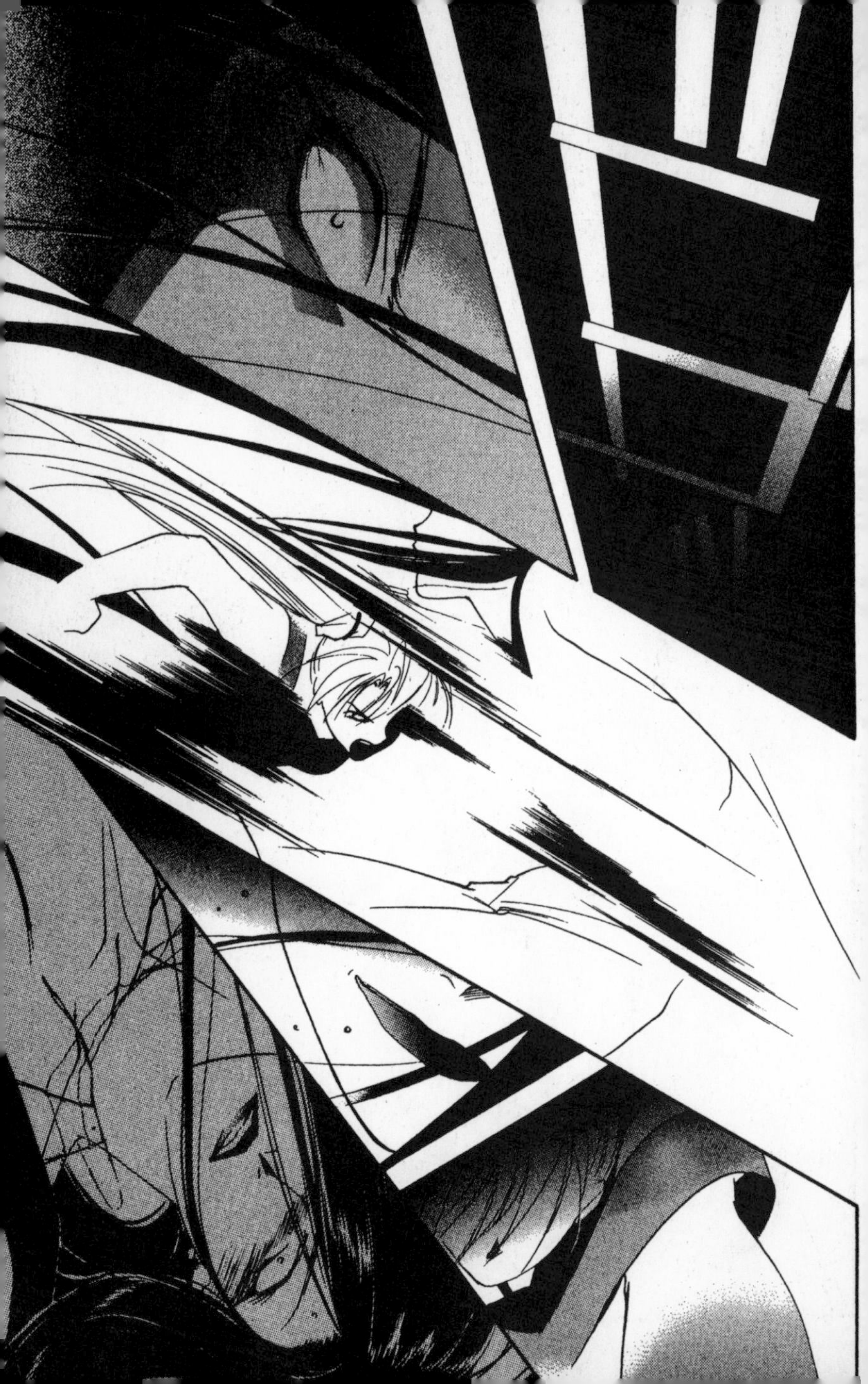

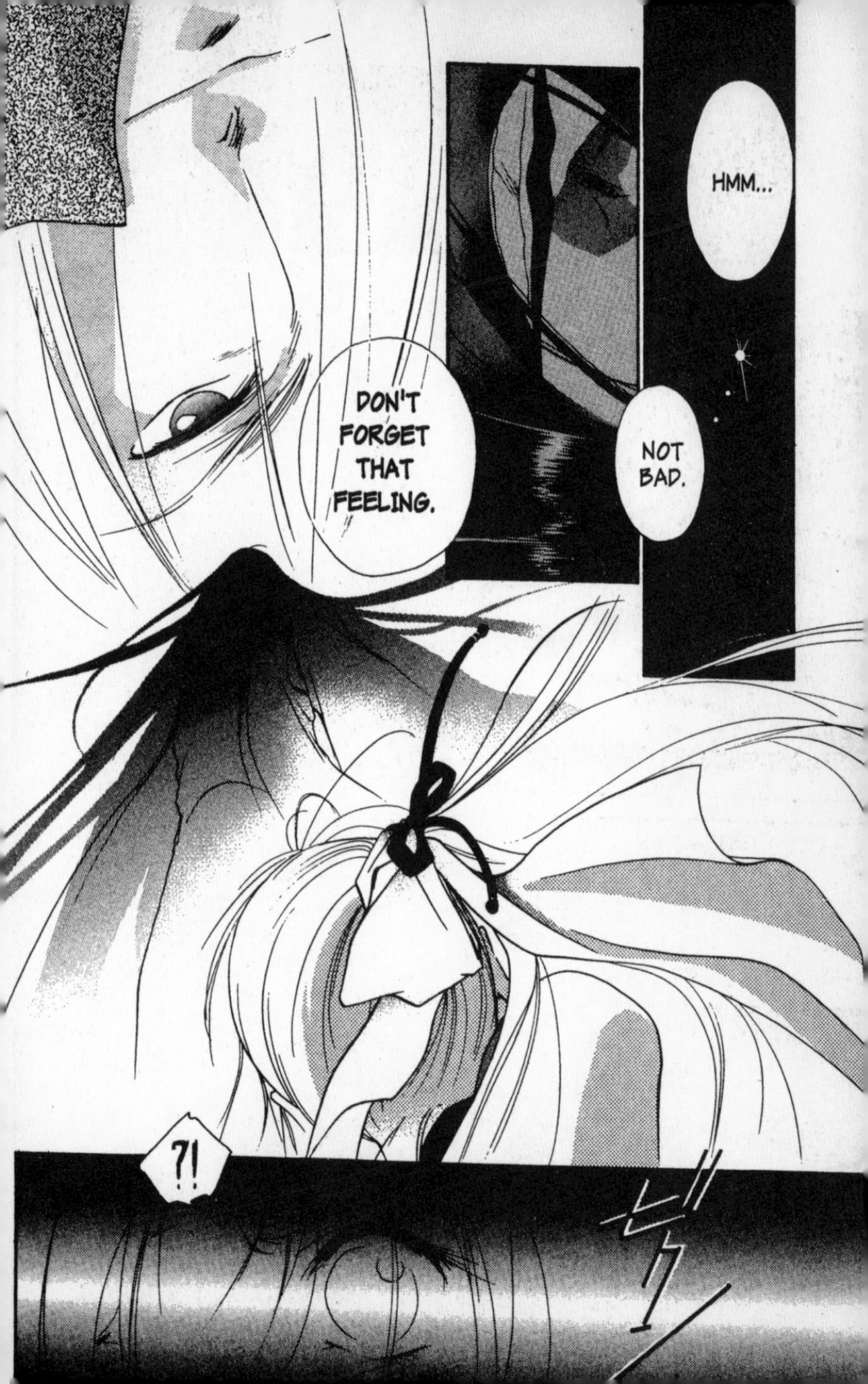
HMM...
NOT BAD.
DON'T FORGET THAT FEELING.
?!

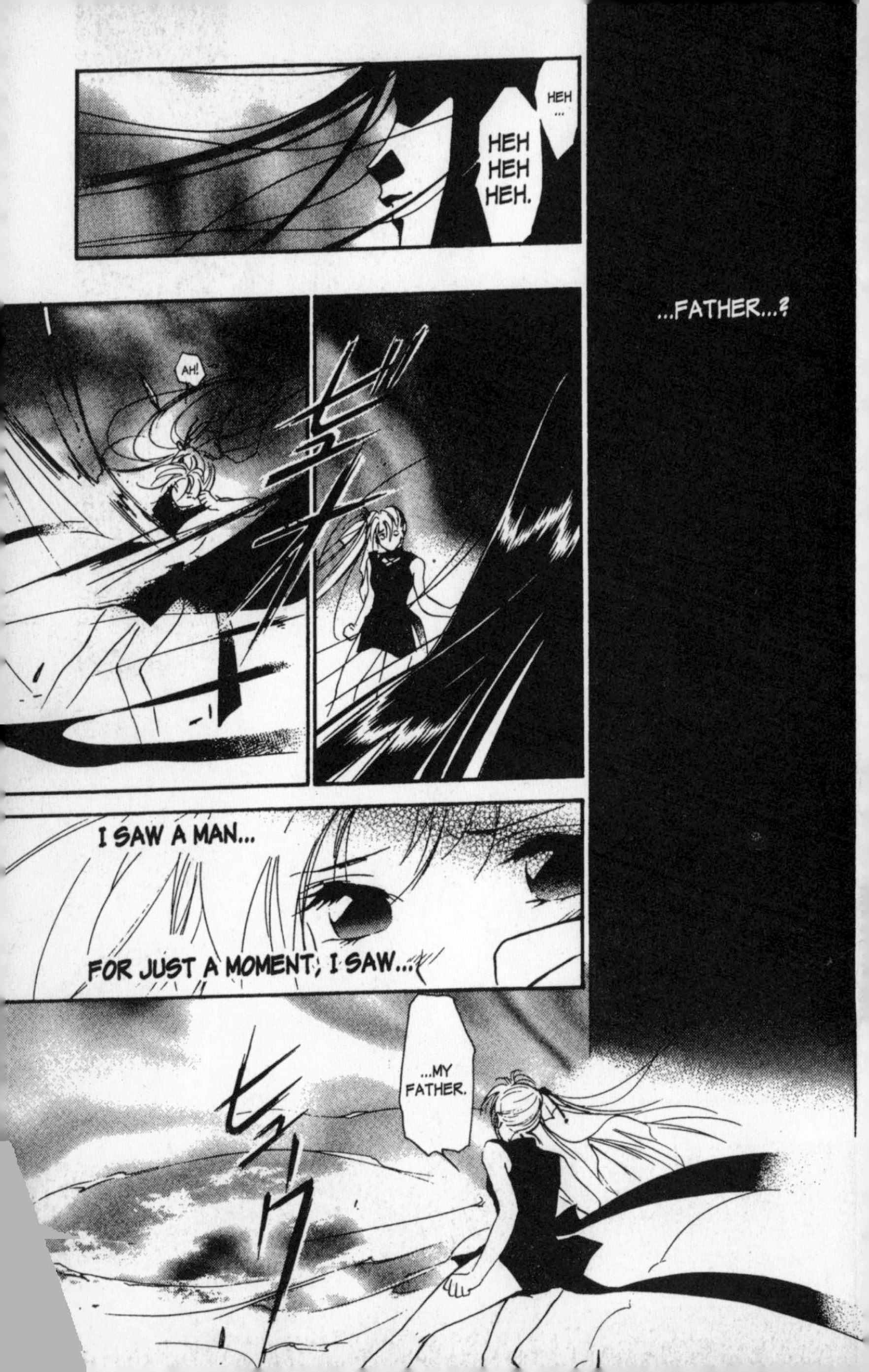
...FATHER...?
HEH ...
HEH HEH HEH.
AH!
I SAW A MAN...
FOR JUST A MOMENT, I SAW...
...MY FATHER.

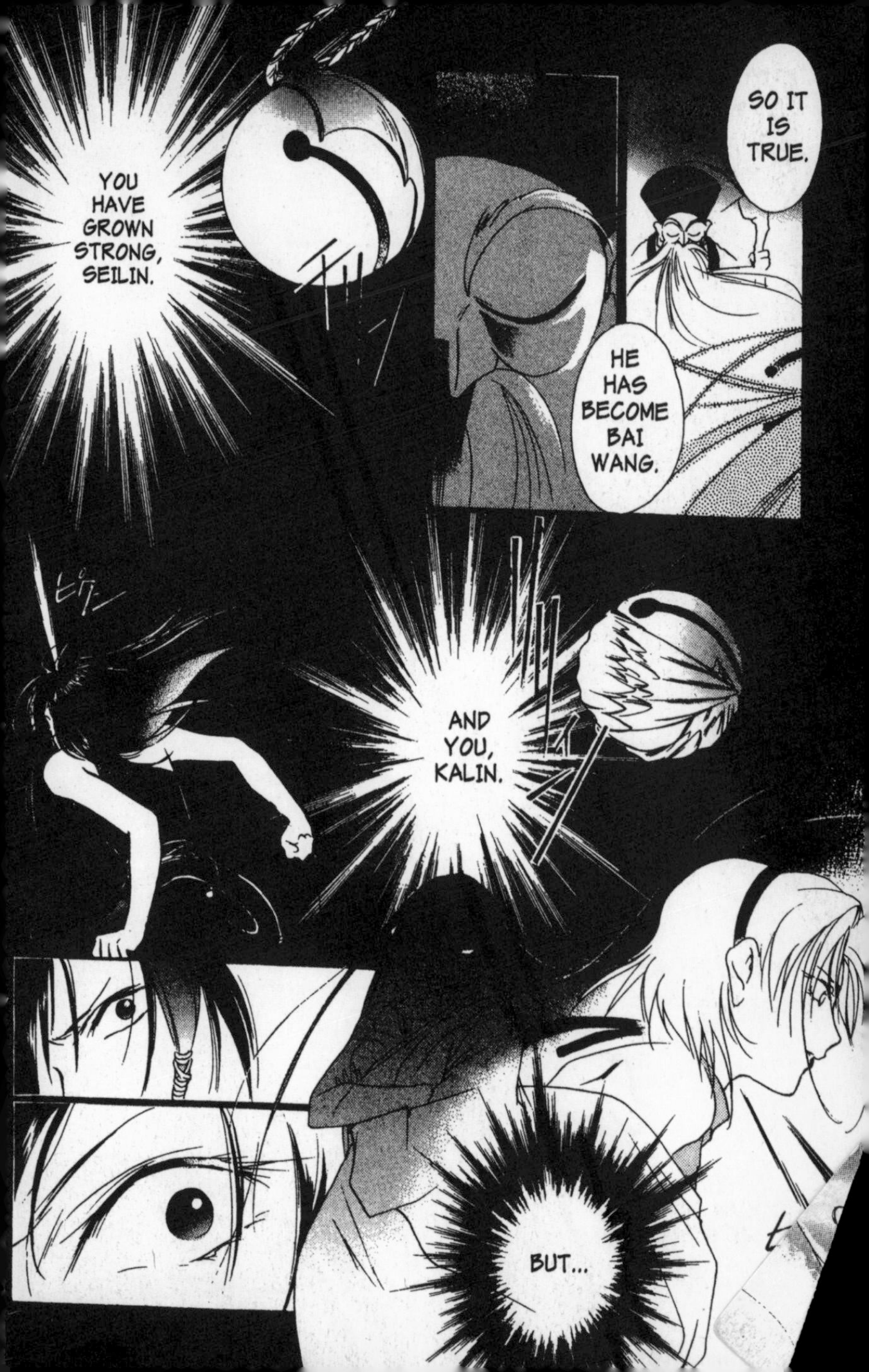
SO IT IS TRUE.
HE HAS BECOME BAI WANG.
YOU HAVE GROWN STRONG, SEILIN.
AND YOU, KALIN.
BUT...

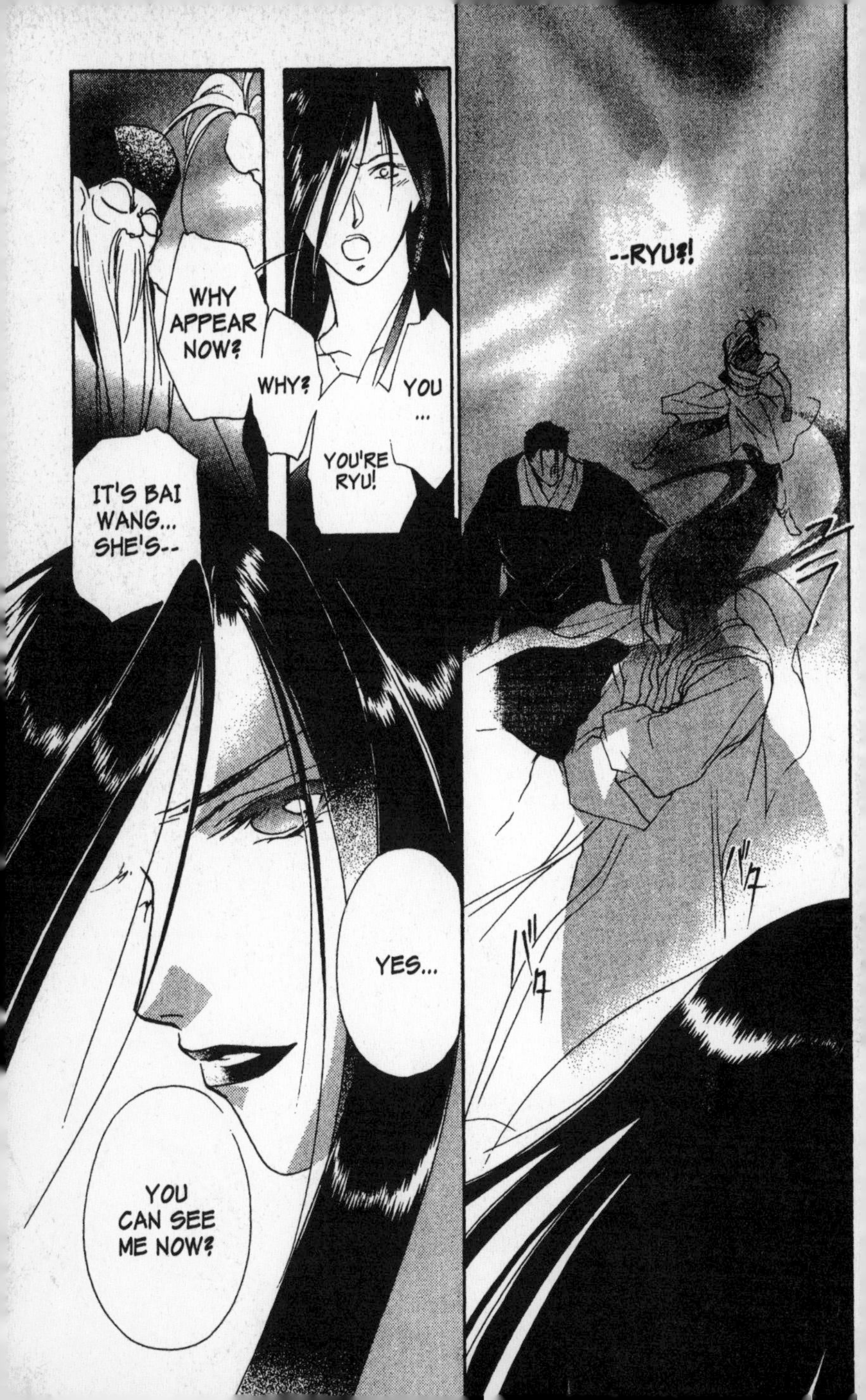
--RYU?!
YOU ...
YOU'RE RYU!
WHY?
WHY APPEAR NOW?
IT'S BAI WANG... SHE'S--
YES...
YOU CAN SEE ME NOW?

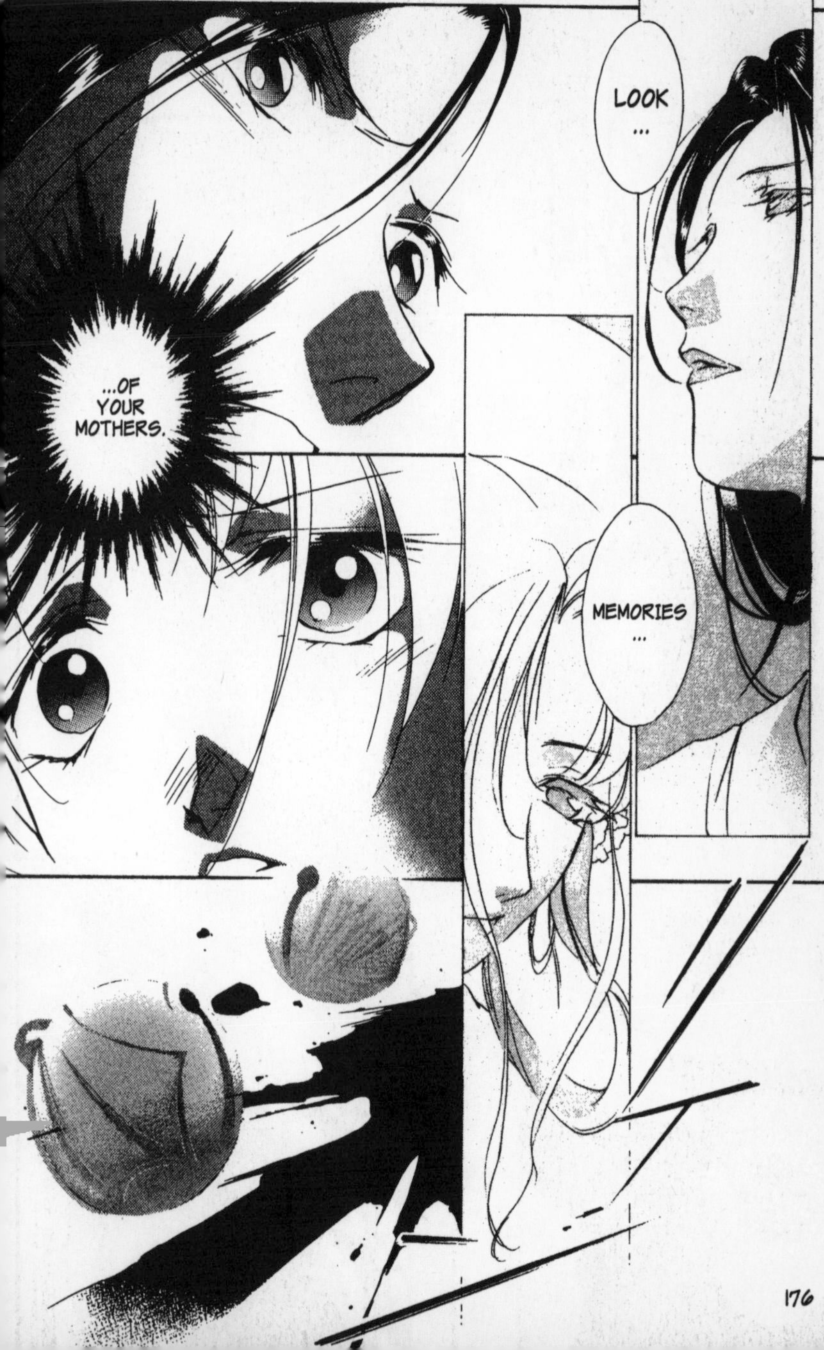
LOOK ...
MEMORIES ...
...OF YOUR MOTHERS.

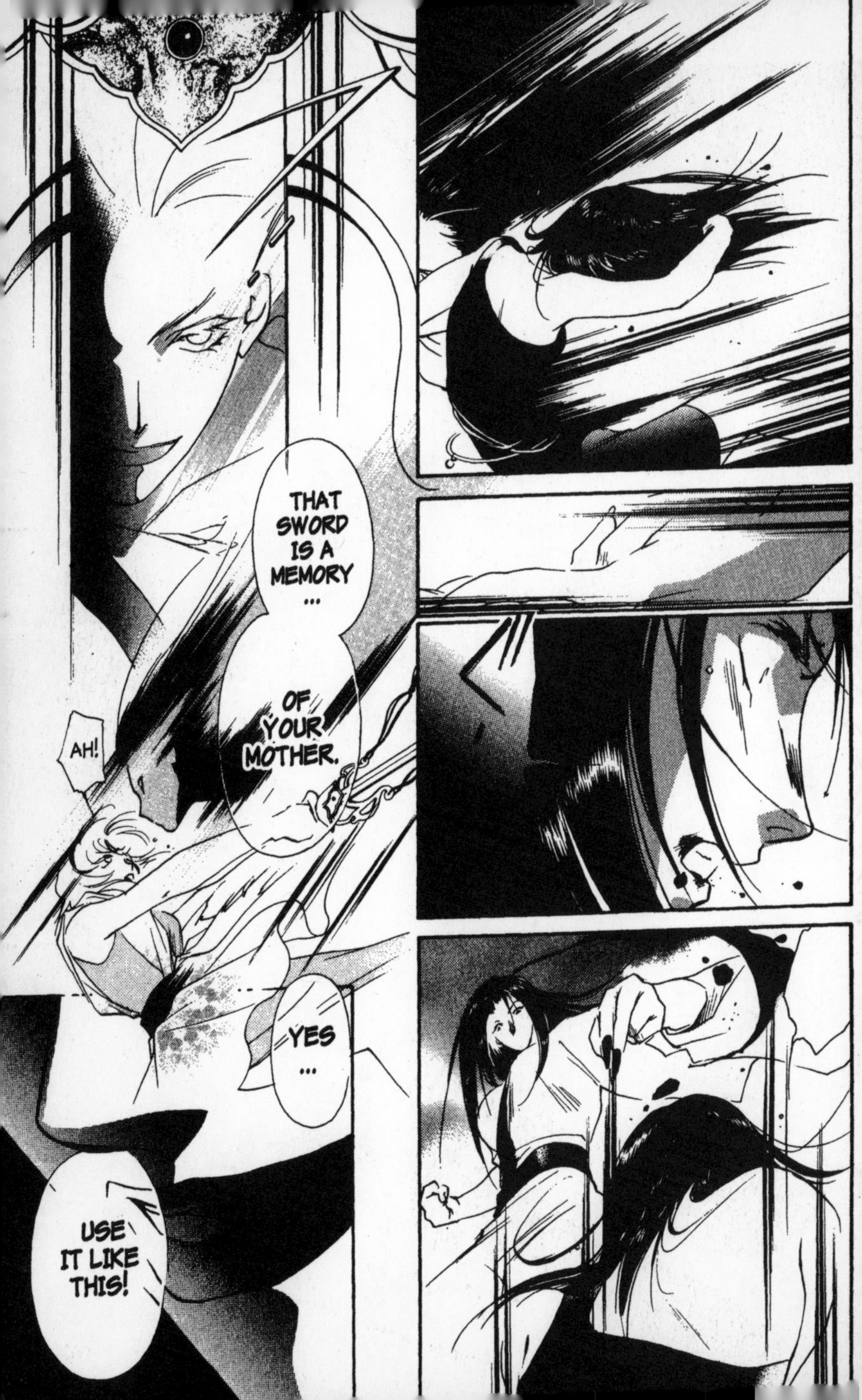
THAT SWORD IS A MEMORY ...
OF YOUR MOTHER.
AH!
YES ...
USE IT LIKE THIS!

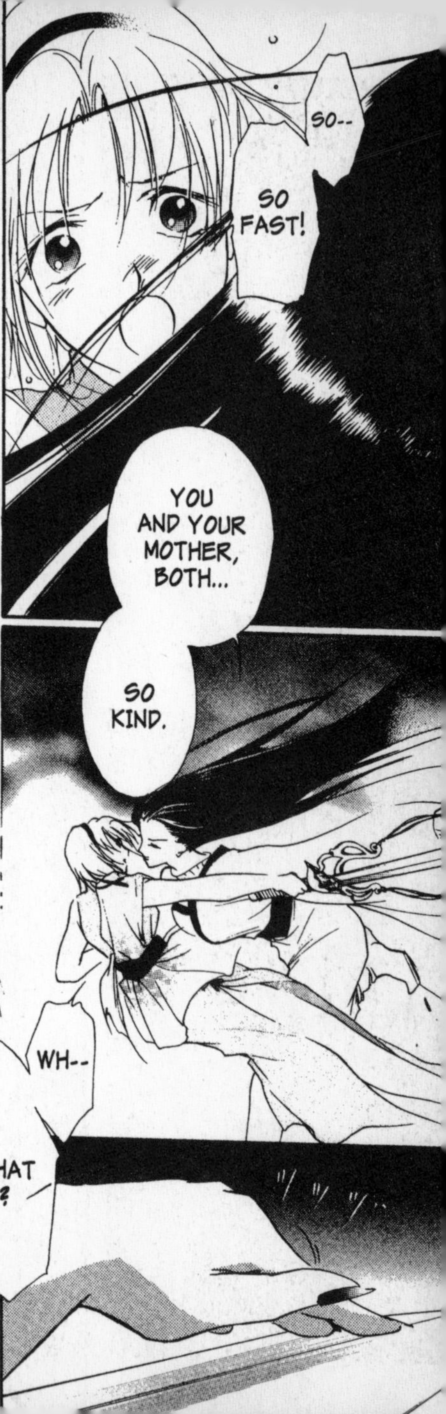
SO--
SO FAST!
YOU AND YOUR MOTHER, BOTH...
SO KIND.
WH--
WHAT?
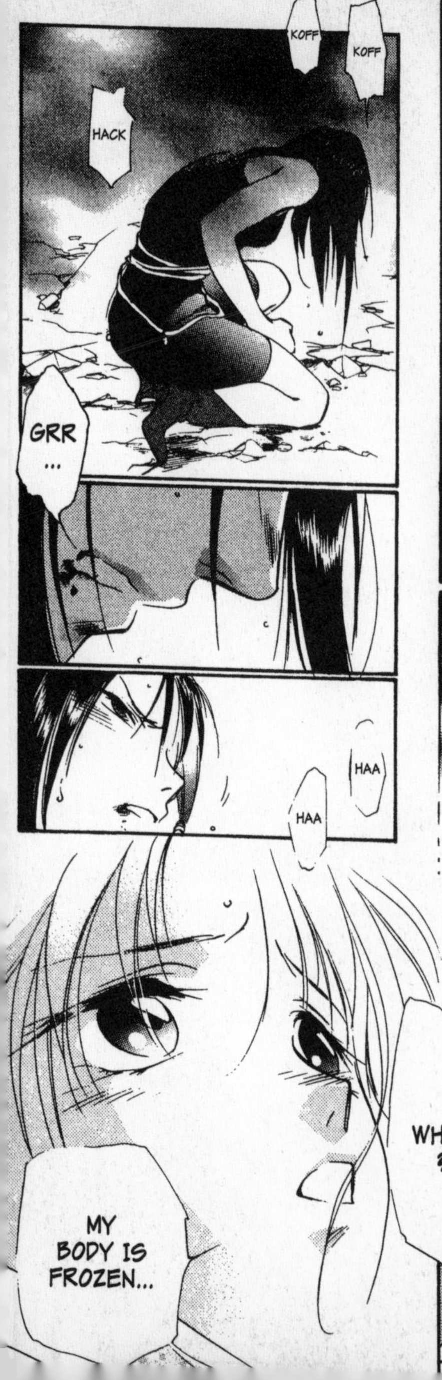
KOFF
KOFF
HACK
GRR...
HAA
HAA
MY BODY IS FROZEN...

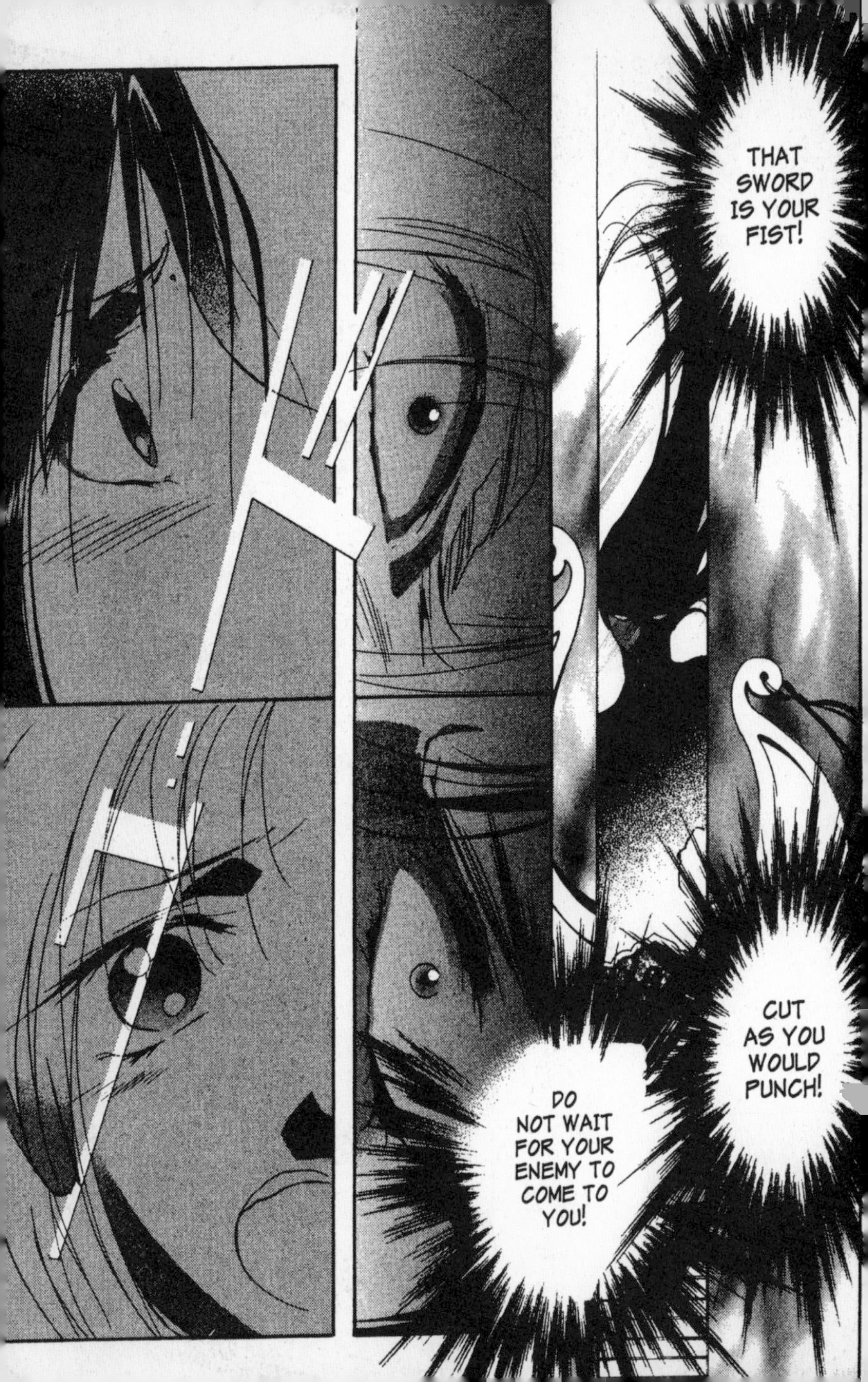
THAT SWORD IS YOUR FIST!
CUT AS YOU WOULD PUNCH!
DO NOT WAIT FOR YOUR ENEMY TO COME TO YOU!

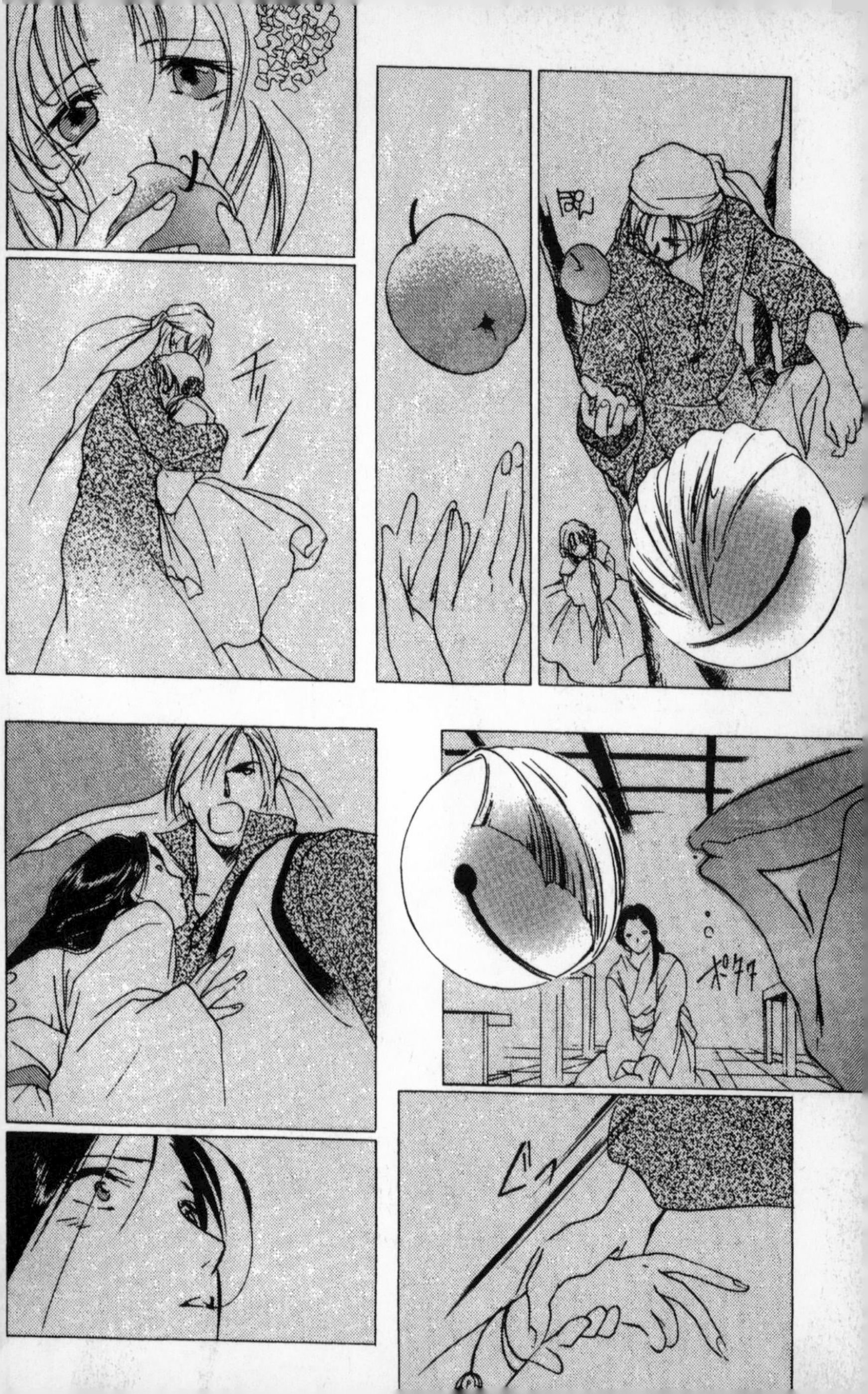
ぽん
チリーン

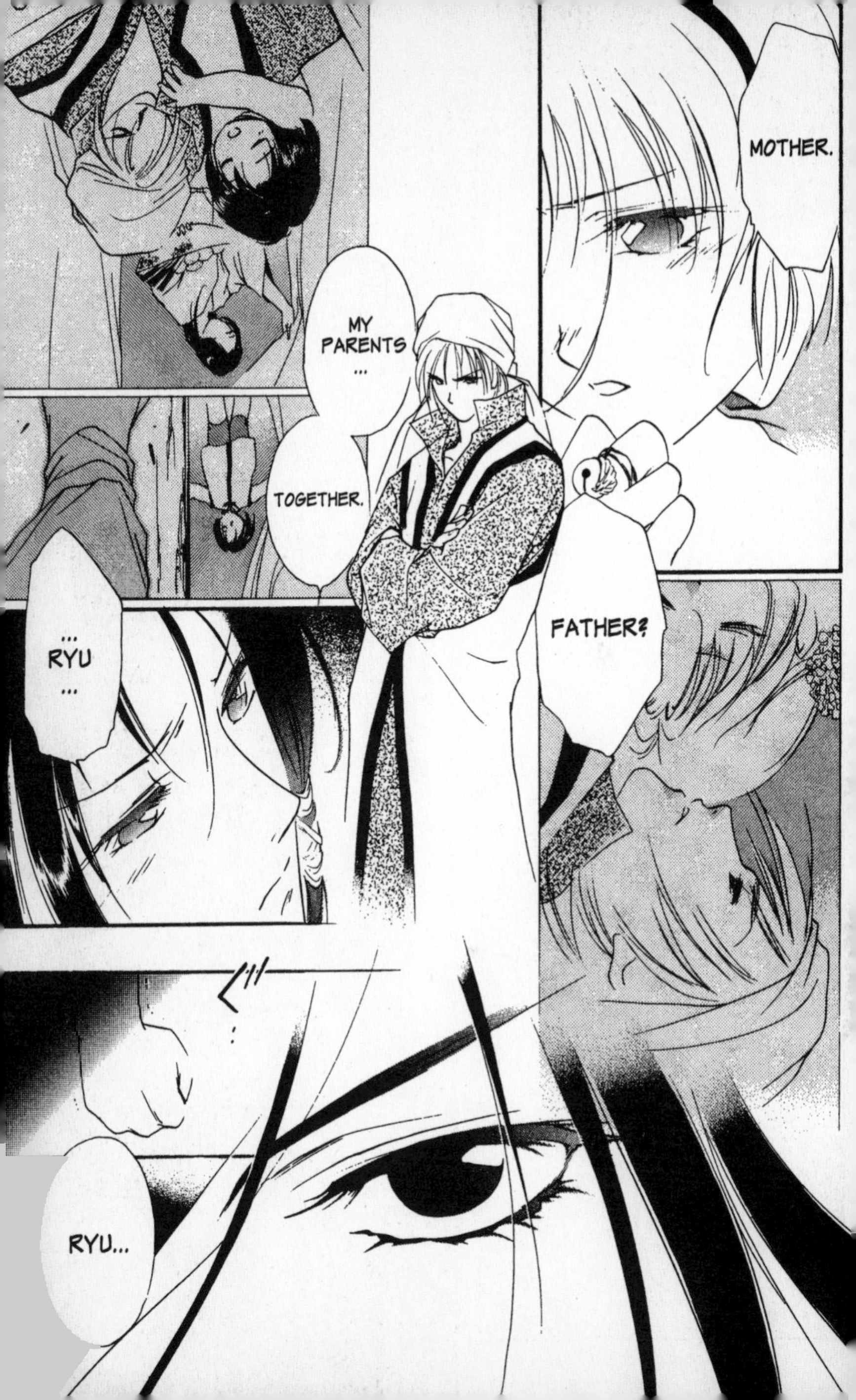
MOTHER.
FATHER?
MY PARENTS ...
TOGETHER.
... RYU ...
RYU...

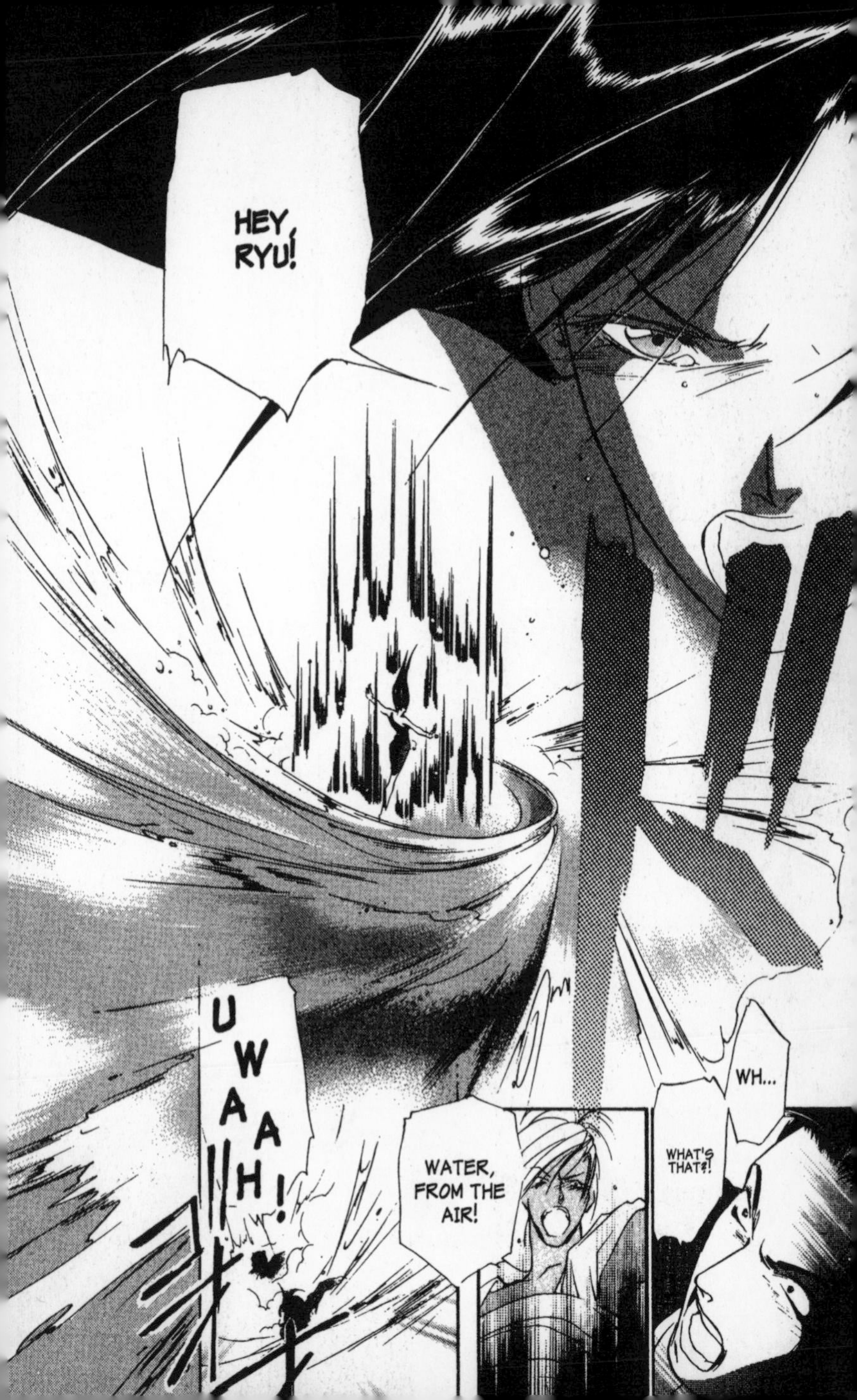
HEY, RYU!
UWAAH!
WH...
WHAT'S THAT?!
WATER, FROM THE AIR!

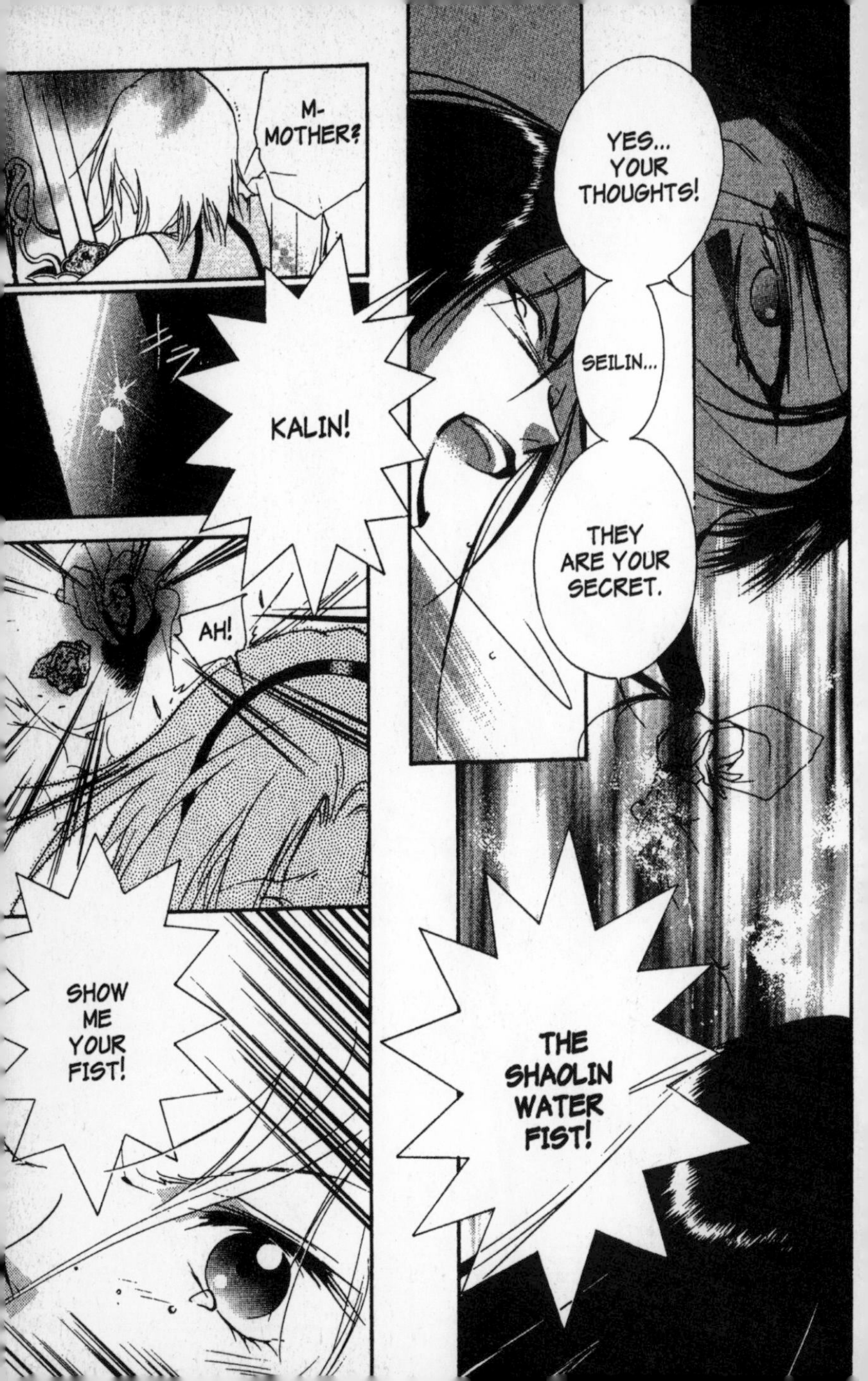
YES... YOUR THOUGHTS!
SEILIN...
THEY ARE YOUR SECRET.
THE SHAOLIN WATER FIST!
M- MOTHER?
KALIN!
AH!
SHOW ME YOUR FIST!

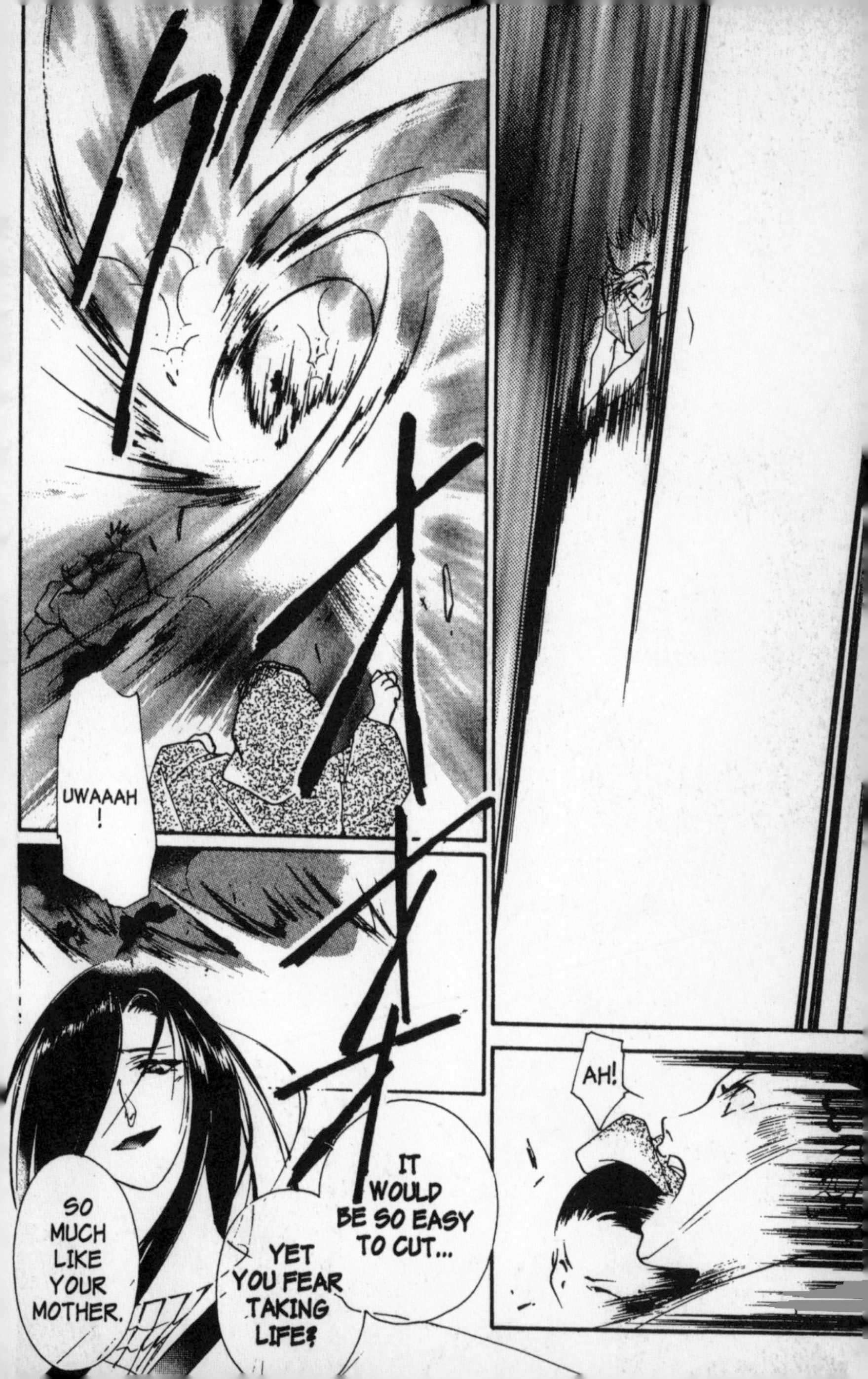
UWAAAH!
AH!
IT WOULD BE SO EASY TO CUT...
YET YOU FEAR TAKING LIFE?
SO MUCH LIKE YOUR MOTHER.

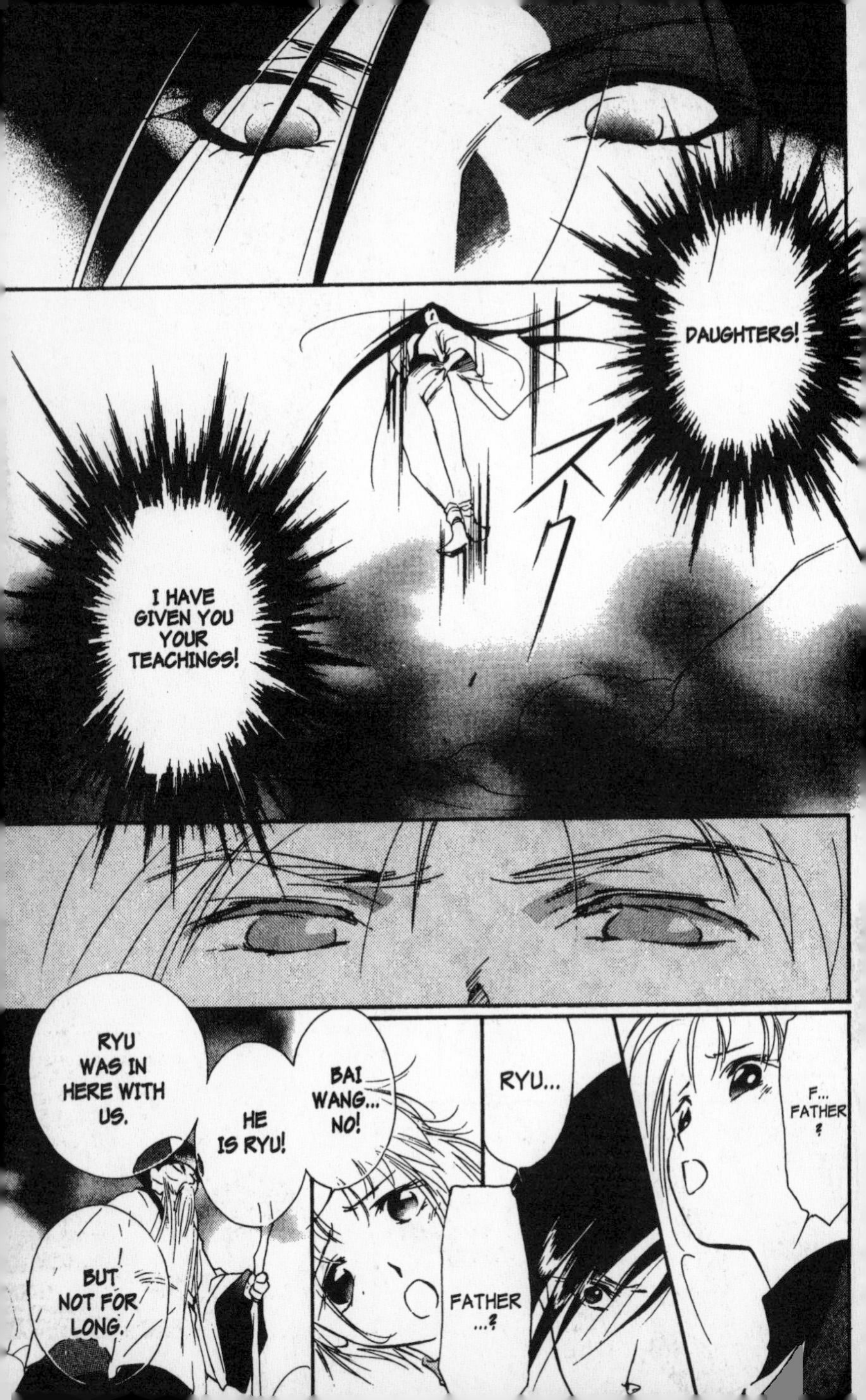
DAUGHTERS!
I HAVE GIVEN YOU YOUR TEACHINGS!
F... FATHER?
RYU...
FATHER ...?
BAI WANG... NO!
RYU WAS IN HERE WITH US.
HE IS RYU!
BUT NOT FOR LONG.

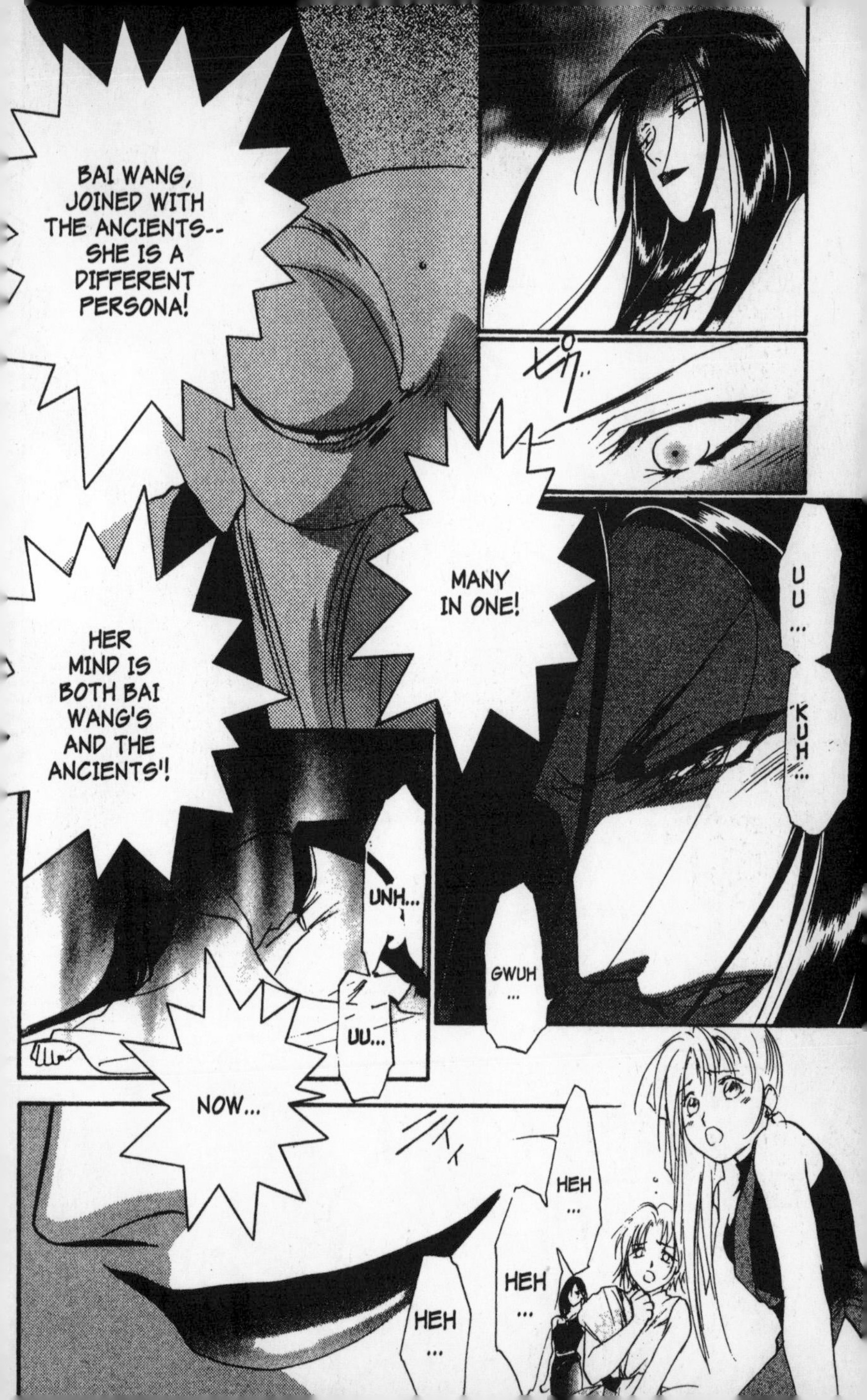
UU... KUH...
GWUH...
BAI WANG, JOINED WITH THE ANCIENTS-- SHE IS A DIFFERENT PERSONA!
MANY IN ONE!
HER MIND IS BOTH BAI WANG'S AND THE ANCIENTS'!
UNH...
UU...
NOW...
HEH...
HEH...
HEH...

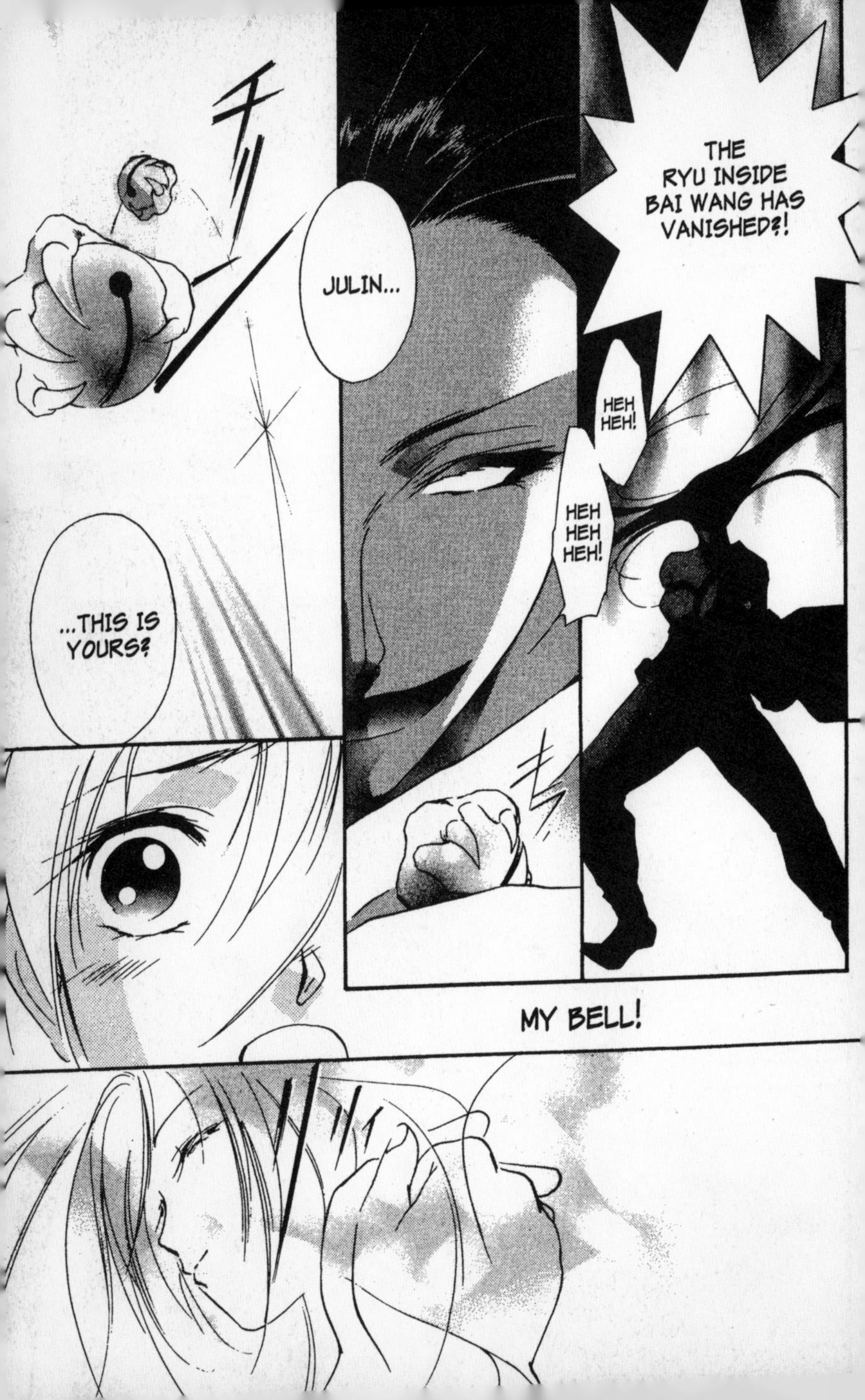
THE RYU INSIDE BAI WANG HAS VANISHED?!
HEH HEH!
HEH HEH HEH!
JULIN...
...THIS IS YOURS?
MY BELL!

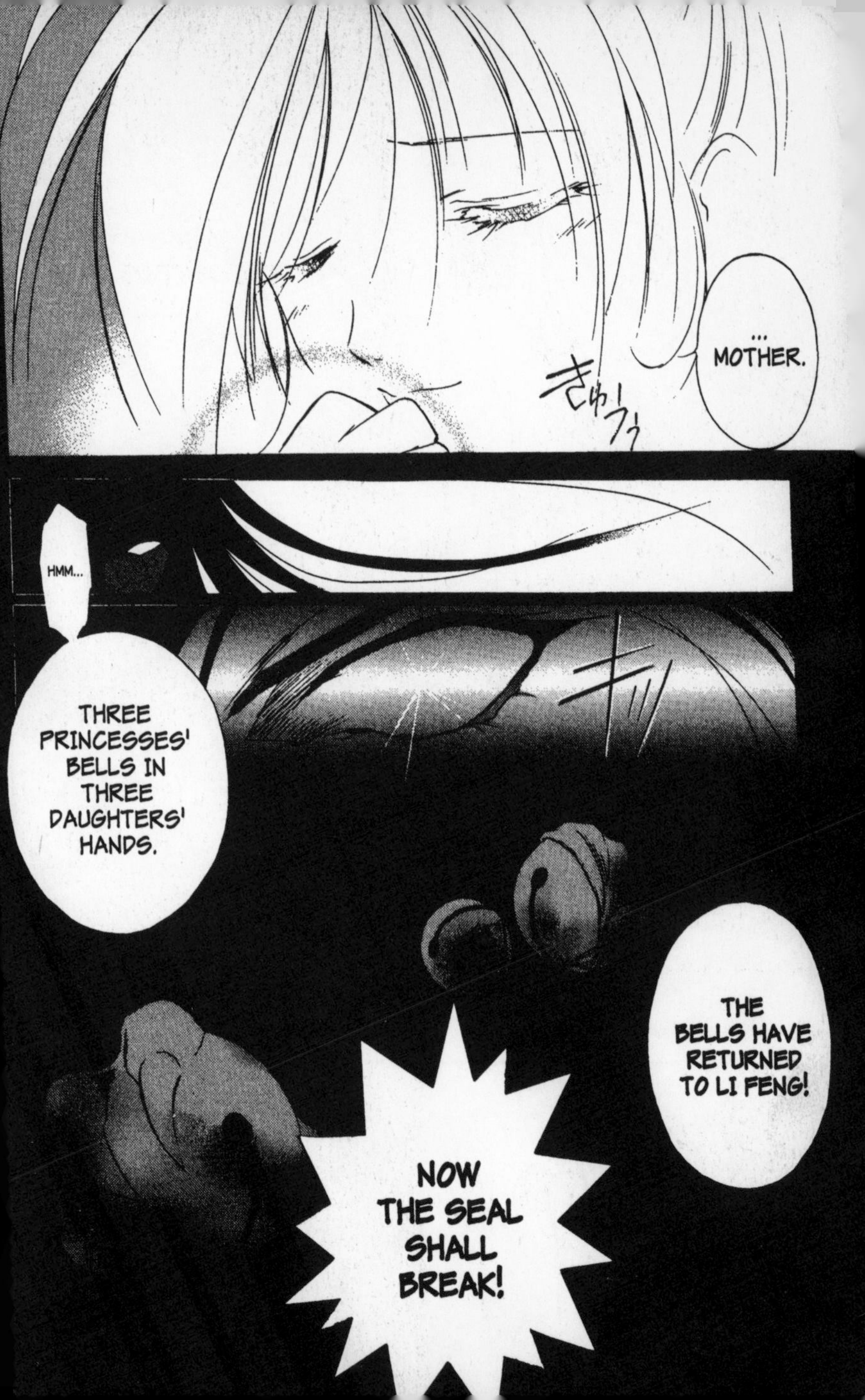
... MOTHER.
HMM...
THREE PRINCESSES' BELLS IN THREE DAUGHTERS' HANDS.
THE BELLS HAVE RETURNED TO LI FENG!
NOW THE SEAL SHALL BREAK!

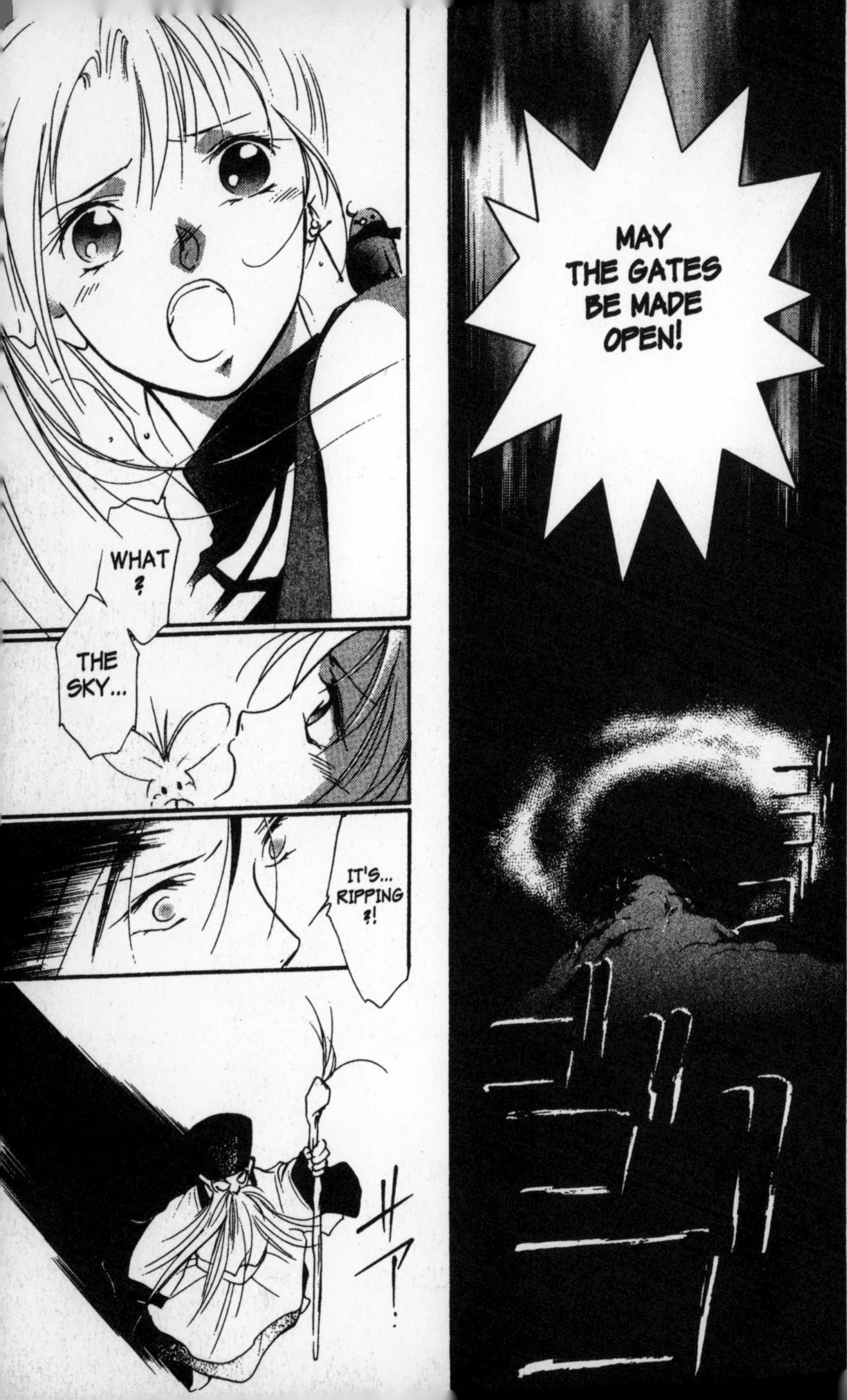
MAY THE GATES BE MADE OPEN!
WHAT?
THE SKY...
IT'S... RIPPING?!

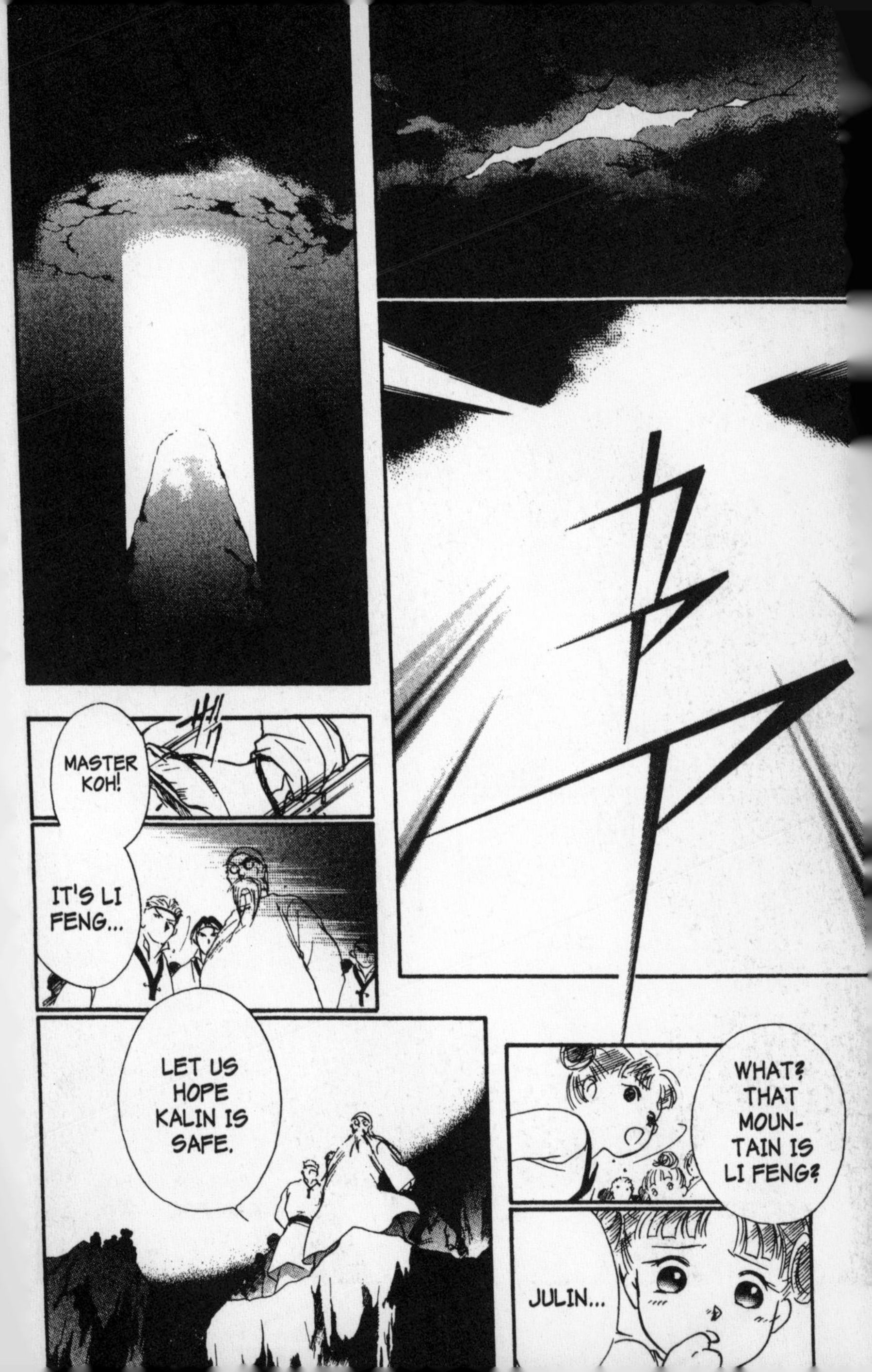
MASTER KOH!
IT'S LI FENG...
WHAT? THAT MOUN-TAIN IS LI FENG?
JULIN...
LET US HOPE KALIN IS SAFE.

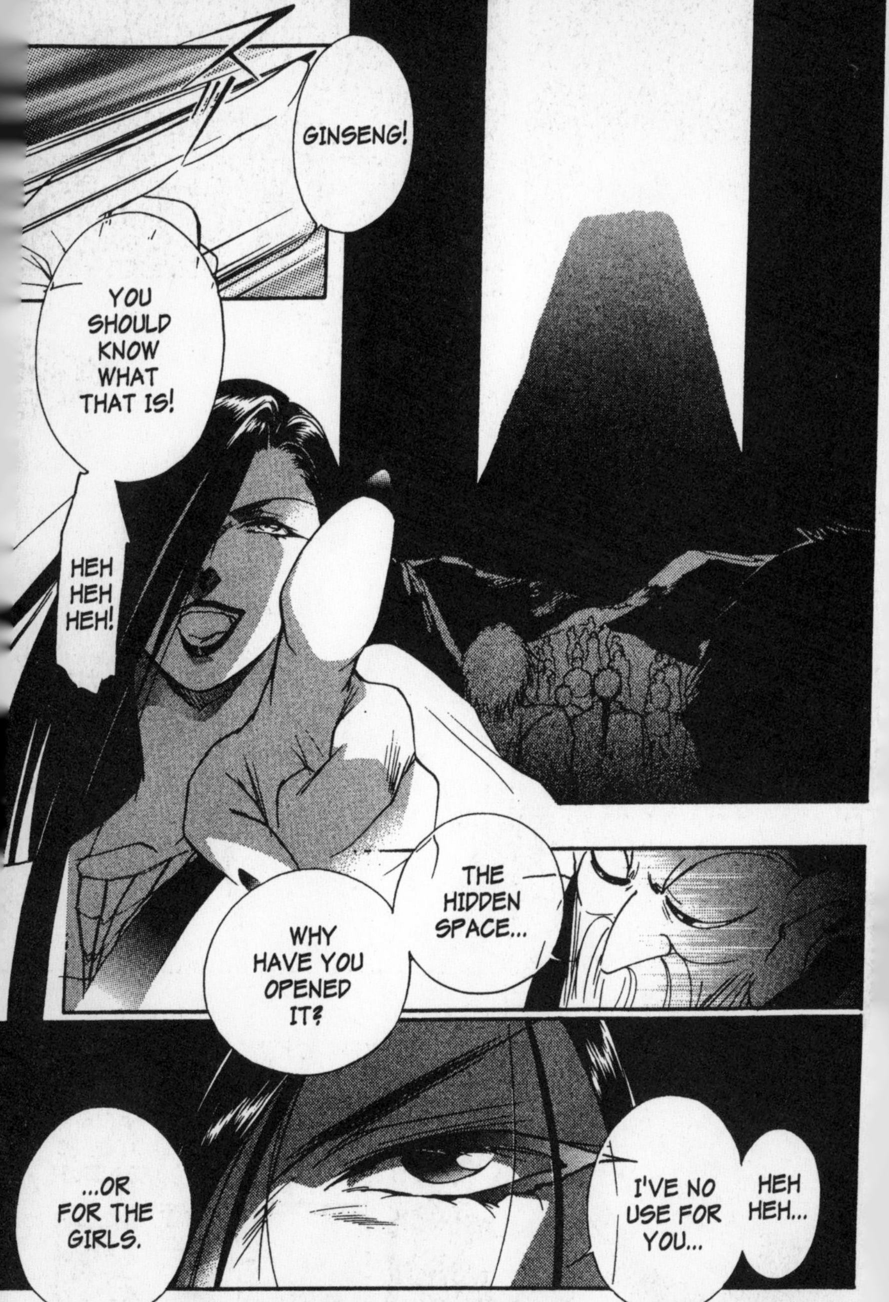
GINSENG!
YOU SHOULD KNOW WHAT THAT IS!
HEH HEH HEH!
THE HIDDEN SPACE...
WHY HAVE YOU OPENED IT?
HEH HEH...
I'VE NO USE FOR YOU...
...OR FOR THE GIRLS.

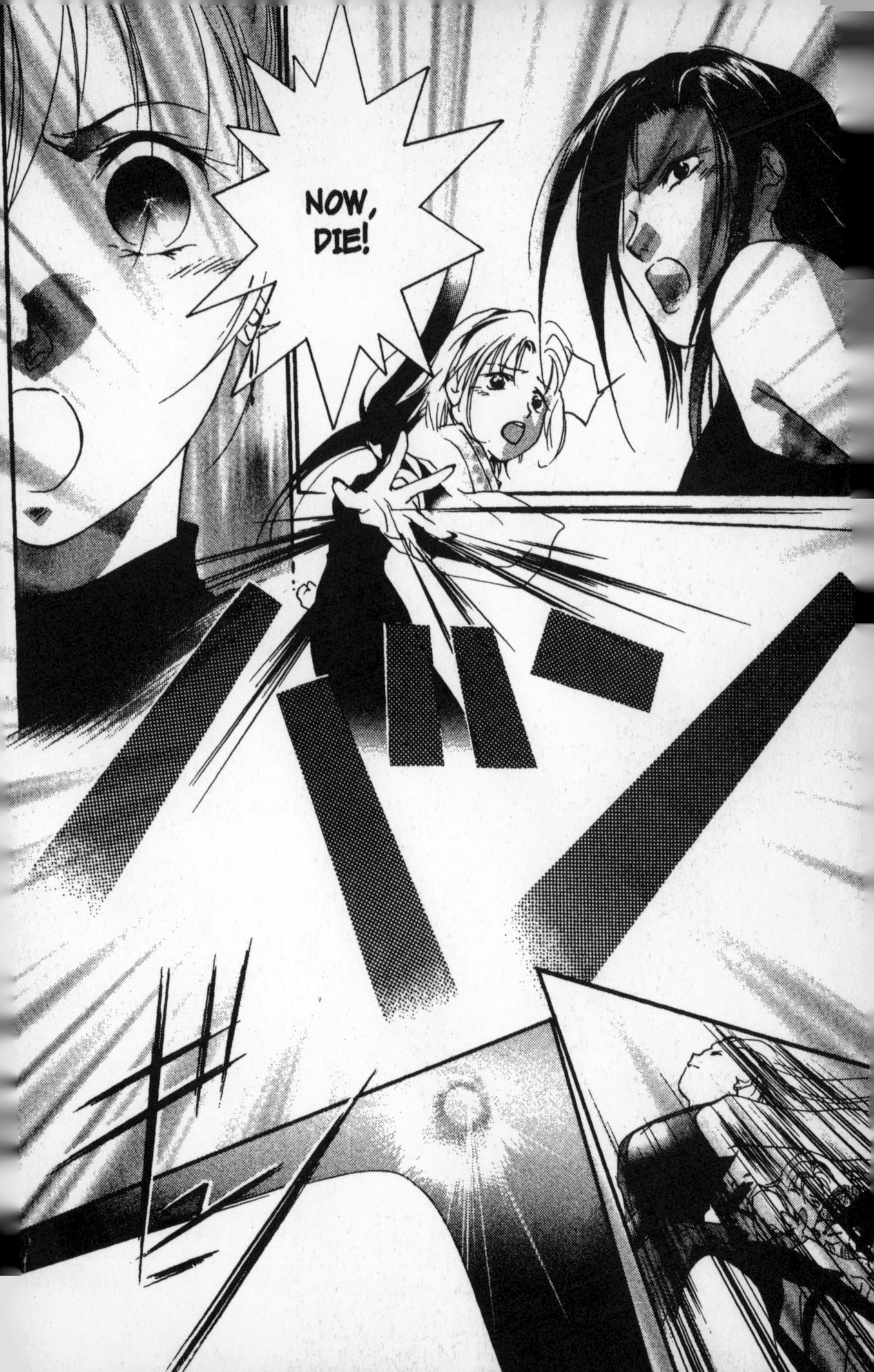
NOW, DIE!

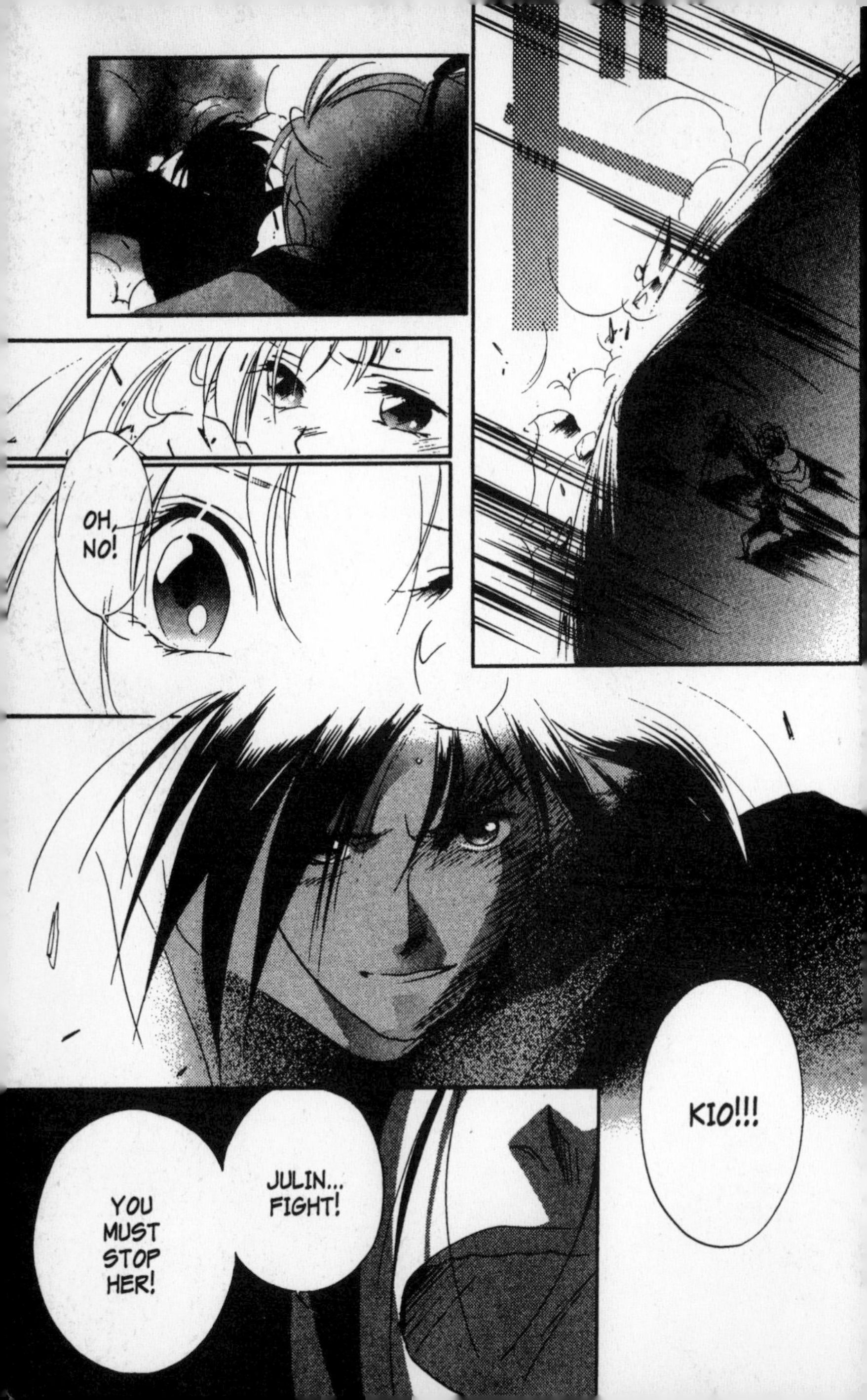
OH, NO!
KIO!!!
JULIN... FIGHT!
YOU MUST STOP HER!

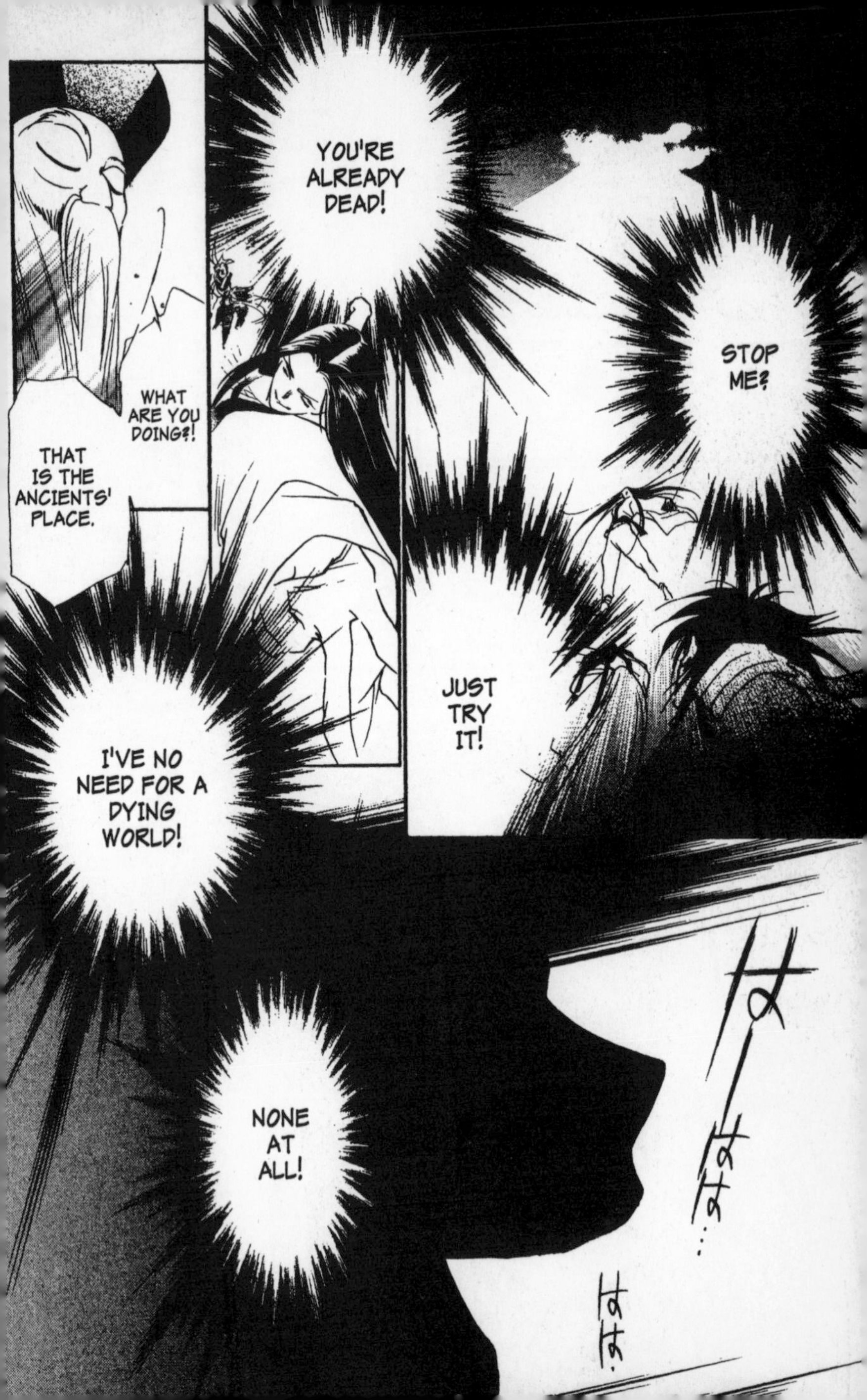
STOP ME?
JUST TRY IT!
YOU'RE ALREADY DEAD!
WHAT ARE YOU DOING?!
THAT IS THE ANCIENTS' PLACE.
I'VE NO NEED FOR A DYING WORLD!
NONE AT ALL!
は—はは…
はは

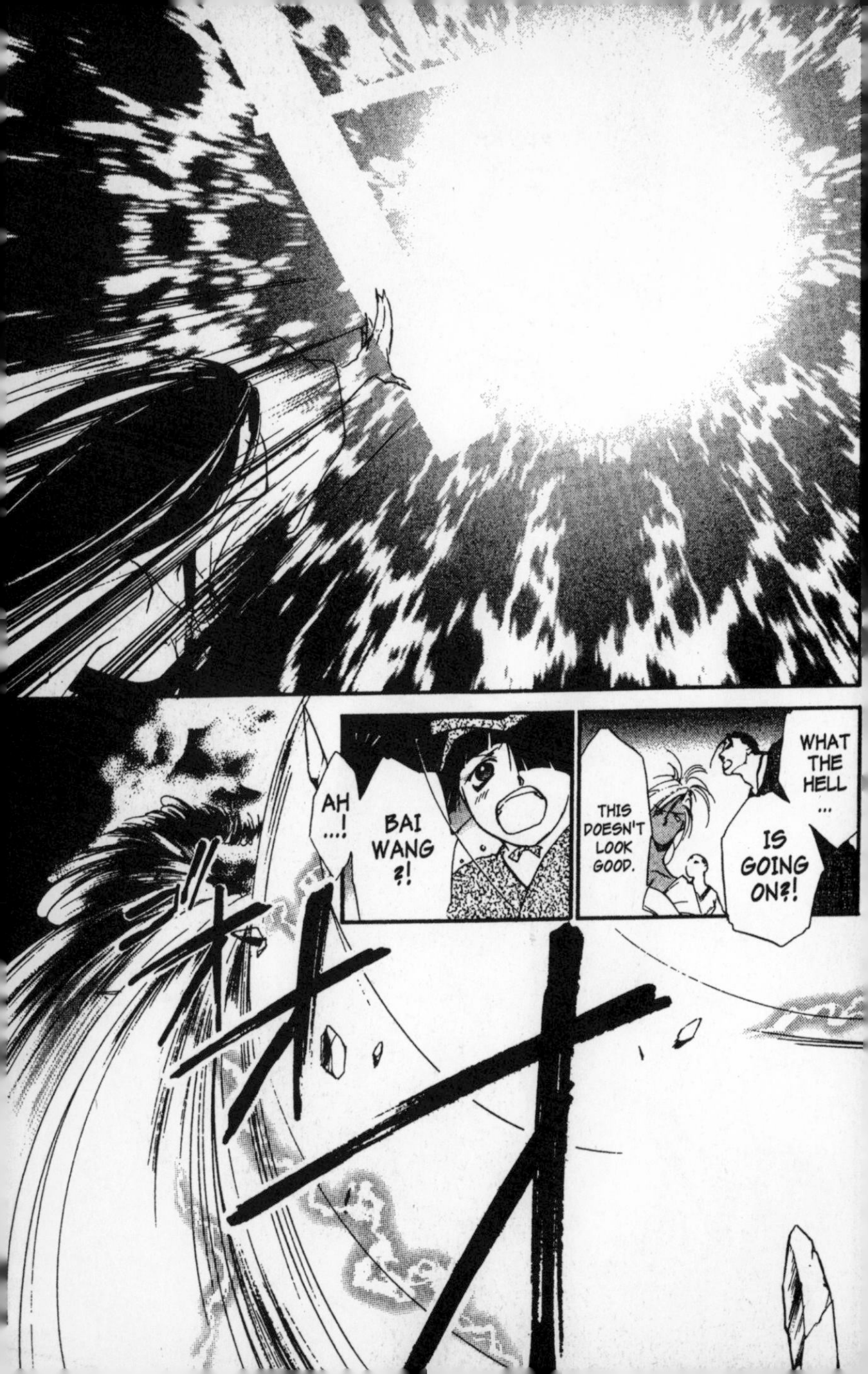
WHAT THE HELL ...
IS GOING ON?!
THIS DOESN'T LOOK GOOD.
BAI WANG ?!
AH ...!

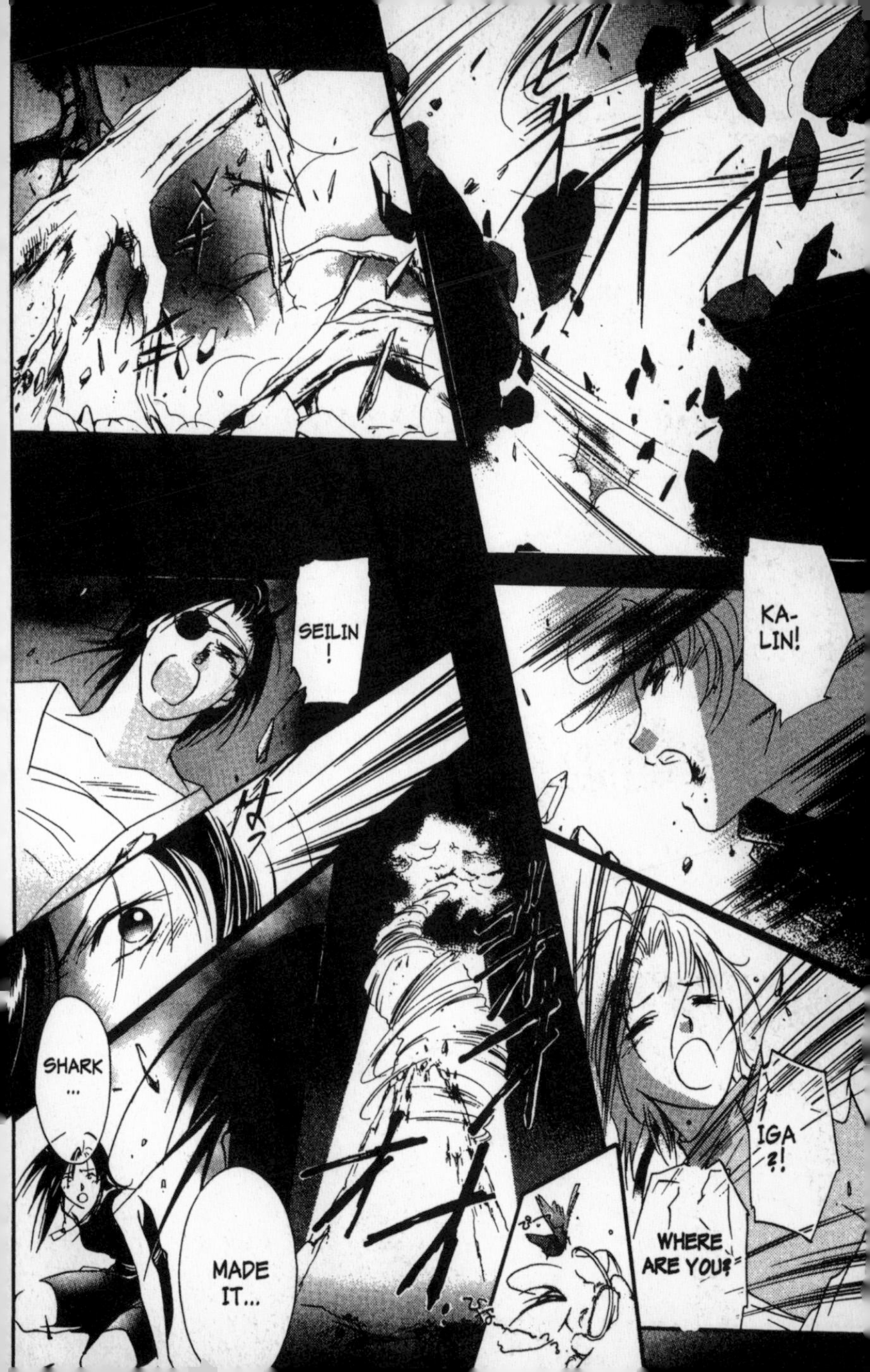
KA-LIN!
SEILIN!
IGA?!
WHERE ARE YOU?
SHARK...
MADE IT...

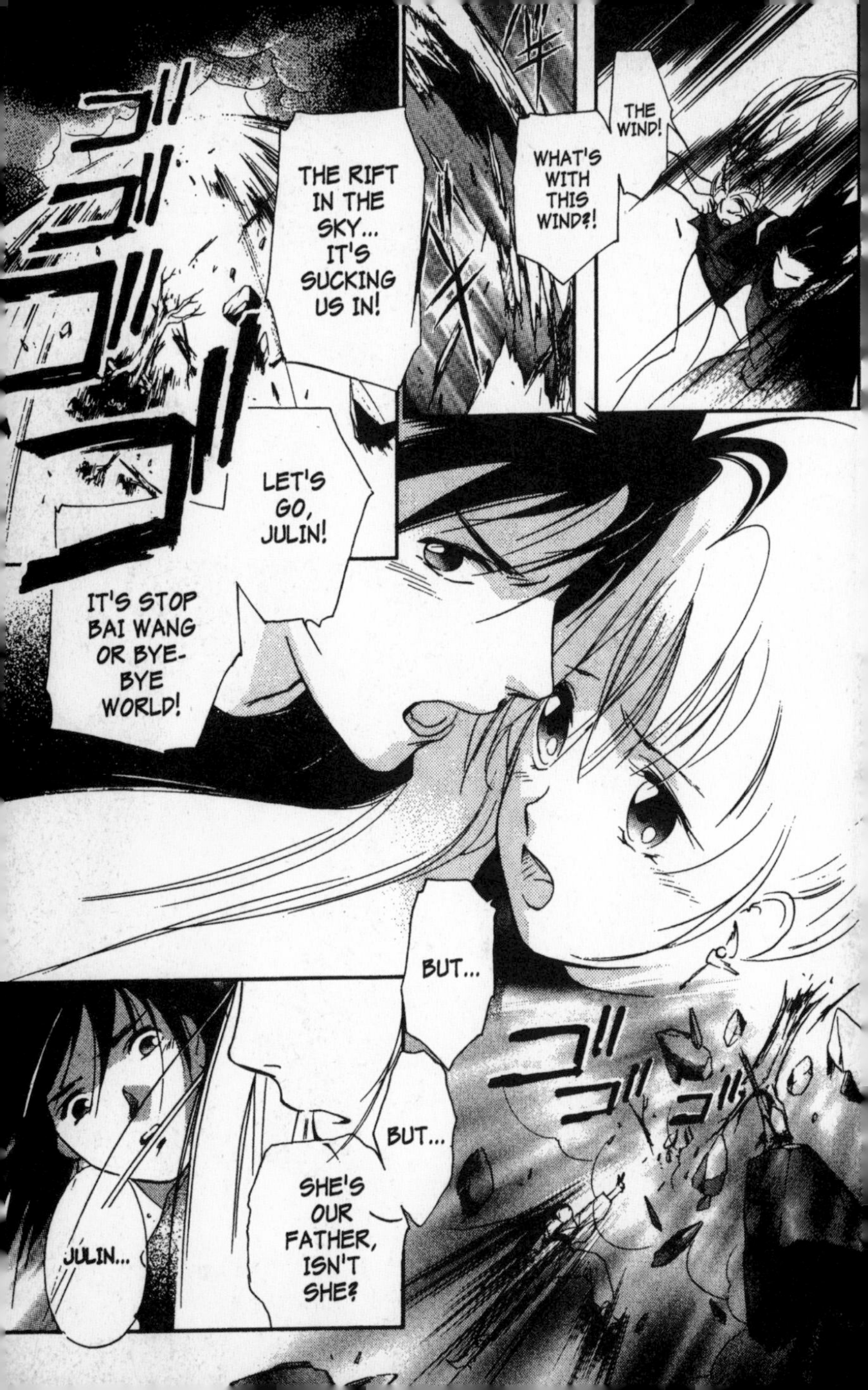
THE WIND!
WHAT'S WITH THIS WIND?!
THE RIFT IN THE SKY... IT'S SUCKING US IN!
LET'S GO, JULIN!
IT'S STOP BAI WANG OR BYE-BYE WORLD!
BUT...
BUT...
SHE'S OUR FATHER, ISN'T SHE?
JULIN...

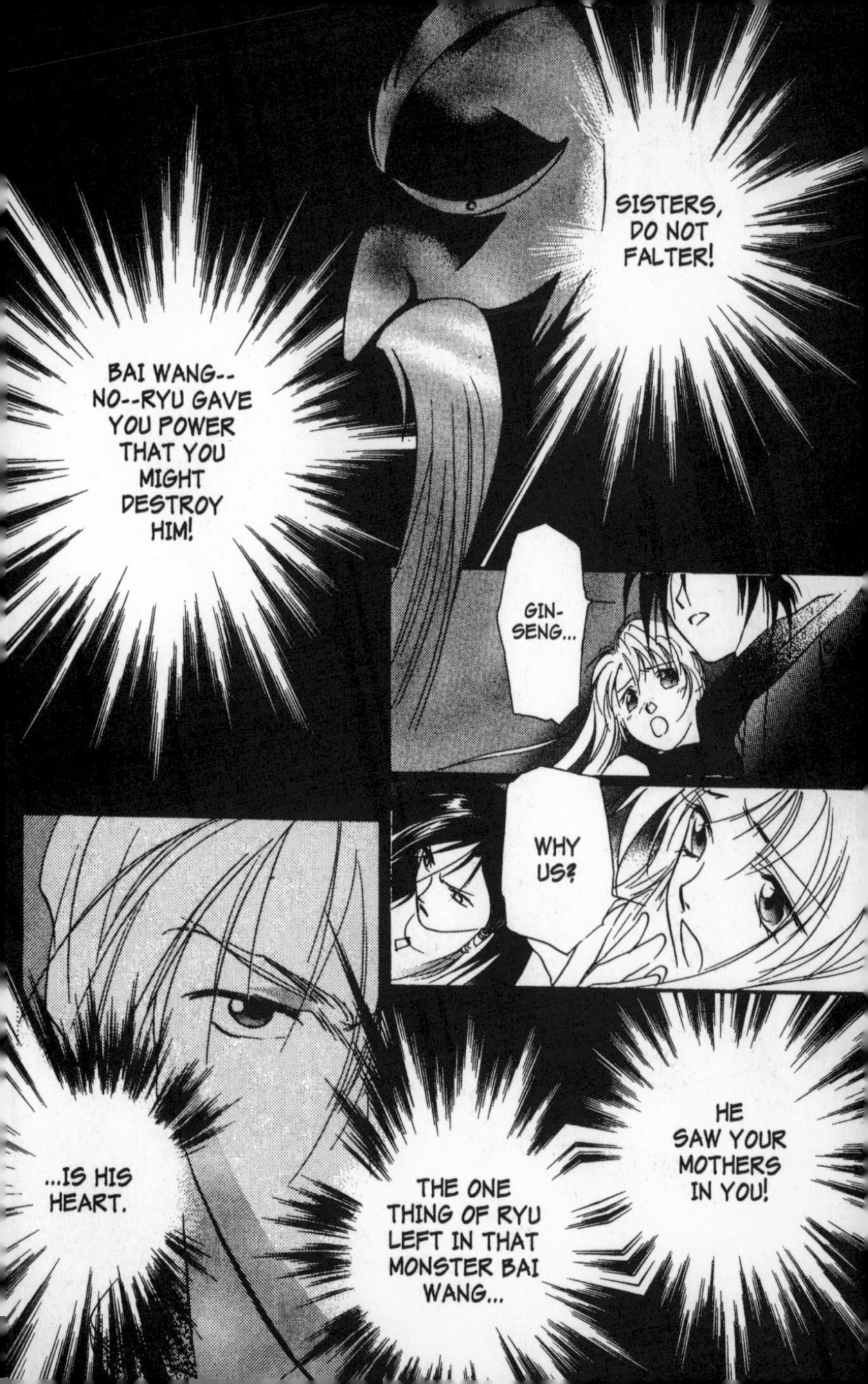
SISTERS, DO NOT FALTER!
BAI WANG--NO--RYU GAVE YOU POWER THAT YOU MIGHT DESTROY HIM!
GIN-SENG...
WHY US?
HE SAW YOUR MOTHERS IN YOU!
THE ONE THING OF RYU LEFT IN THAT MONSTER BAI WANG...
...IS HIS HEART.

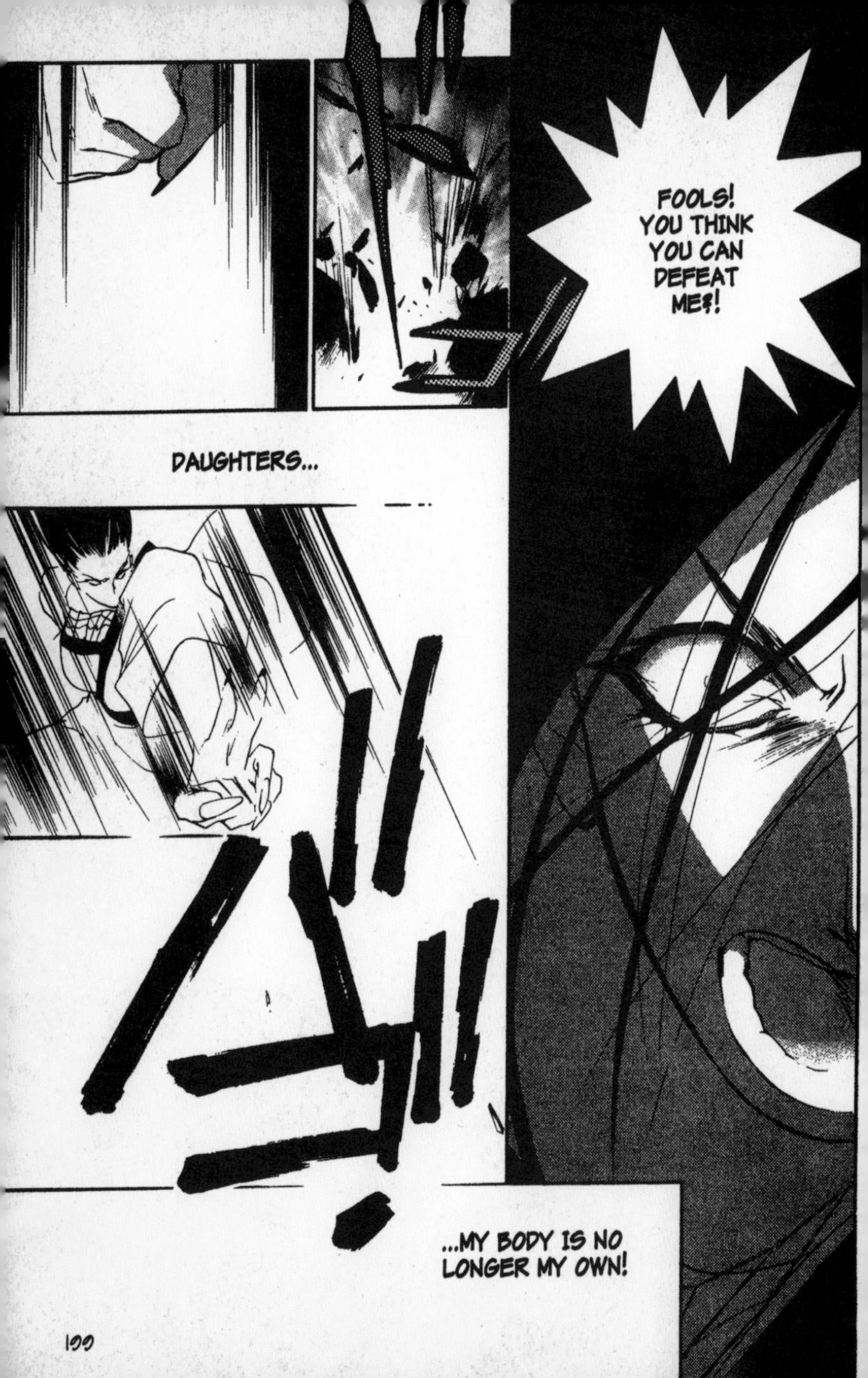
FOOLS! YOU THINK YOU CAN DEFEAT ME?!
DAUGHTERS...
...MY BODY IS NO LONGER MY OWN!

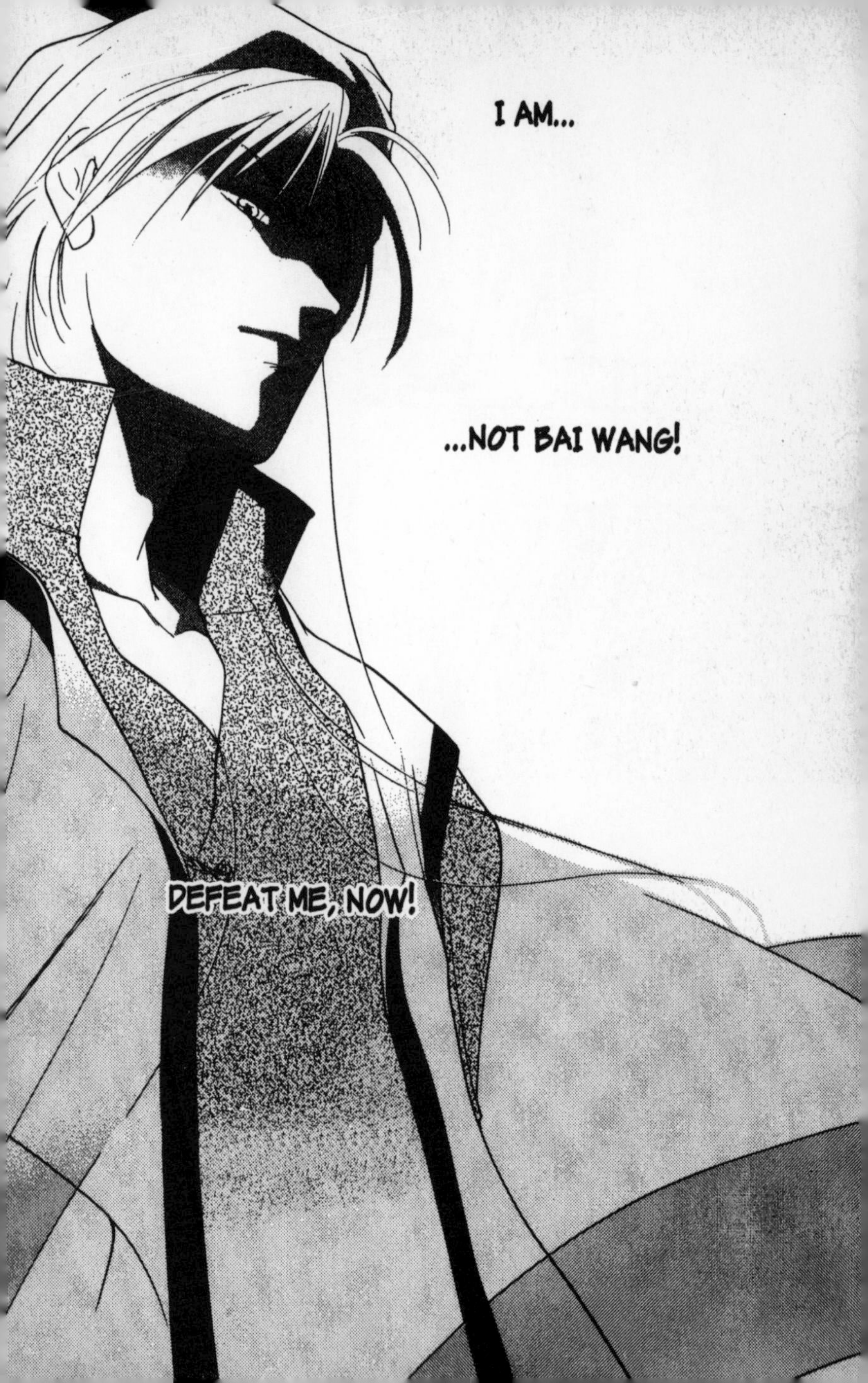
I AM...
...NOT BAI WANG!
DEFEAT ME, NOW!

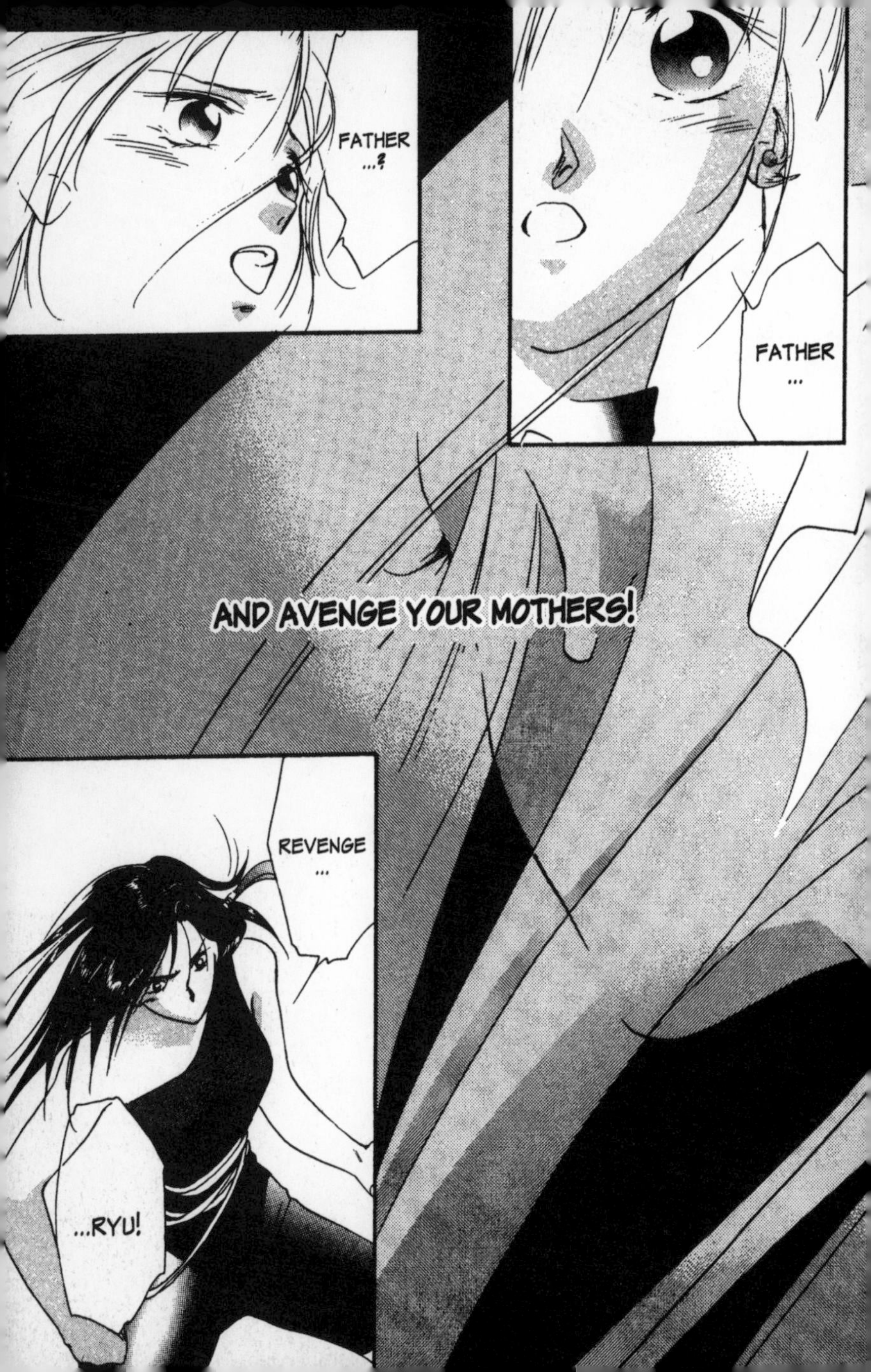
FATHER
...
FATHER
...?
AND AVENGE YOUR MOTHERS!
REVENGE
...
...RYU!

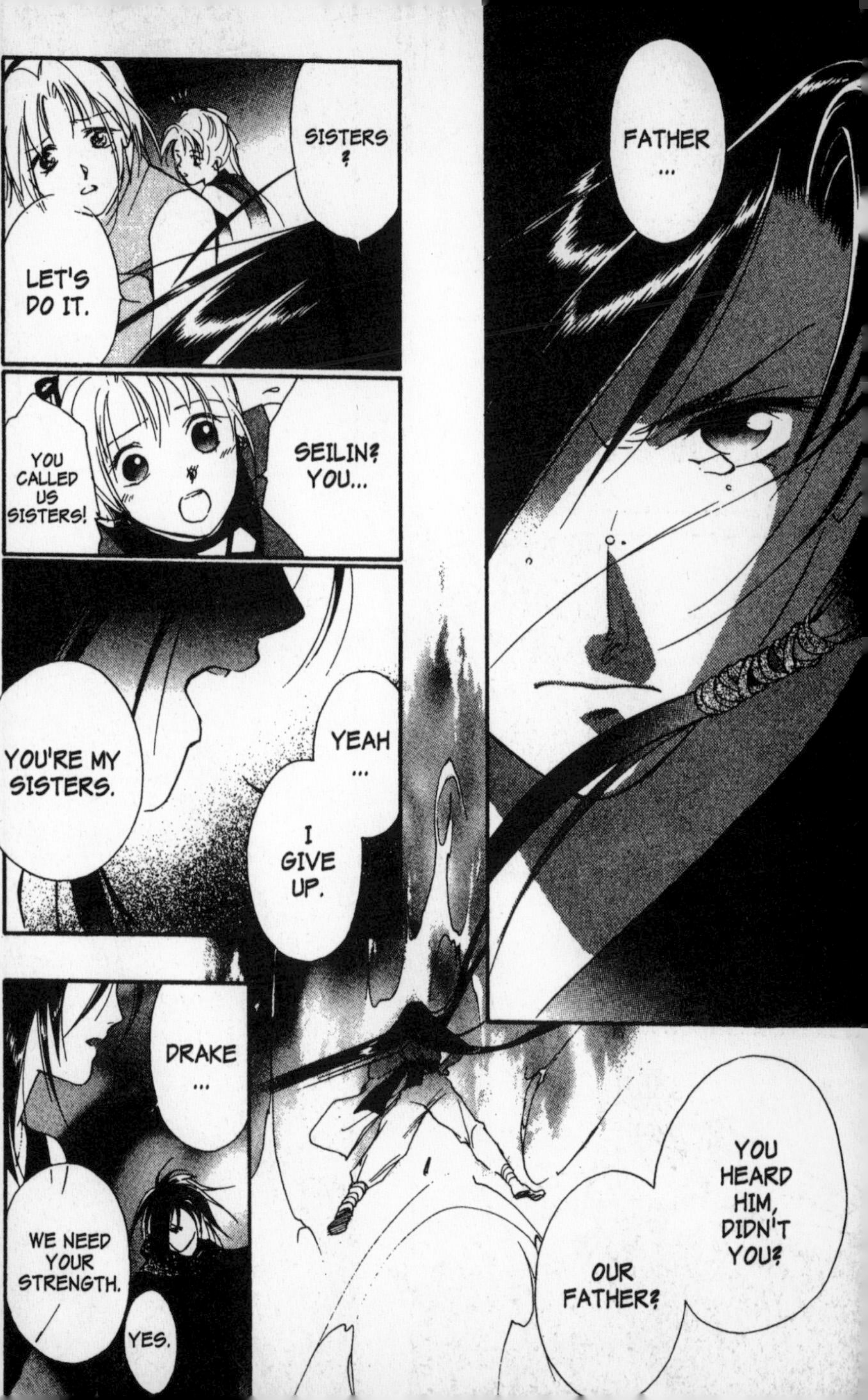
FATHER ...
SISTERS?
LET'S DO IT.
SEILIN? YOU...
YOU CALLED US SISTERS!
YEAH ... I GIVE UP.
YOU'RE MY SISTERS.
YOU HEARD HIM, DIDN'T YOU?
OUR FATHER?
DRAKE ...
WE NEED YOUR STRENGTH.
YES.

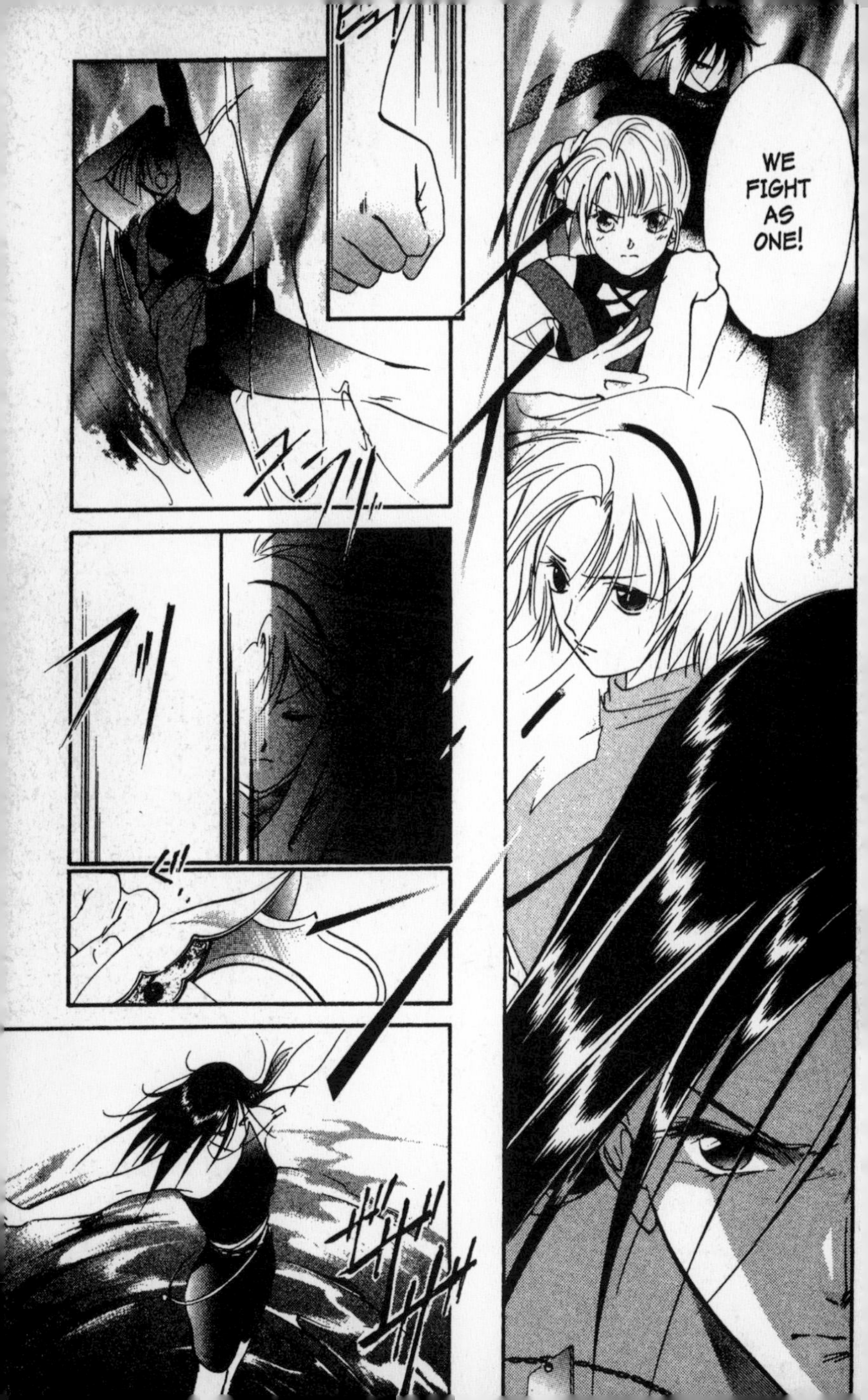
WE FIGHT AS ONE!

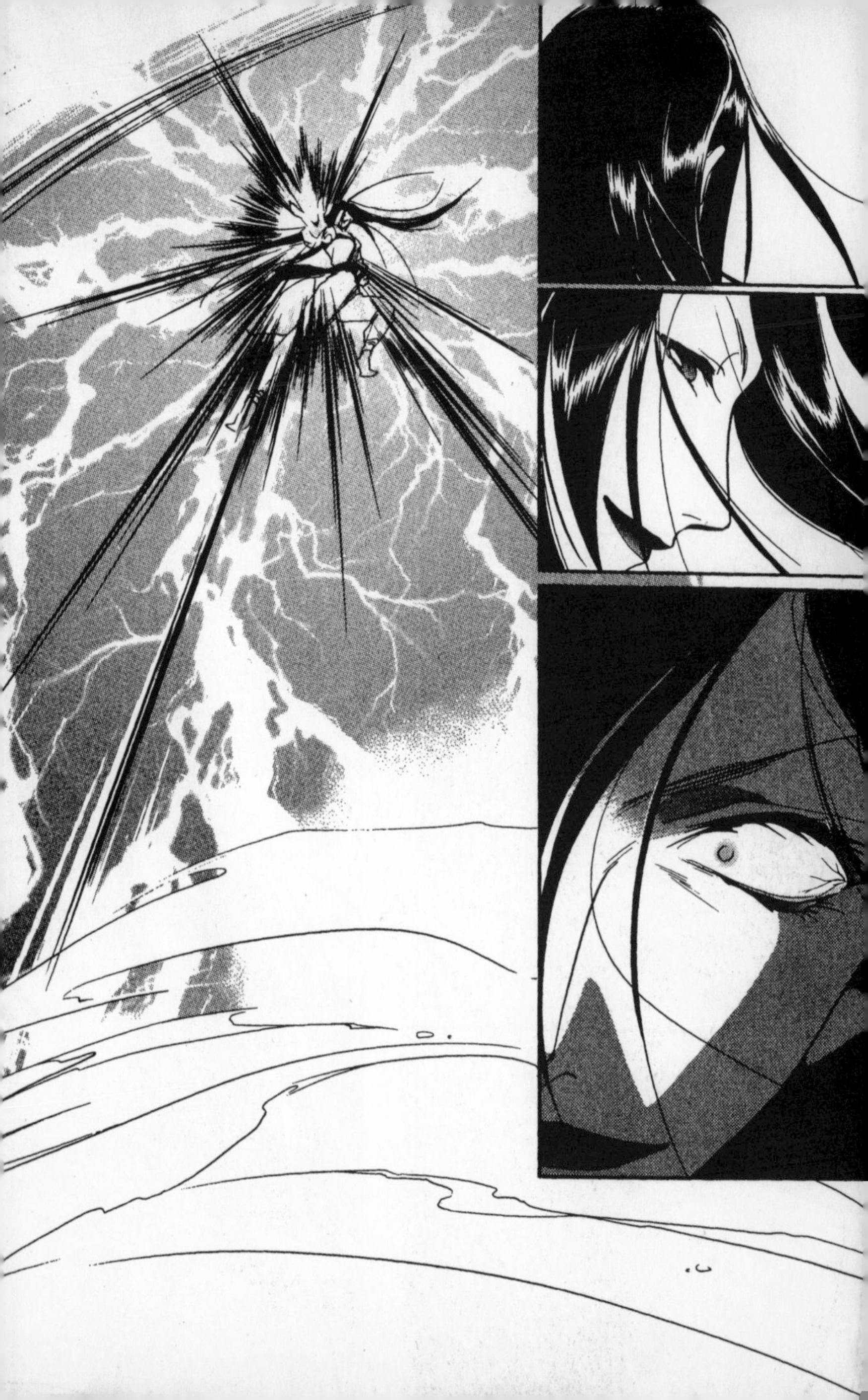

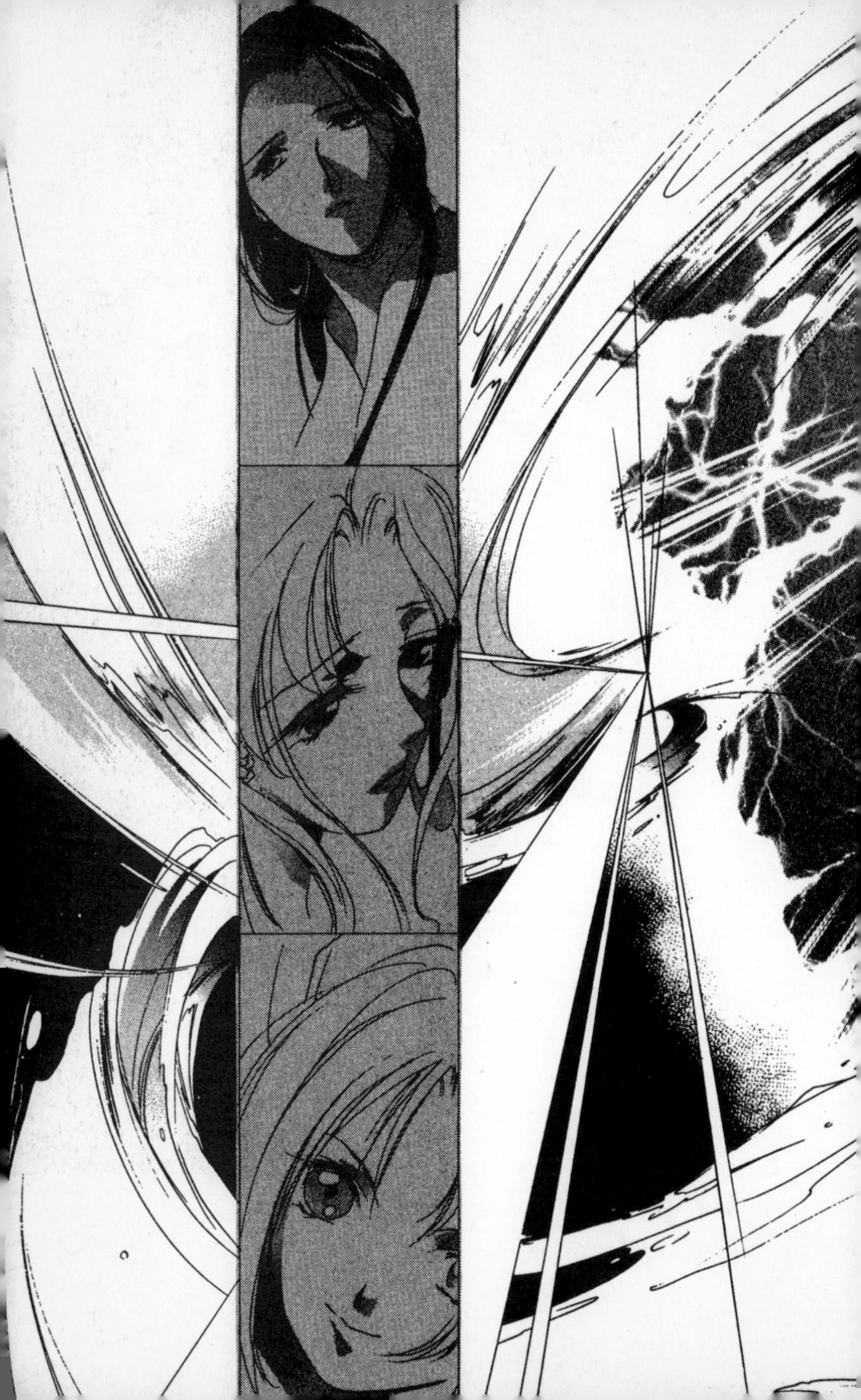

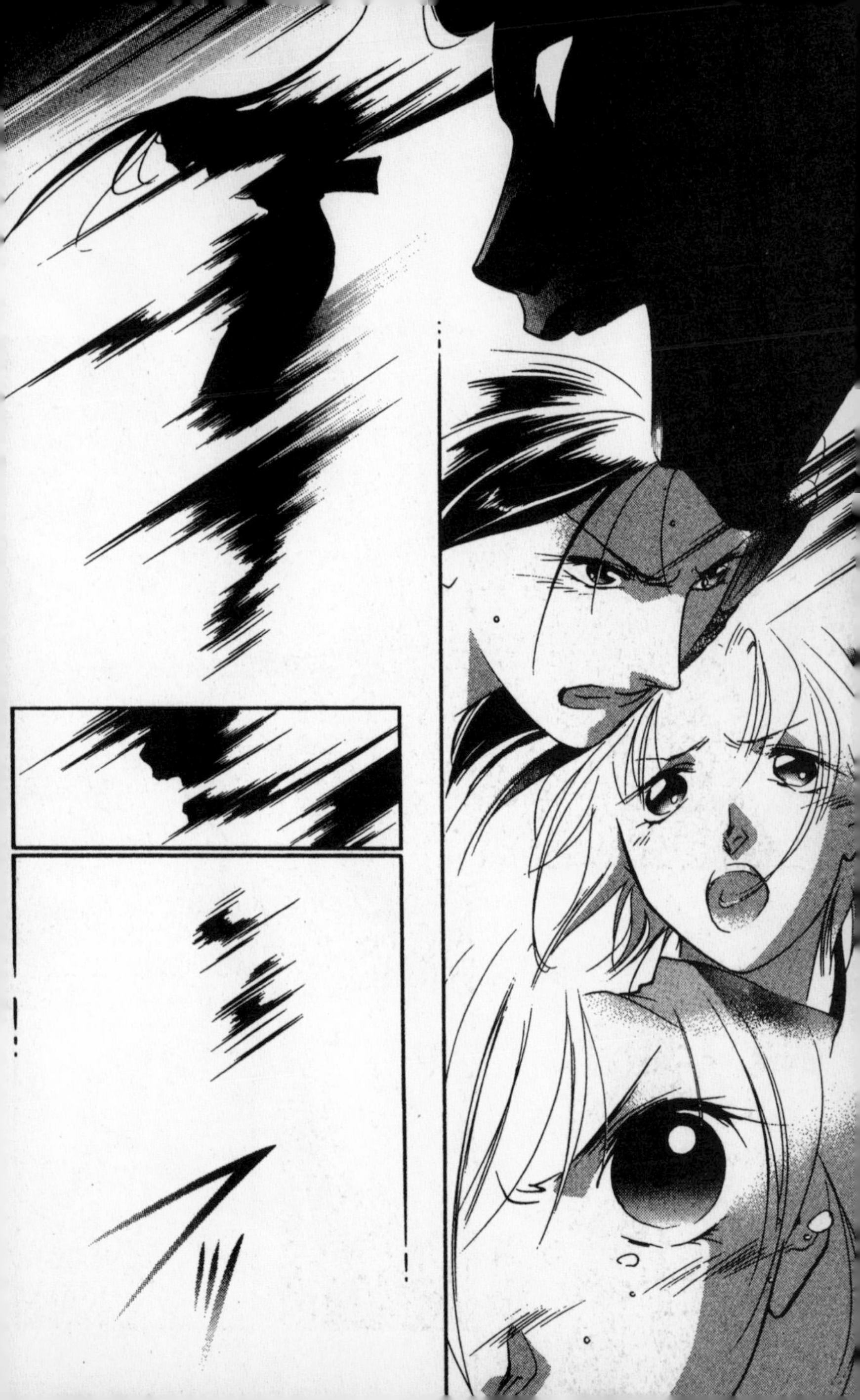

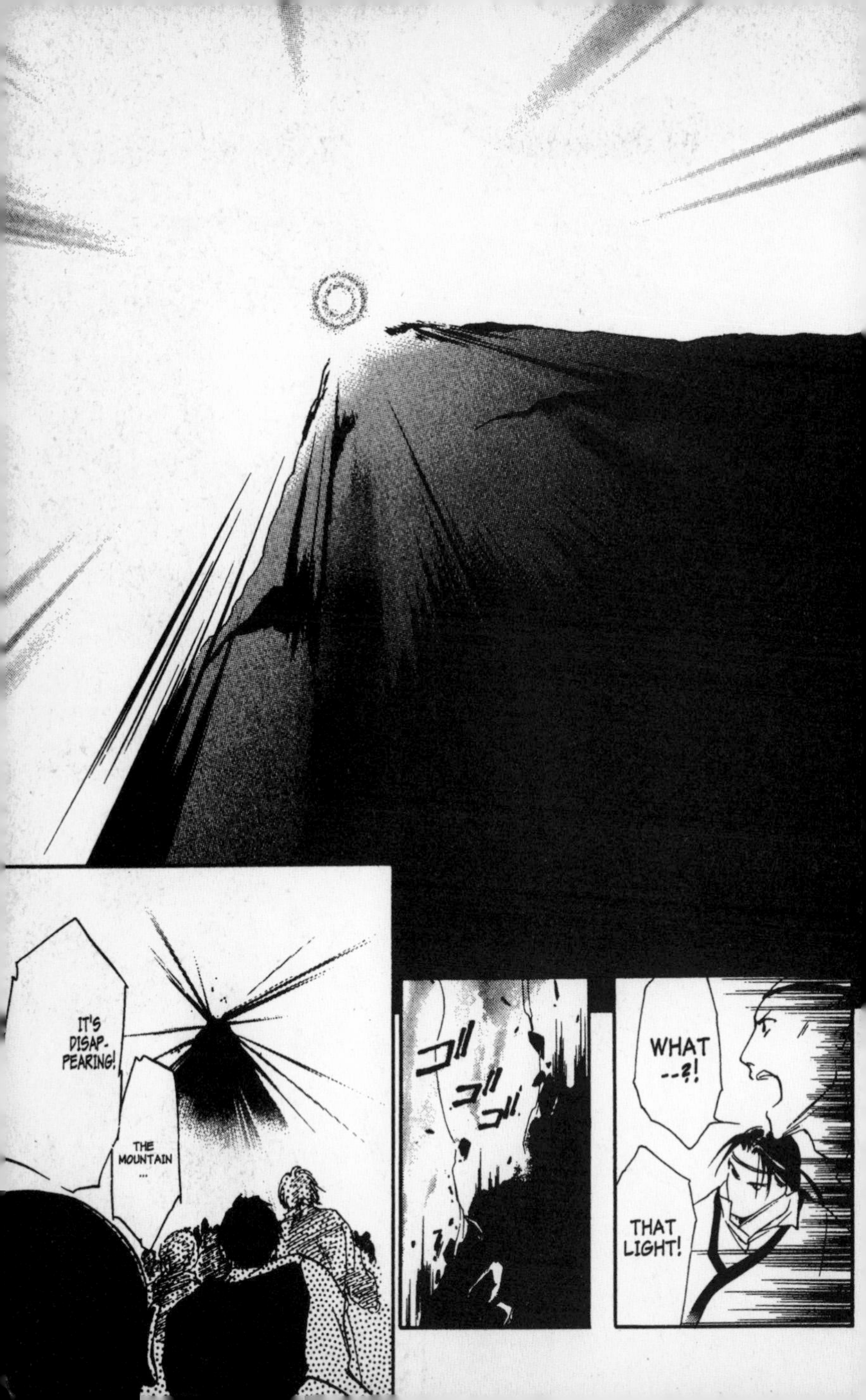
WHAT --?!
THAT LIGHT!
ゴ ゴ ゴ
THE MOUNTAIN ...
IT'S DISAP- PEARING!

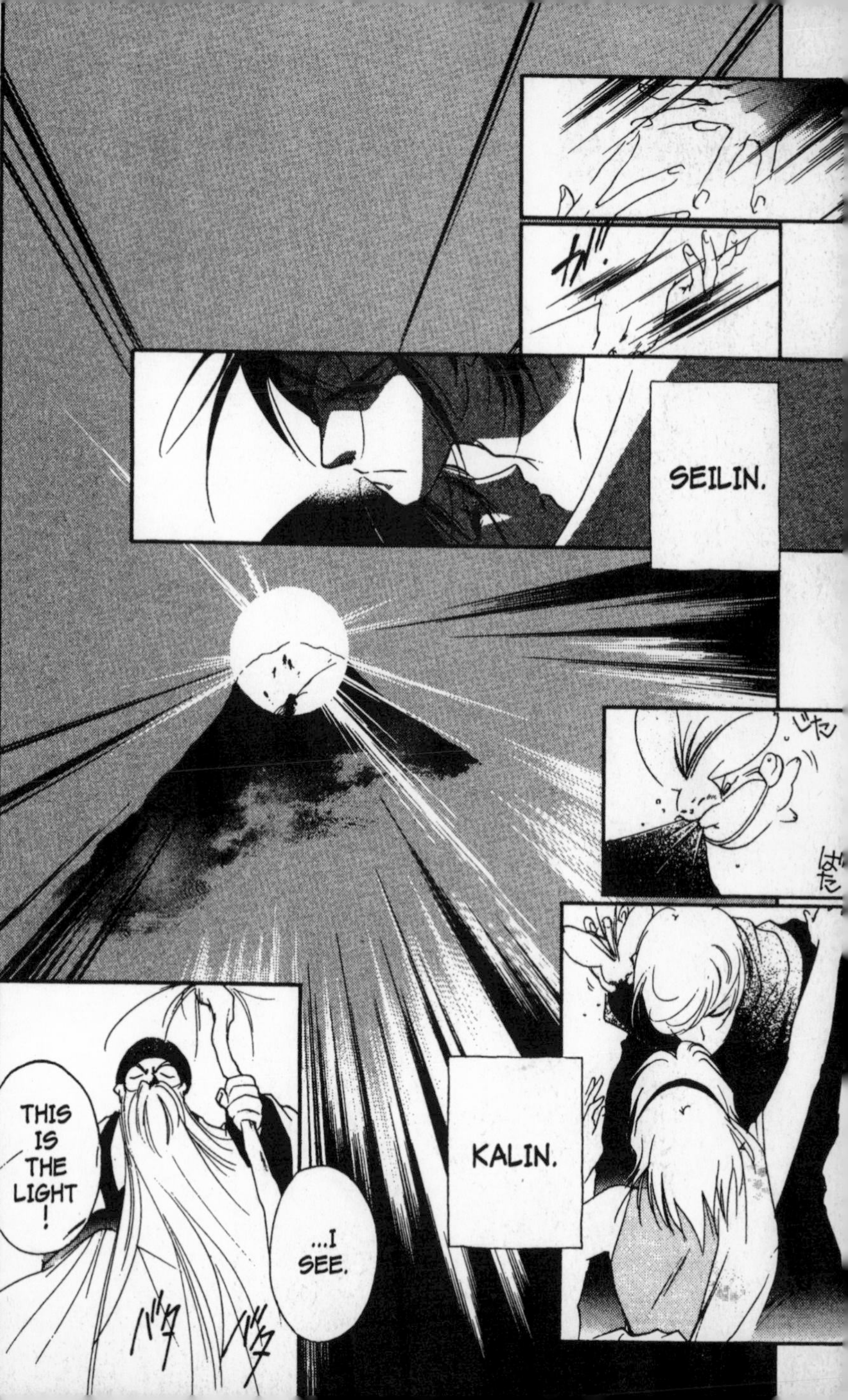
SEILIN.
KALIN.
THIS IS THE LIGHT!
...I SEE.

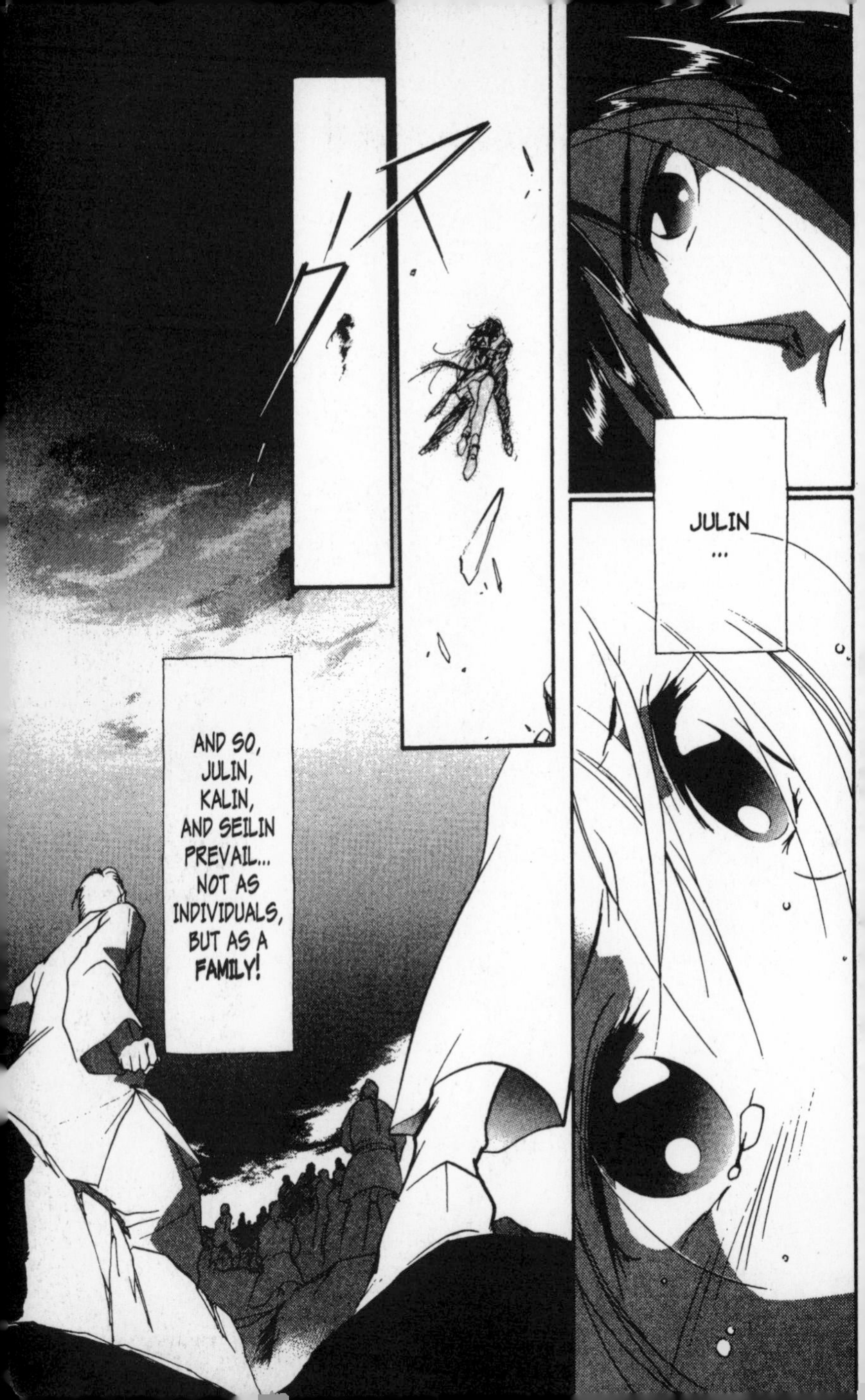
JULIN ...
AND SO, JULIN, KALIN, AND SEILIN PREVAIL... NOT AS INDIVIDUALS, BUT AS A FAMILY!

A new battle begins for the Shaolin Sisters.

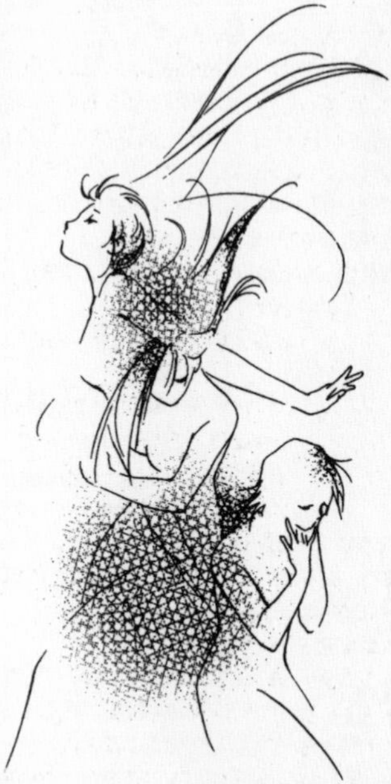

■ Shaolin Sisters 5 - End ■

Q&A Session in Commemoration of SS#1-5! by Toshiki Hirano*

*(actually, I'm asking the questions, too)

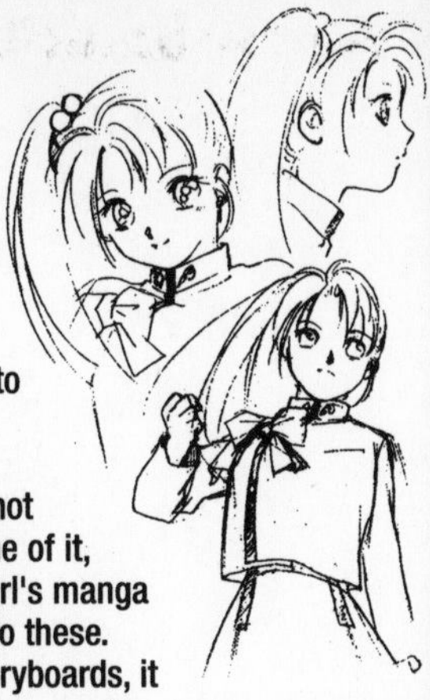

Q: Okay, so spill the beans: you were just sick of doing it, right? That's why you ended it like this!
A: Urp! I mean, there's Dangaioh and all...How can you say that?! Really, things ended pretty much as we planned. We needed a break in the battle, so we decided to stop for now.
Q: So, you're finished. How does it feel?
A: Well, we were aiming for a boy's manga look...but I'm not sure where we ended up. Ms. Kakinouchi had a rough time of it, too; since she usually works in the girl's manga style, it took her twice the time to do these. Since I was just working on the storyboards, it was more or less like doing an anime--made tricky by the fact that we wanted it to be in the style of Hong Kong action films.

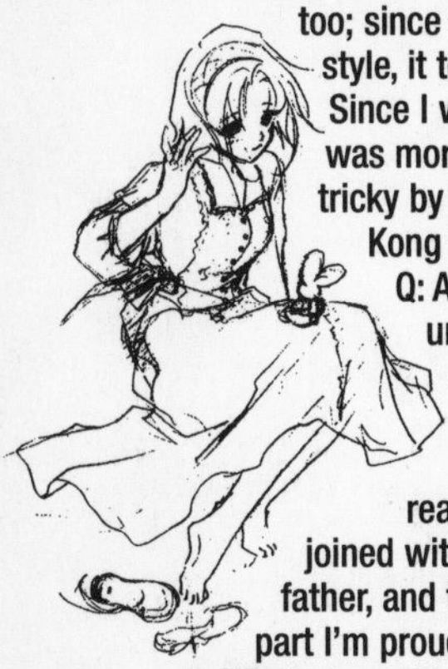

Q: Anything you really wanted to write in the first five volumes?
A: Well, the whole thing is really leading up to the final battle, where the three sisters must join together to fight Bai Wang -- who is, in actuality, their dad! -- after realizing that their real enemy is the ancient spirit that has joined with their father. Only by defeating it may they free their father, and to do this their hearts must be as one. That's really the part I'm proudest about.
Q: What about the anime version?
A: It looks like it might happen, but it's hard to say. It's really speculation at this point, and there are a lot of hurdles to leap, but maybe…? Still, there's more in store for the manga version and I think that, even if we did an anime, I'd like to start with a new story…though I would like to show you all the pilot I did with Ms. Kakinouchi.

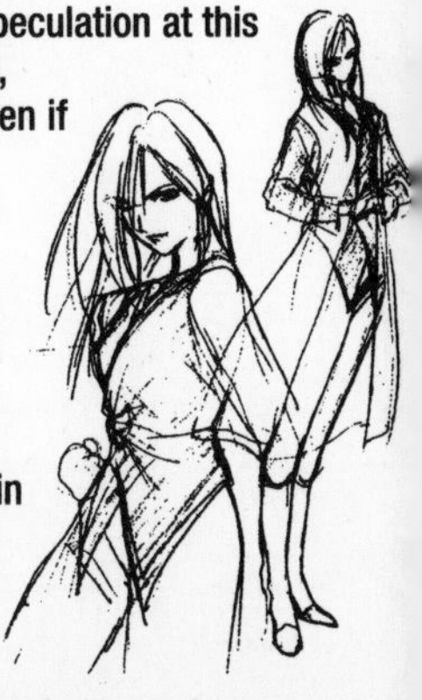

Q: So what's in store for the next Shaolin Sisters series?
A: We're working on that now! It's a pain to change the setting entirely, so I'm still figuring out what to do with the characters.
Q: Just answer the question!
A: Well, we'll probably use the same characters, but move the action into the modern age, with links to what was happening in the past. I want to get the story closer to the world that the readers live in—but please try to keep an open mind about it!
Q: Hmm...sounds like a move for better sales. But hey, if it's interesting, what do I care?
A: Right! And interesting it will be! I promise part two won't let you down!

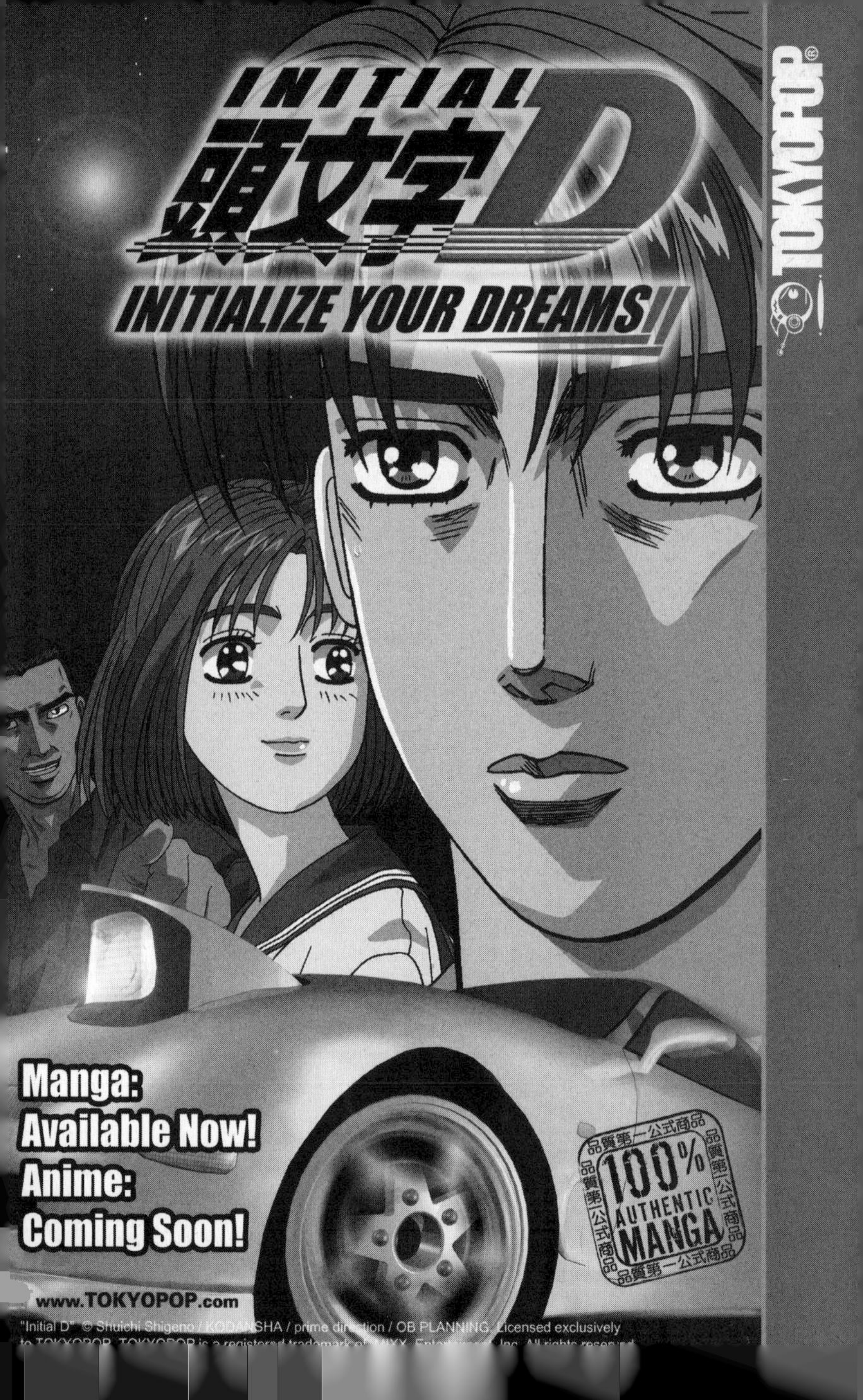
INITIAL
頭文字D
INITIALIZE YOUR DREAMS!!
TOKYOPOP®
Manga:
Available Now!
Anime:
Coming Soon!
100% AUTHENTIC MANGA
品質第一公式商品
www.TOKYOPOP.com
"Initial D" © Shuichi Shigeno / KODANSHA / prime direction / OB PLANNING. Licensed exclusively

TODAY'S HOTTEST MANGA COMES TO AMERICA

KING OF HELL

BY RA IN-SOO

ONLY ONE MAN CAN BRIDGE THE
RIFT BETWEEN HERE & HELL

AVAILABLE NOW AT YOUR FAVORITE
BOOK AND COMIC STORES

T
TEEN
AGE 13+

www.TOKYOPOP.com

GATE-KEEPERS

TOKYOPOP®

100% AUTHENTIC MANGA

By:
Keiji Gotoh

Finding Time to Defend The Earth
Between School & Homework

GET GATEKEEPERS IN YOUR FAVORITE BOOK & COMIC STORES NOW!

www.TOKYOPOP.com

MAY 0 4 2005

SP

STOP!

This is the back of the book.
You wouldn't want to spoil a great ending!

This book is printed "manga-style," in the authentic Japanese right-to-left format. Since none of the artwork has been flipped or altered, readers get to experience the story just as the creator intended. You've been asking for it, so TOKYOPOP® delivered: authentic, hot-off-the-press, and far more fun!

DIRECTIONS

If this is your first time reading manga-style, here's a quick guide to help you understand how it works.

It's easy... just start in the top right panel and follow the numbers. Have fun, and look for more 100% authentic manga from TOKYOPOP®!

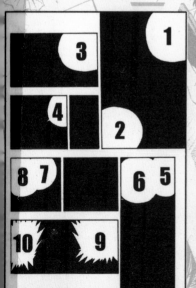